Federal Law Enforcement

Federal Law Enforcement

A Primer

Jeff Bumgarner

Charles Crawford

Ronald Burns

Carolina Academic Press

Durham, North Carolina

Library of Congress Cataloging-in-Publication Data

Bumgarner, Jeffrey B.
  Federal law enforcement : a primer / Jeff Bumgarner, Charles Crawford, and Ronald
Burns.
      pages cm
  Includes bibliographical references and index.
  ISBN 978-1-61163-076-3 (alk. paper)
  1. Law enforcement--United States. 2. Police--United States. I. Crawford, Charles E.,
1967- II. Burns, Ronald G., 1968- III. Title.

  HV8139.B86 2013
  363.20973--dc23

                          2013007024

CAROLINA ACADEMIC PRESS
700 Kent Street
Durham, North Carolina 27701
Telephone (919) 489-7486
Fax (919) 493-5668
www.cap-press.com

Printed in the United States of America

Contents

Part IV · Federal Law Enforcement Agencies: Department of Interior

Part V · Federal Law Enforcement Agencies: Other Agencies

Foreword

As a new federal law enforcement officer, a special agent with the Drug Enforcement Administration (DEA), I took an oath to " ... defend the Constitution of the United States against all enemies, foreign and domestic ..." (Title 5 USC Section 3331). The history of the oath of office dates back to Articles II and VI of the Constitution and the first Act passed by the new Congress of the United States. When I accepted my appointment, all I really knew was that I would enforce the federal narcotics laws. Clearly there was so much more than I was aware of and few informational resources were available that focused on the federal law enforcement community—until now.

Jeff Bumgarner (University of Minnesota, Crookston), Charles Crawford (Western Michigan University), and Ronald Burns (Texas Christian University) have taken that next step; they wrote the book that I would like to have read before I became a special agent. *Federal Law Enforcement: A Primer* examines the history, structure, authority, and jurisdiction of federal law enforcement agencies, and their relationships with state, local, and tribal law enforcement agencies. It focuses first on the origins of federal law enforcement, with the Constitution and the three branches of the federal government. The authors explain how federal law enforcement has evolved since colonial times and how the organizations have changed in response to the needs of a nation in the twenty-first century.

Thanks to Hollywood, everyone seems to know about Crime Scene Investigations (CSIs) and the existence of a DEA, Federal Bureau of Investigation (FBI), Alcohol Tobacco Firearms & Explosives (ATF), and United States Marshals Service (USMS), but little attention is paid to the fact that, unlike many other countries, the United States does not have a national uniformed "police force." The book opens with the history of several "main-line" agencies that are part of the traditional and well-known federal law enforcement community. It quickly takes the reader to the next level by explaining what organizations are responsible for the enforcement of the controversial *USA PATRIOT Act*, the *Immigration Reform and Control Act*, various federal drug laws, security compliance regulations, and numerous other statutes and regulations. There are more organizations within the federal law enforcement community than most people imagine and these chapters tell many of their stories.

There are numerous books on police, patrol and the omnipotent CSIs. Every state or local police officer understands that their powers are delegated from the Governor of a state; their jurisdiction, with the authority to protect and serve rests within each state or township, and is guaranteed by the Constitution. While the language and description of the laws and the procedures may vary slightly among each of the states, law enforcement is a very basic and direct concept. But the same cannot be said for federal law enforcement. The United States does not have and will not have a federal police force, but there are numerous federal agents, investigators, inspectors, and uniformed officers with specific yet limited jurisdiction and authority.

Professors Bumgarner, Crawford and Burns have written an outstanding *"Primer"* on the federal law enforcement community. Few law enforcement officers have a true understanding of the complex and diverse nature of the federal community; the depth of their knowledge is normally based on their professional associations. But the authors paint with a wide brush and introduce the reader to the very diverse federal community, starting with the first federal law enforcement agencies created to collect revenue and provide security to the courts, pursuant to the *Tariff Act of 1789* and the *Judiciary Act of 1789*, respectively. Federal law enforcement has come a long way since the creation of the first federal law enforcement agency, the Marshals Service, to the revitalization of the Federal Air Marshal Service to combat terrorism. I doubt that President George Washington could have imagined the Marshals Service of the twenty-first century when he appointed the first twelve U.S. Marshals.

The expansion of federal law enforcement is based upon changing needs and increasing responsibilities. From tax/tariff collection, to court services, to building security and protecting the postal system, the federal government took full advantage of its powers. The authors have blazed a trail across time and the nation, explaining the origins of the most prominent agencies such as the Secret Service, the FBI, the ATF, and the DEA, as well as lesser known agencies like the Bureau of Indian Affairs, National Park Service, Federal Air Marshal Service, and the ever popular Internal Revenue Service. Although very limited in their jurisdiction, there are several uniformed police services such as the Park Police, Capital Police, Supreme Court Police and the Federal Protective Service. Each organization has a unique history that helps the reader better understand the diverse nature of federal law enforcement.

Each of our military services has police and investigation organizations, one of which has even secured space on prime-time television to tell its stories. While many nations use the military to secure their borders, the U.S. has relies on the Border Patrol and the Coast Guard. Since their inceptions, there have been several changes in these organizations and missions; but after the events of September 11, both are now under the control of the Secretary of Homeland Security.

The growth and development of each federal law enforcement organization is carefully examined. The authors capture the reader's attention as they explain how these agencies have been created, re-organized, and/or merged to meet the latest challenge. Approximately half of the federal officers are involved with investigations and inspections. The remaining officers are spread among police, patrol, security, courts and corrections. Unlike most state and local law enforcement organizations, federal officers are stationed throughout the world fighting crime and protecting American lives.

In addition to discussing the history and structure of these federal agencies, the readers are presented with an overview of the nature of the work performed by these agencies, along with brief summaries of some of their more notable cases. Ensuring that each reader is not left standing alone and wanting more, there are sections in the book regarding where new recruits and senior agents receive training, and how one becomes part of over 100 agencies and sub-agencies that are the federal law enforcement community.

I teach a course in federal law enforcement at Kutzylvania University of Pennsylvania. After reading the draft of *Federal Law Enforcement: A Primer*, I knew I found the perfect text for my course. I trust that you will find reading this book as interesting and informative as I have.

Keith Gregory Logan
Associate Professor, Department of Criminal Justice
Kutztown University of Pennsylvania

Part I
Federal Law Enforcement of the Past and Present

Chapter One

Origins of Federal Law Enforcement in America

Many criminal justice scholars and historians have written about the development of policing as a practice throughout American history. However, generally this history has been focused on local law enforcement. This is understandable because most people associate law enforcement with the uniformed municipal police officer. And certainly, the history of municipal policing in the United States is an interesting and dynamic history to recount. But just as interesting is the development of federal law enforcement in the United States.

The origins of both levels of law enforcement—i.e. local and federal—are rooted in political contexts that enveloped them. Indeed, the histories of these two levels of law enforcement mirror the histories of government generally at the local and federal levels. For example, from the early 19th Century to the early 20th Century, urban municipal policing was characterized by corruption and cronyism—just as local government politics and administration were generally. Police departments in cities such as New York, Boston, Chicago, Cincinnati, and elsewhere were subsidiaries of the local political machines. In fact, police departments were often assigned political duties, including getting voters who were supportive of local politicians out to the polls, or providing favors or protection of rackets operated by supporters of the political machine. Selection and promotion for paid police officers went to the highest bidder, or to those who in some other way loyally had served the machine (Walker, 1977).

Illustrative of this is Cincinnati, which saw 74% of its police department fired after a changeover of the party in power in 1880 (Walker, 1977). Six years later, 80% of the department was let go after another round of political turnover. The overt cronyism and corruption in police departments has diminished over time at a rate commensurate with the diminution of cronyism and corruption generally in local government. With the advent of public administration as a profession and as a scientific and rational approach to the competent management of government and government services during the reform era of the early 20th Century, so too went the way of policing. It was during this time that key police reformers such as August Vollmer and later O.W. Wilson, put forth professional visions for policing that were free from undue political influence and unimpeded by an ill-informed but politically connected laity.

The movement away from institutional corruption in local law enforcement over the past two centuries has been remarkable. But interestingly, federal law enforcement, early in its history, was relatively free of politics. Further, federal law enforcement professionalized with greater speed than did local law enforcement. One major reason for the early insulation from political influence and the rapidity in developing as a profession goes to the nation's historical orientation toward the United States Government—federal power was limited power.

The United States Constitution is the supreme law of the land. But at the same time, it goes to great lengths to limit its own reach, and by extension, the reach of the Executive

Branch of the federal government. It does not confer on the federal government a general police power, but rather grants broad police powers to the states. The 10th Amendment of the Constitution expressly states that powers not delegated to the United States (i.e. powers that are not among the enumerated powers) are reserved to the various states and the people.

But, of course, limited power did not mean *zero* power. Even at the nation's outset, there was a role for federal law enforcement within the context of the enumerated powers of the Constitution. The Constitution was written to establish and define the structure, scope, and responsibilities of the national government of the United States. Given that the Constitution articulates certain acts that are defined as criminal acts, such as Treason under Article III, Section 3, it cannot be said that the federal government had no constitutional law enforcement authority. Further, the Bill of Rights limits the federal government in its relationship to citizens in so far as a number of law enforcement processes are concerned. In these early amendments (ratified in 1791), we find a number of restraints on federal law enforcement, such as protections for the criminally accused against unreasonable searches and seizures (4th Amendment), protection against forced self-incrimination, denial of due process, and the prohibition against double jeopardy (5th Amendment), the right to a speedy and public trial, to be judged by a jury of one's peers, and to have legal representation (6th Amendment), and protection against excessive bail, excessive fines, and cruel and unusual punishment (8th Amendment). The protections would have been unnecessary in the late 18th Century if there had been no federal law enforcement authority to speak of.

Further, the Constitution declares that the federal government is empowered to exercise its responsibilities through all necessary and proper means. The Necessary and Proper Clause of the Constitution, found in Article I, Section 8, states that Congress has the power to "make all Laws which shall be necessary and proper for carrying into the Execution the foregoing Powers, and all other Powers vested by this Constitution in the Government of the United States, or any Department or Officer thereof."

Even so, this clause does not amount to a blank check for federal power. The "foregoing Powers" refers specifically to those expressed powers bestowed on Congress in Section 8, including the power to regulate commerce with foreign nations and among the several states and Indian tribes; to establish a rules regarding immigration and naturalization; to establish rules for bankruptcy in the United States; to provide for the punishment of counterfeiting the securities and current coin of the United States; to define and enforce laws of piracy and other felonies committed on the high seas and offenses against the international law; and to provide for calling out the militia to execute the laws of the union, and to suppress insurrections and repel invasions.

Each of these expressed, enumerated powers of the federal government implies a federal law enforcement function.

Pursuant to the federal government's exercise of its enumerated powers, early American federal law enforcement correlated to four primary responsibilities (Bumgarner, 2006):

1) enforcing taxes and tariffs
2) serving the federal judicial system
3) securing public facilities
4) protecting the postal system

Enforcing Taxes and Tariffs

The Tariff Act of 1789 was signed into law by President George Washington on July 4, 1789. This law was especially important to the fledgling constitutional republic as the country was still reeling in debt from the Revolutionary War. Further, revenue raised under the Articles of Confederation had been negligible. The United States was broke. The Tariff Act authorized the government of the United States to collect duties on imports. And there were a lot of imports to tax in 1789 as European countries sought to capitalize on the needs of a growing nation. But who would collect the tariffs?

A month after the enactment of the Tariff Act of 1789, the Fifth Act of Congress was passed. This legislation created the first federal agency of the Executive Branch—United States Customs. In total, 59 customs districts were created by the law, covering over a 100 ports of entry. "Collectors" were presidentially appointed for each customs district. Each district also was allocated 10 naval officers and nearly 3 dozen surveyors to assist in the collection of duties. Customs was placed under the Department of Treasury where it would remain for over 200 years—until the passage of the Homeland Security Act of 2002 and Customs' partitioned transfer to different corners of the Department of Homeland Security in March 2003 (Saba, 2003).

In addition to personnel, Congress appropriated to Customs 10 warships, or cutters, in 1790. The fleet of cutters operated by U.S. Customs, responsible for Treasury collection efforts on the high seas, came to be known as the Revenue Cutter Service (which is a predecessor to the U.S. Coast Guard—also see Chapter 16). In addition to enforcing customs laws, the Revenue Cutter Service represented the United States' only naval force until 1798 when the Department of the Navy was created. During the first 10 years of its existence, revenues collected by the Revenue Cutter Service rose from $52 to $205 million (USCG, 2002). Beyond revenue collection, the Revenue Cutter Service combated smuggling and piracy. It also enforced anti-slave trafficking laws, which at the time prohibited the use of American-flagged vessels for slave trafficking (beginning in 1794) and barred the introduction of new slaves from Africa into the United States (beginning in 1808).

U.S. Customs served as the primary source of federal funds for the first 125 years of America's history as a nation. By all accounts, U.S. Customs was effective at fulfilling its mission. By 1835, the national debt—seemingly insurmountable only a couple decades earlier—was completely paid off (Saba, 2003). Every state and many large cities could boast the presence of a Customs House. New York City was a particularly important location for U.S. Customs. By the mid-1800s, customs revenues collected in New York City totaled 75% of all customs revenues forwarded to the U.S. Treasury yearly (Saba, 2003).

Serving the Federal Judiciary System

In the same year that U.S. Customs was created, Congress passed the Judiciary Act of 1789. This law created 13 federal judicial districts, federal district and appellate courts, the office of United States Attorney in each district, and the office of United States Marshal in each district. Arguably, the U.S. Marshals (and their deputies) were the first federal law enforcement officers with an exclusively law enforcement mission (also see Chapter 5). The duties of U.S. Marshals resembled those of a local sheriff. They served federal court orders, captured and delivered federal prisoners, and compelled citizens called up for jury duty to serve as jurors. In any given judicial district, the United States Marshal was also the chief federal investigator. U.S. Marshals continued to act in this capacity throughout the 19th Century.

Early federal crimes which fell under the investigative jurisdiction of U.S. Marshals included the Alien Act of 1798 (through which foreigners who were deemed dangerous were arrested and deported), the Sedition Act of 1798 (which effectively criminalized criticism of the federal government), immigration laws, slave trade violations and post-Civil War civil rights violations. In fact the U.S. Marshals had a mixed role in the history of slavery in the United States. Along with Customs, they enforced laws barring the importation of new slaves into the country. But they also enforced the Fugitive Slave Act, which required that slaves who escaped from the South to free states in the north be returned to their southern owners. The first line-of-duty death of a U.S. Marshal occurred in Boston while the marshal was trying to take custody of an escaped slave pursuant to the Fugitive Slave Act. Finally, U.S. Marshals also served as the primary law enforcement authority in unorganized U.S. territories (Calhoun, 1989).

Securing Public Facilities

A visit to Washington, D.C. affords a tourist an opportunity to see many things. One can visit the White House, the U.S. Capitol, the Supreme Court, the Smithsonian Institution, a myriad of national monuments and public parks, and any number of other well-known sites and museums. In visiting these locations, an astute observer would invariably notice a significant police presence. What one might not notice is the fact that a fair number of the law enforcement officers present at these sites themselves come from a number of different agencies. In addition to the Washington, D.C. Metropolitan Police Department, there are several other uniformed police patrol agencies on duty throughout the city. And many of these agencies also have a presence outside of Washington, D.C.—carrying out protection and patrol duties in other cities and locations around the country. Their missions: serving as a police and security force for facilities, parks, and federal reservations controlled by the federal government. These agencies include the U.S. Park Police, the U.S. Capitol Police, the Federal Protective Service, the U.S. Supreme Court Police, the Uniformed Division of the U.S. Secret Service, the FBI Police, the Smithsonian Police, the U.S. Mint Police, and many others (also see Chapter 15). All of the preceding federal police agencies are legacies of one of federal law enforcement's earliest manifestations—going back to the late 1700s.

The United States Congress convened for the first time under the new Constitution in December of 1790. The District of Columbia had been partitioned from Maryland and Virginia, but did not yet have an infrastructure ready to support the United States as its capital. So, Congress met in Philadelphia. Although the capital city of the United States had been New York City under the Articles of Confederation, the Residence Act of 1790 mandated that the United States Government would be seated in Philadelphia for 10 years while public buildings were constructed in the District of Columbia (Senate Historian, n.d.).

While buildings were being constructed in Washington, D.C., there was a need for those facilities to be managed and protected. So, in 1790, Congress appointed a commission to address these concerns. In order to meet the needs of physical security for the real property controlled by the federal government in the District of Columbia, six night watchmen were hired. It was the job of these night watchmen to protect the buildings in the district that would eventually house the United States Government. The buildings included those which would eventually be home to the President, the Congress, the Supreme Court, and several other public offices once the move from Philadelphia to Washington, D.C. took place.

In 1802, a superintendent of public buildings was appointed and given responsibility over the federal buildings in the District of Columbia. The superintendent oversaw the protective activities of the watchmen. Then in 1816, the Office of the Commissioner of Public Buildings was created to replace the superintendent's office. The evolution of management and control of public facilities, including the protection of those facilities, continued for years. Finally in 1849, the Department of Interior was established and assumed organizational control of the Office of the Commissioner of Public Buildings (Senate Historian, n.d.), as well as the policemen serving under that office.

Although Washington, D.C. became the capital of the United States in November of 1800, construction of needed federal buildings continued on for many years after that. And yet, there continued to be only a modest force of watchmen. In fact, the Capitol Building and adjacent grounds were patrolled by only one watchman at any given time. That the public buildings patrol force was understaffed and under-deployed became especially evident after the Capitol Building's rotunda was completed in 1824. The Capitol Building was a huge draw for visitors and dignitaries. The regular influx of visitors was quite taxing on whichever watchman happened to be on duty. Then, a fire in 1825 in the Capitol Building library and an assault on President John Quincy Adam's son in the Capitol rotunda in 1828 caused Congress to re-evaluate the security and protection needs of the Capitol and other federal properties.

On April 29, 1828, Congress passed H.R. 158, An Act Making Appropriations for Public Buildings and Other Purposes. The act declared that a police force for the Capitol and its appurtenant grounds should be created. The duties of the Commissioner and that of his police force were articulated in the federal statute (H.R. 158):

> ... that it shall be his duty to obey such rules and regulations, as may be, from time to time, prescribed by the Presiding Officer of either House of Congress, for the care, preservation, orderly keeping, and police of those portions of the Capitol and its appurtenances, which are in the exclusive use and occupation of either House of Congress, respectively; and, that it shall also be his duty to obey such rules and regulations, as may, from time to time, be prescribed by the President of the United States, for the care, preservation, orderly keeping, and police, of the other Public Buildings and Public Property, in the City of Washington, and the Commissioner and his assistants are hereby authorized and empowered to use all necessary and proper means for the discharge of the aforesaid duties; and the Commissioner and the assistants of the Commissioner shall receive a reasonable compensation for their services, to be allowed by the Presiding Officers of the two Houses of Congress....

At first, these officers of the newly created Capitol police force did not wear uniforms and received very little formal training in law enforcement related duties. The jurisdiction of the force was limited and the responsibilities were fairly intuitive. The mission was essentially, "If you see trouble, or if people need assistance, deal with it." The Capitol police officers regularly found themselves attending to non-law enforcement duties. For example they would often serve as tour guides for visitors to the Capitol. When trouble arose in the form of unrest or demonstrations at the Capitol, this undertrained police force commonly relied on the help of Washington, D.C. auxiliary guard for restoring and keeping the peace (Senate Historian, n.d.). The Capitol police force would continue to find its way and to hone its mission throughout the first half of the 19th Century until eventually moving into the Department of Interior in 1849. From that platform, the uniformed police services of the federal government, exemplified in the Capitol police and in other agencies (such as the U.S. Park Police) would emerge later; these agencies would transform into professional, full-service police organizations which could be modeled by other departments around the country.

Protecting the Postal System

One of the enumerated and exclusive powers of the federal government contained in the U.S. Constitution is the power to establish and regulate a national postal system. But, in fact, America's postal system existed long before the Constitution went into effect in 1789. Indeed, in 1753, Benjamin Franklin was appointed Postmaster General of the colonial postal system. Almost 20 years later, in 1772, Franklin created the position of postal "surveyor." The job of a surveyor was to provide regulatory and audit support in order to ensure the integrity and security of the postal system. The working title of surveyors changed to "special agent" in 1801. The postal system's cadre of special agents in the early 1800s is the forerunner to today's Postal Inspection Service (also see Chapter14).

When the Constitution was adopted in 1789, Congress established a temporary national post office and created the Office of Postmaster General. As a postal system had already existed in Colonial America and under the Articles of Confederation, the new national post office didn't start from scratch. At the time of its creation, there already existed 75 post offices and about 2,000 miles of post roads. In 1792, Congress permanently established the Postal Service as an agency of the United States Government. Postal employees included the Postmaster General, surveyors, an Inspector of Dead Letters, and a couple dozen post riders (USPS, 2007).

Like other federal agencies in the early 19th Century, the Postal Service experienced growth and evolution as the young nation it served likewise grew and evolved. In 1830, the Office of Instructions and Mail Depredations was created within the Postal Service. This unit was established with an explicit law enforcement role—namely, to serve as the investigative and inspection branch of the Postal Service. The special agents assigned to the Office of Instructions and Mail Depredations carried with them significant law enforcement responsibilities. These postal service agents tracked down post office embezzlers, thieves, and robbers who targeted mail riders and mail stagecoaches, steamboats, and trains. In 1853, there were 18 special agents working for the national Post Office. Each agent was assigned a specific territory and possessed a full range of law enforcement authority, including the power to carry firearms and execute warrants as agents of the federal government (USPS, 2007).

Federal Law Enforcement
Expands with the Nation

From the second half of the 19th Century through the early part of the 20th Century, federal law enforcement experienced considerable growth and maturation. This coincided with the growth of the United States as a nation. A total of 29 states joined the Union during the 1800s, including 15 states which joined after 1850. Additionally, three more states joined the Union between 1900 and 1910. The geographic footprint of the nation really took shape during this period of time. As the United States was bound by the Atlantic Ocean to the east and Canada to the North, all of the expansion was westward. And as citizens went west to realize their hopes and dreams, the government of the United States went with them.

Settlers in the American West faced a number of challenging circumstances. The climate of the Great Plains and the western mountain regions was harsh. Nature was largely untamed and there were few amenities of western civilization save for the outposts and small towns. Further, many Native American tribes had not yet relinquished their control of territory; they frequently harassed and challenged settlers through raiding parties and attacks. But there was an additional challenge to western expansion: lawlessness (Johnson and Wolfe, 2003). As the territory of the United States grew, and grew quickly, law enforcement had a difficult time keeping up. Johnson and Wolfe note that federal marshals who policed the unorganized American territories of the West were spread so thin that frequently only a handful of deputy marshals were available to cover geographic areas equivalent to one or more western states today (2003).

The American Frontier West was an ideal place for the criminal element to go. There were very few law enforcement officers in the West. There was also considerable anonymity and freedom for settlers moving out west. No one knew who you were, or where you came from. Nor did most people care. It was an ideal situation for hiding from the law out east, or for turning over a new leaf from one's criminal background or damaged reputation and starting a respectable life.

During the late 1700s and early 1800s, the U.S. Marshals were the primary face of federal law enforcement. Their law enforcement responsibilities were the most plentiful among federal agencies and their authority was the broadest. Throughout the second half of the 1800s, these characterizations remained true. The U.S. Marshals and their deputies were the primary representations of federal police power. And as suggested above, in many western territories, they were the only representation of police power of any kind.

The U.S. Marshals were especially challenged after the Civil War. This was true not only in the South during reconstruction (where U.S. Marshals were reviled for their role in enforcing post-war civil rights laws), but likewise in the ostensibly neutral western territories. In addition to criminal offenders who sought out the West as a playground for new criminal enterprises, western territories hosted many post-Civil War southern veterans who pursued criminal activities out of anger and frustration with their plights during and after the Civil War.

One of the most notorious examples of this was the James Gang, which included famed outlaws Jesse and Frank James. The James Gang committed numerous bank robberies, stagecoach and train robberies, and acts of murder. If federal money or federal property were taken in a robbery, the U.S. Marshals had exclusive jurisdiction in federal territory, or joint jurisdiction with local authorities when the crimes occurred within the boundaries of a state or organized territory.

The U.S. Marshals also had broad law enforcement authority in Indian Territory. Working cases and tracking fugitives in Indian territories was among the most dangerous types of work conditions a U.S. Marshal could find himself in. Between 1872 and 1896 in the Oklahoma Territory, a total of 103 deputy U.S. marshals were killed in the line of duty (Jackson, 1989).

In organized territories and states, general law enforcement authority in the West primarily fell to county and town officers. Even so, U.S. Marshals had investigative authority in those criminal cases in which Indians were alleged to be involved as perpetrators. As already noted, the U.S. Marshals were the only law enforcement officers possessing authority to perform even the most general of police duties in unorganized American territories.

An important point in the history of federal law enforcement was the creation of the U.S. Justice Department. Congress passed a law establishing the Department of Justice in July of 1870. In addition to creating the Justice Department, the statute also gave the department oversight authority regarding federal law enforcement activities. The Office of U.S. Marshal was reorganized to operate under the auspices of the Justice Department. Further reform occurred in July of 1896 when the fee system of compensation for U.S. Marshals and deputy U.S. marshals was eliminated; in its place, the Justice Department established a set yearly salary for U.S. Marshals and deputy U.S. marshals and paid them as department employees.

As important as the creation of the U.S. Justice Department, and its absorption of the U.S. Marshals, was to the history of American federal law enforcement, it wasn't the only significant development in the post-Civil War 19th Century. For example, in April of 1865, the U.S. Secret Service was officially cast into existence as a unit of the Department of Treasury (also see Chapter 9). The primary reason for the creation of the Secret Service was America's huge problem with counterfeit currency. In fact, by some estimates, as much as one-third to one-half of all currency in circulation in the United States was counterfeit in the months that immediately followed the Civil War (Melanson, 2002).

Counterfeiting had been a problem during the Civil War as well. The circulation of counterfeit currency was a weapon used by the South to undermine the economy of the North. And in the 1860s, counterfeiting was relatively easy to do. There wasn't a single currency to be used nationwide. Rather, hundreds of state banks existed around the country that designed and produced their own paper notes. Counterfeiters could either copy legitimate bank notes or simply create fictitious notes of their own. It is estimated that during the early years of the Civil War, there were approximately 7,000 varieties of genuine bank notes and 4,000 varieties of counterfeit notes (Faust, 1991).

Congress addressed the lack of uniformity in American currency by passing three Legal Tender Acts in February and July of 1862 and March of 1863, respectively. The first of these acts authorized the Department of the Treasury to issue $150 million in U.S. Treasury notes. The second and third Legal Tender Acts resulted in a circulation of an additional $300 million in U.S. Treasury notes. The United States began to print its own paper currency. Given the currency's green color, the term "greenback" quickly caught on as slang for American paper money (Faust, 1991).

But even with the adoption of a national currency, counterfeiting continued. Sensing a need for a specific government agency to confront the problem, legislation was passed in 1865 to create the U.S. Secret Service as a bureau of the Treasury Department. The Secret Service's mission was to suppress counterfeiting. And suppress they did. By the conclusion of its first year of existence, the Secret Service had dismantled over 200 counterfeiting operations. In fact, by 1875, the success of Secret Service operations against counterfeiters had effectively made counterfeiting a minor criminal problem—far from the threat to the economy that it once had been (Melanson, 2002).

While the Secret Service was created in 1865 with a single mission in mind—thwarting counterfeiters—the agency did experience an expansion of its authority over time during the latter half of the 19th Century. In 1867, the Secret Service was given investigative jurisdiction to investigate any fraud committed against the United States Government. Interestingly, it was the Secret Service's authority to investigate fraud schemes which ultimately resulted in the agency's famed responsibility of presidential protection. In 1894, the Secret Service informally provided protection for President Grover Cleveland because the President had been the subject of threats relating to a Secret Service fraud case. The suspects in the case were not happy with the federal investigation and had threatened harm against the President as a chief federal executive. Because the threats were related to Secret Service case work, the agency felt a need to provide the President with some protection. Secret Service head William Hazen assigned two agents from the Colorado investigation to work protective detail at the White House. This seemed especially prudent in light of the fact there had already been two presidential assassinations in the preceding 29 years — Abraham Lincoln in 1865 and James Garfield in 1881. Even so, such presidential protection was not yet officially authorized by Congress. Consequently, Hazen was demoted and reprimanded in 1898 for misappropriating Secret Service funds toward the protection of President Cleveland and his family (Kaiser, 1988).

Congress began to adjust its thinking in 1901 when President William McKinley was assassinated by anarchist Leon Czolgosz while visiting the Pan American Exposition in Buffalo, NY. In all of America's history leading up to 1865, no president had ever been assassinated. But with McKinley's death, three presidents had succumbed to assassins' bullets in a 35-year time period.

Congress temporarily authorized the Secret Service to provide protection to the President and the first family while it mulled over what to do. Some members of Congress believed that the United States Army was the proper organization for providing protection to the President, who was after all the commander in chief. Legislation was proposed in the Senate which would have authorized the Secretary of War "to select and detail from the Regular Army a sufficient number of officers and men to guard and protect the person of the President of the United States without any unnecessary display" and to "make special rules and regulations as to dress, arms, and equipment ... of said guard" (Kaiser, 1988).

However, many in Congress opposed this legislation. They saw it as a mechanism for giving the Secretary of War sweeping powers to create a plainclothes, secret service within the army. These legislators were concerned that creating a presidential protection detail, housed in the Army, was a first step toward creating a police-state with the Army at the helm (Bumgarner, 2006). Although the language in the legislation passed in the Senate, it was struck by the House Judiciary Committee when the bill reached the House of Representatives. The sentiments of the House Judiciary Committee are well-reflected in its report (H.R. Report No. 1422, 1902):

> [under the Senate version of the bill] the Secretary of War may detail every man and officer in the Regular Army, under the pretense of protecting the President, dress them to suit his fancy, and send them abroad among the people to act under secret orders. When such laws begin to operate in this Republic the liberties of the people will take wings and fly away.

In lieu of the U.S. Army, the House Judiciary Committee instead recommended that the Treasury Department's Secret Service be permanently authorized to protect the President. The Senate, however, did not agree to this modification, and a final version of the bill did not clear Congress that year. In fact, it wasn't until 1906 that Congress finally agreed to authorize the Secret Service to be the permanent protective agency for the President. Congress, in passing the Sundry Civil Expenses Act for 1907, included language which expressly delegated to the Secret Service this responsibility and appropriated monies to the Department of Treasury for that purpose.

In 1906, the Secret Service also saw its investigative authority expand yet again. This time, the agency was given clearer and broader authority to investigate fraudulent land schemes committed against the federal government or involving federal lands. Commonly, land schemes involved offenders taking federal land, converting it to private ownership (using fraudulent documents), and the selling the land to unsuspecting buyers, or simply converting the federal land's natural resources for one's private use and profit. In the early part of the 20th Century, the U.S. Secret Service investigated a large number of land scheme cases. Through the success of their investigative work, millions of acres of public lands were returned to the government's roster. On November 3, 1907, Secret Service operative Joseph Walker was assigned to a land scheme case when he was killed by subjects of the investigation. Walker was the first Secret Service investigator to be killed in the line of duty (USSS, n.d.).

Public Lands

The turn of the 20th Century was a significant time for law enforcement involving federal public lands. In addition to the robust investigative authority given to the Secret Service to investigate fraudulent land schemes, other federal agencies also saw their own law enforcement authorities on public lands expand. The creation of, and delineation of authority to, the U.S. Forest Service is a case in point. Congress passed the Forest Reserve Act in 1891, which authorized the President of the United States to create federal forest reserves. These reserves were to be timber-covered public lands. The forest reserves, later dubbed national forests, were initially controlled by the U.S. Interior Department. However, the control of the forests was eventually moved to the U.S. Department of Agriculture because timber was an agricultural product. President Theodore Roosevelt signed into law an act creating the United States Forest Service as an agency of the Agriculture Department on February 1, 1905.

On March 3, 1905, Congress authorized employees of the Forest Service to exercise law enforcement authority under Title 16, section 10. Under that authorization (later moved to 16 USC 559), all employees of the U.S. Forest Service of the United States were given the authority ...

> ... to make arrests for the violation of the laws and regulations relating to the national forests, and any person so arrested shall be taken before the nearest United States magistrate judge, within whose jurisdiction the forest is located, for trial; and upon sworn information by any competent person any United States magistrate judge in the proper jurisdiction shall issue process for the arrest of any person charged with the violation of said laws and regulations; but nothing herein contained shall be construed as preventing the arrest by any officer of the United States, without process, of any person taken in the act of violating said laws and regulations.

An interesting feature of this authorization was that the law enforcement authority rested with every Forest Service employee. Early in the Forest Service's existence, all employees were expected to be ready to perform law enforcement duties if the situation required.

Somewhat parallel to the development of the federal interest in public forests for agricultural purposes was the development of the federal interest in public parks for recreational and preservation purposes. In 1872, Yellowstone National Park was established as "a public park or pleasuring-ground for the benefit and enjoyment of the people" and was the first such national park to exist (Kieley, 1940). However, during the 1890s, several more national parks were established. These parks included Yosemite, General Grant, and Sequoia National Parks in California, and Mount Rainier National Park in the State of Washington. National parks were not to be farmed and harvested as national forests were. Hence, lawmakers placed national parks under the control of the Department of Interior. However, each national park still represented a distinct organizational unit within the Interior Department.

On June 8, 1906, the Antiquities Act was signed by President Roosevelt. This statute granted to the federal government additional powers to partition public lands for the enjoyment of the public and for educational purposes. The statute also gave the President the authority to declare historical landmarks, historic and prehistoric structures, and other objects of scientific interest located on public lands or under the federal government's control to be national monuments (Kieley, 1940). National monuments were to be administered and protected by the Department of Interior according to the legislation. The Antiquities Act also established criminal penalties for the theft or destruction of antiquities found on public lands.

On August 25, 1916, Congress saw wisdom in consolidating the individual national parks and monuments—already under the broad control of the Department of Interior—into a single national parks agency within the Interior Department. It was at this time that the National Park Service was created (also see Chapter 11). As a federal agency, the National Park Service was primarily concerned about conservation and recreation. Employees of the National Park Service, like the Forest Service, were given broad law enforcement authority by Congress, found in 16 USC 1a-6. Unlike the Forest Service authority, the police powers only accrued to those employees whom the Secretary of Interior so designated (rather than to all personnel in the organization).

As previously noted, the late 19th Century and early 20th Century was a pivotal time for the growth and expansion of federal law enforcement. The U.S. Marshals moved west and engaged in a full range of police activity on behalf of the United States. The U.S. Secret Service was created with narrow responsibilities but saw its jurisdiction grow significantly over a 40-year period. And two different land management agencies came into existence with robust police powers on those public lands. And yet, still more federal law enforcement "firsts" occurred during this time.

For example, the Bureau of Internal Revenue (renamed the Internal Revenue Service in 1953) had been created on July 1, 1862, but had no law enforcement authority to enforce tax laws. Rather, the U.S. Marshals performed that duty. But on July 1, 1919, the Commission for Internal Revenue created the bureau's Intelligence Unit; its mission was to investigate federal tax fraud and evasion (also see Chapter 13). The Intelligence Unit initially consisted of six U.S. Postal Inspectors who were transferred to the Treasury Department. The Intelligence Unit is the direct ancestor of today's Criminal Investigative Division (CID) of the Internal Revenue Service. The transferred Postal Inspectors, and other agents who would join them in the Intelligence Unit, quickly garnered a reputation for being the most professional and best-trained financial investigators in the world (IRS, 2012).

The late 19th and early 20th centuries were a time of dynamism and flux for the federal law enforcement community. The timeframe saw the growth and refinement of existing agencies and the creation of new ones. Throughout federal law enforcement, authorities were clarified and enhanced by statutes. Law enforcement agents and officers of the U.S.

Marshals, the Secret Service, the Postal Service, U.S. Customs, the Capitol Police, and other organizations were on firmer ground than ever. And yet, no one in law enforcement or government circles could possibly know that all of the advancement of the various federal law enforcement agencies through the early part of the 20th Century would be eclipsed by the transfer of nine Secret Service agents from the Treasury Department to the Justice Department in 1908 for purpose of forming a small detective bureau. This transfer of Treasury personnel constitutes the unheralded but auspicious infancy of what would become the Federal Bureau of Investigation (also see Chapter 3). If some in Congress at the turn of the 20th Century were concerned about the growth of federal police power over the preceding 100 years, they would be stunned at the growth of the next 100 years to come — in no small part thanks to the Justice Department's newly formed detective bureau.

References

Bumgarner, J. (2006). *Federal agents: The growth of federal law enforcement in America.* Westport, CT: Praeger Publishers.

Calhoun, F. (1989). *The lawmen: United States Marshals and their deputies, 1789–1989.* Washington, D.C.: Smithsonian Institution Press.

Faust, P. (ed.) (1991). *Historical times illustrated encyclopedia of the civil war.* New York, NY: Harper and Row.

Internal Revenue Service (2012, March 7). *The history of IRS criminal investigation.* Retrieved from http://www.irs.gov/compliance/enforcement/article/0,,id=107469,00.html.

Jackson, D. (1989). Bicentennial of the U.S. Marshals. *The Smithsonian.* April.

Johnson, H. and Wolfe, N. (2003). *History of criminal justice.* Cincinnati, OH: Anderson Publishing.

Kaiser, F. (1988). Origins of Secret Service protection of the President: Personal, interagency, and institutional conflict. *Presidential Studies Quarterly.* Winter.

Kieley, J. (1940). *A brief history of the National Park Service.* Washington, D.C.: Department of Interior.

Mackintosh, B. (1989). *The United States Park Police: A history.* Washington, D.C.: NPS History Division.

Melanson, P. (2002). *Secret Service: The hidden history of an enigmatic agency.* New York, NY: Carroll and Graf Publishers.

Saba, A. (2003). U.S. Customs Service: Always there ... ready to serve. *U.S. Customs Today.* February.

U.S. Coast Guard (2002). *U.S. Coast Guard: An historical overview.* Washington, D.C.: USCG Historian's Office.

U.S. House of Representatives Report No. 1422, Protection of the President and suppression of crime against government. Report of the House Judiciary Committee, 57th Congress, 1st Session, 1902.

U.S. Postal Service (2007). *The United State Postal Service: An American history 1775–2006.* Retrieved from http://about.usps.com/publications/pub100/welcome.htm.

U.S. Secret Service (n.d.). *Secret Service history.* Retrieved from http://www.secretservice.gov/history.shtml.

U.S. Senate Historian (n.d.). *The Capitol Police.* Retrieved from http://www.senate.gov/artandhistory/history/common/briefing/Capitol_Police.htm.

Walker, S. (1977). *A critical history of police reform.* Lexington, MA: Lexington Books.

Chapter Two

Current State of Federal Law Enforcement in America

Law enforcement in the United States is very decentralized by nature. There are over 12,500 municipal police departments around the country. Additionally, there are over 3,060 county sheriff's departments. With 50 states, the United States also has 50 state police or state patrol organizations. There are also approximately 1,700 special jurisdiction police departments in America, including campus police departments, park police agencies, transit and airport police departments, and other police agencies. State and local police agencies employ over 1.1 million people, with approximately 765,000 sworn officers among them (Reaves, 2011). And then there's the federal law enforcement community with its dozens of federal agencies and 120,000 sworn personnel.

Many observers from other countries look at the United States' system of law enforcement, along with its decentralized, bottom-up nature with bemusement. Why would America choose such an uncoordinated approach to something so important as public safety and the enforcement of public laws? Surely, law enforcement would be more efficiently exercised if centrally managed, or at least regionally managed, with far fewer layers and far less politics.

Critics of a decentralized approach to law enforcement often cite a number of undesirable outcomes. These include (Bumgarner, 2006):

1) Uneven or unequal quality of police service
2) Inability to set national law enforcement policy
3) Disjointed response to crime overlapping jurisdictions
4) Competition and sub-cultural differences between agencies can result in an intentional lack of cooperation

All of these outcomes are a fairly predictable result of decentralized policing and constitute matters of genuine concern for elected officials, law enforcement leaders, and the courts in the United States.

However, there are many practical advantages to the decentralized nature of American law enforcement that cannot be readily dismissed. These advantages parallel those identified by political scientist Thomas Dye when characterizing the nature of America's federal system of government generally, with a premium placed on the benefits of local government control (Dye, 2001).

The chief advantage to a decentralized law enforcement structure in America is that power is dispersed. And it is dispersed not by accident, but by design. The United States adheres to a truly federal system of government, where power is shared by the national and state sovereigns. State sovereignty, by extension, filters down to municipal, county, and special jurisdiction governments which flow from the authorities of their home states and state constitutions. Through the dispersion of police power across the 50 states and thousands of local governments, abuses of power are more easily identifiable and remain confined in reach (i.e. to limited jurisdiction) when they do occur. As such, abuses are more readily susceptible to intervention and corrective measures.

A second advantage of decentralized law enforcement in the United States is the fact that police activity is more manageable and efficient — particularly at the local level. Law enforcement decisions regarding tactics and strategy can be made by officials on the ground and close to the situation or situations at hand without having to consult with bosses in capital cities hundreds or thousands of miles away.

A third advantage of decentralized policing is accountability. This advantage is closely linked to the second. Police leaders who make field decisions in real time and close to the action are not going to be second-guessed by administrators in Washington, D.C. weeks later. Rather, they will be held to account by local officials and the affected public whom they serve in Any-Town, USA. The fact that citizens — real people — can scrutinize law enforcement actions and decisions at the local level and compel changes is a far cry from the lack of influence regular people have over public officials in Washington, D.C., or even over bureaucrats located in the various state capitals. Local governance and accountability can literally begin with a citizen picking up the telephone and lodging a complaint, concern, or suggestion.

A fourth advantaged of decentralized policing in the United States is that decentralization permits the opportunity to observe, chronicle, and study multiple strategies and tactics for policing. The thousands of governmental jurisdictions in the United States provide thousands of governance laboratories for ferreting out policing best practices and practices to avoid. What's more, there is recognition that one size does not fit all. Policing strategies in a smaller community will undoubtedly look very different than strategies in a larger community only a few miles up the road. Through decentralization, law enforcement agencies may tailor their mission, strategies, and activities, to their respective circumstances.

With America's decentralized approach to law enforcement, primacy is placed on crime fighting at the local level — generally where crime occurs. And yet, the United States does maintain a significant federal law enforcement community, constituting about 14% of all gun-carrying, arrest-making law officers in the country. A closer look at just who makes up the federal law enforcement community is in order.

Federal Law Enforcement by the Numbers

The primary federal department responsible for law enforcement at the national level is the U.S. Department of Justice (DOJ). The DOJ organization chart is found in Figure 2.1. Across a swath of agencies, the DOJ employs criminal investigators, prosecutors, civil attorneys, crime and intelligence analysts, correctional officers, victims advocates, and host of others pursuing the DOJ mission, which is (DOJ, n.d.):

> To enforce the law and defend the interests of the United States according to the law; to ensure public safety against threats foreign and domestic; to provide federal leadership in preventing and controlling crime; to seek just punishment for those guilty of unlawful behavior; and to ensure fair and impartial administration of justice for all Americans.

The DOJ's enacted budget for Fiscal Year 2012 was $27.2 billion. This appropriation included funding for 113,521 positions across the department. The Fiscal Year 2013 budget

Figure 2.1 U.S. Department of Justice Organization Chart

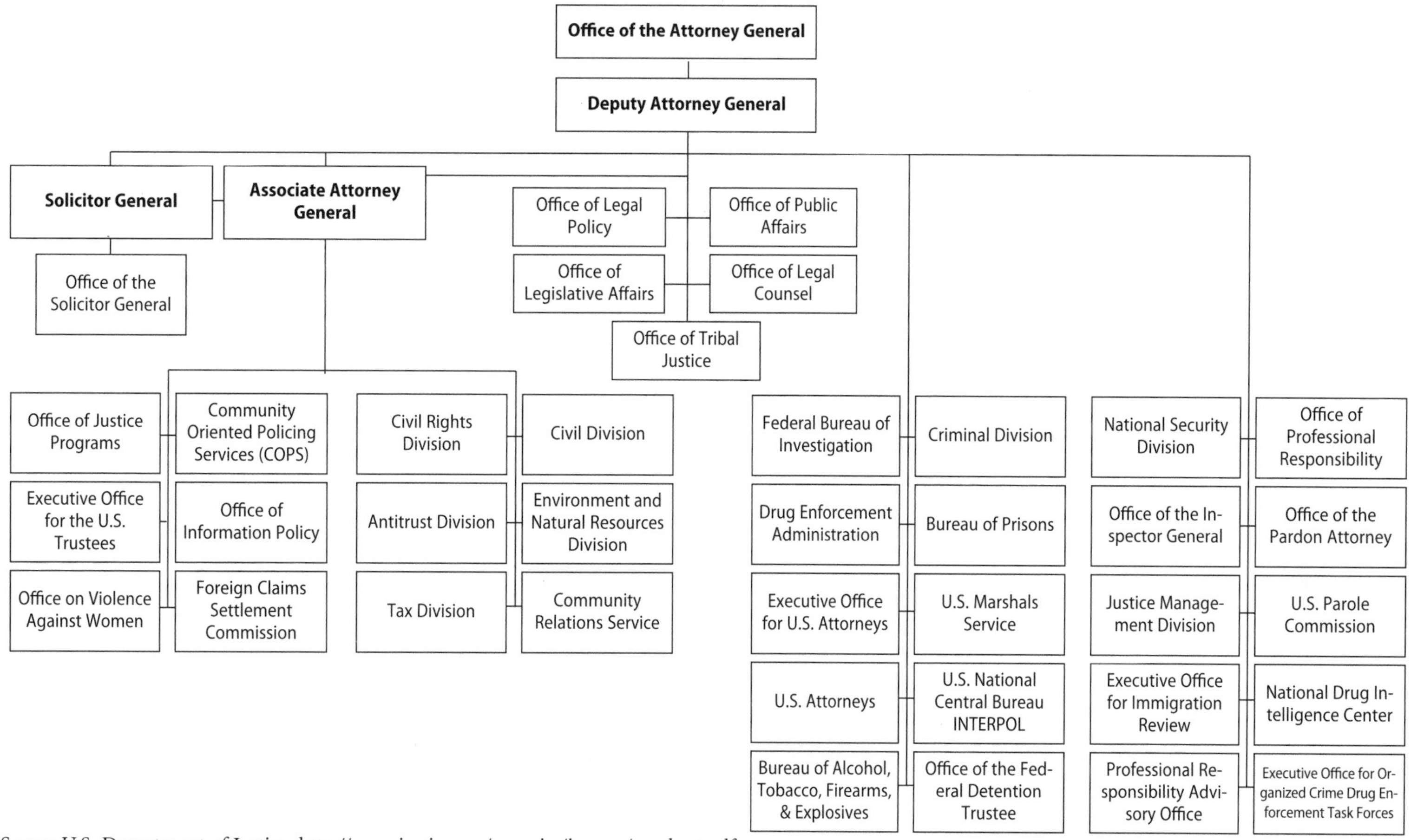

Source: U.S. Department of Justice, http://www.justice.gov/agencies/images/orgchart.pdf.

request was slightly less at $27.1 billion, but included funding for a total staffing level of 114,347 — an increase in personnel of 826. The proportions for spending categories in DOJ's Fiscal 2013 budget were (DOJ, n.d.):

- law enforcement (49%)
- prisons and detention (32%)
- litigation (11%)
- grants (6%)
- administrative and other (2%)

The law enforcement responsibilities of the department constitute DOJ's highest priority as reflected in its discretionary spending. Of course, DOJ is not the only department of the United States Government to engage in a law enforcement mission. As already noted, there are dozens of federal law enforcement agencies spread throughout the federal government investigating crimes and enforcing laws in their respective jurisdictional corners.

In June of 2012, the DOJ's Bureau of Justice Statistics (BJS) released its periodic census of federal law enforcement officers. The report, drafted by BJS statistician Brian Reaves, summarized federal law enforcement data from 2008, collected from 73 federal agencies. Previous census reports, released in 2006 and 2001 covered the years 2004 and 2000, respectively. Consideration of these reports side-by-side presents some interesting observations and trends.

According to the BJS report, there were approximately 120,000 full-time American federal law enforcement officers in 2008. For the purpose of the report, "law enforcement officer" was defined as officers or agents who were authorized by federal law to make arrests and carry firearms in the course of their duties.

Of the 120,000 law enforcement officers, approximately 45,000, or 37%, held positions in which they primarily performed criminal investigative duties. This figure is of similar proportion to the law enforcement data from 2004 when 38% of the 105,000 federal law enforcement officers that year held criminal investigative positions (Reaves, 2006). Interestingly, the percentage of federal officers serving as criminal investigators is down from 2000. In the year 2000, there were 88,000 full-time federal law enforcement officers, 41% of whom occupied criminal investigative positions. While federal law enforcement grew significantly in numbers from 2000 until 2008 (an increase of 36%), the percentage of criminal investigators declined slightly (Reaves and Hart, 2001; Reaves 2012).

In 2008, 23% of federal law enforcement officers, or roughly 28,000, were in positions in which their primary duties were police response and patrol. Many of these uniformed police officers were located in the Washington, D.C. metro area. The percentage of officers working in federal police patrol positions was up slightly from 19% in 2000 and 21% in 2004. Officers primarily performing immigration and inspection duties was also up slightly from 13% in 2000 to 15% in 2008 (Reaves and Hart, 2001; Reaves 2012).

While federal law enforcement is known for consisting of dozens of agencies across all three branches of government, most of the federal law enforcement community is concentrated in a select few agencies. U.S. Customs and Border Protection (CBP) of the Department of Homeland Security employed nearly 37,000 law enforcement officers, including over 17,341 Border Patrol agents. Indeed, the Department of Homeland Security and the Department of Justice combined to employ 80% of all federal law enforcement officers in 2008 (Reaves, 2012).

In addition to the large uniformed force in CBP, the Department of Homeland Security fielded large numbers of criminal investigators. The Bureau of Immigration and Customs Enforcement (ICE) was the Department of Homeland Security's largest investigative agency with 12,446 special agents and enforcement removal officers. ICE saw significant growth among its workforce between 2004 and 2008. In 2008, ICE employed approximately 2,000 more agents than it had in 2004—about a 20% increase. The U.S. Secret Service was DHS's second largest investigative agency with approximately 3,000 special agents.

The Department of Justice is home to the largest federal criminal investigative agency—the Federal Bureau of Investigation (FBI). In 2008, the FBI employed over 12,500 special agents. The Drug Enforcement Administration (DEA) and the Bureau of Alcohol, Tobacco, Firearms and Explosives (ATF) are also Department of Justice investigative agencies and employed 4,308 and 2,541 specials agents in 2008, respectively (Reaves, 2012).

Federal law enforcement has historically been a more inviting environment for women and minorities than figures suggest is the case at the local level. In 2008, approximately 15.5% of federal law enforcement officers were women. This is up only slightly from 2000, when 14.4% were women. However, in local law enforcement, only 12.5% of officers were women in 2007, up about one percent from 2000 (Langton, 2010). In federal law enforcement, women are highly represented among the Offices of Inspector General. Of the 3,500 criminal investigators working for the various Inspectors General throughout the federal government, about 25% of them were women. The federal law enforcement agency with the greatest percentage of female agents or officers was the Internal Revenue Service—Criminal Investigation Division (IRS-CID). Women made up 32% of the special agents working at IRS-CID (Langton, 2010).

Federal law enforcement also has larger shares of racial and ethnic minorities among its ranks than do local law enforcement agencies collectively. In 2008, a little over 34% of all federal law enforcement officers were members of a racial or ethnic minority. This is up from 31% in 2000. In local law enforcement (in 2007), only 1 in 4 officers, or 25%, were members of a racial or ethnic minority. While the representation of minorities has improved in local law enforcement over the years (minorities constituted less than 17% of local officers in 1987), there remains a lag behind the rates of racial and ethnic diversity present in the federal law enforcement community (Reaves 2010; Reaves 2012).

In 2000, there were approximately 88,000 federal law enforcement officers in the United States. In 2008, there were approximately 120,000 federal officers. This amounts to an increase of 35% in less than a decade. Of course, most of that decade occurred within the context of the 9/11 terror attacks existing in our recent past. With the increase in federal law enforcement assets at the line level, one would expect to see a commensurate increase in federal criminal prosecutions. And indeed, federal prosecutions did increase during the first decade of the 21st Century—although not quite on the same trajectory as law enforcement's swelling numbers of personnel might have predicted.

The office responsible for federal criminal prosecutions is the U.S. Attorney's Office in any given federal judicial district. There are 94 judicial districts in the United States, and therefore 94 U.S. Attorneys. Each U.S. Attorney is presidentially-appointed and must be confirmed by the U.S. Senate. The U.S. Attorney is considered the chief federal law enforcement officer for a federal judicial district. However, the U.S. Attorney is not solely a law enforcement official. The responsibilities of the U.S. Attorney Offices are (DOJ, 2010):

- the prosecution of criminal cases brought by the federal government;
- the litigation and defense of civil cases in which the United States is a party;

- the handling of criminal and civil appellate cases before the United States Courts of Appeals; and
- the collection of debts owed the federal government that are administratively uncollectable.

Working for the United States Attorney in every district is a team of Assistant U.S. Attorneys (AUSAs). The AUSAs are the line-level prosecutors for the federal government—much like an assistant county attorney or assistant district attorney is at the local level. In Fiscal Year 2010 (i.e. from October 1, 2009–September 30, 2010), there were nearly 6,000 AUSAs nationwide working in the 94 U.S. Attorney Offices. There were an additional 5,800 employees making up the support staff. In Fiscal Year 2010, a total of 595,680 attorney work hours were directed to court-related activity. Two-thirds of that time was actually spent in court, with 66% of court time logged on criminal cases in U.S. District Court, 22% in U.S. Magistrate Courts, and 4 % on civil cases in U.S. District Court (DOJ, 2010).

In Fiscal Year 2010, federal prosecutors filed 68,591 criminal cases. This was up 21% from the number of criminal cases filed in Fiscal Year 2002—56,658. The criminal cases filed in Fiscal Year 2010 involved a total of 91,047 defendants. The largest share of these criminal cases involved immigration-related crimes; these filings totaled 29,843, or nearly 44% of the total criminal cases filed. There were 14,149 narcotics-related cases filed in Fiscal Year 2010, which were over 20% of the criminal case filings; violent crime cases totaled 11,360, or 16.5% of case filings. Federal prosecutors sustained a 93% conviction rate in Fiscal Year 2010, with 81% of those convicted receiving prison time. More than a quarter of all federal prison sentences were for greater than five years; 53% of prison sentences were for less than three years.

Debate Regarding Constitutional Limits of Federal Police Power

Today in the United States there rages a debate about the scope, purpose, and Constitutional limitations of the federal government, and by extension, federal law enforcement. It is acknowledged by most who are party to the debate that the U.S. Constitution can and does place limits on the federal government and its police powers; therefore, the debate moves to the question of just what does the Constitution require and preclude. Is it the plain language of the Constitution that must be heeded, or are there nuances and evolving and flexible themes embedded in the Constitution which are more permissive than the Constitution's 18th century verbiage would suggest?

The United States adheres to a republican form of government. Indeed, it is often dubbed a constitutional republic. A republican form of government relies on elected representatives of the people serving as government officials. But a constitutional republic goes a step further and ensures that those representatives refrain from tyranny by bounding government's authority within the confines of law—particularly through a constitution which establishes such limits of power. Thomas Jefferson wrote in a letter to Wilson Nicholas in 1803 that "our particular security is in the possession of a written constitution." Constitutional scholar Philip Bobbitt notes that Jefferson, the author of the Declaration of Independence, understood that the Constitution made good the proclamations of the declaration—namely, that the government was the creation of sovereign people, not the other way around (Bobbitt, 1991).

Chief Justice John Marshall certainly echoed this sentiment in his opinion of *Marbury v. Madison* (1803). Justice Marshall, while defending the concept of judicial review, nonetheless articulated that the ultimate authority of the nation is the people, and not Congress, or the President, or the Judiciary. The people possessed ALL authority, and then parceled some authority out through adoption of the Constitution.

That the Constitution is written down is important here. Justice Marshall wrote in part (1803):

> The powers of the legislature are defined and limited; and that those limits may not be mistaken or forgotten, the Constitution is written. To what purpose are powers limited, and to what purpose is the limitation committed to writing, if these limits may, at any time, be passed by those intended to be restrained.

If the American people are sovereign, and the Constitution is the people's instrument for parceling out power to their government, then it must be enduring until such time as the people change it. What's more, the Constitution must mean something if it is to have any efficacy as a check against government abuses of power.

James Madison was the chief author of the U.S. Constitution and vigorously defended it in several written commentaries when the Constitution was a mere proposal being considered to replace the Articles of Confederation. Madison, along with Alexander Hamilton and John Jay, published a number of essays supporting the Constitution which collectively came to be known as the *Federalist Papers*. Madison certainly envisioned a Constitution with enduring and concrete meaning. And he attempted to allay fears in the young, post-monarchist country that was the United State in the late 18th Century; he assured all who would listen that a tyrannical national government could not materialize with the adoption of the Constitution — precisely because the Constitution was clear about what the federal government could do and not do.

In *Federalist 41*, Madison (1788) said in response to those who were concerned that the national government might expand its coercive powers by relying on its mission to provide for the "common defense and general welfare" of the United States (as articulated in the Preamble and in Article I, Section 8) that the common defense and general welfare responsibilities are embodied in the enumerated powers. He specifically said there are no additional powers to be inferred from the preamble or from mention of the "general welfare" in Article I section 8. Madison asked rhetorically why the Constitution would enumerate powers at all if they are merely a sample contained in a general power.

Madison clarified his view of the federal power further in *Federalist 45*. Madison indicated that the powers of the federal government, as permitted in the proposed Constitution, are "few and defined." What's more, these powers relate principally to external objects, such as war, peace, taxation, and matters relating to foreign commerce. On the other hand, the powers of the states are "numerous and indefinite" according to Madison. These powers relate to lives, liberties, and properties of the people, the internal order, improvement and prosperity of the state (Madison, 1788).

Some critics of the proposed Constitution believed it did not go far enough, or was not clear enough, in restraining federal power. They wanted to include a Bill of Rights. Proponents of a Bill of Rights would eventually prevail, but Alexander Hamilton argued against their inclusion. Hamilton wrote in *Federalist 84* that inclusion of a Bill of Rights suggests the need for protection against coercive powers that the federal government doesn't actually have. Hence, the inclusion of a Bill of Rights might have the unintended consequence of validating a claim to broader power held by the federal government (Hamilton, 1788).

These samples from the *Federalist Papers* — a defense of the Constitution by the Framers themselves — certainly imply that the Constitution cannot mean whatever one, or a few, or even a majority of people contemporaneously want it to mean. As Chief Justice William Rehnquist suggested in his 1976 essay "*The Notion of a Living Constitution*," the document has meaning above and apart from a transient majoritarian opinion. In his essay, Chief Justice Rehnquist recalled a brief from a case before him and which was filed on behalf of state prisoners who contended that the conditions of their confinement were unconstitutional.

The brief read in part (Rehnquist, 1976):

> We are asking a great deal of the Court because other branches of government have abdicated their responsibility .... Prisoners are like other 'discrete and insular' minorities for whom the Court must spread its protective umbrella because no other branch of government will do so.... This Court, as the voice and conscience of contemporary society, as the measure of the modern conception of human dignity, must declare that the [named prison] and all it represents offends the Constitution of the United States and will not be tolerated.

Rehnquist observed that this brief epitomized the "living constitution" view. The petitioners wanted non-elected members of the federal judiciary to address a social problem simply because other branches of government failed or refused to do so. Ironically, justices in this case were asked to be the "voice and conscience of contemporary society" while actually being responsible or accountable to a constituency of no one.

Using the brief as a springboard, Rehnquist articulated two broad reasons to avoid the view of the Constitution as a malleable and living document apart from the amendment process. First, the notion of a "living constitution" which permits an expanding view of federal power undermines the sovereignty of the American people. The people adopted the Constitution and its amendments. Rehnquist believed judicial review must not be used to undermine the will of the people. When the Congress, or the President, or the states operate within the authority granted to them, their judgments and not that of the court members must prevail. To this point, Rehnquist drew from John Stuart Mill's classic *On Liberty*, which reads in part (1869):

> The disposition of mankind, whether as rulers or as fellow citizens, to impose their own opinions and inclinations as a rule of conduct on others, is so energetically supported by some of the best and by some of the worst feeling incident to human nature, that it is hardly ever kept under restraint by anything but want of power.

The "restraint" that America has come up with is a system replete with checks and balances, a legislature consisting of members representing different interests found in different parts of the country, and a thorough vetting process for changing the Constitution. The disposition of human beings to impose their will on others, which John Stuart Mill refers to, shouldn't come easier to some just because they are judges.

Likewise, a decision by the President, Congress, or a state to NOT act should not be trumped by an ambitious and wiser judiciary. Rehnquist wrote (1976):

> Surely the Constitution does not put either the legislative branch or the executive branch in the position of a television quiz show contestant so that when a given period of time has elapsed and a problem remains unsolved by them, the federal judiciary may press a buzzer and take its turn at fashioning a solution.

Rehnquist's second reason to avoid viewing the Constitution as a malleable and living document was doing so leads to disastrous decisions. In a decision of supreme judicial activism, Chief Justice Taney invalidated the Kansas-Nebraska Act of 1854 and a whole generation of hard-fought political combat leading up to this law ... a law which had effectively repealed the Missouri Compromise and allowed new territories to decide whether they would permit slavery.

Abraham Lincoln referenced this decision in his first inaugural address in 1861:

> The candid citizen must confess that if the policy of the government, upon vital questions affecting the whole people, is to be irrevocably fixed by decisions of the Supreme Court, the instant they are made, in ordinary litigation between parties in personal actions, the people will have ceased to be their own rulers, having to that extent practically resigned their government into the hands of that eminent tribunal.

For the reasons above, critics of an expansive and flexible view of federal power, and by extension, federal police power, insist that a constitution provides a constitutional republic with its very bedrock. They argue that the limits of power can't be, and shouldn't be, a moving target unless the American people move it. And to ensure that adopting changes is done soberly and not whimsically, the amendment process is a robust one. Constitutional purists note that the amendment process does work and has worked. But it will only continue to work if the Constitution has inherent meaning in the first place.

So, what does the U.S. Constitution say? Most Constitutional scholars agree that the U.S. Constitution does not confer a general police power to federal government, but rather reserves police power to the states. The 10th Amendment of the Constitution declares: "The powers not delegated to the United States by the Constitution, nor prohibited to the States, are reserved to the States respectively, or to the people."

According to the 10th Amendment, States are sovereign governments, and a sovereign can police its own people and territory as it sees fit. By contrast, as previously noted, the federal government's powers are limited and defined. While the responsibilities of collecting taxes, regulating commerce and immigration, and fighting counterfeiting, piracy, and insurrections all connote a need for a coercive police power, these areas of enforcement do not immediately call to mind a role for the federal government in confronting general crimes. And yet, increasingly, this is precisely what the federal government's law enforcement community has done—waded into the waters of general crime fighting.

Of particular importance in the modern history of federal law enforcement has been the power to regulate interstate commerce. This authority given to Congress in the Constitution has been the foundation for most federal criminal statutes (Bumgarner, 2006). The U.S. Supreme Court has had a long history in interpreting the Interstate Commerce clause of the U.S. Constitution. In the case of *Gibbons v. Ogden* (1824), the Supreme Court ruled that the Commerce Clause gave Congress broad authority to regulate commercial matters. Chief Justice John Marshall wrote in the Court's decision that the wisdom and discretion of Congress must be relied upon in determining just how far to take that authority. And, over the dozens of decades that followed, Congress determined in its own wisdom that the authority was fairly expansive.

However in recent years, the U.S. Supreme Court has scaled back Congress' authority to coerce under the power of the Interstate Commerce Clause. In the case of *U.S. v. Lopez* (1995), the U.S. Supreme Court ruled in a 5–4 decision that the Gun Free School Zones Act of 1990 was unconstitutional. The Gun Free School Zones Act had made possession of a gun within 1,000 feet of a school a federal felony. Congress, in passing the law, had justified its authority to do so on the basis of its power to regulate interstate commerce. Government lawyers defending the law before the Supreme Court embraced the same logic. They argued essentially that the presence of guns tend to result in violent crime. What's more, high levels of localized violent crime can have an economic impact which is spread across the country. If students are worried about gun violence at their schools, or are victims of gun violence, then their abilities to secure an education are impeded. Without an education, students will be unable to get a job, thus lacking legitimate income to engage in commerce, including interstate commerce. Further, fear of violent crime generally prevents many from traveling across state lines to areas which are perceived by potential travelers as unsafe. This too affects interstate commerce.

Chief Justice Rehnquist wrote the opinion of the Court in striking down this law. He noted that this logic would permit the federal government to connect virtually any criminal issue to interstate commerce and thereby affords the federal government broad police power. Justice Steven Breyer dissented. He reiterated in his written minority opinion the generally accepted principles of an expansive view toward the Commerce Clause. In particular, he applied 3 principles in his dissent (*U.S. v. Lopez*, 1995):

- First, Congress can regulate local activities if they significantly affect interstate commerce;

- Second, the Supreme Court, in deciding these kinds of cases, must consider not the effect of an individual act, but the cumulative effect of an activity; and

- Third, Congress must be given wide latitude, needing only a rational basis (as opposed to the more stringent "strict judicial scrutiny") for believing that an activity is connected to interstate commerce.

Breyer's view was consistent with the Court's previous decision in *Wickard v. Filburn* (1942). In that case, the Supreme Court said that the federal government could regulate *intrastate* commerce, or even non-commercial activity, if that activity when viewed in the aggregate would affect interstate commerce. But this doctrine was now mortally wounded by the *Lopez* decision and would continue to succumb to additional undermining decisions in the years following *Lopez*.

The U.S. Supreme Court went on to re-affirm the principle of limited power bestowed to the federal government and a limited view of the Commerce Clause in the case of *U.S. v. Morrison* in 2000. In that case, portions of the federal Violence Against Women Act of 1994 were determined to be unconstitutional by the Supreme Court—again in a 5–4 decision. The law, among other things, permitted victims of gender-based violence, such as domestic violence and sexual assaults, to sue their alleged attackers in federal court. Once again, Chief Justice Rehnquist wrote the majority opinion. He said in part (*U.S. v. Morrison*, 2000):

> We accordingly reject the argument that Congress may regulate noneconomic, violent criminal conduct based solely on that conduct's aggregate effect on interstate commerce. The Constitution requires a distinction between what is truly national and what is truly local. In recognizing this fact we preserve one of the few principles that has been consistent since the Clause was adopted. The regulation and punishment of intrastate violence that is not directed at the in-strumentalities, channels, or goods involved in interstate commerce has always been the province of the States. Indeed, we can think of no better example of the police power, which the Founders denied the National Government and reposed in the States, than the suppression of violent crime and vindication of its victims.

The notion of a limited view of the Commerce Clause of the Constitution was yet again upheld in the recent Supreme Court decision regarding the Patient Protection and

Affordable Care Act of 2010. The law, commonly dubbed "Obamacare," included a provision which mandated that most individuals in the United States secure health insurance for themselves and their dependents. Those who were obligated under the law to have health insurance and didn't receive it from their employer would be forced to purchase an acceptable health care insurance policy which would provide for at least "minimally essential" coverage. Any individuals failing to purchase required insurance would be penalized through an assessment collected by the Internal Revenue Service. This provision, known as the "individual mandate" was challenged in court on grounds that such a requirement exceeded Congress' authority under the Commerce Clause. Chief Justice John Roberts wrote the opinion for the Court, upholding the mandate under Congress' taxing authority, but denying the right of Congress to regulate such behavior under the Commerce Clause. Chief Justice Roberts wrote (*National Federation of Independent Businesses, et al. v. Sebelius*, 2012):

> People, for reasons of their own, often fail to do things that would be good for them or good for society. Those failures — joined with similar failures of others — can readily have a substantial effect on interstate commerce. Under the Government's logic, that authorizes Congress to use its commerce power to compel citizens to act as the Government would have them act.
>
> That is not the country the Framers of our Constitution envisioned. James Madison explained [in Federalist 45] that the Commerce Clause was 'an addition which few oppose and from which no apprehensions are entertained.' While Congress's authority under the Commerce Clause has of course expanded with the growth of the national economy, our cases have 'always recognized that the power to regulate commerce, though broad indeed, has limits.' Maryland v. Wirtz, 392 U. S. 183, 196 (1968). The Government's theory would erode those limits, permitting Congress to reach beyond the natural extent of its authority, "everywhere extending the sphere of its activity and drawing all power into its impetuous vortex." [Madison, Federalist No. 48]. Congress already enjoys vast power to regulate much of what we do. Accepting the Government's theory would give Congress the same license to regulate what we do not do, fundamentally changing the relation between the citizen and the Federal Government.

With three major U.S. Supreme Court decisions eroding the broad view of the Commerce Clause in less than 30 years, weighed-in upon by many different justices and under the leadership of two Chief Justices, there is every reason to believe that the federal government has approached its limits on exercising coercive police powers under that provision of the Constitution. But at the same time, there appears to be little to no evidence that the existing variability of roles, responsibilities, and authorities exercised by federal law enforcement agencies — as represented by the sample of agencies in the chapters to follow — will be abated in the future. The mass of federal regulations and laws continue to grow.

In the fall and early winter of 2011, the *Wall Street Journal* ran several articles highlighting the aggrandizing nature of federal law enforcement and the federal criminal code. It noted, with some dismay, that the Code of Federal Regulations had 54,000 pages in 1970 and 165,000 pages today. It estimated that as few as 10,000 and as high as 300,000 regulations were connected to federal criminal statutes and penalties (Radnofsky, Fields, and Emshwiller, 2011). The volume of federal laws and regulations, if they are to be taken seriously, require an ample law enforcement workforce. As the laws flourish, so do the agencies — and in the eyes of many Americans in the political and government classes, they do so to the benefit of the American people and to the detriment of our nation's criminal element. But critics will continue to lament that the "criminal element" with which federal law enforcement is concerned includes a growing number of regular citizens caught up in the web of federal laws and regulations that the nation's framers arguably could never imagine would be the national government's province.

References

Bobbitt, P. (1991). *Constitutional interpretation.* Oxford, UK: B. Blackwell Publishing.

Bumgarner, J. (2006). *Federal agents: The growth of federal law enforcement in America.* Westport, CT: Praeger Publishers.

Dye, T. (2001). *Politics in America.* Upper Saddle River, NJ: Prentice Hall.

Gibbons v. Ogden. 22 U.S. 1 (1824).

Hamilton, A. (1788, July 16). Certain general and miscellaneous objections to the Constitution considered and answered [Federalist 84]. *Independent Journal.*

Langton, L. (2010). *Women in law enforcement, 1987–2008.* Washington, D.C.: Bureau of Justice Statistics.

Lincoln, A. (1861, March 4). First inaugural address. Retrieved from http://wps.prenhall.com/wps/media/objects/107/109640/ch15_a1_d2.pdf.

Madison, J. (1788, January 19). General view of the powers conferred by the Constitution [Federalist 41]. *Independent Journal.*

Madison, J. (1788, January 26). Alleged dangers from the powers of the Union to the state governments considered [Federalist 45]. *Independent Journal.*

Marbury v. Madison. 5 U.S. 137 (1803).

Mill, J.S. (1869). *On liberty.* London: Longman, Roberts, & Green.

National Federation of Independent Businesses, et al. v. Sebelius. 567 U.S. ___ (2012).

Radnofsky, L, Fields, G., and Emshwiller, J. (2011, December 17). Federal police ranks swell to enforce a widening array of criminal laws. *The Wall Street Journal.* U.S. edition.

Rehnquist, W. (1976). The notion of a living Constitution. *Texas Law Review, 54* (693).

Reaves, B. (2012). *Federal law enforcement officers, 2008.* Washington, D.C.: Bureau of Justice Statistics.

Reaves, B. (2011). *Census of state and local law enforcement agencies, 2008.* Washington, D.C.: Bureau of Justice Statistics.

Reaves, B. (2010). *Local police departments, 2007.* Washington, D.C.: Bureau of Justice Statistics.

Reaves, B. (2006). *Federal law enforcement officers, 2004.* Washington, D.C.: Bureau of Justice Statistics.

Reaves, B. and Hart, T. (2001). *Federal law enforcement officers, 2000.* Washington, D.C.: Bureau of Justice Statistics.

U.S. Department of Justice (2010). *United States Attorneys' annual statistical report: Fiscal year 2010.* Washington, D.C.: Executive Office of the United States Attorney, U.S. DOJ.

U.S. Department of Justice (n.d.). *FY 2013 budget performance and summary.* Retrieved from http://www.justice.gov/jmd/2013summary.

U.S. v. Morrison. 529 U.S. 598 (2000).

U.S. v. Lopez. 514 U.S. 549 (1995).

Wickard v. Filburn. 317 U.S. 111 (1942).

Part II
Federal Law Enforcement Agencies

Department of Justice

Chapter Three

Federal Bureau of Investigation (FBI)

To most Americans, no agency more chiefly embodies what federal law enforcement is than the Federal Bureau of Investigation, or FBI for short. In fact, in the eyes of Americans and many around the world, the FBI has come to be known as the premier law enforcement agency on the planet. The reputation has been well-earned. The scope and reach of the FBI and all that it does have grown over the years. Many casual observers of law enforcement stories and activities may be entirely unaware that the FBI is bound by any jurisdictional limitations whatsoever.

But, in fact, the FBI is enveloped by jurisdictional boundaries; as a federal agency, those boundaries remain fairly severe when one considers the entirety of what constitutes the field of policing and subfield of criminal investigation.

Even so, today the FBI has the broadest statutory authority of all American federal law enforcement agencies. This fact is rather remarkable given that the FBI is not, by a long shot, the oldest federal criminal investigative bureau. As Chapter 1 of this text noted, a number of federal law enforcement agencies came into existence and grew in jurisdictional prominence long before the FBI's humble beginning in the first decade of the 20th Century. But the FBI was savvy as agencies go, thanks to its leadership in the early years. It was consistently auspicious. And by the end the 1930s, the FBI's fixture in America's psyche as the face of federal law enforcement and the federal government's response to crime was firmly established.

History

The FBI points to 1908 as its birth year. It was in July of 1908 that the U.S. Justice Department first began to operate an investigative agency of its own. Prior to 1908, it was common practice for the Justice Department to borrow special agents from the U.S. Secret Service. After all, the Secret Service had firmly established by this time its law enforcement bona fides. The Secret Service had acquired, over a period of decades from the 1860s through and beyond 1900, considerable law enforcement jurisdiction.

What's more, the Secret Service was known throughout the federal government to be a professional investigative agency. The U.S. Marshals, on the other hand, were a mixed bag. Although organized under the Department of Justice, each district possessed its own U.S. Marshal, appointed by political processes, and employed deputy marshals beholden to the U.S. Marshal who hired them. And, the U.S. Marshals had their hands full attending to the business and security of the federal courts and policing American territories.

The Secret Service practice of loaning special agents to other government agencies increased considerably in the last decade of the 19th Century. This is because Congress passed a law in 1893 which prohibited the federal government's contracting with the

Pinkerton Detective Agency and other private detective firms. Prior to that time, government agencies were very active in employing the Pinkertons and others to perform investigative, protective, and apprehension duties. After 1893, and thanks to the entrepreneurial and expansion-minded spirit of the Treasury Department, the Secret Service was the only source of investigators to be had (Jeffreys-Jones, 2007).

But this practice of loaning Secret Service agents to other government agencies was not without controversy. Many in Congress were concerned about the expanding and aggrandizing power of the Secret Service. Some of the same concerns about an all-powerful plainclothes federal secret police which had been voiced during the debate about whether the President of the United States needed formal protection and who should do it were raised as the Secret Service continued to peddle its services and involved itself in the non-Treasury business of other agencies. The U.S. Justice Department was one such federal department that had come to regularly rely on Secret Service special agents conducting its investigations.

Some members of Congress were so opposed to the practice of the Secret Service farming out its investigative assets to other government agencies, they equated the practice to government-sanctioned espionage. James Tawney of Minnesota, the chairman of the House of Representatives Appropriations Committee, characterized the practice as a "system of espionage in this country which is entirely inconsistent with the theory of our government." Tawney and others did not want to see federal agents, Secret Service or otherwise, permeating in all corners of the government. Tawney went on to say that Congress would never permit or "… authorize … a secret service bureau in every department" (Fox, 2003).

Ironically, the opposition of Tawney and others to the Secret Service's loaning of special agents would pave the way for precisely the outcome he so dreaded—an investigative bureau in every department. There's little doubt Tawney would be stunned at the multitude of federal law enforcement agencies across the entire landscape of government departments today. But at the time, the concern was to reign in the one agency which seemed poised to become too powerful. So, in the spring of 1908, Congress passed legislation which banned the Treasury Department from loaning Secret Service detectives to any other government department (Jeffreys-Jones, 2007).

Congress' misgivings about the Secret Service presented an opportunity for the Justice Department and its head, Attorney General Charles Bonaparte. Bonaparte had been appointed Attorney General by Theodore Roosevelt in 1907 and had been dismayed from the beginning that the Justice Department had no detective bureau of its own. In fact, shortly after his appointment in 1907, he wrote to Congress about the Justice Department's need for a detective bureau of its own. He wrote in part (DOJ, 1907):

> The attention of the Congress should be, I think, called to the anomaly that the Department of Justice has no executive force, and, more particularly, no permanent detective force under its immediate control. This singular condition arises mainly from the fact that before the office of the Attorney-General was transformed into the Department of Justice a highly efficient detective service had been organized to deal with crimes against the Treasury laws, which force has been, in effect, lent from time to time to this Department to meet its steadily increasing need for an agency of this nature, without, however, being removed from the control of the Treasury Department. I note with pleasure the efficiency and zeal with which these officers have cooperated with the United States attorneys and marshals, as well as with the special representatives of this Department in the interest of their own special and appropriate duties. When emergencies arise requiring prompt and effective executive action, the Department is now obliged to rely

upon the several U.S. marshals; if it had a small, carefully selected, and experienced force under its immediate orders, the necessity of having these officers suddenly appoint special deputies, possibly in considerable numbers, might be sometimes avoided with greater likelihood of economy and better assurance of satisfactory results. I venture to recommend, therefore, that provision be made for a force of this character; its number and the form of its organization to be determined by the scope of the duties which the Congress may see fit to entrust to it. It may well be thought wise to preserve the existing detective organization, especially in view of its highly creditable record and excellent service, and it is not in any wise my purpose to suggest a different view, but it seems obvious that the Department on which not only the President, but the courts of the United States must call first to secure the enforcement of the laws, ought to have the means of such enforcement subject to its own call; a Department of Justice with no force of permanent police in any form under its control is assuredly not fully equipped for its work.

Clear in Bonaparte's report to Congress was his view that it was less than ideal for Secret Service agents, who remained under the control of the Treasury Department, to do the Justice Department's work. Nor was it ideal for the Justice Department to have to rely on the several U.S. Marshals across the country. So, in June of 1908, Bonaparte created a Justice Department investigative unit. He did so by hiring nine Secret Service agents who had previously been contracted by the Justice Department, as well as hiring an additional 25 new agents. He placed Stanley Finch as the head of the new, 34-agent detective bureau. Finch's title was that of Chief Examiner. On July 26, 1908, Bonaparte issued a memorandum to all Justice Department employees. The memorandum required that any Justice Department investigative matter be referred to the Chief Examiner, who would then decide if it was a case that should be handled by one of his agents (DOJ, 2008).

Some in Congress questioned Bonaparte's decision to administratively create an investigative unit within the Justice Department without Congressional approval or appropriation. President Roosevelt also required an explanation. In January of 1909, the Attorney General provided that explanation in the form of a letter to the President. In that letter, Bonaparte highlighted the fact that other federal departments such as Treasury, Interior, and Agriculture all operated law enforcement agencies of their own. As he did in his 1907 report to Congress, he noted that reliance on the U.S. Marshals for investigative business was less-than-ideal due to their district-by-district idiosyncrasies and the limits of their authority under the Judiciary Act of 1789.

Bonaparte's letter to President Roosevelt read in part (Bonaparte, 1907):

There are at present in the Treasury Department, the Post Office Department, and the Departments of the Interior, of Agriculture and of Commerce and Labor, a large number of officers whose duties include the detection of offenses [created by] various criminal statutes on the United States and the collection of evidence for use in the prosecution of such offenders. These officers report to the heads of their respective Departments, are subject to discipline or separation from the service, and receive promotion only through him, and are subject to no direct control by the Department of Justice.

Interestingly, Bonaparte noted that the federal law enforcement community had grown over the years and that every Cabinet-level department of the United States possessed federal law enforcement officers in place to investigate crime. Bonaparte went further in his letter to explain how the responsibilities of the Department of Justice had grown as well, but that there was not a commensurate criminal investigative agency. As Bonaparte noted in his letter, the U.S. Marshals — although organizationally housed within the Department of Justice — were not sufficiently equipped to serve as the Department's investigative arm. He continued in his letter:

> In the meantime, however, the position and duties of the Attorney General have been completely changed. By the Acts approved August 2, 1861, (12 Stat., 285) and June 22, 1870, (16 Stat., 162), the latter creating the Department of Justice, the Attorney General was given supervision and control over all United States Attorneys and Marshals; and by a result of a large number of successive statutes all tending with more or less of conscious purpose, of to the same end, the Department of Justice and the Attorney General, as its head, are now, in substance, the direct agency through which the President discharges his constitutional duty to "take care that the laws be faithfully executed" in all those cases in which proceedings, criminal or civil, in courts of justice constitute the necessary or appropriate means of enforcement. This constitutes already an extremely wide field or duty, and the tendency of Federal legislation has been to steadily increase the burdens and responsibilities of the Department of Justice ever since its organization in 1870.
>
> By reason of this radical change and vast expansion of its duties, it has become, each year, more and more imperatively necessary that this Department should have some executive force directly subject to its orders. The actual arrest of persons charged with crime may, indeed, be required of the several Marshals as part of their duty to execute all civil and criminal process, and they can also be called upon to supply such force as may be needful for the protection of Federal officers in the discharge of their duties or the preservation of public order in localities under the jurisdiction of the United States; but the detection of crime, the collection of evidence, and the conduct of all forms of preliminary inquiries necessary for the enforcement of the law, are not duties imposed by law upon the Marshals or which they could be reasonably expected to discharge with efficiency. It is true that, as above noted, other Executive Departments are supplied with what may be fairly called detective agencies for certain limited purposes, as, for example, the punishment of counterfeiting or frauds upon the revenue, of offenses against the postal laws and of violations of various penal statutes; but a large and increasing residuum of cases exists in which the Department of Justice is obliged by law, and expected as a result of custom, to furnish such services itself; and by a curious anomaly, no specific provision has been made by law to enable it to discharge these difficulties ....

In 1909, William Howard Taft became President of the United States. George Wickersham was appointed Attorney General as a part of the new Taft Administration in March of 1909. Wickersham fully embraced the notion of an investigative unit housed within and under the control of the Justice Department. Shortly after becoming Attorney General, Wickersham gave the name "Bureau of Investigation" to his internal detective agency. With an official name and status as a government bureau, Wickersham signaled his interest in solidifying the investigative authority of this unit and making it a permanent fixture of the Justice Department.

From the Bureau of Investigation's founding through the first half of the 1930s, Congress saw fit to greatly expand the authority and jurisdiction of the Bureau. For example, in 1910, Congress passed the Mann Act. This legislation outlawed human trafficking for forced prostitution and other forms of servitude. The Justice Department's Bureau of Investigation was designated the lead agency for investigating violations of the Mann Act. Because of increasing workload in enforcing this law and others, the fledgling bureau grew significantly in staff. By 1915, Congress had authorized the Bureau's special agent and support staff numbers to grow from 34 to 360 (DOJ, 2008).

Other federal criminal laws were also added to the Bureau of Investigation's repertoire. During World War I, the Bureau of Investigation took on a lead role in confronting foreign spies and saboteurs due to the passage of the Espionage Act of 1917. In October of 1919, the National Motor Vehicle Theft Act was passed. This law made it a federal crime to steal a motor vehicle and take the vehicle across state lines. Again, the primary responsibility of the enforcement of this law was given to the Bureau of Investigation.

Then in 1932, a particularly heinous crime occurred which would secure forever the crowning of the Justice Department's Bureau of Investigation as the lead federal law enforcement agency. It was on March 1st of that year in which the 20-month year old son of Charles Lindbergh was kidnapped in Hopewell, New Jersey. Lindbergh was a world-renowned aviation pioneer and a national hero. Consequently, the attention of the entire country was focused on the investigation of this stunning and tragic crime.

The lead investigative agency in the Lindbergh case was the New Jersey State Police. The investigation focused on the initial ransom note left at the Lindbergh home demanding $50,000 for the Lindbergh baby's safe return. But then, during the month of March, other ransom notes were sent to the Lindberghs modifying the demands. During this period of time in the case, the Bureau of Investigation detailed a number of special agents to assist the New Jersey State Police. There was no federal crime involved, so the role of the special agents was truly a support role.

In May of 1932, the Lindbergh baby's body was found. The baby had been murdered by blunt force trauma to the head. The Lindberghs were devastated and the nation was outraged. Many politicians took an interest in the case. In fact, President Franklin Roosevelt directed the Justice Department to utilize the Bureau of Investigation in any way it could be helpful. Roosevelt further directed the Bureau of Investigation to serve as the lead federal agency to assist in the investigation. The Bureau's presence in the case as partner of the New Jersey State Police paid off. The perpetrators were identified and arrested — in part due to the Bureau's analysis of evidence, including a ransom note. Kidnapper Bruno Hauptmann was convicted and sentenced to die for his role in the kidnapping and murder of the child. He was executed in 1936 — a little over a year after his conviction.

Because of the Lindbergh kidnapping, and the helpful role the Bureau of Investigation played during the unfolding of the case, Congress passed the Federal Kidnapping Act of 1932. This law made it a federal crime to abduct another person and take that person across state lines.

As with the auto theft statute, the requirement that the offenders cross state lines in commission of the crime was a key element of the offense. The interstate nature of the unlawful activity gave Congress the justification for passing a federal law pursuant to its regulation of interstate commerce under the U.S. Constitution. Without the crossing of state lines, auto theft and abduction were mere state-level offenses to be investigated and prosecuted by state and local authorities.

Expanding the Bureau's investigative portfolio even further, Congress passed a federal bank robbery statute in 1934. This law made it a federal crime to rob a bank with holdings insured by the federal government. The investigation of such robberies would be the job of the Justice Department's Bureau of Investigation. Congress also passed laws against interstate flight (i.e. fleeing across state lines to avoid capture and criminal prosecution) and granting statutory authority for Bureau agents to carry firearms and make arrests for crimes committed against the United States (Fox, 2003).

The 1930s were a seminal time for the Bureau. Not only did it receive new law enforcement authorities and expanded investigative jurisdiction, but the Bureau also received considerable public attention and accolades for the work it was doing to fight crime. During the 1930s, special agents of the Bureau of Investigation killed or captured a number of infamous gangsters, including John Dillinger, "Pretty Boy" Floyd, "Baby Face" Nelson, "Machine Gun" Kelly (who coined the term "G-Men" for federal agents), and Ma Barker, Fred Barker, and Alvin Karpis of the Barker-Karpis gang. The death of John Dillinger in particular, who had been dubbed by the Bureau as "Public Enemy #1," played a significant role in galvanizing public support for the Bureau of Investigation. Dillinger, America's most famous bank robber and fugitive at the time, was gunned down on July 22, 1934, outside of the Biograph Theatre in Chicago, by Bureau special agents who had been tracking him.

That the Bureau of Investigation (whose name was changed to the Federal Bureau of Investigation in 1935) captured the American public's collective admiration as the nation's premier crime-fight organization did not happen by accident. Rather, it was done so by way of a calculated and savvy public relations campaign orchestrated by the agency's director, John Edgar Hoover.

J. Edgar Hoover became director of the Justice Department's Bureau of Investigation in 1924. At that time, the Bureau employed approximately 650 people, with about 400 of those serving as special agents in 30 field offices across the country. In Hoover's first 30 years as director (he served a total of 48 years in that position—until his death in 1972), the FBI's special agent cadre grew to over 6,000, working in 59 field offices around the country. As director of the FBI, Hoover's name became synonymous with federal law enforcement, crime fighting, and Cold War counter-espionage. In more recent history, his legacy has been clouded by controversy as more and more is learned about Hoover's tactics, including spying on prominent American citizens and politicians of whom Hoover was suspicious or with whom Hoover disagreed. So who was J. Edgar Hoover?

Hoover, a Washington, D.C. native, was just in his early 20s when he received his master of laws degree from George Washington University in 1917. Shortly after graduation, Hoover began his lengthy career in government service at the Justice Department. His first position was as an attorney with the Justice Department's General Intelligence Division. After only a year in this position, Hoover was named to be the head of the Enemy Aliens Registration Section (FBI, n.d.). In this capacity, Hoover proved to be a tenacious and effective foe of foreign subversives in the United States. His plate was full as threats came from both Kaiser Wilhelm's Germany, with which the U.S. was at war, and Bolshevism—a movement which had just successfully overturned the Czar's reign in Russia and had spawned a red scare in the United States.

Hoover's success in pursuing and prosecuting Communist insurgents in the United States led to yet another promotion in 1919. Hoover was chosen to head the General Intelligence Division—a mere two years after he began his post-collegiate career there.

In 1921, Hoover and his General Intelligence Division were placed under the organizational control of the Bureau of Investigation. Hoover became the deputy director of the Bureau, serving under Director William Burns. In 1924, Burns was forced to resign his post due to scandal—he was one of many officials during the Harding Administration to be marred by the Teapot Dome Scandal—and poor performance as director. Hoover, who was only 29 years old, was then named the director of the Justice Department's Bureau of Investigation.

Hoover, a civil servant who was personally incorruptible, became director of an agency stained by corruption. While Burns had been director, he had used the Bureau of Investigation to provide cover for the Harding Administration by discrediting members of Congress investigating the Teapot Dome Scandal, which related to bribes paid to government officials by oil companies seeking lucrative drilling rights on federal lands (Johnson and Wolfe, 2003). Hoover moved quickly to clean house at the Bureau of Investigation and to create an organizational culture free of corruption and favoritism.

Hoover was driven by the desire to professionalize law enforcement at the Bureau of Investigation. Many of the Bureau's 400 agents were fired because they were incompetent or unqualified in Hoover's mind. Hoover instituted a regime of background checks for the Bureau's special agents, as well as a requirement that agents participate in a law enforcement training academy with rigorous physical fitness standards. Hoover also established the Bureau of Investigation Crime Laboratory in 1932. In the laboratory's first year of operation, it conducted nearly 1,000 examinations—mostly handwriting and firearms analyses (Waggoner, 2007). As noted previously, one of these examinations was a handwriting analysis of one of the Lindbergh kidnapping ransom notes, and which culminated in evidence leading to the conviction of Bruno Hauptmann (DOJ, 2008).

Although J. Edgar Hoover is a historically complicated and controversial figure, his contribution to the professionalization of law enforcement generally, and federal law enforcement specifically, cannot be overstated. Many scholars have written about Hoover and his legacy. In their book *History of Criminal Justice*, Herbert Johnson and Nancy Travis Wolfe identified three areas of law enforcement reform for which Hoover can be credited. These three areas are summarized below (Johnson and Wolfe, 2003):

1) Personnel and Management—
   - special agents were appointed based upon qualifications, not political loyalties
   - special agents were required to possess a college degree in law or accounting
   - discipline was uniform
   - character of the special agents was a job criterion (even off duty)
   - specialized and rigorous training program
   - hierarchical structure with field level supervision (by the Special Agents in Charge of each field office)
   - advancement based upon qualifications

2) Investigative Practices—
   - the work ethic of agents was characterized as persistent and results-oriented
   - special agents relied on advanced technology and science to solve crimes
   - creation of a forensic laboratory
   - maintenance of extensive intelligence files that could be cross-referenced for investigative leads
   - specified investigative procedures, codified into policy, which protected the rights of suspects

3) Law Enforcement Liaison and Training—

- creation of the FBI National Academy in 1935 which provided modern law enforcement investigation and management techniques for state and local police officials
- establishment of the FBI Law Enforcement Bulletin, a professional journal published to provide legal and investigative updates in the field of law enforcement
- creation of the fingerprint identification division which collects and classifies offender fingerprints sent from law enforcement agencies around the country which can be used to identify suspects in new cases

The sum and substance of Hoover's legacy articulated by Johnson and Wolfe is the professionalization of the FBI and the example it serves to the broader law enforcement community. As noted, however, Hoover's leadership includes some blemishes. Hoover and his FBI maintained secret files on political opposition figures. Ostensibly, these files could be used to blackmail politicos into acquiescing to Hoover's will on policy and legislative matters. But what is interesting, if not mitigating, about Hoover's collection of dirt on others is that it was done for the FBI and not for Hoover's personal benefit. Everything Hoover did, for better or worse, was for the protection and advancement of the FBI (Leibovitz, 2003). For 50 years, the FBI was Hoover's. But it can also be said that Hoover truly belonged to the FBI, and Hoover served it for his entire adult life.

Organization and Personnel

The Federal Bureau of Investigation remains today America's premier federal law enforcement agency. It is housed within the U.S. Department of Justice and employed 35,664 people in 2012, including 13,778 special agents and 21,886 support staff. The support staff includes professional positions such as crime and intelligence analysts, language specialists, forensic scientists, computer specialists, attorneys, and others (FBI, 2012).

Historically, FBI special agents were required to have either a law degree or an accounting degree. Additionally, Hoover had required that agents be of "above average intelligence and reputation, of good character, and be above average in personal appearance" (Kessler, 2002, p. 255). For Hoover, sustaining the esteemed public image of FBI agents was as important as what the agents actually did. While special agent applicants today must still be of good character, there is no requirement that agents be attractive. There are also many educational and professional backgrounds from which individuals can become special agents; these still include law and accounting, but also computer science, language fluency, and a diversified path that would include a combination of professional experience and education (such as in law enforcement, the physical sciences, the military, and other backgrounds).

Recruiting FBI agents with foreign language fluency has become an acute priority for the agency. This is especially true with regard to the languages of Arabic and Farsi (the latter of which is spoken in Iran). In the immediate years following the 9/11 terror attacks, intelligence and law enforcement agencies stepped up their information gathering activities and indeed collected reams of raw data. However, the federal government, including the

FBI, lacked sufficient staff with language expertise. At the end of 2004, the FBI had collected 120,000 hours of intercepts in Arabic, Farsi, and other eastern languages, for which it lacked the personnel to translate (Freeh, 2005).

The importance of the FBI as a federal government agency is reflected in the appropriations given it by Congress. In Fiscal Year 2012, the FBI budget totaled $8.1 billion. This was an increase over the previous year's budget by $119 million. What's more, the budget represents a nearly 60% increase over a 10-year period. The FBI's budget in Fiscal Year 2002 was a mere $5.1 billion (Peykar, 2005).

The FBI has a physical presence in all 50 states. In total, the FBI staffs 56 major offices, called field offices, in America's largest cities. Each field office is headed by the Special Agent in Charge of that office, or "SAC." Additionally, the FBI has agents in nearly 400 medium and small cities. These offices are known as "resident offices" or "resident agencies" (RA) and can be staffed by as few as one or two special agents. Every RA is organized under one of the 56 field offices. Special agents in a resident office report ultimately to the SAC of the parent field office.

The FBI is led by a director. J. Edgar Hoover was the agency's 5th director, and there have been 5 directors since Hoover's death in 1972. FBI director Robert Mueller is the second-longest serving director, having taken over the post on September 4, 2001. FBI directors are appointed by the President and confirmed by the Senate. Due to a federal statute passed in 1976, the term of an FBI director is to run no longer than 10 years, after which a new director must be found. However, in July of 2011, at the request of President Barak Obama, the Congress voted to extend Mueller's term for an additional two years. Mueller's directorship is scheduled to end no later than August of 2013.

Organizationally, the FBI is arranged into several branches and offices. See the organizational chart in Figure 3.1 on the next page for a full picture of how the FBI is arranged. The two main operational branches within the FBI are the National Security Branch and the Criminal, Cyber, Response, and Services Branch. The National Security Branch includes divisions dedicated to counterintelligence, counterterrorism, and weapons of mass destruction (WMD). The Criminal, Cyber, Response, and Services Branch include the Criminal Investigative Division, the Cyber Division, a critical incident response group, and an international operations division. In the decade since the 9/11 terrorist attacks, much of the FBI's assets have been moved from the Criminal Investigative Division (which had dealt with general and traditional crimes) to divisions within the National Security Branch. Many of the FBI's critics have lamented this development, claiming that general crimes such as bank robbery and fraud have received insufficient attention and resources.

Other significant divisions within the FBI include the Training Division, the Criminal Justice Information Systems Division, and the Laboratory Division. The Training Division includes oversight of the famed FBI Academy located on the grounds of the Quantico Marine Corps base in Quantico, Virginia, near Washington, D.C. The FBI academy has been located in Quantico since May 8, 1972. Prior to that, special agent trainees used the Marine Base for firearms instruction, but conducted classroom training at the Old Post Office Building in Washington, D.C. and defensive tactics at the Department of Justice Building gym (Kessler, 2002). The FBI Academy runs new-agent and in-service training programs for special agents of the FBI, as well as the National Academy command school for senior level law enforcement officers in state and local police agencies. The FBI Academy also served as the home for many years to the new-agent and in-service training programs

Figure 3.1 The FBI Organizational Structure

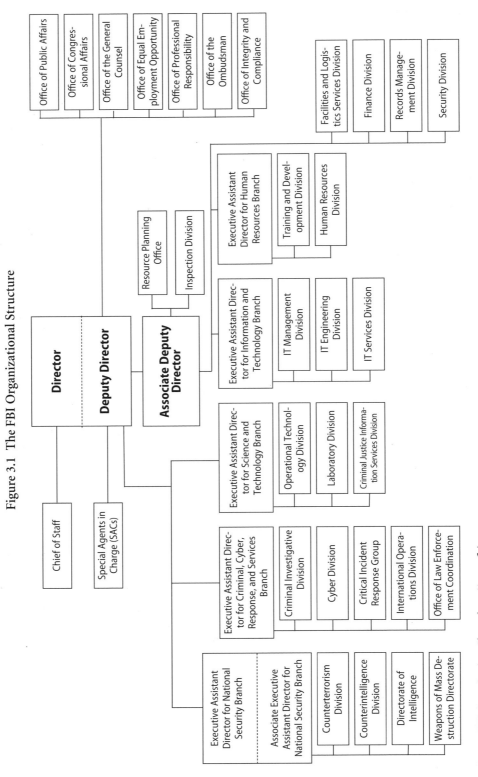

Source: FBI Organization Chart, http://www.fbi.gov.

for the Drug Enforcement Administration (DEA) until 1999, when the DEA completed its own Academy facility at the Quantico Marine Corps Base. However, the DEA still uses some of the training facilities operated at the FBI Academy. The FBI's famed Behavioral Science Unit (which includes FBI profilers) is also housed at the FBI Academy.

The Criminal Justice Information Systems Division (CJIS) is located in Clarksburg, West Virginia, and is home to the largest collection of criminal fingerprints and criminal histories in the world (FBI, 2011). There is probably no element of the FBI that is more utilized by local law enforcement than CJIS. This division is home to the National Crime Information Center (NCIC). Local law enforcement agencies routinely run individuals and property they encounter through NCIC to determined if someone is wanted in another jurisdiction or if property has been stolen. NCIC maintains over 11.7 million active records on wanted, missing, and unidentified persons, as well as stolen property (FBI, 2011).

Of course, local law enforcement officials also frequently check fingerprints collected at crime scenes through the FBI's computerized fingerprint database, known as the Integrated Automated Fingerprint Identification System (IAFIS). Many crimes have been solved because offenders whose prints have been previously collected and are contained in IAFIS have left prints at subsequent crime scenes. IAFIS maintains records on more than 70.2 million criminal fingerprints, 31.7 million civil fingerprints (usually collected as a part of a employment or security clearance background check), and nearly 500,000 unidentified prints which have been collected at crime scenes (FBI, 2011).

The CJIS Division is also responsible for issuing the Uniform Crime Report (UCR) every year. This report is an annual tabulation of the total number of certain types crimes that have occurred throughout the United States. The FBI collects detailed information on more serious crimes, which are called Part I offenses. There are eight Part I offenses; they include homicide, rape, robbery, aggravated assault, burglary, larceny (theft), motor vehicle theft, and arson. The data collected not only relate to the number of these offenses, but also include offender and victim information, as well as information about weapons used. The FBI also collects information (although in less detail) on 21 other crimes, known as Part II offenses. All of the information collected by the FBI for the UCR is gathered by receiving submitted information from participating local law enforcement agencies. In other words, the UCR can only report what local law enforcement reports to the FBI. Approximately 18,000 police agencies submit data to the FBI for the UCR every year. The jurisdictions of these agencies collectively cover approximately 95% of the United States population.

Functions

As already noted, the FBI has the broadest range of law enforcement responsibilities among all federal agencies. There are many federal crimes for which the FBI is statutorily designated as an agency with either exclusive jurisdiction or primary jurisdiction. With regard to virtually all other federal crimes, the FBI at a minimum has concurrent jurisdiction with other federal agencies (e.g. federal drug crimes or firearms crimes, which could be investigated concurrently by the Drug Enforcement Administration or the Bureau of Alcohol, Tobacco, Firearms, and Explosives, respectively).

Given the FBI's broad federal jurisdiction, the agency has found it important to set investigative and operational priorities. The FBI today has identified 10 priorities that principally define its operations. These priorities are (FBI, 2012):

1. Protect the United States from terrorist attack.

2. Protect the United States against foreign intelligence operations and espionage.

3. Protect the United States against cyber-based attacks and high-tech crimes.

4. Combat public corruption at all levels.

5. Protect civil rights.

6. Combat transnational and national criminal organizations and enterprises.

7. Combat major white-collar crime.

8. Combat significant violent crime.

9. Support federal, state, county, municipal, and international partners.

10. Upgrade technology to successfully perform the FBI's mission.

Somewhat interestingly, these priorities have remained relatively stable in the past several years. The exact same priorities were in place as far back as 2005 and had emerged out of the fluctuation relative to the FBI's changing mission in the post-9/11 climate (Bumgarner, 2006).

The priorities highlight the degree of importance that the FBI assigns to securing the nation. Indeed, the top three priorities are national security-related. Crimes that had once been the bread and butter of the FBI, such as organized crime, violent crime (including bank robberies and kidnapping), and fraud all still make the list—but only after most of the other priorities. Drug enforcement isn't listed at all, even though it had been one of the top three priorities during the 1990s. While the order of appearance of these priorities does not necessarily signal their relative importance to one another, neither is it an accident that national security efforts top the list. Clearly, protecting America against threats—especially external threats—has become job #1 for the nation's largest criminal investigative federal law enforcement agency: the Federal Bureau of Investigation.

References

Bonaparte, C. (1909). *Letter to President Theodore Roosevelt concerning the need for a Justice Department investigative agency.* January 14, 1909.

Bumgarner, J. (2006). *Federal agents: The growth of federal law enforcement in America.* Westport, CT: Praeger Publishing.

Federal Bureau of Investigation (2012). *FBI quick facts.* Retrieved from: http://www.fbi.gov/about-us/quick-facts.

Federal Bureau of Investigation (2011). *CJIS annual report.* Retrieved from http://www.fbi.gov/about-us/cjis/annual-report-2011/annual-report-2011.

Federal Bureau of Investigation (n.d.). *J. Edgar Hoover fact sheet.* Retrieved from: http://www.fbi.gov/libref/directors/hoover.htm.

Freeh, L. (2005). *My FBI: Brining down the Mafia, investigating Bill Clinton, and fighting the war on terror.* New York, NY: St. Martin's Press.

Fox, J. (2003). *The birth of the Federal Bureau of Investigation.* Washington, D.C.: Office of Public/Congressional Affairs.

Jeffreys-Jones, R. (2007). *The FBI: A history.* New Haven, CT: Yale University Press.

Johnson, H. and Wolfe, N. (2003). *History of criminal justice.* Cincinnati, OH: Anderson Publishing.

Kessler, R. (2002). *The bureau: The secret history of the FBI.* New York, NY: St. Martin's Press.

Leibovitz, B. (Director). (2003). *The FBI: A revealing inside look at the bureau.* United States: National Geographic.

Pyekar, E. (ed.) (2005). *The FBI: Past, present and future.* New York, NY: Nova Publications.

U.S. Department of Justice (1907). *Annual report of the Attorney General.* Washington, D.C.

U.S. Department of Justice (2008). *The FBI: A centennial history, 1908–2008.* Washington, D.C.: Government Printing Office.

Waggoner, K. (2007). The FBI laboratory: 75 years of forensic science service. *Forensic Science Communication. 9* (4). Retrieved from http://www.fbi.gov/about-us/lab/forensic-science-communications/fsc/oct2007/research/index.htm.

Chapter Four

Bureau of Alcohol, Tobacco, Firearms and Explosives (ATF)

The U.S. Bureau of Alcohol, Tobacco, Firearms and Explosives (ATF) is a federal law enforcement agency housed under the U.S. Department of Justice. Historically, the ATF was part of the Department of Treasury and has been involved in some of the most significant high-profile criminal investigations. The agency has undergone several name changes throughout its history, and its primary focus and responsibilities have emerged and changed over time. Currently, the agency is mainly charged with "administering and enforcing federal laws related to the manufacture, importation, and distribution of firearms and explosives" (Krouse, 2011, p.1). The ATF is also responsible for investigating federal-level arson cases, and addressing federal crimes pertaining to the manufacture, importation, and distribution of alcohol and tobacco.

The nature of the legal jurisdiction maintained by the ATF consistently places the agency in a difficult predicament. For instance, the Second Amendment right of individuals to bear arms has been countered by troubling gun-related violent crime rates, and the ATF is often caught in the middle of respecting individual rights, protecting individuals in society, and regulating the gun industry. For instance, what may appear as overzealous firearms enforcement to some may be viewed as necessary law enforcement practices to others.

Enforcing laws and regulating industries associated with legal goods such as guns, alcohol, and tobacco differs from law enforcement efforts involving strictly illegal goods. Additionally, many in society view the regulation and taxation of alcohol and tobacco as an infringement of their rights and freedoms. Combined, these and other challenges inherent in the responsibilities of the ATF contribute to much controversy, acclaim, and critique directed toward the agency. Ultimately, the ATF is charged "… with fiscal oversight of some of the most controversial topics in Western civilianization" (Herrmann, 1998, p. 39). In summing up the difficulties with the charges of the ATF, Vizzard (1997, p. 215) noted: "The marriage of regulatory and law enforcement functions, linked primarily by historical accident, is unique to ATF, as is the ambiguity of the task environment relating to the firearms mission."

History

The roots of the ATF date back to the origins of the U.S., and the agency garnered much of its prominence in its early history through dealing with tax revenues on foreign-produced alcoholic beverages. The agency would later assume more of its current identity in the late 1960s in response to the passage of the Gun Control Act.

In 1789 the first U.S. Congress imposed a tax on imported spirits to help offset the Revolutionary War debt. The responsibility for overseeing the collection of the taxes fell upon the Department of the Treasury. Congress was impressed with the results of the tax collection efforts and soon augmented the tax by taxing domestic production of spirits in 1791. Taxpayers were particularly discontented with the domestic levy on sprits and they engaged in political resistance, for instance in the form of the Whiskey Rebellion of 1794. Both taxes survived the rebellious efforts, although the taxes came and went on an as-needed basis (Herrmann, 1998).

In 1862 Congress created an Office of Internal Revenue within the Treasury Department. Among the charges for the department was to collect taxes on distilled spirits and tobacco products. Taxation in the U.S. has historically been met with public resistance and tax evasion, which contributed to Congress in 1863 authorizing Internal Revenue to hire detectives to prevent, identify, and enforce the laws pertaining to tax evasion. Tax collection and law enforcement were now under one agency's jurisdiction, and by the end of the decade the Office of Internal Revenue had its own counsel. Thus began the origins of the ATF as we currently know it (Herrmann, 1998).

The regulation of alcohol and tobacco, including the taxation of these products, has been particularly important in U.S. history, leaving the agencies tasked with enforcing the laws surrounding the goods in many particularly challenging situations. The agencies that would become the ATF assumed many important and resource-intensive responsibilities both during and following the Prohibition movement. Accordingly, the origins of the modern day ATF are evident in the Prohibition Unit of the U.S. Treasury Department. The ratification of the Eighteenth Amendment to the Constitution in 1919 (which prohibited the manufacture, sale, transport, import, or export of alcoholic beverages in the U.S.), along with the Volstead Act (which gave the Treasury Department responsibility to enforce the law), brought notoriety and many challenges to the agents charged with enforcing laws pertaining to alcohol. For instance, the years of Prohibition were particularly dangerous for members of the Prohibition Unit relative to other federal law enforcement agents, as far more agents from the agency were killed in the line of duty than were their counterparts in other federal agencies (Moore, 2001).

The Prohibition Unit was part of the Bureau of Internal Revenue (which would later become the Internal Revenue Service [IRS] in 1952) during the 1920s and 1930s. The Prohibition Unit would be transferred to the Department of Justice in 1930 and later returned to the Treasury Department's Bureau of Internal Revenue in 1934 when it assumed the title "Alcohol Tax Unit." The Alcohol Tax Unit (ATU) would then become the "Alcohol and Tobacco Tax Division" (ATTD) in 1952 (Bumgarner, 2006; Herrmann, 1998). The name lasted until 1968 and the passage of the Gun Control Act, which gave the agency responsibility for explosives. The agency's title then changed to Alcohol, Tobacco and Firearms (ATF) Division.

Although the roots of the ATF are grounded in the enforcement of alcohol tax laws, the agency enforces laws pertaining to firearms, tobacco, and explosives as well. The ATF's involvement in the investigation of firearms cases largely began when Congress passed the National Firearms Act in 1934, which provided for the registration and taxing of the transfer of specific types of firearms. Public dismay over the gun violence associated with organized crime groups in response to Prohibition contributed to the enhanced focus on gun control. The taxation aspect of the legislation resulted in the agency becoming the logical choice for enforcement purposes.

Beginning in 1970 it became increasingly apparent that the ATF's law enforcement skills and responsibilities did not necessarily reflect the IRS's revenue-collecting efforts, thus there was a move to give the ATF independence from the IRS. Retired ATF agent

James Moore (2001, p. 142) stated: "In 1970 ATF was still a division of the Internal Revenue Service, an agency that viewed the world through tax-colored glasses; an enormous bureaucracy led by men with little use for a unit no longer needed to protect the alcohol revenue." He added that ATF agents largely sought to separate from the directed focus of IRS officials on tax collection and there was an increasing division between the ATF and other units within the IRS (Moore, 2001). In 1972, the functions, powers, and duties related to alcohol, tobacco, firearms, and explosive were transferred from the IRS to the ATF (Herrmann, 1998), and it became a stand-alone agency within the Treasury Department.

Although taxation regarding firearms had been part of the ATF's charges for decades, it wasn't until the 1960s and 1970s that firearms tax enforcement became a priority for the agency. The increased amount of violent crime, including gun and bomb-related violence, resulted in Congress passing the Gun Control Act of 1968 which amended the National Firearms Act by extending coverage and providing cost-prohibitive taxes on explosives. The act also imposed new and stricter penalties for federal crimes committed with firearms. The ATTD was the lead investigative agency for firearms violations, and thus enhanced its efforts in this area (Bumgarner, 2006).

Passage of the Gun Control Act largely impacted the ATF. For instance, between 1968 and 1972 the agency doubled its law enforcement force, refocused its mission from alcohol to firearms, and assumed additional jurisdiction in explosives. Licensing requirements for firearms and explosives dealers were being developed during this time and the licensing and regulatory responsibilities of the agency expanded (Vizzard, 1997). The bureau became increasingly law enforcement-oriented and focused less on tax or regulatory enforcement (Zimring, 1975).

Despite the agency's long history of upstanding law enforcement services, the ATF was recently criticized for several of its actions, particularly in relation to high-profile incidents that attracted negative attention to the bureau. Specifically, the ATF was criticized for its involvement in two incidents in which federal authorities were attempting to serve a warrant and the situations escalated into deadly violence. The first of these incidents occurred in 1992 in Ruby Ridge, Idaho and began with an ATF investigation and ended in the deaths of three individuals, including a U.S. Marshal. The Ruby Ridge incident began with an ATF investigation into illegal firearms deals, and eventually escalated into an eleven-day siege which drew nationwide attention, including protests from anti-government activists who strongly believed the federal agents were imposing on citizen's rights.

Another incident that also negatively impacted the agency occurred in Waco, Texas in 1993. It involved the siege of the Branch Davidian compound and the death of 76 individuals. The incident in Waco was preceded by a standoff lasting 50 days and the deaths of four ATF special agents and six Branch Davidians. Numerous other ATF agents were wounded (Bumgarner, 2006). Aside from the physical harms and criticism directed at the ATF and other federal law enforcement groups, the incident resulted in the unscheduled retirement of ATF's top management, widespread characterization of the law enforcement efforts as "inept," and some individuals in society viewing the incident as a symbol of abuse of government authority. The incident was also identified as an inspiration for several subsequent incidents of domestic terrorism, including Oklahoma City's Murrah Federal Building bombing in 1995 (Vizzard, 1997, p. 1).

The Ruby Ridge and Waco incidents attracted much national attention, particularly as the news media were present for the raid on the Branch Davidian compound. Images of the heavily armed ATF agents contributed to the belief among some groups and individuals in society that the U.S. government was too intrusive and invasive with regard to individual rights and liberties. Such claims were voiced loudly following the Ruby Ridge incident and perpetuated by the incident in Waco. To be sure, the criticism in the Ruby Ridge and Branch Davidian incidents was directed at several federal law enforcement agencies, not just the ATF.

More recently, the bureau has been the primary target of an incident in which illegal guns were willingly sold to low-level gun dealers who then escaped ATF surveillance efforts. "Operation Fast and Furious" has directed much negative attention to the ATF, as the bureau, in conjunction with the FBI, DEA, and other agencies, sought to follow the trafficking of illegal guns into Mexico and build cases against Mexican traffickers and weapons brokers. The operation began in Phoenix in 2009 as a gun sting operation in which small-time gun traffickers were permitted to distribute firearms to middlemen, who then passed the guns along to Mexico. However, the low-level gun dealers evaded surveillance and the illegal guns, numbering between 1,500 and 2,500, were assumedly used in numerous crimes including the shooting death of Border Patrol Agent Brian Terry. The incident resulted in major changes in the leadership of the ATF, including the replacement of the Acting Director and the Deputy Director of the agency.

The events surrounding the "Fast and Furious" gun sting have been deemed "the worst blow (to the ATF) since the agency's botched 1993 raid on the Branch Davidian compound ..." (Freedman, 2011), and have renewed arguments that the ATF should be disbanded—arguments that have surrounded the agency since the 1970s (Bumgarner, 2006). Earlier suggestions that the ATF should be abolished were inspired by the efforts of several interests groups, including the National Rifle Association (NRA) and government leaders. Prominent among the government groups was the Reagan administration, which moved into the White House in 1981. The NRA, in its efforts to protect the rights of gun owners, provided numerous challenges to the ATF, and has been, and remains particularly influential in lobbying politicians to protect what the NRA perceives to be Second Amendment rights regarding the use and possession of firearms (Moore, 2001). The Reagan administration, conservative in its political approach, believed that the ATF infringed on the rights of legitimate gun owners, and the administration was supported by gun lobbyists (Vizzard, 1997).

The arguments offered for the dissolution of the ATF generally related to the varied objectives of the ATF, including its responsibility for enforcing various types of laws and regulating taxes. The Treasury Department earlier suggested that ATF agents and law enforcement responsibilities should be merged with the U.S. Secret Service, primarily because the agents of both agencies took the same civil service test and studied at the same academy. Such a move, the Treasury argued, would save taxpayers $39 million annually and would improve several federal law enforcement functions, including counterterrorism and the suppression of bombings and counterfeiting (Moore, 2001; Vizzard, 1997).

The effects of the negative attention directed toward the ATF were compounded by a lack of strong leadership, as the administration often sought to avoid problems as opposed to innovatively address them (Vizzard, 1997). Claims that the ATF should merge with another agency or be notably reorganized persist (Vizzard, 1997), for instance as it was recently suggested that the ATF should be merged with the FBI (Yager, 2011).

The ATF's budget and staffing were reduced in the period immediately following the earlier move to eliminate the agency; however, the 1980s were largely successful for the ATF. Particularly, a series of events and forces resulted in the revitalization of the ATF.

The revitalization was, in large part, attributed to the efforts of Senator James Abnor, who was influential in the ATF not being abolished, and was able to help increase the agency's budget through Congress. Senator Abnor was influential in gaining support for the agency from the Reagan and Bush administrations.

The appointment of Steve Higgins as director of the bureau also benefitted the agency, which experienced a near doubling in staff size between 1984 and 1992. The agency's staff size had decreased regularly beginning with the Carter administration and reached a low during the early part of the Reagan administration. Higgins and his administrative staff helped centralize the agency's dual charges of law enforcement and tax regulation, and garnered public and political support. Concurrently, the violent crime rate and drug trafficking were increasing in the U.S., which helped the bureau gain recognition as a vital component of federal law enforcement. Further, firearms prosecutions were gaining higher priority among U.S. attorneys than during any period in the past (Vizzard, 1997).

The ATF's revitalization during this time was also enhanced as the firearms lobby redirected its attention and efforts to the pending Brady Bill and reduced its efforts directed toward the ATF. Additionally, the alcoholic beverage industry supported the agency while the firearms industry offered little resistance to ATF efforts (Vizzard, 1997). The agency gained greater prestige within the Treasury Department as Customs became the target of criticism, and the ATF was able to better move out of the shadow of the U.S. Secret Service, particularly since the Secret Service had limited jurisdiction over violent crime and drug trafficking—two of the primary social concerns of the time (Vizzard, 1997).

In the mid-1990s, the ATF prioritized the investigation of the 64 black church burnings in the southern portion of the U.S. The fires were initially believed to be racially motivated. Ultimately, two members of the Ku Klux Klan were arrested, but thirty other arrests in relation to the burnings were deemed to have no racist motives (Moore, 2001).

The ATF underwent additional changes with the beginning of the 21st century. For instance, part of the major restructuring of the organization of federal law enforcement following the terrorist attacks against the U.S. in 2001 involved Congress transferring ATF's enforcement and regulatory functions for firearms and explosives from the Department of the Treasury to the Department of Justice (DOJ). This move, as part of the Homeland Security Act, added "Explosives" to the agency's title in reference to the agency's responsibility for investigating bombings and other explosives-related offenses, and removed from the agency its responsibilities for regulating and collecting revenue from the alcohol and tobacco industries (Lluberes, 2005). Despite the name change to include the term "explosives," the agency's acronym remains ATF.

It was believed by many that the ATF would become part of the newly created Department of Homeland Security during the major reorganization of federal law enforcement, however the interrelatedness of the responsibilities of the FBI and the ATF and the need for greater cooperation between the agencies resulted in the ATF becoming part of the DOJ (Bumgarner, 2006). The ATF remains the lead federal agency with regard to the enforcement of laws pertaining to firearms crime, arson, explosives, and trafficking alcohol and tobacco.

In summarizing the challenges historically and currently facing the ATF, Moore (2001, xiv) noted that "The history of this bureau is crammed with conflict and controversy. Aside from the battles with bad guys, there's been friction between agents and their revenue-oriented chiefs, antagonism between ATF agents and the FBI, and outright hostility initiated by the well-oiled gun lobby and its lackeys in Congress."

Organization and Personnel

Akin to many other federal law enforcement agencies, the ATF employs a relatively low number of employees. The agency, however, is growing in size. The low relative number of employees persists despite the agency's extensive tasks and responsibilities. As of FY 2010, the ATF had 5,107 employees, of which 2,562 (50.2%) were special agents, 1,738 (34.0%) provided administrative, professional, and technical support, and 624 (12.2%) were industry operations investigators (Bureau of Alcohol…, 2011a). The 2,562 special agents as of 2011 represented an increase from the 2,373 full-time individuals in the ATF with arrest and firearm authority as of 2004. The number of individuals with such powers increased from by about 2% from 2002 to 2004 (Reaves, 2006), and by 7.1% between 2004 and 2008 (Reaves, 2012).

Historically, the ATF has not been a particularly diverse agency. Until 1971, women were not considered for appointment to agent positions; nor were they considered for agent positions in any other major federal law enforcement agency (Vizzard, 1997). The ATF has long employed both Black and Hispanic agents, although the agents located in the Southeastern Region of the U.S., where over half of all the agency's employees were until 1971, were mostly white males. In addition, minorities were underrepresented in the other regions, which resulted in a notably non-diverse agency. The historical lack of diversity within the agency is consistent with some other law enforcement agencies, and stems from the historical lack of diversity within policing and law enforcement in general. The ATF (and many other federal law enforcement agencies) hire individuals with policing experience, and the historical lack of diversity within policing at the state and local levels has resulted in the bureau generally lacking a great deal of diversity. Affirmative action programs intensified during the 1970s and 1980s, which ultimately helped diversify the ATF. The bureau, similar to many other law enforcement agencies, has had more success actively recruiting ethnic and racial minorities than it has recruiting females (Vizzard, 1997).

As of 2004, females were slightly underrepresented in the ATF relative to other federal law enforcement agencies. For instance, only 13.0% of full-time individuals with arrest and firearms authority in the agency as of 2008 were female, compared to the average of 15.5% among all federal law enforcement groups. The percentage of full-time sworn officers who were women in the ATF decreased slightly between 2004 (13.3%) and 2008 (Reaves, 2006; 2012).

Racial and ethnic minorities were also underrepresented in the ATF, accounting for 18.9% of full-time individuals with arrest and firearms authority in 2008. This percentage falls far short of the 34.3% average for all federal law enforcement agencies. Hispanics/ Latinos were notably underrepresented in the agency (5.8% in the ATF; 19.8% among other federal law enforcement agencies; Reaves, 2012).

The ATF has historically undergone a great deal of organizational change. Between the repeal of Prohibition and 1977, the ATF and its predecessors were reorganized 17 times, leading to much inconsistency within the bureau (Moore, 2001). More recently, the ATF maintained 25 field divisions across the U.S. and in FY 2009 maintained a presence in 11 international offices in eight countries. The internationalization of the ATF is evidenced in the agency providing firearms-related training to 885 Mexican police and prosecutors, and over 4,000 members of the international law enforcement community in FY 2007–2008 (Bureau of Alcohol..., 2011a). The organizational design of the ATF is noted in Figure 4.1 on p. 54.

The enacted budget for the ATF for FY 2010 was roughly $1.12 billion. From FY 2001 to FY 2010, Congress increased ATF appropriations from $771.0 million to roughly $1.158 billion (Krouse, 2011). The number of personnel within-, and budget appropriations for the agency continue to increase, for instance as the ATF's budget in 1973 was less than $74 million to support the efforts of 3,829 full-time employees, including 1,622 special agents and 826 industry operations investigators (Bureau of Alcohol..., 2011b). The ATF has been one of the most cost-effective federal law enforcement agencies, as it maintains roughly a 35–1 return on every dollar it spends, which is the best cost-to-collection ratio among federal law enforcement agencies (Herrmann, 1998).

Functions

The ATF organizes its activities into 10 core areas of interest. Within each of these areas the bureau has identified particular performance goals. These areas and goals include:

- Alcohol and Tobacco — Reduce the loss of tax revenues caused by contraband alcohol and tobacco trafficking.
- Criminal Groups and Gangs — Reduce the risk to public safety caused by criminal organizations and gangs.
- Explosives, Bombs, and Bombings — Reduce the risk to public safety caused by bombs and explosives.
- Explosives Industry Operations — Improve public safety by increasing compliance with Federal laws and regulations by explosives industry members.
- Fire and Arson — Reduce the risk to public safety caused by the criminal use of fire.
- Firearms Criminal Prosecution and Use — Reduce the risk to public safety caused by criminal possession and use of firearms.
- Firearms Industry Operations — Improve public safety by increasing compliance with Federal laws and regulations by firearms industry members.
- Illegal Firearms Trafficking — Reduce the risk to public safety caused by illegal firearms trafficking.
- Modernization — Modernize business processes and systems for improved mission effectiveness and transparency.
- Workforce — Attract, develop, and retain an expert workforce to execute the ATF mission ("Strategic Plan," 2010).

The latter two functions ("Modernization" and "Workforce") are administrative in nature; the preceding functions are more oriented toward law enforcement.

Perhaps the most effective means to understand the responsibilities of the ATF are to examine the agency's strategic goals. In outlining its strategic plan and goals for 2010–2016, the ATF identified six primary areas of focus, including:

1. Illegal Firearms Trafficking, with the goal of reducing violent firearms crimes by strengthening firearms trafficking intelligence gathering, analysis, inspection, and investigative activity.

Figure 4.1 ATF Organizational Structure as of 4/26/2006

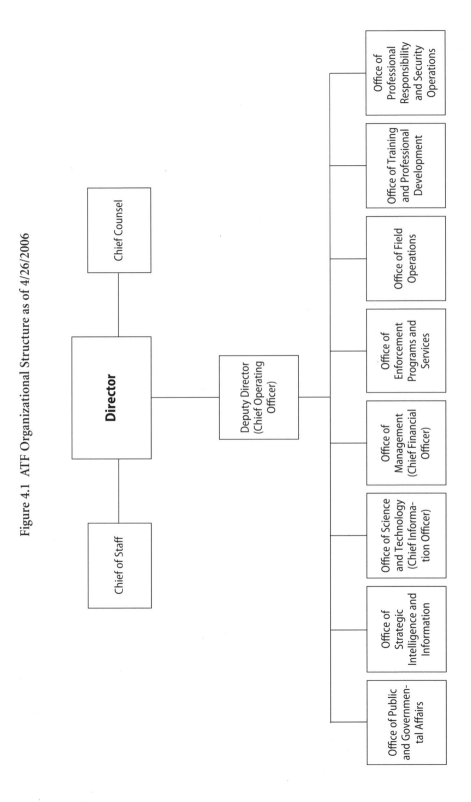

Source: http://www.atf.gov/about/organization/.

2. Criminal Groups and Gangs, with the goal of making communities safer by expanding efforts to identify, target, and dismantle criminal gangs and organizations that use firearms and explosives in committing crime. For instance, the ATF has successfully completed numerous investigations into outlaw motorcycle gangs (e.g., Queen, 2005).

3. Explosives, Bombs, and Bombings, with the goal of advancing domestic and international explosives expertise to prevent, detect, and investigate acts of violent crime and terrorism and to enhance public safety.

4. Fire and Arson, with the goal of advancing the science of fire investigation globally by setting and delivering the highest standards in response, research, information sharing, and training.

5. Modernization, with the goal of modernizing business processes and systems for improved information sharing, knowledge management, and use of innovative technologies in support of ATF's critical missions.

6. Workforce, with the goal of attracting, developing, and retaining an expert workforce to execute the ATF mission in the emerging business environment ("Strategic Plan...," 2010).

Within each of these areas and goals are a series of anticipated efforts by the bureau in its attempt to become increasingly professional and to address its wide array of responsibilities.

Federal law enforcement agencies changed their focus of attention toward terrorism and the enforcement of terrorism-related activities following the 2001 terrorist attacks against the U.S. Accordingly, the ATF is largely concerned with preventing and responding to terrorist attacks against the U.S. These concerns are not entirely new to the bureau. For instance, the ATF was instrumental in the investigations of the World Trade Center bombing in 1993 and the bombing of the Alfred P. Murrah Federal Building in Oklahoma City in April 1995. Nevertheless, the agency's role in enforcing the laws pertaining to the illegal use and trafficking of firearms and explosives has become even more pronounced following the 2001 attacks. Its enforcement efforts in relation to tobacco and alcohol have also become increasingly important as terrorists seek various means to support their activities and have engaged in bootlegging various regulated products as part of their financing efforts. As part of their approach toward anti-terrorism, ATF special agents are participates in the Department of Justice's Joint Terrorism Task Forces.

The ATF remains, of course, concerned with issues aside from terrorism. For instance, in FY 2010 the ATF recommended 17,893 cases for prosecution, most of which were not directly related to terrorism. Of all cases (both terrorism and non-terrorism-related) referred for prosecution, 5,322 (30%) were convicted. Of those convicted, 54% were given prison sentences of which the mean prison sentence was 147 months. Sixteen offenders were sentenced to death and 41 received a life sentence (Bureau of Alcohol, 2011a). The ATF is well-known for referring individuals for criminal prosecution, and refer more individuals for federal prosecution per agent than any other federal law enforcement agency (Kingsbury, 2008).

Despite the dangerous nature inherent in some of the ATF's responsibilities, the agents have been relatively safe from the physical harms inherent in law enforcement. For instance, in 2010 only three of the 24 ATF agents assaulted in the line of duty were injured, and there were no deaths. The number of agents assaulted decreased from 2009 when 35 agents were harmed (FBI, 2011a). Two-thirds of the agents assaulted in 2010 were making an arrest or issuing a summons at the time of the attack (FBI, 2011b), and a firearm (83%) was used most often in the assaults on the agents. The number of ATF agents assaulted in 2010 constituted 11.5% of all assaults against federal law enforcement officers within the Department of Justice and 1.3% of assaults against federal law enforcement officers (FBI, 2011c).

Much of the ATF's resources are devoted to its firearms compliance and investigations program, which differs from the primary responsibility of enforcing the taxes associated with alcohol that was placed upon the agency upon its creation (e.g., Kingsbury, 2008, Vizzard, 1997). With regard to firearms compliance, the bureau periodically checks the records of federally licensed gun dealers. However the primary focus of the firearms program has been on reducing firearms-related violence. In FY 2010 the ATF initiated 10,072 criminal investigations pertaining to firearms cases, including illegal possession and firearms trafficking, compared to 564 cases pertaining to arson and explosives, 95 alcohol and tobacco diversion cases, and 24 explosives theft cases. Further, the agency conducted 10,538 federal firearms licensee inspections, compared to 3,925 federal explosives licensee inspections (Bureau of Alcohol..., 2011a). The bureau regulates the explosives industry and addresses explosives-related crime. It has statutory authority to oversee roughly 12,000 explosives licensees and permit holders, and 106,000 federal firearms licenses (Lluberes, 2005).

As part of its public outreach and general law enforcement efforts, the ATF facilitates and participates in several crime prevention and enforcement programs. For instance, the ATF is a full partner in the President's Project Safe Neighborhoods, which was created in FY 2001. Project Safe Neighborhoods is a large-scale initiative to reduce gun crime and involves ATF personnel working with state and local law enforcement agencies to examine violent firearms-related issues and incidents. The ATF works with DOJ attorneys, other federal law enforcement agencies, and state and local law enforcement groups to prosecute offenders, particularly armed violent and career offenders. The ATF also heads the U.S. Attorney General's Violent Crime Impact Teams (VCITs) in attempt to reduce the number of homicides and other violent crimes committed with firearms in various U.S. cities. The VCITs primarily assist state and local agencies by investigating all firearms-related leads; responding to all street recoveries of firearms and interviewing individuals involved to identify the source of the firearms; and focusing on violent and career criminals (Bureau of Alcohol..., 2005).

As part of its violent crime prevention responsibilities, the ATF created a community outreach prevention program which would eventually become known as the Gang Resistance Education and Training (GREAT) program, which is now funded by the Office of Justice Programs. GREAT encourages children and youth to avoid involvement in delinquency and violent gang activities. Since 1991, the program has graduated over 5 million school children, and over 10,000 law enforcement officers and professionals have been certified as instructors for the program (Bureau of Alcohol..., 2011a). The program is facilitated in cooperation with local law enforcement agencies and other federal law enforcement agencies. Participants in the program learn about the importance of making good decisions, resisting negative influences, and developing more positive attitudes regarding law enforcement (Lluberes, 2005).

The ATF facilitates "one of the most sophisticated crime laboratory systems in the world" (Bagley, 2007, p. 47). Their National Laboratory Center includes a fire research lab that assists with fire scene investigation, and two additional forensic laboratories that focus on forensic evidence pertaining to firearms, alcohol, explosives, tobacco, and arson. The agency also maintains the Arson and Explosives National Repository, which oversees the Bomb and Arson Tracking System and facilitates information sharing among law enforcement agencies regarding bomb and arson cases (Lluberes, 2005).

The ATF houses one of the government's oldest law enforcement labs, which in 1984 became the first federal laboratory to win the approval of the American Society of Crime Laboratory Directors. The Society only approves labs that meet notably strict standards (Moore, 2001). Among other contributions and services, ATF labs have developed a technically advanced computerized method of matching bullets with the guns that fired them, and can reconstruct and test arson and fire scenarios. In FY 2010, ATF laboratories processed 3,329 forensic cases, and 101 fire research cases (Bureau of Alcohol..., 2011a). The agency also facilitates the Canine Enforcement Training Center which includes training for accelerant and explosives detection canines from national and international law enforcement agencies.

Partnerships and cooperative efforts have become increasingly important in all levels of law enforcement, particularly in light of concerns for homeland security (e.g., Gerspacher, 2008). Within the law enforcement community, the ATF is recognized for two particular qualities: two-way cooperation with other agencies, and outstanding undercover work (Moore, 2001). With regard to the former, the ATF partners with various agencies with regard to training, law enforcement, regulatory efforts, and forensic services. Among the groups they partner with are other law enforcement agencies, regulatory agencies, professional organizations, international groups, academia, community groups, and industry personnel. For instance, licensed gun dealers provide a valuable resource to the ATF in the sense that they are involved in the industry and have a similar interest in removing illegal guns from society. Gun laws and cooperative relationships between the ATF and other law enforcement agencies have largely contributed to the ATF's successes in the fight against organized crime (Moore, 2001).

An example of the ATF's cooperative efforts involves the bureau's rapid-response National Response Teams, which can be deployed to assist law enforcement agencies at all levels in large-scale arson and/or explosives incidents. As experts in these areas, ATF personnel provide valuable assistance whenever and wherever necessary. The bureau provides a great deal of explosives training to all levels of law enforcement both nationally and internationally (Lluberes, 2005).

The ATF in the twenty-first century has, like many other federal law enforcement agencies, been primarily focused on terrorism and concerns for homeland security. The bureau remains vigilant in its fight against gun trafficking and other gun-related crimes, and the nature of these and other responsibilities of the ATF has resulted in the bureau engaging in more international crime fighting efforts.

The ATF has undergone many changes since its inception. Its responsibilities have shifted in relation to changes in society at large. Tasked with regulating industries and enforcing laws related to issues (i.e., alcohol, tobacco, firearms, and explosives) that often generate passion among and prosperity for various groups in society, the agency has, at times, been in the center of controversy and scrutiny. Ultimately, the agency provides many very important contributions to the law enforcement community and society at large.

References

Bagley, P. D. (2007). *The everything guide to careers in law enforcement.* Avon, MA: Adams Media.

Bumgarner, J. B. (2006). *Federal agents: The growth of federal law enforcement in America.* Westport, CT: Praeger.

Bureau of Alcohol, Tobacco, Firearms and Explosives. (2005). *Violent crime impact teams: Best practices.* U.S. Department of Justice. ATF Publication 3501.1. Accessed online January 12, 2012 at: http://www.atf.gov/publications/download/p/atf-p-3501-1.pdf.

Bureau of Alcohol, Tobacco, Firearms and Explosives. (2011a). *Fact sheet: Facts and figures (FY2010).* Accessed online October 12, 2011 at: http://www.atf.gov/publications/factsheets/2010-factsheet-facts-and-figures.html.

Bureau of Alcohol, Tobacco, Firearms and Explosives. (2011b). *ATF fact sheet: ATF staffing and budget.* Accessed online October 12, 2011 at: http://www.atf.gov/publications/factsheets/041411-factsheet-atf-staffing-and-budget.pdf.

Bureau of Alcohol, Tobacco, Firearms and Explosives. (2011c). *Heraldry of the ATF seal.* Accessed online December 2, 2011 at: http://www.atf.gov/about/history/heraldry-of-seal.html.

Federal Bureau of Investigation. (2011a). *Uniform Crime Reports: Law enforcement officers killed & assaulted, 2010.* Table 76: Federal Law Enforcement Officers Killed and Assaulted. Accessed online December 2, 2011 at: http://www.fbi.gov/about-us/cjis/ucr/leoka/leoka-2010/tables/table76-federal-leoka-department-agency-by-extent-of-injury-06-10.xls.

Federal Bureau of Investigation. (2011b). *Uniform Crime Reports: Law enforcement officers killed & assaulted, 2010.* Table 81: Federal Law Enforcement Officers Killed and Assaulted. Accessed online December 2, 2011 at: http://www.fbi.gov/about-us/cjis/ucr/leoka/leoka-2010/tables/table81-federal-leoka-department-agency-by-activity-10.xls.

Federal Bureau of Investigation. (2011c). *Uniform Crime Reports: Law enforcement officers killed & assaulted, 2010.* Table 80: Federal Law Enforcement Officers Killed and Assaulted. Accessed online December 2, 2011 at: http://www.fbi.gov/about-us/cjis/ucr/leoka/leoka-2010/tables/table80-federal-leoka-department-agency-by-type-weapon-10.xls.

Freedman, D. (2011, June 30). "Fast and Furious" sparks new gun control debates. *Houston Chronicle.* Accessed online October 12, 2011 at: http://www.chron.com/news/article/Fast-and-Furious-sparks-new-gun-control-debates-1446773.php.

Gerspacher, N. (2008). The history of international police cooperation: A 150-year evolution in trends and approaches. *Global Crime, 9*(1–2), 169–184.

Herrmann, V. (1998). Alcohol, Tobacco and Firearms, Bureau of. Pp. 39–41 in G.T. Kurian (ed.), *A Historical Guide to the U.S. Government.* NY: Oxford.

Kingsbury, A. (2008, October 27). Taking on the gun traffickers and the gangs. *U.S. News & World Report, 145*(9): 20.

Krouse, W. J. (2011). *The Bureau of Alcohol, Tobacco, Firearms and Explosives (ATF): budget and operations for FY2011*: Congressional Research Service. Document Number R41206. Accessed online October 12, 2011 at: www.fas.org/sgp/crs/misc/R41206.pdf.

Langton, L. (2010). *Women in law enforcement, 1987–2008.* Washington, D.C.: U.S. Department of Justice, Bureau of Justice Statistics. NCJ 230521.

Lluberes, A.L. (2005). Inside the new ATF. *Police Chief,* 72(11): 40–44.

Moore, J. (2001). *Very special agents: The inside story of America's most controversial Law enforcement agency — The Bureau of Alcohol, Tobacco, and Firearms.* Champaign, IL: University of Illinois Press.

Queen, W. (2005). *Under and alone: The true story of the undercover agent who infiltrated America's most violent outlaw motorcycle gang.* NY: Random House.

Reaves, B. A. (2006). *Federal law enforcement officers, 2004.* Washington, D.C.: U.S. Department of Justice, Bureau of Justice Statistics. NCJ 212750.

Reaves, B.A. (2012). *Federal law enforcement officers, 2008.* U.S. Department of Justice, Bureau of Justice Statistics. NCJ 238250.

Strategic Plan: Bureau of Alcohol, Tobacco, Firearms and Explosives: FY 2010–FY 2016. (2010, October). Report Number ATF P 1000.5. Accessed online October 12, 2011 at: http://www.atf.gov/publications/download/sp/2010-2016/2010-2016-strategic-plan-complete.pdf.

Vizzard, W.J. (1997). *In the cross fire: A political history of the Bureau of Alcohol, Tobacco, and Firearms.* Boulder, CO: Lynne Reinner.

Yager, J. (December 2, 2011). Rep. Issa examining ways to reorganize ATF. *The Hill.* Accessed online December 20, 2011 at: http://thehill.com/homenews/house/196865-issa-wants-to-reorganize-atf.

Zimring, F. E. (1975). Firearms and federal law: The Gun Control Act of 1968. *Journal of Legal Studies,* 4(1), 133–198.

Chapter Five

U.S. Marshals Service

U.S. Marshals are recognized by many as being the oldest federal law enforcement agency in the United States, and have served the U.S. since 1789 when the Office of the United States Marshal was created. Since that time the agency has been among the most versatile federal agencies and has provided a wealth of law enforcement services in many different capacities.

The 94 U.S. Marshals oversee the activities in each of the 94 federal judicial districts within the United States. U.S. Marshals are presidentially appointed and confirmed by the Senate. They are assisted by over 4,000 Deputy U.S. Marshals and Criminal Investigators, and 1,628 administrative employees and detention officers (U.S. Marshals Service, 2009b; U.S. Marshals Service, 2009c). U.S. Marshals work in each of the 94 districts, 218 sub-offices, and four foreign field offices (U.S. Marshals Service, 2009b). In accord with many discussions of the U.S. Marshals Service, this chapter will not always distinguish between U.S. Marshals and deputy U.S. marshals. Generally, the term "U.S. marshal" or simply "marshal" is often used to refer to deputy marshals. Distinctions are provided, however, in areas where notable differences between the positions exist.

The Marshals Service has been termed "The Silent Service" in response to the lack of publicity attributed to the agency. The limited publicity received by the agency is largely the result of the Marshals historically not having a public information office (McKinney & Russo, 2009) and the general lack of sensationalism that surrounds the many valuable services the agency provides. Nevertheless, the agency has been represented in various television shows and motion pictures. Popular culture has included numerous depictions of U.S. Marshals in both print and electronic media, with many accounts of Marshals portrayed as lawmen "possessing supernatural characteristics of strength, poise, and speed in drawing their pistols" (Zohra and Walker, 2008, p. 2). Media depictions of the marshals are found in popular films such as *The Fugitive* (1993) and the sequel *U.S. Marshals* (1998), both of which focus on the operations of a fictional group of U.S. Marshals. The 2010 movie *True Grit*, a remake of the 1969 film starring John Wayne, follows a deputy U.S. Marshal as he pursues a fugitive. Television shows such as *Eureka, In Plain Sight, Justified, Manhunters: Fugitive Task Force*, and *Chase* also depict marshals engaging in various law enforcement pursuits. Several literary works focus on the U.S. Marshals, including *Out of Sight*, a novel which depicts the relationship between a U.S. Marshal and a bank robber, and was later made into a motion picture. These and other media accounts have largely shaped public perceptions of the U.S. Marshals and provide some historical context to the agency.

History

The origins of the U.S. Marshals Service began with the passage of the Judiciary Act of 1789, following which then-President George Washington appointed the first 13 U.S.

Marshals. U.S. Marshals were to be appointed by the President on the consent of the Senate (Lenior, 2008). The number of Marshals appointed by Washington expanded to 16 by 1791; or one Marshal for each district within the United States. Washington's choices for individuals to serve as U.S. Marshals set the standard for the Marshals that followed in the sense that they were all prominent, politically active men in their respective states, and most were veterans of the Revolutionary War who supported the Federalist Party (Newton, 2011). The Marshals were appointed based on their loyalty, dedication, and leadership in relation to the government (Zohra and Walker, 2008).

The primary responsibility of the early Marshals was to provide security for the federal courts (Newton, 2011), but the Judiciary Act also gave the U.S. Marshals broad powers to enforce the law, including the right to carry firearms, make arrests, and conduct searches and seizures in accord with court-approved warrants (Bumgarner, 2006). Specifically, the responsibilities for the early Marshals included transporting and supervising federal prisoners, managing the jails where federal inmates were housed, collecting payments of court costs, protecting the courts, overseeing federal executions, and serving court notices and warrants. Marshals also conducted the United State's first nine federal censuses from 1790 to 1870 (Turk, 2008) and collected taxes in the state or territory of their jurisdiction. Congress codified the extensive law enforcement powers applied by the early marshals in statutes that gave the agency sheriff-like responsibilities and powers to enforce federal laws and perform specific duties (Lenior, 2008).

The absence of any other federal law enforcement agency that was strictly devoted to crime fighting meant that the marshals were the primary law enforcement agency for the federal government and were responsible for enforcing the criminal laws that existed during the early history of the United States. The offices of the U.S. Marshal and the deputy marshals were the first federal law enforcement agency that had law enforcement as a primary function, although other federal agencies such as postal surveyors and customs personnel had also law enforcement powers (Turk, 2005).

The Marshals had broad law enforcement powers, yet received little financial support. In response, they often called upon citizens to assist them with their responsibilities. Citizens who were deputized and recognized as special deputy U.S. marshals were given temporary authority to perform law enforcement operations pertaining to the mission for which they were summoned (Lenior, 2008). Deputizing citizens as marshals is a historical practice that continues today, albeit on a limited basis.

The history of the U.S. Marshals Service was largely shaped by societal events and legislative efforts. Among the societal events that shaped the U.S. Marshals Service was slavery, including the need to investigate and apprehend violators of the Fugitive Slave Law of 1850. Marshals following this act were required to capture runaway slaves and return them to their masters. Marshals played a significant role during the United State's Civil War, for instance through guarding against espionage and generally assisting the federal government, which sought to preserve the Union and confront Southern subversives. That role would continue following the war, particularly in light of the 13th, 14th, and 15th amendments to the United States Constitution which outlawed slavery; made freed slaves citizens and afforded them due process of law, and; granted former slaves the right to vote, respectively (Bumgarner, 2006).

Early marshals were instrumental in the establishment of the United States in other ways, as they provided various law enforcement services on an emerging basis. For example, marshals were called upon to enforce the Sedition Act of 1798, which made criticism of the United States government and its officials punishable. Marshals also investigated and arrested individuals accused or suspected of engaging in counterfeiting of federal currency; a responsibility that would later be transferred to the United States Secret Service. Early marshals were also instrumental in assisting Internal Revenue agents (who lacked arrest powers) as they enforced the whiskey tax law in the early 1870s, and provided assistance during the 1894 Pullman strike by helping to keep train service running.

Marshals played a significant role in ensuring peace in the unsettled western portion of the United States during the late 1700s and 1800s, particularly as the United States increased in geographical size (e.g., the expansion of the United States following the Louisiana Purchase in 1803) and conflict between settlers and Native Americans persisted. The lack of established towns, cities, and police departments in the west, and generally in areas that the United States accumulated, resulted in marshals being tasked with enforcing the laws and protecting settlers who often only had each other, and perhaps local sheriffs and/or the military to rely on. The lack of a strong law enforcement presence in the largely unsettled areas and the need to escape law enforcement attention encouraged several outlaws and groups of outlaws to head west where they could more easily avoid law enforcement detection and engage in criminal behavior (Bumgarner, 2006). The role of marshals in helping to settle the wild west contributed to the legendary status of marshals such as Wyatt Earp, Edward and Bat Masterson, and James Butler Hickok (aka "Wild Bill"). These individuals and several other legendary marshals are depicted in many accounts as "drifters who came into town, apprehended the outlaws, and moved on in search of new adventures" (Zohra and Walker, 2008, p. 3).

The Marshals expanded as an agency in jurisdiction and became increasingly professional in the second half of the 19th century and the first decade of the 20th century. Among other developments, they were placed under the authority of the United States Attorney General in 1861, and in 1870 the marshals became part of the newly created United States Department of Justice where they are housed today. In 1890 the Supreme Court ruled that the President had the power through the Attorney General to assign a marshal to protect federal judges. Further, the fee system that had been used to pay marshals was replaced by a system in which marshals received an annual salary as of 1896. Prior to giving all marshals a salary, agents working in the field received a commission for the tasks they completed (Turk, 2008).

During this period the agency further refined and defined its missions, particularly as other federal law enforcement agencies emerged and specialization within federal law enforcement became increasingly prominent. The enhanced specialization in federal law enforcement ultimately reduced the responsibilities of the marshals, for instance as the FBI, DEA, Postal Inspection Service, Border Patrol, and other agencies assumed specialized missions and duties and adopted some of the responsibilities traditionally maintained by marshals.

The United States Secret Service became increasingly established as a federal law enforcement agency during the early part of the 20th century, and in several ways replaced the Marshals Service as the primary federal law enforcement agency in the United States. The Secret Service eagerly expanded its jurisdiction and marshals, on the other hand, were still appointed and directly accountable to the President and heavily influenced by politics (Bumgarner, 2006). Years later and remaining today, many of the marshals' historical investigative and enforcement responsibilities were dispersed to other federal law enforcement agencies such as the FBI and the Secret Service. Nevertheless, marshals continued to serve many prominent roles and regularly received new assignments, such as protecting the United States from enemy aliens, spies, and saboteurs during World War I, and arresting bootleggers during Prohibition. With regard to the latter, it is suggested that pursuing liquor tax evaders was the most dangerous task performed by marshals, as it contributed to numerous marshal fatalities, particularly during 1869 and 1935 (Newton, 2011).

Marshals were also tasked with ensuring the safe integration of African-Americans into public schools in the South following the United States Supreme Court's historical decision in the 1954 case *Brown v. Board of Education*. Marshals provided much service, law enforcement, and order maintenance in a series of civil rights demonstrations during the 1960s and into the 1970s, and have historically been called on to help quell civil disturbances and provide a law enforcement presence during tumultuous times. For instance, they were heavily involved in controlling public protests regarding the war in Vietnam and securing federal buildings in response to protest demonstrations regarding the Persian Gulf War.

A series of airline hijackings in the late 1960s and early 1970s brought about a new responsibility for marshals. Marshals, at the time, were the only federal agents with the wide range of powers necessary to safeguard airlines and airline passengers. In 1969 the roots of the Sky Marshal Program emerged in the Miami office of the marshals. The operation began with five deputies who worked to develop an anti-hijacking strategy. The program would expand to include over 230 deputies during the four years it was in operation. Administration of the Sky Marshal Program was transferred to the Federal Aviation Administration in 1973, primarily in response to the lack of resources maintained by marshals, who were still responsible for a host of other law enforcement functions at the time (McKinney & Russo, 2009). Today, the Transportation Security Administration runs the Federal Air Marshal Program, which is designed to meet the same goals as the Marshals' Sky Marshal Program.

Organization and Personnel

The U.S. Marshals Service is headed by a director, who is assisted by a deputy director. The Office of the Director and Deputy Director of the Marshals Service provides vision, direction, and leadership for the agency; establishes the policy and procedures for the agency; sets goals and oversees operations and the performance of the agency, and; oversees the general functioning of the agency. The U.S. Marshals Service provides many significant federal law enforcement functions and the agency's contributions are perhaps best reflected by the fact that it makes more arrests of criminal offenders in the United States than do all other federal law enforcement groups combined (Lenior, 2008). In 2009, the U.S. Marshals arrested and booked a record 183,986 suspects for violations of federal law (Motivans, 2011).

The 3,313 U.S. marshals with arrest and firearms authority as of 2008 represented an increase of 2.5% from the number of marshals in 2004 (Reaves, 2012). Marshals have jurisdiction over, and are located throughout, the entire United States; however an earlier Bureau of Justice Statistics report noted that the greatest number of marshals were employed in Texas, California, New York, Washington, D.C., and Florida. (Reaves, 2006).

The varied responsibilities of the U.S. Marshals Service often means that individuals who work for the agency be skilled in a variety of areas. Depending on one's position within the agency, employees are expected to engage in investigations, arrests, and all other aspects of law enforcement. Among other requirements, candidates for deputy U.S. marshal positions undergo a 17.5 week basic training program at the U.S. Marshals Service Training Academy in Glynco (GA), which is at the Federal Law Enforcement Training Center. They must also pass a structured interview, an in-depth background investigation, a medical exam, and a physical fitness test. Individuals who are selected by the agency are hired at the GL-5 or GL-7 levels. Such extensive training is needed given that Marshals are involved in almost all aspects of the federal justice system, as they conduct fugitive investigations, protect judges and courthouses, serve court papers, and transport prisoners.

Although there is a certain element of danger in all law enforcement positions, some positions are more vulnerable to violence and danger than others. Marshals, relative to other federal law enforcement personnel, seemingly face higher level of violence primarily due to the nature of their work. For instance, in 2004, marshals had the third highest rate of assaults (1.5 per 100 officers) among federal law enforcement personnel, and had the third highest rate of assaults with injury (.7 per 100 officers) among the same group. These numbers dropped from 2004 to 2008, as the rate of assault decreased to .6 and the rate of assault with injury dropped to .1. No marshal was feloniously killed during 2004 or 2008 (Reaves, 2006, 2012).

More recent data indicate that 165 marshals were assaulted in 2010 and there were no line-of-duty deaths during the year. The largest percentage of marshals (41.2%) who were assaulted were making an arrest or issuing a summons at the time of their victimization. The number of marshals assaulted constituted 79% of all assaults against federal law enforcement officers within the Department of Justice, and 8.7% of assaults against all federal law enforcement officers (FBI, 2011).

In one of the few research studies on federal law enforcement agents, Newman and Rucker-Reed (2004) assessed stress levels of deputy U.S. marshals through surveying one hundred deputies from offices across the United States. They found that deputies generally scored low on the State-Trait Anxiety Inventory. The primary stressors identified by the deputy marshals related to organizational variables, including concerns with management, inept bosses, and the work environment. Deputies who were inclined to think about job-related illnesses or being injured on duty, and those who faced retirement or disliked their current assignments experienced more stress than their counterparts. Results from this study suggested that deputy marshals experienced similar levels of stress and responded similarly to the same types of stressors as police officers. Similar to police officers, deputies seemingly prefer specific aspects of their job, including chasing criminals and risking their life; generally, tasks that the much of the general public would find stressful.

Aside from deputy U.S. marshals, the Marshals Service employs individuals who perform a wide array of duties. For instance, the agency employs airplane pilots who fly aircraft in support of Justice Prisoner and Alien Transportation System (JPATS), and Aviation Enforcement Officers who help transport prisoners, search prisoners, respond to disturbances, and process prisoners who are transported via aircraft. Detention Enforcement Officers within the Marshals Service transport prisoners, conduct searches of inmates, manage cellblocks, and process prisoners. In addition to these and other positions, the Marshals Service also employs a host of administrative personnel, including Human Resource Specialists and Assistants; Management and Program Analysts; Budget Analysts; Investigative Research Specialists; Administrative Support Personnel, and; Accountants. The organizational design of the U.S. Marshals Service is depicted in Figure 5.1.

Compared to most other federal law enforcement agencies, the U.S. Marshals Service has had lower levels of diversity. In 2004, females accounted for 15.5% of all federal officers with arrest and firearm authority, while racial and ethnic minorities accounted for 34.3%. The percentages of females (10.2%) and minorities (19.4%) employed by the U.S. Marshals were well below the overall average for all federal law enforcement agents

Figure 5.1 United States Marshals Service

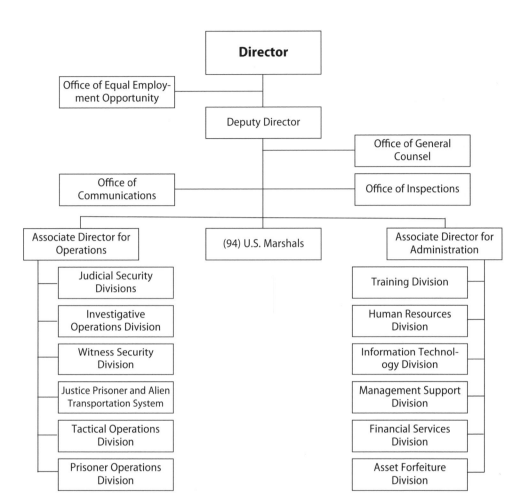

Source: U.S. Marshals Service, http://www.justice.gov/jmd/mps/manual/usms.htm.

(Reaves, 2012). The agency has made efforts to diversify its ranks, for instance as in 2000 John Marshall, the son of former Supreme Court Justice Thurgood Marshall (the first African-American Supreme Court Justice), became the first African American director of the U.S. Marshals Service. Marshall not only became the first African-American to head the Service, but the first former U.S. marshal to assume the role (Starling, 2000). Stacia Hylton was later sworn in on December 31, 2010 as the Marshals Service's first female director.

Functions

Marshals provide numerous important law enforcement functions and have often been called on by the federal government to fulfill law enforcement responsibilities on an emerging basis and in response to issues that may not fit directly within the jurisdiction of other federal law enforcement agencies. The agency's role as the enforcement arm of the federal courts system results in marshals being involved in a large number of law enforcement endeavors. In its description of the Position Classification Standards for the "U.S. Marshal Series" (GS-0082), the United States Office of Personnel Management (United States Office..., 1973) noted that:

> This series covers positions involving a range of law enforcement responsibilities including serving a variety of civil writs and criminal warrants issued by Federal courts; tracing and arresting people wanted under court warrants; seizing and disposing of property under court orders; safeguarding and transporting prisoners; providing for the physical security of court facilities and personnel; providing for the physical security of jurors and key Government witnesses and their families; preventing civil disturbances or restoring order in riot and mob violence situations; and performing other special law enforcement duties as directed by a court order or by the Department of Justice.

Particularly, marshals are responsible for providing judicial security; conducting fugitive investigations; operating the Witness Security Program; operating the JPATS; federal prisoner operations; asset forfeiture, and; special missions and programs. The wide array of responsibilities of marshals contributes to the Marshals Service being one of the more flexible and vital components of federal law enforcement.

Judicial Security

U.S. marshals assume many of the same responsibilities as local sheriffs, including the provision of judicial security. A primary mission for the Marshals Service is to provide judicial security, including protecting federal judges, United States Attorneys, Assistant United States Attorneys, jurors, and other individuals involved in federal court cases. The Judicial Security Division of the Marshals Service provides protection for the judicial process and is organized according to two program areas: Judicial Operations and Judicial Services.

Judicial Operations encompasses several programs led by a Deputy Assistant Director who oversees: (1) the National Center for Judicial Security, which provides educational, operation, and technical support regarding judicial security; (2) the Office of Protective Operations, which provides protective support for the judiciary; (3) the Office of Protective Intelligence, which provides guidance, coordination, and recommendations regarding threats or harms to the judiciary, and; (4) the Office of Management and Administration, which manages the businesses processes of the Judicial Security Division.

Judicial Services is a program in the Judicial Security Division, and is also led by a Deputy Assistant Director who oversees programs funded by the Administrative Office of the United States Courts (AOUSC) court security appropriation. The funding provides support for: the Court Security Officer (CSO) program; security equipment and systems for space occupied by the Judiciary, and; U.S. Marshals Service employees to administer the daily functions. Judicial Services is organized into four oversight areas: (1) the Office of Court Security, which is responsible for the daily operations and personnel management of the CSO program; (2) the Office of Security Contracts, which performs the daily contract responsibilities with the private contractors and the district Contract Officer Technical Representatives; (3) the Office of Security Systems, which is responsible for all security and monitoring systems for judicial space; and (4) the Office of Financial Management, which has the daily oversight responsibility of a budget of approximately $335 million.

Generally, marshals are responsible for ensuring safe judicial proceedings in federal courts, and protect over 2,000 federal judges and about 5,250 other court officials at over 400 court facilities. They are also responsible for protecting the Director of the Office of National Drug Control Policy, and the Deputy Attorney General in Washington, D.C. and when they travel. Marshals are also responsible for protecting the United States Supreme Court Justices when they leave Washington, D.C., and provide protective details for foreign officials when they visit the United States during the United Nations General Assembly Sessions (U.S. Marshals Service, 2009b).

The agency's Court Security Officer program is largely comprised of experienced, former law enforcement officers who are contracted and receive limited deputations as special Deputy U.S. Marshals. They work with deputy U.S. marshals and senior inspectors to ensure safety at federal courthouses. In addition to security, Marshals also serve the federal courts through delivering subpoenas, indictments, and other court papers notifying individuals of court appearances.

Fugitive Apprehension

Beginning in 1979 and by a memorandum of understanding with the FBI, marshals assumed the lead responsibility of apprehending federal fugitives. The agency is the United States government's primary source for executing fugitive warrants and investigations. In FY 2010 marshals apprehended over 36,100 federal fugitives and cleared roughly 39,100 felony warrants (U.S. Marshals Service, 2011a). Marshals also work closely with state and local law enforcement agencies in the apprehension of fugitives at the state and local levels, as they led fugitive task forces with agencies from these levels to arrest an additional 81,900 state and local fugitives, and cleared roughly 108,200 state and local felony warrants. Marshals led 75 district fugitive task forces and seven regional fugitive task forces as of 2011 (U.S. Marshals Service, 2011a).

Aside from providing assistance to state and local law enforcement agencies in apprehending fugitives, marshals provide expertise and training in the area to all levels of law enforcement, including international agencies. Further, the agency's "15 Most Wanted" fugitive program assists with the apprehension of the most dangerous and high-profile fugitives. As of FY 2009 marshals had captured 204 fugitives identified as one of the "Most Wanted" (U.S. Marshals Service, 2009b).

Marshals apprehend both domestic and international fugitives, and the Marshals Service is the primary agency responsible for administering extraditions to and from the United States. The agency coordinated 805 extraditions and deportations from 67 countries in FY 2010. The Marshals Service has foreign field offices in Jamaica, Mexico, Colombia, and the Dominican Republic to support its international effort (U.S. Marshals Service, 2011a), and has been deemed by INTERPOL and the United States Department of Justice as the primary agency responsible for apprehending international fugitives believed to be in the United States.

Marshals worked with INTERPOL to assemble the first international fugitive operation, which included agencies in England, Mexico, and Canada. The result was the International Affairs Fugitive Task Force, which sought to apprehend fugitives wanted by the involved countries. The task force created international warrants, which had not been attempted prior, through receiving assistance from INTERPOL task force members. The warrants were then executed, which enabled the marshals to apprehend fugitives outside of the United States. The operation resulted in the arrest of over two hundred fugitives within eight weeks (McKinney & Russo, 2009).

The U.S. Marshals Service targets specific types of offenders in addition to its more general role of fugitive apprehension. Specifically, the agency targets sex offenders who fail to comply with the provisions in the Adam Walsh Child Protection and Safety Act of 2006, fugitives with gang affiliations, and organized crime groups, for instance through its involvement in the Organized Crime Drug Enforcement Task Force. The latter is a primary component of the United States Attorney General's drug-supply reduction strategy. Marshals apprehended 10,019 sex offenders in FY 2009 under the Adam Walsh Child Protection and Safety Act (U.S. Marshals Service, 2009b), and their efforts directed toward gangs is part of the Department of Justice's more general efforts to address gang violence. Marshals also conduct financial surveillance as an investigative tool to identify funds and assets used by fugitives to commit crime and avoid apprehension.

Marshals have always had broad authority to enter into partnerships with state and local law enforcement to pursue fugitives, although doing so was never specifically funded until 2002 when Congress appropriated funds to form regional task forces. The task forces focus on apprehending fugitives accused of violent crimes. The appropriation of funds resulted in greater cooperative efforts between the marshals and state, county, and local law enforcement agencies. Such cooperative efforts are evidenced in several high profile initiatives, including a series of concerted, collaborative efforts between marshals and other law enforcement agencies. For instance, from April 4 through April 10, 2005, the marshals collaborated with public safety agencies at the federal, state and local levels to execute a large number of arrest warrants. The effort, known as Operation FALCON (Federal and Local Cops Organized Nationally), involved over 3,000 law enforcement officers from 25 federal agencies, and 934 state, county, and local agencies. The operation resulted in 10,518 arrests of fugitives accused of committing crimes such as murder, child molestation, rape, armed robbery, sexual assaults and other serious crimes (Finan, 2005).

The success of Operation FALCON contributed to additional cooperative efforts between marshals and other law enforcement agencies. Among those efforts were Operation FALCON II and III (both of which occurred in 2006 and focused on the apprehension of fugitives) and FALCON 2007, which focused on gang members and gang-related crime in urban areas. FALCON 2008 resulted in the capture of 55,800 fugitive felons; the largest number of fugitives apprehended during any of these Operation FALCON efforts (U.S. Marshals Service, 2011d).

Witness Security Program

The Marshals Service is well-known for its facilitation of the Witness Security Program (WITSEC), through which the agency provides protection for witnesses who testify for the government in cases involving significant criminal activities. The program was authorized by the Organized Crime Control Act of 1970 and later amended by the Comprehensive Crime Control Act of 1984 (U.S. Marshals Service, 2009d). Marshals have protected, relocated, and provided new identities to over 8,200 witnesses and more than 9,800 of their family members since 1971 (U.S. Marshals Service, 2009c). The agency is recognized as one of the world's leading and foremost authorities on witness security practices, and offers training and guidance in the area to government agencies from around the world.

Witnesses and family members who enter the WITSEC are typically provided new identities and authentic documentation. They receive housing, subsistence for basic living expenses, medical care, and in some cases job training and employment assistance. Not all who apply for the program are accepted, as candidates must meet certain criteria (McKinney & Russo, 2009). No participant in the WITSEC who has followed the security guidelines has been harmed while under the protection of marshals (U.S. Marshals Service, 2009d). The program, however, has been criticized for "coddling" sometimes dangerous felons, being costly in terms of the resources needed to facilitate that program, and encouraging individuals to lie under oath. There have also been claims that individuals have been deceived into joining the program and failed to receive services and goods promised to them as part of their involvement (Newton, 2011).

JPATS

Marshals have historically been responsible for transporting federal prisoners. Early marshals were required to transport prisoners by horseback, mule, and automobile. With regard to the latter, marshals were earlier required to use their own automobile to transport prisoners and were reimbursed for mileage and other associated costs (McKinney & Russo, 2009). The U.S. Marshals Service and the Immigration and Naturalization Service merged air fleets to create the JPATS in 1995. The merger resulted in a concerted effort to transport prisoners and criminal aliens. Marshals manage the program, which is sometimes informally referred to as "Con Air" and handles over 977 requests each day to move prisoners between judicial districts, correctional facilities, and foreign countries. The agency is one of the largest transporters of inmates in the world (Wojdylo, 2005).

JPATs is responsible for over 350,000 prisoner and alien movements each year via coordinated air and ground systems (U.S. Marshals Service, 2009c), and transports sentenced prisoners who are in the custody of the Federal Bureau of Prisons to court appearances, hearings, and detention facilities via a network of aircraft, cars, vans, and buses (U.S. Marshals Service, 2011b). Most transports within JPATs occurred via air in FY 2010 (206,358; 57.9%), although there was a substantial number of ground movements (150,245; 42.1%) (U.S. Marshals Service, 2011b). JPATS is the only government-operated, regularly scheduled passenger airline in the United States, and it assists the military and other law enforcement agencies by transporting their prisoners between jurisdictions at a reduced cost of what commercial airlines would charge (U.S. Marshals Service, 2011b). The large majority of JPATS transports, however, involve federal prisoner movements.

JPATS transports federal detainees and criminal aliens between Federal Bureau of Prison facilities and U.S. Marshal offices, and flies deportable aliens to their international destinations. The services are also provided, at a reasonable cost, to move military, state, and local prisoners per cooperative agreements between the Marshals Service and other agencies. The Marshals Service makes about 3,000 cooperative movements per year to assist local and state law enforcement agencies as they seek to extradite individuals wanted for prosecution or to serve sentences. JPATS regularly serves roughly 40 domestic and international cities, and other cities as necessary. Prisoner-movement scheduling is conducted at JPATS headquarters, which is located in Kansas City, MO (Wojdylo, 2005).

The Marshals Service used its aircraft that was typically reserved to transport prisoners to deploy deputy marshals and special deputy U.S. marshals to secure critical, at-risk installations immediately following the 2001 terrorist attacks against the United States. Special deputy U.S. marshals were assembled from law enforcement agencies throughout the United States and were deputized as federal marshals for their assignments (Lenior, 2008).

Prisoner Operations

The U.S. Marshals Service houses roughly 63,000 federal detainees each day in federal, state, local, and private facilities across the United States. In FY 2010 marshals received 225,329 prisoners (U.S. Marshals Service, 2011c). Over 80% of the inmates are housed in 1,800 state, local, and private jails across the United States. The remaining prisoners are placed in Federal Bureau of Prisons facilities (U.S. Marshals Service, 2011c). Cooperative Agreement Funds are used to pay local jails for their services in housing inmates in areas where detention space is scarce. The funds may be used to improve jail conditions and/or expand capacities.

Asset Seizure and Forfeiture

The Comprehensive Crime Control Act, passed by Congress in 1984, gave federal prosecutors forfeiture provisions to help combat crime. The legislation created the United States Department of Justice's Asset Forfeiture Program, through which marshals are responsible for managing and disposing seized and forfeited properties acquired by offenders through criminal behavior. The materials include real property, vehicles, businesses, jewelry, aircraft, and various other goods. Marshals regularly manage roughly 18,000 assets valued at more than $2 billion (U.S. Marshals Service, 2009b), and seek to maximize the net returns from the forfeited and seized properties and reinvest the proceeds into law enforcement endeavors (U.S. Marshals Service, 2009c). Cash and financial instruments account for 79% of the value. Vehicles comprise 26 percent of the inventory items (U.S. Marshals Service, 2009b).

The specific goals of the Asset Forfeiture Program are to strip criminals of their ill-gotten gains, improve law enforcement cooperation, and enhance law enforcement through equitable revenue sharing (U.S. Marshals Service, 2009a). Proceeds from sales of the seized items are typically shared with the law enforcement agencies that were involved in the investigations that contributed to the seizure. An estimated $5.2 billion has been shared with state and local agencies since FY 1985. In FY 2009, equitable sharing payments were approximately $395 million (U.S. Marshals Service, 2009b). Marshals attempt to minimize the amount of time an asset remains in inventory, and maximize the net return for the sale of goods by contracting with qualified vendors (U.S. Marshals Service, 2009a).

Special Missions and Programs

The Tactical Operations Division (TOD) of the U.S. Marshals Service is responsible for responding to national emergencies and crises involving homeland security, and engages in special law enforcement assignments, security missions, and various types of crises. It is comprised of several programs, including the:

- Office of Crises Services, which provides support to persons impacted by crisis or traumatic situations such as mass shootings;
- Office of Emergency Management, which consists of several national program areas and is the point of contact for several sensitive and classified missions pertaining to homeland security and national emergencies;
- Office of Resource Management, which provides financial expertise to TOD management and manages the business processes of TOD;
- Office of Security Programs, which is responsible for managing and coordinating several Marshals Service security programs and plans, such as communications security and personal identity verification;
- Office of Strategic Technology, which provides technical support and wireless communications to Marshals Service missions;
- Strategic National Stockpile Security Operations, which assists with securing the United States' medical countermeasures, and;
- Special Operations Group, which is a specially trained and equipped tactical unit deployed in high-risk and sensitive law enforcement situations, national emergencies, civil disorders, and natural disasters (U.S. Marshals Service, 2010).

The Special Operations Group is a specially trained tactical unit that was established in 1971 and responds to emergencies anywhere in the United States or its territories. It is a self-supporting response team comprised mostly of full-time deputy marshals from across the United States who have volunteered to be members. The members are on call at all times and "have demonstrated that they can meet rigorous standards of physical and mental ability" (De Lucia & Doyle, 1998, p. 30). The group also maintains a full-time operational cadre housed at the Marshals Service Tactical Operations Center at Camp Beauregard, a Louisiana National Guard installation (U.S. Marshals Service, 2009b, 2011e).

The U.S. Marshals Service is one of, if not the oldest, federal law enforcement agencies in the United States. It has historically provided a variety of law enforcement services and has filled in the gaps where no specifically designated law enforcement group had jurisdiction over important law enforcement matters. Accordingly, the agency's focus and responsibilities have shifted over time, and the Marshals have been quite flexible and effective in meeting their responsibilities.

References

Bumgarner, J. B. (2006). *Federal agents: The growth of federal law enforcement in America*. Westport, CT: Praeger.

De Lucia, R. C., & Doyle, T. J. (1998). *Career planning in criminal justice* (3 ed.). Cincinnati, OH: Anderson.

Federal Bureau of Investigation. (2011b). *Uniform Crime Reports: Law enforcement officers killed & assaulted, 2010*. Table 81: Federal Law Enforcement Officers Killed and Assaulted. Accessed online December 2, 2011 at: http://www.fbi.gov/about-us/cjis/ucr/leoka/leoka-2010/tables/table81-federal-leoka-department-agency-by-activity-10.xls.

Finan, R. J. I. (2005). Fugitive investigations. *The Police Chief, 72*(8).

Lenior, J. (2008). The U.S. Marshals' posse: A model for the 21st century. *The Federal Lawyer, 55*(7), 34–35.

McKinney, L., & Russo, P. (2009). *One marshal's badge: A memoir of fugitive hunting, witness protection, and the U.S. Marshals Service.* Washington, D.C.: Potomac Books.

Motivans, M. (2011). *Federal justice statistics, 2009.* U.S. Department of Justice, Bureau of Justice Statistics, NCJ 234184.

Newman, D. W., & Rucker-Reed, M. L. (2004). Police stress, state-trait anxiety, and stressors among U.S. Marshals. *Journal of Criminal Justice, 32*, 631–641.

Newton, M. (2011). *U.S. Marshals.* New York: Chelsea House.

Reaves, B.A. (2006). *Federal law enforcement officers, 2004.* Washington, D.C.: U.S. Department of Justice, Bureau of Justice Statistics. NCJ 212750.

Reaves, B.A. (2012). *Federal law enforcement officers, 2008.* U.S. Department of Justice, Bureau of Justice Statistics. NCJ 238250.

Starling, K. (2000). 'Marshal Marshall': Thurgood Marshall's son is first black to head U.S. Marshals Service. *Ebony, 55*(10), 110–114, 160.

Turk, D. (2005). *United States Marshals Service: Historical perspective.* Washington, D.C.: USMS Historian Office.

Turk, D. (2008). A brief primer on the history of the U.S. Marshals Service. *The Federal Lawyer, 55*(7), 26–27.

U.S. Marshals Service. (2009a). *Fact sheet: Asset forfeiture program.* U.S. Marshals Service Office of Public Affairs.

U.S. Marshals Service. (2009b). *Fact sheet: Facts and figures.* U.S. Marshals Service Office of Public Affairs.

U.S. Marshals Service. (2009c). *Fact sheet: U.S. Marshals Service.* U.S. Marshals Service Office of Public Affairs.

U.S. Marshals Service. (2009d). *Fact sheet: Witness Security Division.* U.S. Marshals Service Office of Public Affairs.

U.S. Marshals Service. (2010). *Fact sheet: Tactical Operations Division.* U.S. Marshals Service Office of Public Affairs.

U.S. Marshals Service. (2011a). *Fact sheet: Fugitive operations.* U.S. Marshals Service Office of Public Affairs.

U.S. Marshals Service. (2011b). *Fact sheet: Justice Prisoner and Alien Transportation System.* U.S. Marshals Service Office of Public Affairs.

U.S. Marshals Service. (2011c). *Fact sheet: Prisoner operations.* U.S. Marshals Service Office of Public Affairs.

U.S. Marshals Service. (2011d). *Historical timeline.*

U.S. Marshals Service. (2011e). *Tactical operations.* Retrieved April 30, 2011, from http://www.usmarshals.gov/duties/ops.htm.

United States Office of Personnel Management. (1973). *Position classification standard for U.S. Marshal series, GS-0082.* Accessed online December 5, 2011 at: http://www.opm.gov/fedclass/gs0082.pdf.

Wojdylo, J. R. (2005). Con air: America's high-flying paddy wagon. *Sheriff, 57*(2), 22–25, 56.

Zohra, T. & Walker, J.T. (2008). Gun fighters: U.S. Marshals of the old west. Pp. 1–26 in J. Bumgarner (ed.), *Icons of Crime Fighting: Relentless Pursuers of Justice*, volume 1. Westport, CT: Greenwood Press.

Chapter Six

Drug Enforcement Administration

The Drug Enforcement Administration (DEA) is the nation's primary-jurisdiction law enforcement agency for enforcing federal controlled substance laws. Its focus of attention is fixed squarely on disrupting significant drug trafficking organizations and the money-laundering, drug violence, and narco-terrorism associated with the drug trade (DOJ, 2012). Illicit drug use touches a wide swath of the American people. In 2009, nearly 9% of Americans 12 years old or older (i.e. 21.8 million people) were considered current users of illegal drugs (NDIC, 2011). The estimated costs to society, in terms of public costs related to crime, health care, lost productivity, and damage to the environment, totaled $215 billion (GAO, 2011).

The DEA is housed within the U.S. Department of Justice and has been a part of that department since 1968 (when it was organized as the Bureau of Narcotics and Dangerous Drugs). However, the heritage of the DEA goes back considerably further in the nation's historical timeline. What's more, the function of drug enforcement really began in the Treasury Department rather than the Justice Department.

History

Drug enforcement in the United States at the federal level began with the passage of the Harrison Act of 1914. This law mandated that anyone who produced, imported, manufactured, dispensed, sold, distributed, or gave away opium or coca leaves, as well as their salts and derivatives, register with the federal government. The purpose of registration under this law was not to advance public health by discouraging the narcotics trade. Rather, the purpose of registration was to enable the federal government to collect a special tax on the production and sale of these narcotics. Given that the law was rooted in the federal government's desire to collect tax revenue, enforcement responsibility of the Harrison Act was given to the U.S. Department of the Treasury (Bumgarner, 2006).

In 1919, the U.S. Constitution was amended to prohibit the manufacture, sale, and transportation of alcoholic beverages in the United States. The prohibition of alcohol, established by the 18th Amendment and codified into federal criminal law by the National Prohibition Act—also known as the Volstead Act—was not about the collection of revenue, but rather about the public health and morality. Prohibition proponents had lobbied and carried successfully the argument that intoxicating liquor caused all sorts of social and moral hazards, and individuals, families, and the country at large would be better off without it. Despite the lack of connection to revenue, the U.S. Treasury Department was given the responsibility of enforcing the Volstead Act—quite probably because of its history and experience in regulating certain narcotics since the passage of the Harrison Act five years earlier.

In order to enforce criminal laws relating to alcohol and other controlled substances, the Treasury Department created a Prohibition Unit within its Bureau of Internal Revenue in 1920. Later, in April of 1927, the Prohibition Unit separated from the Bureau of Internal Revenue into a distinct bureau of its own—the Bureau of Prohibition. It was this bureau that became famous for its effort to fight organized crime and the "speak easy" businesses in the Chicago area during the 1920s and early 1930s. Special Agent Eliot Ness and his band of "Untouchables," who brought down gangster Al Capone and about whom many movies have been made, were members of the U.S. Treasury Department's Prohibition Unit (Bumgarner, 2006).

During the prohibition era of the 1920s, Congress had developed an affinity toward controlling or prohibiting substances. In 1925, heroin was federally outlawed. And in 1930, marijuana was also outlawed. The bans on heroin and marijuana remained in effect even after 1933 when the prohibition of alcohol was repealed by the 21st Amendment.

With prohibition a thing of the past, the Treasury Department's Prohibition Unit was disbanded. However, a new federal law enforcement agency was created in its place to continue to investigate crimes relating to controlled substances. The new agency, named the Bureau of Narcotics, operated as a part of the Treasury Department for over 30 years.

Then, in 1968, the Bureau of Narcotics was merged with the Bureau of Drug Abuse Control—a unit which had been a part of the Food and Drug Administration, itself a part of the U.S. Department of Health, Education, and Welfare. The merger of these two bureaus resulted in the new Bureau of Narcotics and Dangerous Drugs (BNDD). The BNDD was organizationally placed in the U.S. Department of Justice, where it has remained ever since. In 1973, the BNDD changed its name to its current moniker—the Drug Enforcement Administration. Along with the name change, the agency absorbed additional drug enforcement personnel from across the federal bureaucratic landscape (Bumgarner, 2006).

Although there have been several pieces of federal legislation relating to narcotics and other pharmacological substances over many years beginning with the Harrison Act of 1914, there is no single piece of legislation which has been more profound in its impact on federal law enforcement, and perhaps on the entirety of the federal criminal justice system, then the Controlled Substances Act of 1970.

The Controlled Substances Act is actually a section of a larger bill passed by Congress—the Comprehensive Drug Prevention and Control Act of 1970. The Controlled Substances Act is found in Title II of this large bill. It is the Controlled Substances Act that has become the foundation for drug-related law enforcement in the United States. The Controlled Substances Act replaced or consolidated over 50 different distinct and disparate drug laws. All drug prohibitions were consolidated into this single law, thus making drug enforcement more rational and uniform. The Bureau of Narcotics and Dangerous Drugs was identified in statute as the primary jurisdiction law enforcement agency for the enforcement of federal drug laws. Later, the act was amended to reflect that the Drug Enforcement Administration would fulfill this role.

The rise of drug enforcement as an activity of federal law enforcement has been meteoric over the past century. The United States has transitioned from a time when unregulated narcotics and other substances were considered remedies to physical ailments and depression to the present day when narcotics and other substances are controlled and are an interwoven component to violent crime, gang activity, and even terrorism. Through the growth and maturation of the federal drug enforcement community, all of federal law enforcement has been impacted.

Drug enforcement in recent years has also had a significant impact on the federal courts and correctional system in the United States. The "War on Drugs," which began in the 1980s and has continued largely unabated since, has resulted in stiff federal penalties for controlled substance violations. The expression "war on drugs" is more than a euphemism. The United States actually did declare a war of sorts on the trafficking of controlled substances. On April 8, 1986, President Ronald Reagan issued National Security Decision Directive 221, which declared that the manufacture and trafficking of drugs constituted a national security threat to the United States. Concomitant to NSDD 221 was a commitment to aggressively target drug traffickers in the United States and abroad (DEA, 2009).

The emphasis on drug enforcement during the 1980s and 1990s paid dividends in the form of significant increases in drug prosecutions and convictions. Most of the federal prison population prior the 1980s and the War on Drugs consisted of those who had engaged in organized crime, mail fraud, defrauding the federal government, and other white collar offenses with relatively high socio-economic backgrounds. But in the wake of the War on Drugs, the prison population changed considerably. By the mid-1990s, approximately 60% of the federal prison population consisted of federal drug offenders (Cole and Smith, 2001).

Organization and Personnel

The DEA has seen significant growth in numbers and resources over the years. In 1973, the newly created DEA had 1,470 special agents. Most of these agents had already been employed as BNDD special agents and merely changed titles. But the agency quickly began to hire new employees who only knew the organization as the DEA. In 1975, the DEA employed 2,135 special agents. By 2005, the numbers had more than doubled. In 2005, the DEA fielded over 5,200 special agents and an additional 5,500 support staff (including intelligence analysts, crime analysts, regulatory investigators, drug classifications specialists, crime laboratory technicians and scientists, and others). By 2012, the numbers of special agents declined slightly to just under 5,000 (DEA, 2012). This number included both direct authorized positions paid for out of DEA's appropriated budget, and reimbursable special agent positions funded from external sources. In Fiscal Year 2012, the DEA received direct authorized funding for only 4,053 special agents.

The Department of Justice's budget proposal for the DEA in fiscal year 2013 asked the agency to decline even further in its authorized strength. The DOJ requested funding for 3,958 special agents — a drop of over 100 special agents from the previous year. However, the budget also predicts the number of fee-funded and reimbursable special agents to equal 1,235, bringing the total special agent cadre for Fiscal Year 2013 to 5,193. Even when accounting for the fee-funded and reimbursable special agent positions, the total number of 5,193 is a 2% drop from the total in Fiscal Year 2012 — 5,312. DOJ also requested funding for 1,013 intelligence analysts — up slightly from 999 in Fiscal Year 2012 (DOJ, 2012).

Looking at the trend over decades, staffing levels at the DEA have grown arithmetically. However, the budget has grown exponentially. In 1975, the DEA annual budget was $141 million. It jumped to nearly $207 million by 1980 (DEA 2009). However, in 2011, the DEA's annual budget was in excess of $2 billion. The budget has continued to hover around $2 billion ever since. The Fiscal Year 2012 budget was $2.035 billion. The Fiscal Year 2013 budget request put forth by the DOJ was $2.051 billion (DOJ, 2012). This funding supports a far-flung network of field offices around the country and attaches' in foreign countries. The DEA has 226 field offices located in the United States, organized under 21 divisions. Each division is led by a Special Agent in Charge (SAC). The DEA also has 85 offices abroad, located in 65 countries (DEA, 2012).

The DEA also operates the El Paso Intelligence Center (EPIC). This unit of the DEA was established in 1974 after a government report highlighted weaknesses in intelligence gathering and analysis along the Southwest border with Mexico. At the time of its founding, EPIC was staffed by personnel from the DEA, U.S. Customs, and the Immigration and Naturalization Service. However, since then, many more federal, state, and local law enforcement agencies have assigned personnel to work at EPIC and serve as intelligence liaisons to the broader law enforcement community. In addition to the DEA and Immigration and Customs Enforcement (ICE), participating agencies include the FBI, the U.S. Coast Guard, U.S. Customs and Border Protection (CBP), the U.S. Secret Service, the U.S. Marshal Service, the Bureau of Alcohol, Tobacco, Firearms, and Explosives (ATF), the Internal Revenue Service (IRS), the U.S. Defense Department, the U.S. Interior Department, the Texas Department of Public Safety, the Texas National Guard, the El Paso County Sheriff's Department, and several task forces, among others (DEA, n.d.). The purpose of EPIC is to collect, analyze, and disseminate information on drug trafficking, illegal immigration, and human trafficking.

EPIC is but one of DEA's many specialized offices and divisions. Figure 6.1 offers a complete look at the organization chart of the DEA with its many sub-organizations, and the relationships of these units to the leadership and to one another.

All DEA special agents receive their initial training at the DEA Training Academy, which is co-located with the FBI Training Academy on the grounds of the Quantico Marine Base in Quantico, VA. From 1985 until 1999, the DEA utilized the facilities of the FBI Academy. However, the growth in both agencies and ever-expending content of initial-entry and in-service training made it difficult to deliver all necessary training within the confines of the existing facilities. Consequently, Congress authorized $29 million to build a distinct training complex for the DEA at the Quantico Marine Base. The complex, known as the Justice Training Center, was completed in April 1999 (DEA, 2009). The DEA Training Academy provides initial service and advance training to special agents, diversion investigators, forensic scientists, and other staff.

Functions

The DEA identifies for itself a 3-pronged mission (DEA, 2012):

1) to enforce the controlled substances laws and regulations of the United States;

2) to bring to the criminal and civil justice system of the United States, or any other competent jurisdiction, those involved in the illegal growing, manufacture, or distribution of controlled substances that are a part of or destined for illicit drug markets in the United States; and

3) to recommend and support non-enforcement programs aimed at reducing the availability of illicit controlled substances on domestic and international markets.

The exclusivity and single-mindedness of the DEA mission — to combat drug violators — makes the agency among the most controversial in all federal law enforcement. For one, the DEA's purpose for existing is centered on criminal laws that many Americans believe involve no real victims. Indeed, a large minority of Americans in the United States views drug violations as victimless crime; what's more, critics of drug laws posit that ancillary violent crime, such as gang and weapons offenses, would be considerably less if the need for the black market drug trafficking enterprises no longer existed (Bumgarner,

Figure 6.1 DEA Organizational Chart

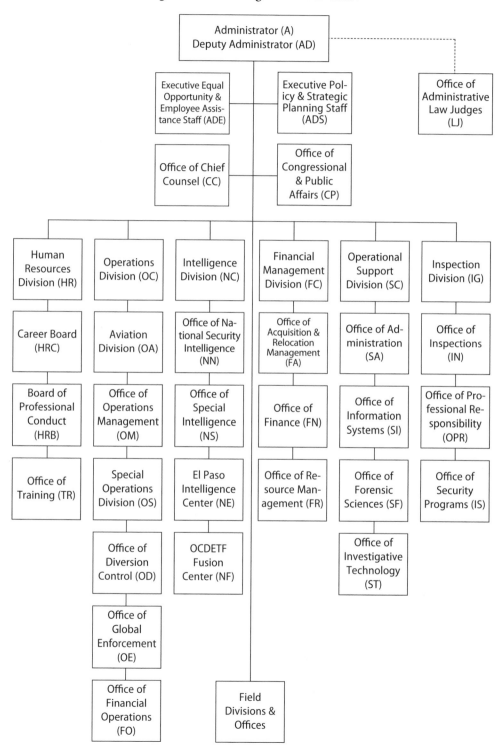

2006). It is easy to imagine why many in the United States would view drug violations differently from other kinds of criminal activities. The DEA estimates that as many as 74 million Americans have used illegal drugs (Bumgarner, 2006).

Critics also like to highlight high-profile cases involving alleged abuse of power by the DEA. Many accuse the DEA of being cavalier and cowboy-ish in its approach to drug investigations, often conducting (unnecessarily, say the critics) large-scale raids and dynamic no-knock warrants on routine rather than judicious occasion. On April 21, 2012, the DEA conducted a raid at a San Diego, California, residence and took nine suspects into custody. The raid resulted in the seizure of 18,000 ecstasy pills and weapons. One person arrested, but never formally charged, was an engineering student at the University of California—San Diego. Daniel Chong had gone to that house the night before to smoke marijuana with some friends. Chong was taken to the DEA office in San Diego and placed handcuffed in a holding cell after being questioned. DEA agents told him he would be released. However, the agents forgot about him and left him in the holding cell for five days before he was accidently discovered by another agent. Chong had been in the cell without food or water. He drank his own urine as dehydration set in. Upon finding him, the DEA quickly got him medical attention. Chong was hospitalized for five days while being treated for dehydration, a perforated esophagus, and liver failure. On May 3, 2012, Chong filed a lawsuit against the DEA for $20 million (Goldman, 2012).

Ironically, it was one of the DEA's predecessor agencies that make it likely that the DEA, and possibly individual agents, will pay heavily for forgetting about Chong. In particular, it was the Treasury Department's Bureau of Narcotics, through the ineptitude of some of its agents, that the principle of sovereign immunity for federal agents was abolished. In 1965, Bureau of Narcotics agents in New York arrested Webster Bivens and searched his home for controlled substances. The search was without a warrant and the arrest was without probable cause. Bivens sued the federal agents involved in the case for damages and for emotional harm and suffering. In 1971 case of *Bivens v. Six Unknown Narcotics Agents*, the U.S. Supreme Court found that federal agents who, through gross negligence or intentionality, violated the civil rights of citizens could be subject to civil liability under the Federal Tort Claims Act, thus eliminating the principle of sovereign immunity for federal law enforcement (*Bivens v. Six Unknown Narcotics Agents*, 1971).

Occasional missteps notwithstanding, the DEA has not been deterred from aggressively pursuing its mission. The DEA has identified a number of priorities which help operationalize the mission of the organization. The DEA's operational priorities are as follows (DEA, n.d.):

- Investigation and preparation for the prosecution of major violators of controlled substance laws operating at interstate and international levels.

- Investigation and preparation for prosecution of criminals and drug gangs who perpetrate violence in our communities and terrorize citizens through fear and intimidation.

- Management of a national drug intelligence program in cooperation with federal, state, local, and foreign officials to collect, analyze, and disseminate strategic and operational drug intelligence information.

- Seizure and forfeiture of assets derived from, traceable to, or intended to be used for illicit drug trafficking.

- Enforcement of the provisions of the Controlled Substances Act as they pertain to the manufacture, distribution, and dispensing of legally produced controlled substances.

- Coordination and cooperation with federal, state and local law enforcement officials on mutual drug enforcement efforts and enhancement of such efforts through exploitation of potential interstate and international investigations beyond local or limited federal jurisdictions and resources.

- Coordination and cooperation with federal, state, and local agencies, and with foreign governments, in programs designed to reduce the availability of illicit abuse-type drugs on the United States market through non-enforcement methods such as crop eradication, crop substitution, and training of foreign officials.

- Responsibility, under the policy guidance of the Secretary of State and U.S. Ambassadors, for all programs associated with drug law enforcement counterparts in foreign countries.

- Liaison with the United Nations, Interpol, and other organizations on matters relating to international drug control programs.

Interestingly, the DEA has elected to not explicitly reference among its priorities the battle against terrorism. Clearly, the DEA has played a significant role in the war on terror. The intelligence collection and analysis at EPIC and in other corners of the organization have contributed to thwarting many acts of terror. And, of course, the DEA is the lead American law enforcement agency in fighting drug cartels in Latin America and Asia. Many of the actions of the cartels have been dubbed "narco-terrorism." Drug cartels have waged violent campaigns against government officials, journalists, rival organizations, law enforcement, and the general public for years in Mexico, Central and South American, and in Asia—especially Afghanistan. The violence resembles other forms of terrorism as it is clearly intended to intimidate and influence the political and social order of the countries within which the drug cartels operate. Crimes like kidnapping, mass murder, and bombings have all been carried out by drug trafficking organizations.

After 9/11, many federal law enforcement agencies highlighted and emphasized before Congress their own contributions to homeland security and the war against domestic and international terrorism. The DEA certainly could do the same thing. And yet, at least in its priorities, the agency appears content to emphasize its role as the lead counter-drug law enforcement agency. If fulfilling that function sweeps up some terrorists in the process, then all the better.

The U.S. Department of Justice, in its strategic plan for FY 2007–2012, identified three major goals which it would pursue:

1) the prevention of terrorism and the promotion of national security;

2) the prevention of crime, the enforcement of federal laws, and the representation of the rights and interests of the American people; and

3) ensuring the fair and efficient administration of justice.

The DEA certainly has found elements of its own mission reflected in all three DOJ strategic goals. But clearly, Goal #2 serves as the umbrella for most of what the DEA does and has done in recent history. In fact, a specific strategic objective identified by the DOJ under Goal #2 is the reduction of the threat, trafficking, use, and violence associated with illegal drugs (DOJ 2007). The DOJ goes on in its strategic plan to identify a number of particular strategies to achieve this strategic objective. These strategies include: targeting drug traffickers and organizations with the investigative resources and asset forfeiture authority of the Organized Crime Drug Enforcement Task Forces (OCDETFs) located around the country, targeting major international drug trafficking organizations, utilizing the OCDETF Fusion Center (an OCDETF clearinghouse of drug and financial intelligence information), interdicting drugs and drug money before reaching the United States from source countries, bolstering counterdrug efforts on the border, specifically targeting methamphetamine trafficking, and several other strategies.

While the DEA is on point as the lead counter-drug agency in pursuit of the objective listed above, the DOJ favors a multi-jurisdictional and multi-agency approach to the drug war. The OCDETF program is the chief mechanism for accomplishing this approach. OCDETF task forces include representation from the DEA, Federal Bureau of Investigation, Bureau of Alcohol, Tobacco, Firearms, and Explosives, U.S. Marshal Service, Bureau of Immigration and Customs Enforcement, U.S. Coast Guard, and the Internal Revenue Service—Criminal Investigation Division. Additionally, officers and agents from state and local police agencies and sheriff's departments also serve on these task forces (DOJ, 2007).

The OCDETF program was born in 1982. Task forces were set up in 12 different cities and were modeled after the South Florida Task Force, which had proven quite successful. The purpose of the OCDETFs were to target drug traffickers, drug-related money laundering, and organized crime syndicates connected to the drug trade with a multi-agency agency/multi-expertise approach (DEA, 2009).

The High Intensity Drug Trafficking Area (HIDTA) program is another important part of DEA's strategy to confront drug trafficking—particularly within the boundaries of the United States. The HIDTA program was created with the passage of the Anti-Drug Abuse Act of 1988 and is actually administered by the White House Office of National Drug Control Policy. The purpose of the HIDTA program is multi-pronged (ONDCP, n.d.):

1) To facilitate cooperation among federal, state, local, and tribal law enforcement agencies to share information and implement coordinated enforcement activities;

2) To enhance law enforcement intelligence sharing among federal, state, local, and tribal law enforcement agencies;

3) To provide reliable law enforcement intelligence to law enforcement agencies to facilitate the design of effective enforcement strategies and operations; and

4) To support coordinated law enforcement strategies that make the most of available resources to reduce the supply of illegal drugs in designated areas of the United States and in the nation as a whole.

By the end of 1990, only five HIDTAs had been created. However, the number of areas within the United States that were deemed to be high-intensity trafficking areas grew. In 2012, there were 28 HIDTAs. The HIDTAs tend to be found in urban areas with large populations, and along the border. The 28 HIDTAs cover only 16% of the nation's counties, but 60% of the U.S. population (ONDCP, n.d.). Each HIDTA is managed by a board made up of law enforcement representatives in that given area. On an annual basis, the HIDTAs identify their own unique drug trafficking problems, craft strategies for confronting those problems, and seek and secure federal funding to pay for implementing those strategies.

The DEA has had a mixed record of collaboration with other law enforcement agencies. In 1982, a concerted effort was made enhance cooperation between the FBI and the DEA on drug investigations. The FBI was given concurrent jurisdiction with the DEA for investigating drug violations. What's more, the director of the DEA was ordered by Attorney General William French Smith to no longer to report directly to the Justice Department, but rather to the director of the FBI. The goal was to reduce duplication of effort between the two agencies and to realize economies of scale. But in that same year, 1982, the U.S. General Accounting Office (now the Government Accountability Office, but still known as GAO) issued a report chronicling unsuccessful efforts in cooperation between the DEA and FBI. The report highlighted the fact that FBI-DEA task forces in Chicago and New York were failures and that the task forces were disbanded. The report noted that inherent differences in the investigative methods of the two agencies created conflict between DEA and FBI personnel (GAO, 1982).

The DEA and FBI never actually implemented the policy of the DEA director reporting to the FBI director. During the 1980s, additional efforts to collaborate were pursued. In 1990, the GAO once again examined the collaborative relationship between the DEA and the FBI. The GAO found that the DEA and FBI continued to maintain their own investigative priorities and intelligence systems during the 1980s and that collaboration, with a few exceptions, was more informal and ad hoc than formal. Both agencies tended to prefer it that way (GAO, 1990).

By contrast, there has been considerable cooperation between the DEA and the Department of Homeland Security's Bureau of Immigration and Customs Enforcement (ICE). In 2009, the DEA and ICE entered into an agreement which streamlined the process by which ICE special agents could be cross-designated with the authority to investigate federal drug laws. Without cross-designation, ICE special agents are confined to enforcing customs and immigration laws. Drug charges emerging from customs and immigration cases have long been under ICE's purview (and that of the U.S. Customs Bureau and U.S. Immigration and Naturalization Service, respectively, before the creation of ICE). But to the extent the drug connection in customs and immigration cases takes on a life of its own, ICE's investigative jurisdiction is limited without cross-designation.

Under the agreement between DEA and ICE, a total of 3,100 ICE special agents were cross-designated to investigate controlled substances violations. This more than doubled the number of ICE agents receiving that authority prior to 2009 (GAO, 2011). The agreement also established a number of protocols to follow when ICE agents uncover evidence of drug crimes, and likewise, when DEA special agents uncover evidence of non-drug related offenses of interest to ICE (e.g. human trafficking, smuggling of weapons and contraband other drugs, etc). The protocols were about more than each agency protecting their own investigative turf. The protocols in the agreement were put in place to enhance officer safety (especially undercover officers) and to prevent one agency's law enforcement operations and activities from compromising an ongoing investigation of the other agency (GAO, 2011).

The DEA is very active in the exercise of its law enforcement authorities. DEA special agents receive their police powers from Title 21 of the United States Code, Section 828. Most of the nation's laws relating to controlled substances can be found in Title 21. Section 828 states:

(a) Any officer or employee of the Drug Enforcement Administration or any State or local law enforcement officer designated by the Attorney General may—

(1) carry firearms;

(2) execute and serve search warrants, arrest warrants, administrative inspection warrants, subpoenas, and summonses issued under the authority of the United States;

(3) make arrests without warrant (A) for any offense against the United States committed in his presence, or (B) for any felony, cognizable under the laws of the United States, if he has probable cause to believe that the person to be arrested has committed or is committing a felony;

(4) make seizures of property pursuant to the provisions of this subchapter; and

(5) perform such other law enforcement duties as the Attorney General may designate.

Many proponents and critics of the DEA have noted with interest that subsection (a) (5) gives the Attorney General of the United States broad authority to use special agents of the DEA in any ways he or she sees fit. Federal law enforcement critics see in that language opportunities for mission-creep, and by extension, general federal mischief. They argue that the DEA and other federal agencies empowered by similarly-worded statutes can be used in any way, whimsical or otherwise, that the Attorney General so choses. This is inconsistent with the notion that federal law enforcement agencies have authorities and responsibilities which are narrowly defined.

However, the flexibility of authority in the statute has been used for admirable purposes on many noteworthy occasions. For example, in the wake of Hurricane Katrina, which struck New Orleans, Louisiana, and other locations along the gulf coast in August of 2005, the DEA deployed 113 special agents to the region to assist local and state law enforcement agencies in securing order and tending to the humanitarian crisis which emerged. In fact, DEA agents are credited with being the first federal law enforcement officers to deploy after the hurricane struck. The special agents came from offices in Dallas, Houston, Atlanta, St. Louis, and Miami, and engaged in police patrol, search and rescue assistance, and the delivery of medicine (DEA, 2009).

Regardless of the merit one places in the enforcement of the nation's drug laws, as noted previously, there is little doubt that they have significantly impacted the federal criminal justice system as a whole. According to the U.S. Justice Department, from October 1, 2008–September 30, 2009 (i.e. Fiscal Year 2009), there were a total of 183,986 suspects arrested and booked with the U.S. Marshals Service for federal offenses. A full 17% of these suspects, or 30,928, were arrested for drug violations. Arrests for drug offenses were the second-largest category of reasons for arrest; immigration-related criminal offenses is the largest category with 84,749 arrestees, or 46% of the total (Motivans, 2012).

A large share of the formal arrests for drug-related offenses in Fiscal Year 2009, and which resulted in booking by the U.S. Marshals, was made by special agents of the DEA. Nearly 12,000 of the 30,928 arrests for drug offenses were made by DEA criminal investigators. Additionally, DEA made thousands of arrests which did not result at that time in booking through the U.S. Marshals Service. Rather, the booking and tracking was completed within house at the DEA. In all, DEA special agents arrested a total of 29,896 suspects from October 2008 through September of 2009 (which includes the 12,000 arrestees booked through the U.S. Marshals Service). All but 3,565 of these arrests were for drug offenses. In other words, arrests made by DEA special agents totaled 26,331 for drug-related crimes. Cocaine-related offenses constituted the largest share of arrests by the DEA. A total of 8,491 and 2,870 arrests were made for powder cocaine and crack cocaine, respectively. Arrests for crimes related to the possession, manufacture, or distribution of methamphetamines totaled 4,701.

Marijuana-related arrests totaled 7,294, or 24% of all DEA arrests in Fiscal Year 2009. Marijuana has been a particularly interesting issue for the DEA to navigate as marijuana possession remains a federal felony, but is a misdemeanor or less under the laws of many states. In January of 2011, the DEA published in report fashion the agency's position on marijuana. The agency deemed it necessary to explain the legal status of marijuana as 15 states by that time had enacted laws permitting the medical use of marijuana. In its position statement, the DEA noted that marijuana as a controlled substance remains in Schedule I—which means that marijuana is highly susceptible to abuse and has no known potential medical use or value. The DEA noted in its statement that there is no widely held recognition in the scientific or medical communities that smoked marijuana is anything but harmful to users (DEA, 2011).

The DEA, in its position paper, also challenged the notion that it targeted for investigation and prosecution "every-day" people who happen to use marijuana. It noted that in 2008, over 25,000 were sentenced in federal court for drug crimes; among those sentenced, 25% were for marijuana violations. However, only 1.6% of the marijuana-related convictions and sentences were for simple possession. In Fiscal Year 2006, 96% of all marijuana-related charges in federal courts related to trafficking offenses (DEA, 2011).

Many critics of the DEA have also claimed that, whether by intention or by the nature of the laws they enforce, minorities are disproportionately targeted by the agency. Among those arrested by the DEA in Fiscal Year 2009, 69% were white. Only 28% of the arrestees were black. However, a significant number of the white offenders arrested were Hispanic. According to the Justice Department, Hispanics constituted over 45% of all those arrested by the DEA that year. Having said that, this is still a lower percentage than one might predict given the percentage of Hispanics among all federal offenders convicted (for all types of federal crimes) in Fiscal Year 2009, which is 54%.

DEA investigations tend to culminate in significant sentences for those convicted of drug offenses. According to the Administrative Office of the U.S. Courts, from October of 2008 through September of 2009, the average sentence for convicted drug offenders was 83.7 months. The average sentence for weapons offenses was 87.2 months; for violent federal crimes, the average sentence was 115.8 months. By contrast, the average sentence for fraud, which had at one time been the mainstay of federal crimes, and which typically involve amounts in excess of several hundred thousand dollars (less the cases be declined), was a mere 31.9 months. Of course, in many fraud cases offenders have no prior criminal record, which results in shorter sentences (Motivans, 2012).

Going forward, the DEA will continue to operate as the nation's premier counter-drug law enforcement agency. While in recent years in the post-9/11 era, the agency's resources haven't grown as rapidly as it had in years prior to 9/11, neither has the agency's resources and posture among the federal law enforcement community diminished in any significant way. The DEA continues to add value to the broader federal law enforcement community through its expertise in controlled substance violations, its diversion programs, its forensic capabilities, and ultimately its track-record of successful investigations, arrests, and convictions of drug traffickers in the United States and abroad.

References

Bumgarner, J. (2006). *Federal agents: The growth of federal law enforcement in America.* Westport, CT: Praeger Publishers.

Bivens v. Six Unknown Narcotics Agents. 403 US 388 (U.S. Sup Ct, 1971).

Cole, G. and Smith, C. (2001). *The American system of criminal justice.* Belmont, CA: Wadsworth.

Drug Enforcement Administration (2009). *Drug Enforcement Administration: A tradition of excellence 1973–2008.* Washington, D.C.: Government Printing Office.

Drug Enforcement Administration (2012). *DEA fact sheet.* Washington, D.C.: Office of Public Affairs.

Drug Enforcement Administration (2011). *The DEA position on marijuana.* Washington, D.C.: Office of Public Affairs.

Drug Enforcement Administration (n.d.). *El Paso intelligence center.* Retrieved from http://www.justice.gov/dea/programs/epic.htm.

Drug Enforcement Administration (n.d.). *DEA mission statement.* Retrieved from http://www.justice.gov/dea/agency/mission.htm.

General Accounting Office (1982). *FBI-DEA task forces: An unsuccessful attempt at joint operations.* GGD-82-50.

General Accounting Office (1990). *Justice Department: Coordination between DEA and the FBI.* GAO/GGD-90-59.

Goldman, R. (2012, May 3). Student abandoned in DEA cell for 5 days to sue for $20 million. *ABC News World Report with Diane Sawyer.* Retrieved from http://abcnews.go.com/US/student-abandoned-cell-days-sue-20-million/story?id=16273815.

Government Accountability Office (2011). *Combating illicit drugs: DEA and ICE interagency agreement has helped to ensure better coordination of drug investigations.* GAO-11-763.

Motivans, M. (2012). *Federal justice statistics 2009—statistical tables.* Washington, D.C.: Bureau of Justice Statistics.

National Drug Intelligence Center (2011). *National Drug Threat Assessment 2011.* Retrieved from http://www.justice.gov/archive/ndic/pubs44/44849/44849p.pdf.

Office of National Drug Control Policy (n.d.). *High intensity drug trafficking areas (HIDTA) program.* Retrieved from http://www.whitehouse.gov/ondcp/high-intensity-drug-trafficking-areas-program.

U.S. Department of Justice (2012). *Drug Enforcement Administration (DEA).* Retrieved from http://www.justice.gov/jmd/2013summary/pdf/fy13-dea-bud-summary.pdf.

U.S. Department of Justice (2007). *Strategic plan: Stewards of the American dream.* Washington, D.C.: U.S. Dept. of Justice.

Part III
Federal Law Enforcement Agencies

Department of Homeland Security

Chapter Seven

U.S. Immigration and Customs Enforcement (ICE)

There are an estimated 11 million unauthorized aliens living in the United States, with hundreds of thousands more entering the country illegally, some seeking freedom and economic opportunity, and others who may seek to do harm to the nation. No matter what their motivations may be behind illegally entering the United States, all are in violation of immigration laws (Siskin et al., 2007). Debates and political posturing around the issue of immigrants and immigration enforcement have existed in the United States since the mid 1800s. The country has often been divided over the needs of national safety and border control, and the need for low paid unskilled laborers. Having undocumented populations is troublesome as it is difficult to know who may be a potential terrorist and who is seeking employment and a better life. Immigration enforcement is essentially controlling those who are in violation of the Immigration and Nationality Act (INA). Enforcement in the past has been a difficult balancing act as agents had to assist with both legal entry and deny violators of the INA. While the debates over the most effective way to address national security and assist lawful immigration will continue, the context was forever changed during the course of one event. The terrorist attacks of September 11, 2001 (9/11) would permanently change the views and structure of immigration enforcement in the United States.

After 9/11, immigration enforcement was made a national priority. The Bush administration would pass the Homeland Security Act that would not only restructure numerous federal law enforcement agencies, but would also pass sweeping reforms for the nation's immigration policy. Prior to this major overhaul of federal law enforcement and immigration, the Immigration and Naturalization Service (INS) under the U.S. Department of Justice was the agency responsible for immigration law enforcement, benefits, and handling refugees. After the 9/11 attacks it was discovered that the individuals who led the hijackings were in the United States under either student visas or the Visa Waiver program. The thought that terrorist could be hidden and supported within the borders of the United States was a frightening proposition for both citizens and government officials.

Ultimately the blame would fall on INS and their failure to track students who were no longer in compliance with the student visa program. The National Commission on Terrorist Attacks Upon the United States, which investigated the 9/11 attacks, stated that after reviewing all the hijackers' applications they could have been denied visas because they were not filled out completely. Furthermore, the Commission felt that had State Department officials required more information in such cases, they would have discovered more grounds for denial such as the false statements on the applications of at least three of the hijackers (2004). The attack left the nation in shock and understandably there was a new focus placed on border security. Congressional hearings were held, and INS's model and effectiveness as an agency were severely criticized (Powell, 2005). As one former INS agent pointed out, there appeared to be little concern from upper level supervisors as funds seemed to be squandered, and for years INS was plagued by high attrition rates with highly motivated recruits becoming quickly disillusioned and fleeing to other agencies (Weissinger, 2005).

History

President George W. Bush signed the Homeland Security Act on November 25, 2002. The Act abolished the Immigration and Naturalization Service effective March 2, 2003 and transferred many of its functions to three agencies within the Department of Homeland Security: Customs and Border Protection (CBP), Bureau of Citizenship and Immigration Services (BCIS), and U.S. Immigration and Customs Enforcement (ICE). The mission of assisting immigrants with obtaining citizenship and assimilating into the country and culture would remain important, but with the reshuffling and absorption of INS this would not be the primary focus of ICE. These traditional functions would be placed in other agencies within the Department of Homeland Security (DHS) and former INS employees would be absorbed into this new structure.

The creation of ICE also reflected a new attitude towards immigration enforcement in a post 9/11 United States. American citizens were calling for a more hard-lined approach to immigration enforcement with appropriate resources to carry out this new function. In the mind of most Americans including government officials, fighting illegal immigration was the same as fighting the war on terror. To this end, the newly formed agency would play a role distinct from its INS predecessor. Immigration and Customs Enforcement was created in March of 2003 and would become the largest investigative branch of the DHS. However, ICE would also begin amid controversy with the appointment of its first director Julie Meyers in 2005. The Bush Administration selected Meyers whose experience included serving two years as a federal prosecutor, and four years at the White House as special assistant to President Bush, and at the departments of Commerce, Justice and Treasury. There were accusation that her selection was due to cronyism and she simply lacked the requisite managerial experience to head such a large agency. Statutes required the head of ICE to have at least five years of experience in both law enforcement and management, and Meyers' resume did not appear to reflect these requirements. Despite law enforcement and Senate opposition the 36 year-old Meyers was appointed as the first director of ICE (Eggen & Hsu, 2005).

By 2004 ICE would have more than 10,000 employees including investigators or special agents and detention and transport officers. The agency had an operating budget of nearly $3 billion (BJS, 2004; DHS, 2004). Today ICE operates with a budget of nearly $6 billion, with more than 20,000 employees working in more than 400 offices in the United States and around the world. The primary mission of the newly created agency is to promote public safety and national security by deterring illegal immigration, preventing immigration related crimes, and removing persons who entered the United States illegally through its two principal operating components—Homeland Security Investigations (HSI) and Enforcement and Removal Operations (ERO) (Bullock, et al., 2009). However, the mission has expanded greatly over the agency's short existence to include a wide variety of criminal enforcement efforts that may be connected to terrorism. Currently ICE enforces both immigration and customs laws including money laundering, weapons trafficking, child pornography, cyber crimes, identity theft, and the theft of cultural property (Deputy Associate Director, 2011).

Organization and Personnel

To accomplish the goals of national security and safety, ICE contains distinct offices and suboffices, and directors that work in a coordinated fashion. The structure of ICE has changed quickly moving from six operation branches to four essential ones, the Director's Leadership Offices, and three primary investigation and operation offices: Enforcement and Removal Operations (ERO), Homeland Security Investigations (HSI), and Management and Administration (M&A). Each of these offices has their own missions and subcomponents that work in conjunction with the larger goals of ICE. The Director's Office contains six leadership offices:

- The Office of Public Affairs—The OPA is committed to outreach to the media, telling the story of ICE, and building public support for ICE's mission.

- The Office of Congressional Relations—The OCR handles outreach to Congress and promoting greater understanding of ICE operations, policies, and programs among members of Congress, Congressional committees and their staffs.

- The Office of the Principal Legal Advisor—The OPLA is the largest legal program in the Department of Homeland Security and provides legal advice, training and services in cases related to the ICE mission, and is the legal representative for the U.S. government in exclusion, deportation, and removal proceedings.

- The Office of Professional Responsibility—The OPR upholds DHS standards for integrity and professionalism by investigating allegations of employee misconduct, inspecting and reviewing ICE offices, operations and processes. OPR also oversees the agency's detention functions to ensure compliance with agency standards.

- The Office of Detention Policy and Planning—ODPP is responsible for designing a detention system that meets ICE's unique needs as well as reforming the current system through long term improvements and providing detainees with appropriate medical care.

- The Office of State, Local and Tribal Coordination—The OSLTC is responsible for building, improving and coordinating with state, local, and tribal governments, law enforcement agencies, and non-governmental organizations (ICE Leadership Offices, 2011).

In addition to the director's leadership offices, ICE's two operations offices are critical to their primary mission of national security and immigration enforcement. The main duty of Enforcement and Removal Operations is to identify, apprehend, and when possible remove illegal aliens from the United States. ERO prioritizes the apprehension of criminals who threaten the security of the nation. Furthermore, ERO transports and manages aliens held in custody, and provides legal resources to groups and individuals who are to be deported. In addition, the ERO contains sub-offices and programs to assist with ICE's overall mission and ERO's direct mandates:

- ICE Health Service Corps—Provides medical care and public health services to more than 15,000 detainees in transit or housed in one of 24 designated facilities throughout the nation, and oversees medical care to an additional 17,000 detainees housed at non-ICE staffed detention facilities.

- Detainee Locator—ICE maintains a detainee locator service on their website where the public can locate individuals in ICE custody over the age of 18 or who have been released in the last 60 days.

- Secure Communities—Removes convicted alien criminals by using the existing relationship between ICE and the FBI. Annual appropriations from Congress allow the ERO through Secure Communities to prioritize the removal of illegal aliens convicted of committing a crime. As of 2011, the Secure Communities program has removed more than 77,000 legal and illegal convicted immigrants (ICE Enforcement and Removal Operations, 2011).

Homeland Security Investigations is a critical directorate for ICE's mission. HSI special agents investigate a wide range of criminal violations connected to smuggling people and goods across borders such as drug smuggling, human rights violations, and cyber crimes. HSI agents conduct investigations to protect critical infrastructure and industries that may be the target of terrorist attacks as well as activities that may threaten legitimate trade in the United States. To meet this critical directive HSI contains three important sub-offices.

- The ICE Homeland Security Investigations Intelligence Office—HSI-Intel employs cutting edge technology to collect, analyze and share strategic and tactical data for use by DHS, ICE leadership, and operational units. It also supports federal, state, local, tribal and international law enforcement partners.

- ICE International Affairs—IA enhances national security by conducting and coordinating investigations involving transnational criminal organizations and serving as the agency's liaison to counterparts in local government and law enforcement in nearly 50 countries around the world. IA is the largest international investigative component in DHS.

- The National Intellectual Property Rights Coordination Center—IPR Center is a task force that responds to global intellectual property (IP) theft through information sharing, developing initiatives, and conducting investigations related to IP theft (ICE Homeland Security Investigations, 2011).

The final component of ICE's operation and investigations offices is Management and Administration (M&A). The primary focus of M&A is to coordinate ICE's administrative and managerial functions including overseeing the budget, human resources and personnel, recruitment, and procurement of equipment and property and tracking agency performance. To accomplish these support roles, M&A contains nine sub-offices under its directorate.

- Freedom of Information Act Office—The FOIA Office is a centralized office that receives, tracks, and processes all freedom of information requests according to the law.

- The National Firearms and Tactical Training Unit—The NFTTU ensures that ICE personnel have the necessary firearms, protective equipment, and training.

- The ICE Office of Acquisition Management—The OAM is the acquisition arm of ICE, procuring law enforcement services and products, temporary housing, food, clothing and transportation, computers, telecommunications equipment, security equipment, and software.

- The Office of the Chief Financial Officer—The OCFO manages all of ICE's financial resources through implementing best business practices and linking strategic planning, budgeting and performance reporting.

- The Office of the Chief Information Officer—The OCIO provides information technology (IT) services, products, and solutions that enable ICE and DHS to meet their respective missions.

- The Office of Diversity and Civil Rights—The DCR directs and integrates the application of the Civil Rights Act of 1964 to ensure that applicants and employees are treated in a non-discriminatory manner in compliance with established laws, regulations and executive orders.

- The Office of Human Capital—The OHC is responsible for attracting, developing and retaining a talented and diverse workforce ensures that ICE's managers are in compliance with human resources' policies procedures.

- The Office of Policy—The OP is responsible for identifying, developing and effectively communicating ICE's organizational priorities and policies by focusing on key areas such as risk and strategic management, operations, international affairs, and management policy.

- The ICE Office of Training and Development—The OTD establishes and maintains standards for ICE's training programs, and oversees the training delivered to ICE personnel and ICE's online training programs.

- The ICE Privacy Office is responsible for ICE's compliance with federal privacy laws and policies (ICE Management & Administration, 2011).

ICE's organizational structure reflects the agency's approach to dealing with the multiple fronts on which it operates and carries out its missions of enforcing federal immigration laws, targeting illegal people and goods, and dismantling the support networks of terrorism and international crime. Like all federal law enforcement agencies, the ability of ICE to carry out its mission is based on hiring and retaining high quality personnel. ICE's homeland security mission is carried out with more than 20,000 employees working in a variety of roles from law enforcement to support professions working in intelligence and management. ICE is a large federal law enforcement agency with several key career paths.

Generally, agents and officers that are employed by ICE must attend the ICE Detention and Removal Division Basic Training Program (ICE-D) at the Federal Law Enforcement Training Center in Glynco, GA, for 12 to 17 weeks, and complete a five-week Spanish Language Training Program (SLTP) or pass an oral Spanish language proficiency test. The requirements for each position vary by the grade level to which the candidate is applying. Typically a bachelor's degree is required or a combination of education and experience. Candidates must be under the age of 37 at the time of application although this may be waived in some cases. Candidates must pass all exams with at least a 70% and successfully complete the Physical Abilities Assessment (Immigration and Customs Enforcement, 2008). Currently there are six key law enforcement-related positions in ICE: Deportation Officers, Detention and Deportation Officers, HSI Special Agents, Immigration and Enforcement Agents, Intelligence Careers, and Investigations Support Positions.

Deportation Officers

Deportation Officers conduct legal research to support decisions on deportation/exclusion cases and assist attorneys in representing the Government in court actions. Deportation officers also work with other federal law enforcement officials to identify, locate and/or apprehend aliens and ensure their physical removal from the United States. Deportation officers also conduct complex investigations, surveillance work, prepare investigative reports and assist in difficult and sensitive seizures (USA Jobs, 2008).

Detention and Deportation Officers

Detention and Deportation Officers (DDO) take criminals and illegal aliens into custody, and direct and execute detention and removal activities. DDOs may recommend administrative procedures and policies, participate in long-range planning, and provide guidance on detention and removal operations. DDOs may also develop budget estimates and justifications, analyze programs to recommend improvements, and assist in investigations (Occupations, 2011).

Homeland Security Investigations Special Agents

Special Agents are required to attend 22 weeks of paid training at the Federal Law Enforcement Training Center in Glynco, Georgia. Special agents are involved in a variety of challenging criminal and civil investigations involving national security threats, terrorism, public safety, drug smuggling, child exploitation, human trafficking, illegal arms export, financial crimes, identity fraud, and more. Special agents are required to carry and routinely qualify with firearms, and complete regular physical examinations. They are also subject to random drug testing. New special agents are assigned to their first duty station based on the needs of the agency and serve a minimum of three years before being eligible to change locations (Become a Criminal Investigator, 2011). HSI activities and agents are organized in one of 26 Special Agent in Charge (SAC) principal field offices throughout the United States.

Immigration and Enforcement Agents

Immigration and Enforcement Agents (IEA) are the uniformed presence of immigration enforcement within the U.S. interior. IEAs are responsible for arresting, processing and removing aliens from the United States to their country of citizenship. Additional responsibilities for the IEA may include: visiting holding and correctional facilities, implementing the Criminal Alien Program, initiating criminal proceedings against violators of the Immigration and Nationality Act, gathering intelligence, conducting investigations, and performing enforcement functions related to the detention and deportation and the apprehension of absconders (Occupations, 2011).

Intelligence Careers

Several job tracks fall under the umbrella of Intelligence Careers within ICE. Intelligence Officers are responsible for analyzing and evaluating information and preparing intelligence reports, providing on-site intelligence to field offices involved in major criminal investigations, and coordinating with other ICE components and the larger intelligence community. Intelligence Research Assistants are responsible for technical and administrative support, and assisting intelligence operations through procedural work and data gathering. Intelligence Research Specialists collect, analyze, and distribute strategic and tactical intelligence for internal offices (Occupations, 2011).

Investigations Support Positions

The final law enforcement-related career path in ICE are the Investigations Support Positions. These include several posts such as auditors who conduct highly complex financial reviews of criminal organizations, work site investigations, and business entities to aid ICE investigators. Criminal Research Specialists perform several duties for criminal, civil, and administrative investigations revolving around financial crimes, smuggling, critical infrastructure, national security, arms and strategic technology, and human smuggling. Investigative Assistants provide technical, administrative, and clerical support to the ongoing investigations (Occupations, 2011).

Functions

The career paths and positions within ICE are designed to work in a coordinated effort to accomplish the basic functions of the agency of ensuring the security of the nation and enforcing immigration laws. While these two basic responsibilities are straightforward as the previous section on structure and personnel illustrates, the mission that must be carried out through multiple investigative and enforcement fronts. Yet in many cases it is the critical work of ICE's Homeland Security Investigations (HSI) special agents that uncover some of the most egregious human rights violators, dangerous alien offenders, and related criminals. In addition, ICE's Enforcement and Removal Unit essentially operates on the front lines of the criminal justice system creating partnerships through several key programs that seek to identity, detain and remove individuals within the borders of the United States.

Homeland Security Investigations

HSI special agents typically conduct complex investigations to uncover immigration law and human rights violations. Consider the associated crimes that fall under the mission of ICE and HSI: bulk cash smuggling, cyber-crimes, human trafficking, trade violations, and worksite enforcement. Many of these investigations result in high profile and successful apprehensions and removals of violent offenders and war criminals that have sought illegal refuge in the United States. ICE is handling more than 1,900 human rights-related cases involving suspects from 95 countries. HSI has more than 200 active human rights investigations, which may support criminal charges or removal proceedings (Statement of John P. Woods, 2011).

HSI Notable Cases

In 2004, HSI special agents investigated Thierry Rugamba who reportedly immigrated to the United States in 2000, as a victim of the 1994 Rwandan genocide. During the extensive investigation Rugamba's real identity of Jean-Marie Vianney Mudahinyuka was revealed, and six witnesses identified Mudahinyuka as a perpetrator of the Rwandan genocide. One witness allegedly witnessed Mudahinyuka committing murder and rape. Mudahinyuka was arrested and sentenced to 51 months in federal prison for immigration violation and assaulting an HSI agent. After completing his sentence, ICE successfully removed Mudahinyuka to Rwanda in January 2011, and handed him over to the Rwandan National Police to face charges of genocide and war crimes (Statement of John P. Woods, 2011).

In May 2009, the HSI Human Rights Violators and War Crimes Unit identified Juan Miguel Mendez, a citizen of Argentina, as the subject of an INTERPOL Red Notice (Red Notices are international wanted notices). Mendez was wanted in Argentina for his participation in torture, disappearances, and extrajudicial killings while he served in the Argentine military. ICE arrested him on June 10, 2009, ordered him held without bond, and in 2010 removed him to Argentina. Mendez was transferred into the custody of Argentine law enforcement officials where he is awaiting trial for human rights violations. ICE's HSI was able to complete the investigation, arrest, and removal of an international war criminal within 18 months. This speed and efficiency received recognition among many federal agencies and the international media (Statement of John P. Woods, 2011).

HSI special agents have also worked closely with the Department of Justice in joint investigations to apprehend perpetrators of the massacres at Dos Erres in Guatemala where soldiers killed more than 200 men, women, and children. In 2010, Gilberto Jordan, a naturalized U.S. citizen, was arrested by HSI special agents in West Palm Beach, Florida on the charge that he unlawfully obtained his U.S. citizenship by lying about his prior service with the Guatemalan military and concealing his involvement in the massacres at Dos Erres, resulting in a statutory maximum of a 10-year sentence. HSI has arrested other individuals alleged to be former members of the Kaibiles who participated in the Dos Erres massacre. ICE has had numerous other investigation successes that stem from their close partnership with local, federal, and international agencies. While ICE may have the spotlight and lead the investigations into the immigration violation that connects to various offenses, the cooperative efforts often involve other Department of Justice components, including the Human Rights and Special Prosecutions Section, the National Security Division's Counterterrorism Section, United States Attorney's Offices, and the Office of International Affairs.

In addition to organizations and agencies within the United States, ICE works in collaboration with several international governments and units. For example, HSI maintains close relationships with a number of United Nations-sponsored tribunals and war crimes organizations in Argentina, Australia, Bosnia and Herzegovina, Germany, Peru, Rwanda, and the United Kingdom among others. ICE's investigation efforts are important work as the agency points out they must work quickly and professionally as the stakes are high. The statute of limitations for visa fraud is five years. If the fraud is not exposed within the five-year time limit ICE has a major obstacle to prosecution and ultimately an offender may evade punishment for their crimes. The United States has sheltered millions of refugees who have fled oppressive regimes, ethnic cleansing, and open conflict in their home countries. Creating a safer United States for every citizen requires removing individuals who are dangerous or have committed human rights violations (Statement of John P. Woods, 2011).

Cases such as the ones outlined in this chapter are clear examples of the important work conducted by HSI special agents. Another interesting component of the work done by HSI is worksite enforcement. While worksite enforcement may not always have the limelight of other investigative efforts, effective worksite enforcement has several goals and benefits according to ICE. It is a critical aspect of protecting the infrastructure of the United States. For example, unauthorized workers employed in critical infrastructure facilities such as airports, shipping ports, and nuclear plants could pose serious homeland security threats. Worksite enforcement also protects illegal workers from abusive employer practices such human smuggling, exploitation, and threats. HSI worksite enforcement strategies examine both employers who knowingly hire illegal workers, as well as the workers themselves. Worksite enforcement detent typically involves intricate investigations that may take months and in some cases years as a complex web of activities are uncovered. As of fiscal year 2008 ICE made more than 1,100 arrests stemming from investigations and worksite enforcement (Fact Sheet: Worksite Enforcement, 2011).

Enforcement and Removal Operations

The investigations of immigration law violations and connected crimes have garnered HSI special agents well deserved attention. As a part of the overall mission and the result of HSI operations offenders must eventually be removed from the United States. At this point it is ICE's Enforcement and Removal Operations (ERO) that becomes involved. The ERO is responsible for enforcing the nation's immigration laws in a fair and efficient manner. The mandate of ERO is to enhance the security of the United States through removing aliens who pose a threat to public safety. Since 2009, ERO has had record levels of enforcement with nearly 400,000 removals each year with convicted criminals representing more than half of these removals. Their crimes ranged from homicide and drug trafficking to sexual offenses (ICE, 2011).

ERO operate two types of programs to target criminal aliens: Jail Enforcement Programs and Task Force Programs. The Criminal Alien Program (CAP) is a component of the Jail Enforcement Program. ERO officers assigned to CAP work to identify, processes and remove criminal aliens incarcerated in federal and state prisons, and local jails throughout the United States. The purpose of this program is to prevent criminal aliens from being released into the general public (Criminal Alien Program, 2011).

Within CAP there are four additional programs that work in a coordinated effort to screen inmates, place detainers on criminal aliens, and process them for removal. The Violent Criminal Alien Section (VCAS) screens recidivist criminal aliens that are discovered through CAP and interagency partnerships. Once identified through VCAS, ERO seeks federal criminal prosecution of these criminal aliens in coordination with the U.S. Attorney's Office to deter and reduce felony violations and illegal reentry after deportation. The second program within CAP is the Joint Criminal Alien Removal Taskforces (JCART). JCART works with other agencies such as probation and parole offices, the United States Marshal's Service, ICE's Office of Investigations (OI), U.S. Customs and Border Protection (CBP), the Federal Bureau of Prisons (BOP), and local law enforcement to conduct special operations to locate and arrests at-large criminal aliens who have been released from federal, state, or local custody (Skinner, 2010).

The third component of CAP is Detention Enforcement and Processing Offenders by Remote Technology (DEPORT). ERO created the DEPORT center in Chicago to assist in processing non-U.S. citizens in the federal correctional system. ERO officers working in the DEPORT Center conduct interviews of BOP inmates nationwide using video tele-conference equipment to process criminal aliens from all 114 federal detention facilities and take them into ERO custody upon completion of their sentences. The final component of CAP is Rapid Removal of Eligible Parolees Accepted for Transfer (REPAT). The REPAT program is designed to accelerate the removal of criminal aliens from the United States by allowing selected inmates currently serving a sentence to accept early release in exchange for voluntarily returning to their country of origin and waiving their right to an appeal (Skinner, 2010).

Outside of CAP, ERO also operates the Secure Communities program. Secure Communities operates in more than 2,700 jurisdictions and works in a partnership with existing federal agencies. For decades local law enforcement has sent fingerprints to the FBI for analysis in the past. Under the Secure Communities program the FBI automatically sends the fingerprints to ICE to check against its immigration databases. If these checks reveal that an individual is in the United States illegally or has a criminal conviction that would result in removal, ERO begins the process of prioritizing their removal. The priorities are based on the individual's potential threat to public safety, the severity of their crimes, criminal history, and the frequency of having violated immigration laws. ICE generally issues a detainer on the person, requesting that the state or local jail facility hold the individual up to an extra 48 hours to allow for an interview. Following the interview, ICE decides whether to seek the person's removal. Between October 2008 and October 2011, the number of convicted criminals that ICE removed from the United States increased 89% with a significant contribution coming from the Secure Communities program (Secure Communities, 2011).

ICE and ERO realize the importance of partnerships and taskforce operations in dealing with immigration enforcement. One successful example of a partnership approach is the § 287(g) program. The Illegal Immigration Reform and Immigrant Responsibility Act of 1996 added Section 287(g) that allows for the performance of immigration officer functions by state officers and employees. Under the § 287(g) program local corrections officers with ICE training conduct immigration screenings during the booking process in jail, and work in conjunction with local law enforcement including state patrol officers, detectives, and investigators to detain or assist in the deportation of dangerous offenders and repeat immigration violators. This partnership has led to the identification and removal of thousands of potentially dangerous criminal aliens from the United States (287(g) Success Stories, 2011).

The removal of criminal aliens is a significant aspect of ERO. To further enhance this key mission ICE created the National Fugitive Operations Program (NFOP) in 2003. The NFOP was created to expand the agency's ability to locate, arrest, and remove fugitive aliens, or those aliens who have failed to leave the United States after an order of removal, deportation or exclusion, or who failed to report to ICE after receiving a notice. The NFOP utilizes 104 fugitive operations teams that search the databases of National Crime Information Center (NCIC) and other intelligence sources to pursue criminal aliens and other NFOP priority cases. Their efforts have resulted in 40,000 arrests from joint operations (Fact Sheet: ICE Fugitive Operations Program, 2011).

Enforcing immigration and customs laws has always represented a unique challenge in the United States. It has been a difficult balancing act of welcoming legal immigrants, promoting legitimate international trade and commerce, and securing the nation's borders. Within this historic framework the terrorist attacks of September 11, 2001 would forever change the views of violating immigration laws and the potential risk it poses to national security. With one act, federal law enforcement in the United States would undergo one the most significant changes in modern history. With more than 20,000 employees and an operating budget of nearly $6 billion, U.S. Immigration and Customs Enforcement became the largest investigative arm of the Department of Homeland Security and second in size only to the Federal Bureau of Investigation. While the mission of ICE is straightforward with the statement of promoting homeland security and public safety through the criminal and civil enforcement of federal laws governing border control, customs, trade, and immigration, it is a complex and challenging task that requires a creative and expansive organization to match.

While ICE as an agency is less than a decade old, it has had an enviable and impressive track record of detection, apprehension, and removals of criminal aliens, notorious war criminals, and individuals who pose threats to the nation's safety. ICE plays a critical role in the mission of the Department of Homeland Security. Immigration and Customs Enforcement has carried out intricate and often high profile investigations along with active frontline work that will undoubtedly serve as a role model for interagency partnership and professionalism. ICE is also one of the newest agencies in federal law enforcement and only history will show the true impact of its actions on national security and immigration enforcement.

References

287(g) Success Stories (2011). Retrieved from http://www.ice.gov/287g/success-stories.htm.

Become a Criminal Investigator (2011). Retrieved from http://www.ice.gov/careers/occupations/investigator/.

Bullock, J., Haddow, G., Coppola, D., and Yeletaysi, S. (2009). *Introduction to homeland security: Principles of all-hazards response.* Burlington, MA: Elsevier Inc.

Criminal Alien Program. (2011). Retrieved from http://www.ice.gov/criminal-alien-program/.

Deputy Associate Director Homeland Security Investigations, Peter T. Edge. (2011). Retrieved from http://www.ice.gov/about/leadership/hsi-dad-bio/peter-edge.htm.

Eggen, D. and Hsu, S. (2005, September 20). Immigration nominee's credentials questioned. *Washington Post.* Retrieved from http://www.washingtonpost.com/wp-dyn/content/article/2005/09/19/AR2005091901930.html.

Fact Sheet: ICE Fugitive Operations Program (2011). Retrieved from http://www.ice.gov/news/library/factsheets/fugops.htm.

Fact Sheet: Worksite Enforcement (2011). Retrieved from http://www.ice.gov/news/library/factsheets/worksite.htm.

Fugitive Operations (2011). Retrieved from http://www.ice.gov/fugitive-operations/.

ICE (2011). *ICE total removals.* Retrieved from www.ice.gov/doclib/about/offices/ero/pdf/ero-removals.pdf.

ICE Enforcement and Removal Operations (2011). Retrieved from http://www.ice.gov/about/offices/enforcement-removal-operations/.

ICE Homeland Security Investigations (2011). Retrieved from http://www.ice.gov/about/offices/homeland-security-investigations/.

ICE Leadership Offices (2011). Retrieved from http://www.ice.gov/about/offices/leadership/.

ICE Management & Administration (2011). Retrieved from http://www.ice.gov/about/offices/management-administration/.

Immigration and Customs Enforcement (2008). Detention and removal operations training division basic immigration law enforcement training program. Retrieved from www.ice.gov/doclib/about/offices/ero/pdf/ice_d_handbook.pdf.

National Commission on Terrorist Attacks upon the United States. (2004*). The Nine/ eleven Commission report, final report of the National Commission on Terrorist Attacks Upon the United States.* New York: W.W. Norton and Company Inc.

Occupations. (2011). Retrieved from http://www.ice.gov/careers/occupations/.

Powell, J. (2005). *Encyclopedia of North American immigration.* New York: Facts on File Inc.

Secure Communities. (2011). Retrieved from http://www.ice.gov/secure_communities/.

Siskin, A., Bruno, A., Nunez-Neto, B., Seghetti, L., and Wasem, R. (2007). Immigration enforcement within the United States. In B. Isenburg (Ed.*) Immigration Enforcement and Policies* (pp. 1–72). New York: Nova Science Publishers.

Skinner, R. (2010). Performance of 287(g) agreements between Immigration and Customs Enforcement and state and local law enforcement agencies. Washington, D.C.: Office of the Inspector General.

Statement of John P. Woods, Deputy Assistant Director, National Security Investigations Division, Homeland Security Investigations, U.S. Immigration and Customs Enforcement, before the House Committee on Foreign Affairs, Tom Lantos Human Rights Commission: "No Safe Haven: Law Enforcement Operations Against Human Rights Violators in the U.S." (2011). Retrieved from http://www.dhs.gov/ynews/ testimony/20111013-woods-no-safe-haven.shtm.

USA Jobs. (2008). Retrieved from http://www.usajobs.org/jobarchive.jsp?page=37.

Weissinger, G. (2005). *Law enforcement and the INS: A participant observation study of control agents.* Lanham, Maryland: University Press of America Inc.

Chapter Eight

United States Customs and Border Protection

The security of any nation relies on its ability to control and regulate borders. A border is more than just a line of division and geographic boundary; it also represents legal jurisdiction, sovereignty, and citizenship. Safeguarding a country's borders is a delicate balancing act, as security does not often support the free flow of people, goods, and trade. The United States is no exception and represents a unique nation with more than 80,000 miles of coastline, and more than 7,500 miles of border with two of its largest trading partners, Canada and Mexico (Warner, 2010). Historically border protection for a nation has been viewed in military terms with preparation for repelling an external threat. Clearly, citizens desire this level of security and protection from foreign danger, however globalization and the technology of the 21st century have changed the views and landscape for border safety.

Internal threats to national security have shaped the perspective of what it means to secure the borders of the United States. The first attack on the World Trade Center in 1993, followed by the bombing of the Murrah Building in Oklahoma City in 1995, and the second terrorist attacks on the World Trade center September 11, 2001 showed the citizens of the United States and many nations around the world that a new era of protecting a country's borders had begun. In this new era, terrorism became inextricably linked to transnational groups, organized crime, the smuggling of drugs and weapons, human trafficking, and illegal entry into the country.

The terrorist actions on 9/11 altered life in the United States, spawning new legislation, focusing government and military action on known terrorist groups and locations. While terrorism may have dominated the discussions of national security and border safety during the first decade of the twenty-first century, by the second decade an increasing threat to border safety was coming from drug cartels and organized crime in Mexico, as their form of high profile violence turned border towns into war zones. The mix of cartel drug violence, corruption, and the smuggling of drugs, cash, and weapons across U.S. borders may present the most tangible threat to national security at this point in time. These actions also demonstrated the need for transnational cooperation for the security of both nations.

History

The history of Customs and Border Protection begins with the U.S. Border Patrol. It is a history that has been shaped by politics, nationalism, fear, and security. These are forces that would ultimately turn borders into sites of constant struggle. Immigration has always been a part of American history and was viewed as a key element to life in the United States. Accordingly, the federal government did little to regulate immigration in the early years of the nation. However there were laws pertaining to naturalization such as the 1790 Naturalization Act which allowed all "free white persons" who had been in the country for two years to be naturalized in any American court (Kettner, 1978). This racialized view of citizenship would frame the discussion over immigration in the United States for decades. During the 1850s waves of immigrants triggered xenophobic reactions within the country as citizens and government officials grappled with the concepts of national identity, sovereignty, and controlling the borders. From 1880 to 1920 nearly 24 million people immigrated to America from Central, Eastern, and Southern Europe, as well as Asia (LeMay and Barkan, 1999).

This tremendous shift in the nation's population turned immigration into a political issue as the federal government expanded its role and capacities. Several groups would face restrictions on entry and access to citizenship in the United States. The Page Act of 1875 and the Chinese Exclusion Act (1882), both at the federal level, restricted Asian laborers and those considered "undesirable" from entering the country. Furthermore, the Naturalization Act would prevent Asians from becoming citizens as they could not meet the standard of being "White" (Lee, 2011). The Chinese represented the first group to be targeted for exclusion based on race and class. The legislation that restricted Chinese immigration provided a framework for how immigration should be handled with other groups as the debate continued into the twentieth century. The Page and Chinese Exclusion acts legalized restrictions based on race and created new bureaucracies and officials that were now needed to inspect and process newly arriving aliens, effectively turning the United States into a gatekeeping nation (Lee, 2011).

Early Immigration Enforcement

Controlling the flow of people along the U.S. borders had proved problematic with various groups. For example in the late 1880s, Geronimo and the Apache Chiricahua tribe raided territories in the United States along the Mexican border making it clear that the southern border of the United States would need protection. As early as 1904, mounted watchmen of the U.S. Immigration Service patrolled the border to prevent illegal crossing. A small group of inspectors, referred to as mounted guards, operated out of El Paso, Texas and patrolled as far west as California trying to restrict the flow of illegal Chinese immigration. The resources of these early inspectors were limited and frequently required assistance from U.S. military troops and the Texas Rangers who were assigned to border patrol duties (Border Patrol History, 2011). It was a difficult process patrolling nearly 2,000 miles of border particularly as border crossing from Mexico increased. Prior to the Mexican Revolution of 1910 most Mexican immigrants that came to the United States were landless peasants. However, after the revolution nearly 50,000 Mexican immigrants a year including landowners, professionals, and intellectuals began to cross the border (Nathan, 2003).

While the Page and Chinese Exclusion acts may have defined immigration practices for the 19th century, with the massive movement across the Southern U.S. border, the immigration issues of the twentieth century would revolve around the borders between the United States, Mexico, and Canada. Between the 1920s and 1950s more than 1.4 million Canadians and 5.5 million Mexicans entered the United States, the vast majority of whom were temporary laborers who migrated in response to the labor shortages created by the restrictions on Asians and other groups (Ueda, 1994). Several forces coincided further illustrating the need for enhanced security along the border. The passage of the Eighteenth Amendment, which would prohibit the transportation of alcohol, and the

Immigration Acts of 1921 and 1924 which placed quotas on less "desirable" immigrants meant the federal government now had to enforce these laws and pay considerable attention to the borders north and south of the United States eventually leading to creation of the U.S. Border Patrol.

Creation of the U.S. Border Patrol

The numerical limitations of the Immigration Acts resulted in increased attempts to enter the United States illegally when legal avenues failed. Therefore, the mission of the Border Patrol became more important to the U.S. Government. On May 28, 1924, Congress passed the Labor Appropriation Act of 1924, officially establishing the U.S. Border Patrol with appropriations for 450 Patrol Inspectors. This marked the beginning of the effort in the United States to gain complete control of the borders by intercepting both illegal immigrants and contraband (Haddel, 2010). The Border Patrol was a component of the Bureau of Immigration and was therefore authorized by Congress to execute any warrants regarding the admission or deportation of any illegal immigrant as well as the power to arrest any alien attempting to enter the country illegally in the officer's presence. In addition, the new agency now had the power to board and search any sea vessels or vehicles in U.S. territory that were suspected of smuggling immigrants (Nevins, 2002).

The newly created force would primarily patrol along the U.S.-Mexican border on horseback. Officers also patrolled the Gulf coast of Florida to prevent illegal entry from Cuba. (Navarro, 2009). Officers were quickly recruited for the new positions and many of the early agents were recruited from the Texas Rangers, local sheriff's offices, and appointees from the Civil Service Register of Railroad Mail Clerks. Border Patrol recruits were issued a badge and revolver, but were not uniformed until 1928. Officers furnished their own horse and saddle while the federal government supplied oats and hay for the horses. The agents were paid an annual salary of $1,680 (Border Patrol History, 2011).

In 1932 the Border Patrol was placed under the authority of two directors, one in charge of the Mexican border office in El Paso, Texas and the other in charge of the Canadian border office in Detroit, Michigan. The Detroit office had the majority of Border Patrol agents as liquor smuggling from Canada was the primary government concern at the time. The Border Patrol academy opened on October 16, 1934 at Camp Chigas in El Paso, Texas, which became known as the El Paso District Training School. The first session of training began on December 3, 1934 with 32 male recruits. The initial curriculum consisted of lecture courses on immigration law, citizenship, documentation, and Spanish. Classroom instruction lasted four hours per day with no physical training program. Three afternoons per week classes were devoted to rifle, pistol, and horsemanship training. The first session graduated March 17, 1935 (Border Patrol Academy, 2011).

After the repeal of Prohibition in 1933 the focus of the Border Patrol shifted from stopping the smuggling of contraband liquor to the prevention of unauthorized entry by Mexican immigrants (Nevins, 2002). Prior to the creation of the Border Patrol, Mexican citizens could freely cross the border as they were waived from the quotas of the Immigration Acts. However, the creation of the Border Patrol and the new focus on the U.S.-Mexican border now meant it was a crime for Mexicans to enter the United States without proper documentation. This also meant that any Mexican living north of the border would be viewed with suspicion (Nathan, 2003). The Border Patrol would also incorporate new technology during the 1930s and 1940s utilizing motorized patrol, airplanes, helicopters, and radios.

World War II had a significant impact on Border Patrol in the United States. Within the Roosevelt Administration there was fear that saboteurs and foreign agents might attempt to enter the United States illegally, so securing the border took on a new urgency and was viewed as a national security issue. Accordingly, the Border Patrol, which was housed in the Immigration and Naturalization Service was transferred to the Department of Justice and given a larger budget to increase the number of officers to well over 1,500 and purchase necessary equipment to aid in their mission. The duties of the Border Patrol during wartime expanded to guarding enemy alien detention camps and securing the coast against possible Axis-power invasions (Nivens, 2002). Another impact of World War II was the signing of a bilateral agreement (The Bracero Program) between the United States and Mexico that allowed Mexican citizens to work in the United States temporarily due to labor shortages. Between 1942 and the 1960s, more than 4 million Mexican citizens came to the United States under this program. This would ultimately create illegal aliens as workers overstayed their permits further increasing national concern about illegal entry into the country (Nathan, 2003).

Change in Policy Towards Immigrants and Immigration

By the end of World War II the Border Patrol would once again focus on illegal entry from the Mexico and undocumented workers currently in the United States. In response, INS would launch of its most aggressive and controversial programs in 1954—Operation Wetback. The program was essentially a crackdown on illegal immigration; however, officers rounded up over one million legal citizens and residents along with illegal immigrants and deported them to Mexico (Anderson, 2010). The late 1950s and 1960s represented significant shifts in the operation of the Border Patrol in the United States. Substantial numbers of illegal aliens began entering the U.S. on private aircraft in the late 1950s from Cuba, which increased during the early 1960s due to the Cuban missile crisis. To curb this activity the federal government assigned the Border Patrol to track suspicious flights.

This was also a time period of several attempted hijackings, and illegal drugs were now accompanying the smuggling of illegal aliens. The Border Patrol was tasked with protecting domestic flights and working with other agencies on drug interdiction efforts (Border Patrol History, 2011). The 1980s and 1990s would bring an increased growth in illegal immigration into the United States and the Border Patrol met the challenge with technology and personnel employing the use of night vision and seismic equipment to detect and apprehend those who crossed the border illegally. The Border Patrol would also expand its capabilities and roles in new areas during this time period with the inclusion of anti-smuggling units and search and rescue. While Border Patrol has had several milestones and events that have shaped the role and mission of the agency, the terrorist attacks of September 11, 2001 would bring the most significant restructuring of the agency in nearly half a century.

The security of the nation's borders would take center stage after the attacks and the federal government would once again reassess how the borders of the United States should be monitored and protected. With the creation of the Department of Homeland Security (DHS) on March 1, 2003, the U.S. Border Patrol became part of U.S. Customs and Border Protection (CBP), a component of DHS. The creation of CBP incorporated parts of U.S. Customs with a history spanning over two centuries and elements of the Immigration and Naturalization Service in an attempt to streamline federal law enforcement and co-operation. CBP became a frontline agency for national security with the broad mission of preventing terrorists, terrorist weapons, narcotics, and agricultural threats from entering the United States. In addition, the current CBP mission includes apprehending criminals with outstanding warrants, gathering intelligence, and protecting the borders and airspace of the country (Schied, 2010).

Organization and Personnel

U.S. Customs and Border Protection is a key component of the DHS and represents one of its most complex agencies. In addition to carrying out its primary mission of keeping terrorist and their weapons from entering the United States, CBP also secures trade and travel while enforcing hundreds of U.S. regulations, immigration, and drug laws. To accomplish this multi-dimension mission CBP has an equally multi-faceted structure to match. A commissioner appointed by the President of the United States heads CBP. The Office of the Commissioner is responsible for securing and managing the borders of the United States and oversees nearly two-dozen offices in charge of various aspects of immigration, trade, border security, and operations. The CBP contains six Commissioner staff offices that assist in supporting the overall mission:

- Office of the Chief of Staff—The OCS serves as the liaison to the DHS for all issues involving the CBP, and assists the commissioner in planning and implementing policies (Schied, 2010).

- Office of Chief Counsel—The OCC provides legal advice and legal representation of CBP officers in matters relating to their duty. The Office also ensures compliance with legal requirements, preparing formal legal opinions, preparing or reviewing responses in all court actions involving CBP, and developing, implementing, and evaluating nationwide programs, policies, and procedures (Commissioner's Staff Offices, 2011).

- Office of Diversity and Civil Rights—The ODC is responsible for ensuring compliance with federal civil rights statutes, regulations, and executive orders governing federal employment and federally funded and/or assisted programs. The ODC also formulates and implements policies and programs in the areas of workforce diversity and inclusion (Commissioner's Staff Offices, 2011).

- Office of Policy and Planning—The OPP advises the executive staff on policy related to the CBP mission as well as strategic and tactical planning. The OPP also proposes creative and innovative solutions for planning, statistical research, and evaluation (Commissioner's Staff Offices, 2011).

- Office of Trade Relations—The OTR provides accurate information to the international trade community on CBP trade policy and the resolution of trade issues (Commissioner's Staff Offices, 2011).

- Non-Government Office Liaison—The NGO Liaison is the agency's principal liaison to non-governmental organizations and facilitates dialogue on behalf of CBP to the NGO community (Commissioner's Staff Offices, 2011).

In addition to the six Commissioner's offices, CBP also contains 13 separate offices that are headed by Assistant Commissioners. The following provides a brief description of each office:

- Office of Air and Marine—The mission of the Office of Air and Marine is to protect the American people and the critical infrastructure of the United States through air and marine forces to detect and prevent acts of terrorism, and the unlawful movement of people across the Nation's borders (Assistant Commissioners' Offices, 2011).

- Office of Border Patrol—The OBP is the primary enforcement organization for CBP and is responsible for preventing terrorist, weapons of terrorism, drugs and illegal aliens from entering the United States. The OBP is organized into 20 sectors along the northern and southern borders, and coastal points of entry (Shied, 2010).

- Office of International Trade—The OIT provides a unified strategy for international trade policy and program development. Specifically, the OIT directs national enforcement responses, targeting of illegal goods crossing the border as well as punitive actions against companies participating in predatory trade practices (Assistant Commissioners' Offices, 2011).

- Office of Congressional Affairs—The OCA advises CBP administrators on all legislative and congressional issues, and assists members of Congress in understanding CBP programs (Shied, 2010)

- Office of Field Operations—The OFO enforces CBP laws and regulations and oversees operations in 20 field offices, 327 ports of entry, 15 preclearance stations in Canada, Ireland and the Caribbean, Immigration policy and programs, and Agricultural Quarantine Inspection (AQI) at all ports of entry in order to protect the health of U.S. plant and animal resources (Assistant Commissioners' Offices, 2011).

- Office of Administration—The OA administers financial management activities including accounting, budgeting, procurement, logistics, financial systems, policy, planning, and audit oversight (Assistant Commissioners' Offices, 2011).

- Office of Human Resources Management—The HRM is responsible for providing human resources support within CBP and a safe and fair work environment (Assistant Commissioners' Offices, 2011).

- Office of Information and Technology—The OIT is responsible for implementation and worldwide support of information technology, communications, research and development, and technological strategies for meeting mission-related needs of CBP (Assistant Commissioners' Offices, 2011).

- Office of Intelligence and Investigative Liaison—The OIIL is responsible for the entire intelligence cycle, including planning, collection, processing, analysis, production and dissemination of all-source intelligence (Assistant Commissioners' Offices, 2011).

- Office of Internal Affairs—The OIA is responsible for ensuring compliance with all CBP programs and policies relating to corruption, misconduct, or mismanagement and for executing the internal security, integrity, and management inspections program (Assistant Commissioners' Offices, 2011).

- Office of International Affairs—The INA is responsible for supporting and coordinating CBP's foreign programs and activities that promote anti-terrorism and global border security (Assistant Commissioners' Offices, 2011).

- Office of Public Affairs—The OPA informs the public, foreign officials and investors, international travelers and government stakeholders about CBP missions and activities through a variety of media outlets (Assistant Commissioners' Offices, 2011).

- Office of Training and Development—The OTD is responsible for leadership and direction of all CBP training programs, ensuring the workforce is prepared to carry out the missions and strategic plans of the agency (Assistant Commissioners' Offices, 2011).

U.S. Customs and Border Protection is a complex agency and its organization reflects the ever-evolving needs and difficulties of securing the borders and seacoast points of entry into the United States. CBP has also experienced unprecedented growth over the last few years to accomplish its primary mission and is now better staffed than at any time in its history, or in the history of its legacy agencies (primarily INS and Customs). CBP operates with an annual budget of more than $11 billion making it one the largest federal law enforcement agencies with numerous employment opportunities in integral positions (Securing America's Borders, 2011).

U.S. Customs and Border Protection is currently the largest law enforcement agency in the DHS with nearly 60,000 employees. In general, CBP has two categories of careers: frontline law enforcement and mission-critical occupations. The majority of CBP personnel are employed in frontline law enforcement positions. This includes over 20,000 Border Patrol Agents, nearly 1,000 Air and Marine Interdiction Agents, over 2,200 CBP Agriculture Specialists, and 2,500 employees in CBP revenue positions. CBP also has 8,000 employees working in dozens of mission-critical positions in careers including intelligence research specialists, sector enforcement specialists, paralegals, human resource specialists, and mechanics that support frontline occupations (We are CBP!, 2011)

Becoming a Frontline Officer in Customs and Border Protection

In general, candidates seeking to work in a frontline law enforcement position must pass a thorough background investigation and an intensive pre-screening process. Depending on the position and background of the applicant, candidates must attend 8 to 17 weeks of training in one of the most intense training programs in federal law enforcement at either the Federal Law Enforcement Training Center (FLETC) in Glynco, Georgia or the recently renovated advanced training facility in Artesia, New Mexico. If candidates are not fluent in Spanish they must remain an additional 40 days to attend Spanish Task-Based Language Training. All courses must be passed with a 70% or better to successfully complete the academy (Border Patrol Academy, 2011). Applicants in most cases must be under the age of 37, but exceptions are made for key positions and for applicants with prior military experience. The educational requirements for most frontline positions is a bachelor's degree in any field from an accredited college or university, however relevant work experience may be substituted for the degree. The frontline law enforcement positions are Border Patrol Agent, Customs Border Protection Officer, Agricultural Specialist, and Air & Marine Agent.

Border Patrol Agents

Border patrol agents conduct one of the most important activities of CBP—line watch. This involves the detection and apprehension of terrorists, undocumented aliens and human traffickers at or near the borders of the United States. Border patrol agents conduct surveillance from covert positions, investigate leads, and respond to electronic sensors, camera systems, and aircraft sightings indicating illegal activity. Other major activities are farm, traffic, and transportation checks, city patrol, and anti-smuggling operations. Border Patrol Agents work under arduous and at times dangerous conditions. In 2010, one Border

Patrol officer was killed in the line of duty and more than 1,000 officers were assaulted (Officers Killed and Assaulted, 2011). Overtime is mandatory for Border Patrol Agents and working 10–16 hour days is not uncommon. Border Patrol Agents are required to carry and be proficient with firearms, and be fluent in Spanish (Border Patrol Agent, 2011).

Customs Border Protection Officers

Customs Border Protection officers detect and prevent terrorists and weapons of mass destruction from entering the United States, while facilitating the orderly flow of legitimate trade and travelers. CBP Officers enforce laws related to revenue and trade, seize contraband, interdict agricultural pests, and determine the admissibility of people. CBP Officers perform a full range of inspection of passengers and cargo, and carry out law enforcement activities related to the arrival and departure of persons, merchandise and conveyances such as cars, trucks, aircraft, and ships at ports of entry. CBP Officers must wear a uniform, work overtime, and conduct their duties under demanding conditions. They must also regularly qualify with and carry firearms, and are subject to random drug testing (CBP Officer, 2011).

Agricultural Specialists

Agricultural specialists are skilled technicians and their training and requirements are different from other frontline positions. The applicants for this position must have a bachelor's or higher degree with a major field of study in biological sciences (including botany, entomology and plant pathology), agriculture, natural resource management, chemistry or any field directly related to the position or a combination of experience and education. Successful new hires must complete 10 to 12 weeks of training at the Professional Development Center located in Frederick, Maryland. Agricultural Specialists serve as experts and technical consultants in the areas of inspection, analysis, examination and law enforcement activities related to the importation of agricultural/commercial commodities and conveyances. Agricultural Specialist may also plan, implement, and supervise remedial actions such as treating and decontaminating various types of prohibited materials (Agriculture Specialist, 2011).

Air and Marine Agents

There are two separate career paths within the Air & Marine Division: air interdiction agents and marine interdiction agents, both of whom play a critical role in the CBP mission of preventing terrorism and illegal entry into the United States. Air interdiction agents may either pilot CBP manned or unmanned aircraft. Applicants must possess a valid FAA commercial pilot's license with instrument ratings appropriate for the position. Air interdiction agents work with multiple law enforcement agencies, and may pilot multiple types of aircraft working with the latest sophisticated detection systems to track and apprehend suspect aircraft, sea vessels, vehicles and people along the northern and southern borders, and coastal regions of the United States (Air Interdiction Agents, 2011). Marine interdiction agents patrol oceans, lakes, and rivers to prevent the illegal entry of terrorist and their weapons, illegal narcotics and undocumented aliens. Marine interdiction agents command various CBP vessels in some of the most challenging situations often at night and in adverse sea conditions. They also conduct covert and overt operations against terrorist activities and conduct operations with some of the nation's top law enforcement agencies, and deploy to natural disaster areas to help those in need (Marine Interdiction Agents, 2011).

Functions

The organization and personnel of CBP are structured to carry out its dual missions of securing the nation's borders while facilitating legitimate trade and travel. They are missions that frequently place employees in difficult and dangerous situations. CBP must continuously evolve and revise strategies as groups that threaten the United States also change their structures and plans. This level of vigilance has led to numerous successful apprehensions and strengthened security at the borders.

Border Patrol

While U.S. Customs and Border Protection carries out many different functions to accomplish its dual missions, the core activity of the agency involves active control of the southern, northern, and coastal borders of the United States. Border patrol activities consist of five main strategies: (1) increase the probability of apprehending terrorists and their weapons as they attempt to enter illegally between the ports of entry; (2) deter illegal entries through enforcement; (3) detect, apprehend, and deter smugglers of humans, drugs, and other contraband; (4) employ "Smart Border" technology to multiply the effect of enforcement personnel; and (5) reduce crime in border communities.

The southern border with Mexico is approximately 2,000 miles, and stretches through some extremely inhospitable and harsh terrain. Each year hundreds of aliens die as a result of failed attempts to enter the United States undetected. Within these 2,000 miles of border, there are three primary smuggling corridors: the South Texas corridor, the West Texas/New Mexico corridor, and the California/Arizona corridor. More than 90% of the one million plus annual arrests made by Border Patrol occur within these smuggling corridors (Office of Border Patrol, 2011). Border Patrol currently uses a mix of agents, information, and technology to secure the borders. Agents patrol on all-terrain vehicles and horseback, and are assisted by infrared and night vision cameras, biometric systems, seismic sensors, and aerial platforms resulting in noteworthy apprehensions and seizures along the southern border.

Notable Border Patrol Cases

During 2011 agents in the Tucson Sector, which is the busiest sector of CBP, apprehended 123,285 illegal immigrants between the ports of entry, seized 1,039,443 pounds of marijuana, rescued 509 individuals in distress, and confiscated $3,630,219 of U.S. currency (CBP U.S. Border Patrol Tucson Sector, 2011). In December of 2011 CBP officers at the Pharr-Reynosa International Bridge encountered a maroon Freightliner tractor and trailer at the CBP cargo facility. Examination by CBP officers in a secondary inspection revealed 423 packages of marijuana concealed within the trailer with a street value of $2,464,760. In November of 2011, CBP officers working at the Hidalgo/Reynosa International Bridge in Hidalgo, Texas arrested a male U.S. citizen for attempting to smuggle a 10-year-old Mexican national child into the United States. The driver presented a U.S. birth certificate for himself and his presumed minor female daughter. The vehicle and occupants were referred to secondary for further inspection and it was there that CBP officers discovered that the child was not related to the adult traveler but was in fact a Mexican national with no valid documents to enter or reside in the U.S. The man was arrested and later incarcerated. CBP officials were able to locate the child's biological parents in Mexico and she was reunited with her family (CBP Officers at the Hidalgo, 2011). Along the same bridge in February, border patrol agents intercepted a 23-year-old Texas man who was attempting to deliver six AK-47 rifles to the Gulf Cartel in Reynosa for $300. In custody the man admitted to delivering weapons on at least 50 other trips (Chapa, 2011).

When citizens consider the activities of CBP they visualize the highly publicized actions as described in the previous section and the debated policies along the Southern Border with Mexico. However, the U.S.-Canada border is more than 4,000 miles including the Great Lakes and Native American reservations, and requires cooperation with Canadian and tribal law enforcement officials. While the volume of illegal crossing of the northern border pales in comparison to the southern border, the U.S. border with Canada has well-organized smuggling operations that could potentially support the movement of terrorists and their weapons. For example, the CBP Seattle Field Office manages 67 ports with more than 1,400 agents and 120 agricultural specialists. During 2011 agents in the Seattle office discovered $3.2 million in unreported currency, seized more than 400 pounds of illegal drugs and 115,000 prohibited plant and animal products, and made 1,613 arrests (CBP Seattle Field Office, 2011). The Detroit Sector of CBP was awarded the "Most Notable Law Enforcement Interdiction or Arrest" trophy in 2011 for the dramatic apprehension of three armed suspects attempting to cross the St. Clair River from Canada into Detroit. The suspects were initially detected using new video monitoring screens in a camera control center located at the Selfridge Air National Guard base northeast of Detroit (U.S. CBP wins, 2011).

Notable Air and Marine Cases

Border Patrol works with a variety of law enforcement agencies, such as the U.S. Coast Guard, to address potential illegal entry and maritime smuggling of both people and cargo. In May 2011 the crew of a CBP Caribbean Air & Marine Branch DHC-8 aircraft detected a vessel without navigational lights, traveling east towards the Northern coast of Puerto Rico. The crew notified marine agents aboard a CBP Mayaguez Marine Interceptor, which stopped the suspect vessel approximately nine-miles northwest of Arecibo, Puerto Rico. Agents boarded the vessel and determined there were 26 passengers from the Dominican Republic; there was also debris floating in the water near the boat that was later discovered to be six bricks of cocaine. Six of the passengers were charged with attempted illegal re-entry into the United States (CBP U.S. Air and Marine Agents, 2011).

Another aspect of controlling border spaces is patrolling the skies over the United States, and CBP's air division is charged with this task. Air interdiction agents operate aircraft such as the King Air 350, twin engine Multi-role Enforcement Aircraft (MEA) to accomplish the mission of securing the nation's air space. In April of 2011 the Air and Marine Operations Center (AMOC) in Riverside, California alerted air interdiction agents in Texas of a suspicious aircraft. A San Angelo Air Unit launched an aircraft asset to pursue small plane. Upon landing in Sonora, Texas, the pilot of the suspect aircraft consented to a search, which yielded $218,000 worth of marijuana (Air and Marine Agents in Texas, 2011).

Unmanned aircraft also play a key role in supporting border patrol. CBP currently operates nine Predator Bs: six total from the National Air Security Operations Center

(NASOC)—Sierra Vista (Arizona) and NASOC—Corpus Christi (Texas); two from NASOC—Grand Forks (North Dakota); and a maritime variant of the Predator B, the Guardian, from NASOC—Cocoa Beach (Florida). The number of CBP unmanned aircraft is second only to that of the United States Air Force. Skilled FAA certified agents pilot the aircraft in real time. Since the inception of the UAS program, CBP has flown more than 12,000 hours in support of border security operations and emergency responses, leading to the total seizure of approximately 46,600 pounds of illicit drugs and the detention of 7,500 individuals suspected in engaging in illegal activity along the Southwest border (CBP Receives Fourth, 2011).

Customs Enforcement

While the actions of the Border Patrol, and Air and Marine agents are newsworthy and critical in securing the nation, controlling the flow of goods, commodities, and agriculture into the United States is equally important. Cargo entering the United States from any foreign territory has been subject to physical examination to verify that it complies with U.S. laws and regulations. After the terrorist attacks of 9/11 this mission took on greater urgency. CBP works with thousands of companies who are members of the Customs Trade Partnership Against Terrorism to strengthen security in the supply chain. CBP uses intelligence from a number of sources to identify high-risk shipments in order to concentrate its inspection resources on them.

Notable Customs Enforcement Cases

During 2011 U.S. Customs and Border Protection agents seized more than 1,700 fake drivers licenses coming through international mail at the Chicago O'Hare Airport. The counterfeits were ordered online from China and were high quality reproductions of licenses from Illinois, Ohio, South Dakota, Wisconsin, Florida, Georgia, and Pennsylvania. The majority appeared to be purchased by college students. Both federal and local authorities expressed concern over the ease with which the fakes could be ordered and their potential threat to national security (More than 1,700 fake driver's licenses, April 2011). Between January and March of 2011, Customs and Border Patrol Protection seized more than $30 million in counterfeit checks and money orders at DHL facilities in Cincinnati. The fraudulent checks and counterfeit money orders originated from West Africa as a part of international financial scams designed to steal money from U.S. citizens ($30 million in counterfeit funds seized at DHL, March 2011).

Threats to legitimate U.S. trade and intellectual property are also a concern for CBP. In June of 2011, CBP agents discovered nearly $1 million worth of counterfeit SanDisk portable memory chips hidden inside more than 1,900 karaoke machines being shipped into the Port of Long Beach from China. Once the chips were discovered to be counterfeit they were destroyed and the importers who violated the trademark laws were subject to civil and criminal penalties (Customs agents seize, June 2011). In 2010, CBP agents in the Otay Mesa community of San Diego detected nine separate shipments containing nearly 14,000 counterfeit toys including Barbie Dolls, Lego sets, and Spiderman masks with a value of nearly $200,000. The toys were of inferior quality, did not have the appropriate licensing agreements, and were destined for Mexico (Thomas, Dec 2010). In a separate seizure in Otay Mesa in 2011, CBP authorities confiscated 100,000 counterfeit Major League Baseball caps, and remote-controlled toys. Although they were of inferior quality and lacked licensing, the fakes would have sold for more than $200,000 in Mexico. Had they been legitimate products, their value in the United States would have been well over $1 million (Repard, 2011).

Controlling the flow of people and products into any nation is vital for security. Protecting the borders of the United States has always been a serious and contentious issue and epitomizes one of the most difficult challenges in federal law enforcement. The southern border with Mexico poses several unique problems as smugglers and human traffickers implement the use of tunnels to aid illegal entry, and small submersible vessels and ultra-light aircraft are used to move drugs across the borders. These current actions must be considered within the context of the terrorist attacks of 9/11. Illegal entry into the country and the smuggling of prohibited items took on new dimensions in the face of terrorism leading to the creation of U.S. Customs and Border Protection to handle these new threats.

Globalization during the 21st century has also revealed the interconnected nature of trade, and the need for a high level of planning, interagency, and international cooperation to control the flow of people and goods. Globalization has also increased the awareness of the multiple sources of threats to national security produced by new technologies and innovations from transnational groups whether they are terrorist organizations, crime syndicates, or international drug cartels. U.S. Customs and Border Protection will continue to develop groundbreaking procedures and technologies for patrolling the land, air, and waters of the United States and methods to gauge the success of their practices as the frontline guardians of economic trade security and points of entry into the nation.

References

$30M in counterfeit funds seized at DHL (2011). Retrieved from http://www.bizjournals. com/cincinnati/morning_call/2011/03/30m-in-counterfeit-funds-seized-at-dhl.html.

Agriculture Specialist (2011). Retrieved from http://www.cbp.gov/xp/cgov/careers/ customs_careers/ag_spec/.

Air and Marine Agents in Texas Find 86 Pounds of Marijuana Hidden in Small Aircraft (2011). Retrieved from http://www.cbp.gov/xp/cgov/newsroom/news_releases/archives/ may_2011/05032011_2.xml.

Air Interdiction Agents (2011). Retrieved from http://www.cbp.gov/xp/cgov/careers/ customs_careers/air_marine/air_interdiction/.

Anderson, S. (2010). *Immigration (Greenwood guides to business and economics)*. Santa Barbara, CA: Greenwood.

Assistant Commissioners' Offices (2011). Retrieved from http://www.cbp.gov/xp/cgov/ about/organization/assist_comm_off/.

Border Patrol Academy (2011). Retrieved from http://borderpatrolacademy.com/.

Border Patrol Agent (2011). Retrieved from http://www.cbp.gov/xp/cgov/careers/customs_ careers/border_careers/.

Border Patrol History (2011). Retrieved from http://www.cbp.gov/xp/cgov/border_securi-ty/border_patrol/border_patrol_ohs/history.xml.

CBP Officer (2011). Retrieved from http://www.cbp.gov/xp/cgov/careers/customs_careers/border_careers/.

CBP Officers at the Hidalgo International Bridge Disrupt Child Smuggling Attempt-Man Arrested (2011). Retrieved from http://www.cbp.gov/xp/cgov/newsroom/news_releases/local/11222011_xml.

CBP Receives Fourth Predator-B in Arizona (2011). Retrieved from http://www.cbp.gov/xp/cgov/newsroom/news_releases/national/12272011.xml.

CBP Seattle Field Office Outstanding Year End Results (2011). Retrieved from http://www.cbp.gov/xp/cgov/newsroom/news_releases/local/12202011_4.xml.

CBP U.S. Air and Marine Agents Intercept Vessel With 26 Undocumented Aliens Near Arecibo; Narcotics Found Floating Nearby (2011). Retrieved from http://www.cbp.gov/xp/cgov/newsroom/news_releases/archives/may_2011/05252011_8.xml.

CBP U.S. Border Patrol Tucson Sector Announces Fiscal Year-End Accomplishments (2011). Retrieved from http://www.cbp.gov/xp/cgov/newsroom/news_releases/local/12162011_15.xml.

Chapa, S. (2011). Edinburg man caught delivering AK-47s to Gulf Cartel. Retrieved from http://www.valleycentral.com/news/story.aspx?id=585454.

Commissioner's Staff Offices (2011). Retrieved from http://www.cbp.gov/xp/cgov/about/organization/comm_staff_off/.

Customs agents seize 1,932 karaoke machines in Los Angeles (2011). Retrieved from http://www.reuters.com/article/2011/06/02/us-karaoke-seizure-idUSTRE7516SG20110602.

Haddal, C. (2010). *People crossing borders: An analysis of U.S. border protection policies.* Washington, D.C.: Congressional Research Service.

Import Specialist (2011). Retrieved from http://www.cbp.gov/xp/cgov/careers/customs_careers/import_specialist/.

Lee, Erika (2003). A Nation of immigrants and a gatekeeping nation: American immigration law and policy. In R. Ueda (Ed.) *A Companion to American Immigration* (pp. 5–35) UK: John Wiley & Sons.

Kettner, J. (1978). *The development of American citizenship, 1608–1870.* Chapel Hill: University of North Carolina Press.

LeMay, M., and Barkan, E. (1999). *U.S. immigration and naturalization laws and issues: A documentary history.* Westport, Conn., Greenwood Press.

Marine Interdiction Agents (2011). Retrieved from http://www.cbp.gov/xp/cgov/careers/customs_careers/air_marine/marine_interdiction/.

More than 1,700 fake driver's licenses seized at O'Hare Airport (April, 2011). Retrieved from http://www.suntimes.com/news/crime/4830764-418/story.html.

Nathan, D. (2003). Immigration, Mexico. In L. Stacy (Ed.) *Mexico and the United States.* Tarrytown, NY: Marshall Cavendish.

Navarro, A. (2009). *Nativism, armed vigilantism, and the rise of a countervailing movement.* Lanham, MD: Altamira Press.

Nevins. J. (2002). *Operation Gatekeeper: the rise of the "illegal alien" and the making of the U.S.-Mexico border.* New York: Routledge.

Office of Border Patrol (2011). *National border patrol strategy.* Retrieved from www.cbp.gov/linkhandler/cgov/ ... /national_bp_strategy.pdf.

Officers Killed and Assaulted (2011). Retrieved from http://www.fbi.gov/about-us/cjis/ucr/leoka/leoka-2010/federal-officers-killed-and-assaulted.

Repard, P. (2011). Fake-logo caps, toys headed into Mexico seized. Retrieved from http://www.utsandiego.com/news/2011/jun/14/fake-logo-caps-toys-headed-mexico-seized/?print&page=all.

Schied, E. (2010). *U. S. Customs and Border Protection: Performance and accountability report: fiscal year 2009*. Darby, PA: Diane Publishing.

Securing America's Borders (2011). Retrieved from http://www.cbp.gov/xp/cgov/border_security/bs/border_sec_initiatives_lp.xml.

Thomas, D. (2010). Fake Barbie dolls, Lego's and more toys seized at Otay Mesa Border. Retrieved from http://cdn2-b.examiner.com/news-in-san-diego/fake-barbie-dolls-lego-s-and-more-toys-confiscated-at-otay-mesa-border.

Ueda, R. (1994). *Postwar immigrant America: A social history*. Boston: Bedford Books of St. Martin's Press.

U.S. CBP wins "Most Notable Interdiction/Arrest" award for northern border SBI arrests on St. Clair River (2011). Retrieved from http://www.gsnmagazine.com/node/25135.

Warner, J. (2010). *U.S. Border security: A reference handbook*. Santa Barbara, CA: ABC-CLIO, LLC.

We are CBP! (2011). Retrieved from http://www.cbp.gov/xp/cgov/careers/customs_careers/we_are_cbp.xml.

Chapter Nine

United States Secret Service

Financial security is essential for the survival of any nation. There are several agencies that work in partnership or may have a secondary mission of ensuring the integrity of the economic system of the United States. However, the United States Secret Service is the only agency that was created with the specific mission of safeguarding and protecting the currency of the country. The physical currency of a country is not only its lifeblood but it is a tangible representation of wealth and government stability. Like any country's infrastructure or natural resource currency is vulnerable to attack, typically in the form of counterfeiting. According to the Bureau of Engraving and Printing, 23.5 million notes are produced each day with a face value of approximately $453 million (Annual Production Figures, 2011). The shear volume and value of the printed currency in the United States alone has made the American dollar a target for counterfeiting.

While the currency of a nation is paramount for its survival and trade, the government leaders of a country are perhaps even more important for security and strength. The loss of a nation's leader is devastating and may impact numerous countries around the world. Even a high profile attempt on a leader's life may deeply affect a nation. Protecting leaders and the integrity of the nation's currency may be two of the most challenging tasks assigned to any agency in the United States' government. In the light of the terrorist attacks of 9/ 11, each of these missions would be profoundly changed, and the United States Secret Service would have its role expanded with increasingly technical investigations involving numerous agencies, the private sector, and academia.

History

The creation of the Secret Service is a story rooted in national crisis. By the beginning of the American Civil War (1861) the United States was not only facing one its bloodiest conflicts, but was also reeling from a currency quagmire. In 1861 there were 1,600 banks that were designing and printing their own money. As a result there were literally thousands of different genuine bank notes circulating around the country. This was an unprecedented time for counterfeiters. Criminals were able to open their own banks, hire printers, and begin churning out their own money with legitimate looking seals and names. This was a major blow to economic trade in the United States. Merchants and citizens had a difficult time distinguishing between legitimate and bogus notes, resulting in people hoarding coins with the belief they were the only safe currency. In response to the hoarding of coins, banks had to produce fractional bills to represent the coins, which in turn further added to the confusion of currency in the country. The United States was at a point where even the crudest counterfeits could pass inspection due to the sheer variety of notes (Melanson, 2005).

Business leaders and bankers were convinced that a single legal tender bill was necessary. However, there was opposition to the thought of the government printing its own money.

Examples of the time which gave people pause included the depreciating Confederate currency and that of the Revolutionary continentals. However, three-fourths of the Republicans, the Secretary of the Treasury, and the Finance Committee supported the creation a single currency. The United States Congress with Lincoln's signature passed the Legal Tender Act of 1862. The act created a new national currency, changed the money structure of the United States, and restored investor confidence. The act resulted in the sale of nearly $500 million in bonds and the printing of more than $300 million worth of greenbacks (McPherson, 2003). The new legal tender would range in denominations from one dollar to one thousand dollars with a new printing technology and the use of green ink on both sides of the notes. Congress hoped that the use of this improved printing process would eliminate counterfeiting, however they underestimated the ingenuity of "coney" men who began creating high quality fake greenbacks immediately (Melanson, 2005).

Creation of the Secret Service

Throughout the Union counterfeit currency began appearing with regularity, and by 1862 it was estimated that nearly one-third to one-half of the money in circulation was counterfeit (Gaines, 2001). It became clear very quickly that state and local law enforcement was simply ill equipped to deal with the volume and severity of counterfeiting. Bankers, governors, and business leaders pleaded with the federal government to intervene. The new national currency would require national level protection and security. In 1863 the Treasury Department began sending employees across the country to pursue counterfeiters. The employees essentially worked like detectives, tracking down leads and conducting investigations to discover the origins of fake currency. These early enforcement efforts led to many arrests and high profile apprehensions of some notorious "coney" men. April 4, 1865 President Abraham Lincoln met with the Secretary of the Treasury Hugh McCullough who suggested there needed to be a permanent force whose job it would be to end counterfeiting. Lincoln agreed, and it would be the last meeting the two men would have as the president was assassinated that night.

President Johnson supported the idea of creating an anti-counterfeiting force, and on July 5, 1865 the United States Secret Service was created. Treasury Secretary McCullough appointed William P. Wood as the first Director of the Secret Service Division of the Treasury Department. Director Wood would oversee ten newly appointed operatives who were all sworn in along with him. Wood insisted that every operative be on call 24 hours a day, be ready to deploy on short notice, stay in top physical condition, and swear unconditional obedience. William Wood was unconventional and exceptional as Director of the Secret Service. He hired additional personnel including criminals who were master forgers, as he believed they truly understood the craft of counterfeiting and would be valuable assets to investigations. Under Wood's leadership from 1865 to 1869, Secret Service Agents apprehended more than two hundred counterfeiters. Wood expanded his force with former soldiers, detectives, and police officers and established the Secret Service headquarters in Washington, D.C., with field offices in 11 cities (Melanson, 2005).

Early Secret Service agents used a variety of investigative techniques to uncover and apprehend counterfeiters. Agents used disguises, changed their names, and moved into areas suspected of harboring counterfeiters. Agents would work undercover taking on the role of a counterfeiter to arrest criminals attempting to purchase fake currency; other times the agents would pose as potential buyers of bogus greenbacks. Agents intercepted suspects' mail, sought informants willing to turn against other counterfeiters, and followed suspected counterfeiters in hopes of catching them purchasing supplies or materials to print currency. Agents were not issued badges at this time and the federal government only paid for their handcuffs. Agents were responsible for purchasing and providing their own weapons. For identification, Secret Service Agents carried letters on Treasury Department letterhead.

These letters of identification were often met with derision and were subject to being counterfeited. In 1871 a con man obtained written correspondence from the Secretary of the Treasury, washed the letter, retained the signature and wrote a new letter identifying him as an Agent-in-Charge. The con man attempted to use this forged credential to retrieve counterfeit bills from a Secret Service office in California. Although the forged document appeared valid and the con man looked the part, the office administrator contacted Washington to verify the information and the con man was arrested. The result of this was a decree that all Agents would now have to carry an official badge to thwart any future impersonations. The Secret Service authorized a five-pointed star in August 1875. Agents were required to place a deposit of $25 for the cost of their badge to be refunded upon retirement. Agents were soon given official credentials provided by the Bureau of Engraving and Printing to accompany their badges (Melanson, 2005).

Duties of the Early Secret Service

Despite a meager budget, grueling work schedules, and little support from Congress and the public, the Secret Service would go on to distinguish itself with numerous high profile apprehensions, seizures, and arrests of counterfeiters that threatened the financial security of the United States. The Secret Service had largely won the public's trust and dealt a serious blow to counterfeiting. The Secret Service was the only purely investigative agency of the federal government at the time and was the best equipped to handle threats as they emerged against the United States (Jones, 2011). For example, in 1866 a new group of rabble-rousers were emerging in the south calling themselves the Ku Klux Klan. By 1871 Congress had officially condemned the actions of the Klan and the Attorney General ordered the Director of the Secret Service to send agents to investigate the organization in several southern states. Klan leaders were followed to discover membership and meeting locations resulting in nearly 1,000 arrests, prosecutions, and numerous members sentenced to prison (Melanson, 2005). The Secret Service continued to have its authority expanded to investigate many other violations, and engaged in a new range of activities. For example, during the Spanish American War, and World War I the Secret Service gathered intelligence and prevented espionage and sabotage (Jones, 2011). This responsibility led the Secret Service into new territory that would become the mission primarily associated with the agency—protecting the President of the United States.

In 1894 the Secret Service became aware of a plot to assassinate President Grover Cleveland and assigned two agents to a detail to protect the president and investigate the plot. The agents followed Cleveland's carriage in a buggy. Political opponents criticized Cleveland for his security and unauthorized use of the Service so he dismissed the agents. However, the threats to Cleveland's life increased and the president's wife insisted the protection be continued at the White House. The Secret Service began to informally assign agents to expand the security detail at the White House and when the president traveled. Although the Secret Service was now providing a force to protect the president, it would not save the next Commander-in-Chief William McKinley. William McKinley had a protection detail assigned to him when he was shot September 6, 1901 at a reception in

Buffalo New York. Two Secret Service Agents were in front of the president when a 28 year-old anarchist joined the greeting line, drew a concealed pistol and shot the president twice in the chest and stomach. McKinley would die from complications eight days later. This tragedy prompted the Secret Service to officially take on the fulltime task of protecting the president in 1902 even though the agency did not have the authority to do so. Congress would not allocate the funds for this mission until 1906 (Kessler, 2010).

Protecting the President

Prior to formal Secret Service protection, presidents essentially protected themselves. For example, when the White House first opened a deranged man entered and threatened to kill President John Adams. Without calling for help Adams invited the man into his office and calmed him down. President Andrew Jackson physically defended himself on at least two occasions. Protecting the president in the nineteenth and early twentieth century was a difficult task. Congress had not yet made assassination of the president a federal crime, and members of the public were still allowed to freely roam the White House during daylight hours. By the end of World War II three presidents had been assassinated or died from complications from an assassination attempt (Lincoln, Garfield, and McKinley) and four others were in either immediate danger (Jackson, Franklin Roosevelt, Truman) or survived the attempt (Theodore Roosevelt) (Oliver and Marion, 2010). One critical event would solidify the full-time protection of the president and immediate family—the assassination attempt on President Harry Truman.

Due to needed remodeling in the White House, President Truman had his family relocated to the Blair House that was traditionally used as the guest quarters for the White House. On November 1, 1950 two men, Oscar Collazo and Griselio Torresola planned to assassinate Truman in order to bring attention to the cause of separating Puerto Rico from the United States. The pair discovered Truman was not in the White House and made their way to the nearby Blair quarters. White House police officer Donald Birdzell was stationed at the front entrance while Cazollo came up behind him and fired his automatic pistol. The pistol misfired, but would eventually discharge a round into Birdzell's knee. Agent Floyd Boring and Officer Joseph Davidson responded and opened fire on Cazallo killing him. The second gunman Torresola fired upon Officer Leslie Coffelt in the west security booth, and turned on another officer shooting him three times.

At this point President Truman was sleeping and agents retrieved weapons and secured the hallways and elevators to protect him. Torresola ran towards the Blair house and encountered the wounded Birdzell who fired upon the gunman, but missed. In a last act of courage the wounded Officer Coffelt propped himself up against his security booth, took aim and fired a round in to Torresola's ear killing him. Coffelt died four hours later in surgery and was placed on the Secret Service honor roll of those killed in the line of duty. Truman was never harmed but the incident demonstrated the need to protect the president. On July 16, 1951 Congress finally passed legislation to permanently authorize the Secret Service to protect the president, his immediate family, the president-elect, and the vice president if requested (Oliver and Marion, 2010).

With this new congressionally approved mission the Secret Service began to strengthen their training and professionalism. In 1953 the first special agent training school was opened. It was a three-week course covering basic investigations and protection responsibilities appropriate for the 1950s. Prior to this pre-service training, agents merely toured the Bureau of Engraving and Printing, attended a basic two-week Treasury program, and received informal lectures. The vast majority of special agent training was on the job or in-service (Holden, 2006). Congress expanded the authority of the Secret Service after other crises including the assassination of Senator Robert Kennedy. Senator Kennedy's assassination resulted in extending protection to major presidential and vice presidential candidates. After the assassination of President Kennedy in 1963, the Secret Service reexamined its approach to protection details and the training needed to carry out this critical mission.

Lessons Learned from the Kennedy Assassination

The training of presidential protection details prior to Kennedy's assassination consisted of war stories told by older agents and the short three-week course offered by the agency. Kennedy's death revealed several glaring problems with this approach to such an important task. During the November 22, 1963 assassination critical mistakes were made. Only two agents were sent ahead to Dallas to coordinate with local law enforcement, and there was no inspection of the surrounding buildings along the motorcade route. The agent in charge of driving the limousine had no training in evasive skills and slowed down waiting for commands after the first shot rather than speeding up to escape an ongoing attack (Kessler, 2010). Furthermore, several of the agents failed to recognize the sound of gunfire during the attack. Their only exposure to gunfire came during training on the range with hearing protection; they thought they were hearing a backfire or firecracker (Melanson, 2010). The loss of President Kennedy under their watch due to the combination of missteps and mistakes devastated the Secret Service but the agency would recover, improve, and grow from the difficult lessons learned in Dallas.

The training of Secret Service agents would increase dramatically over the decades and include new technology and approaches to teaching and preparation. Prior to the 1970s and the Kennedy assassination in 1963, Secret Service training lacked elements of realism. This would soon change with the James J. Rowley Training Center opened in Beltsville, Maryland. Established in 1971, the Rowley Training Center is a nearly 500 acre complex designed to simulate protection detail scenarios including training in buildings, helicopters, and passenger planes to prepare for various threats on land and sea. The intricate facility is based upon the two-prong approach of developing instinctive combat-ready skills for the agents, and the investigative tools needed to assess, detect, and stop violent threats and financial crimes.

The 1970s through the 1990s were periods of notable changes in Secret Service structure and missions. In 1971 Congress authorized Secret Service protection for visiting heads of a foreign state or other official guests. The Executive Protective Service was officially renamed the Secret Service Uniformed Division in 1977. In 1984 Congress authorized the Secret Service to investigate violations related to credit and debit card fraud, federal-interest computer fraud, and fraudulent identification documents. By the year 2000, the Secret Service was authorized to conduct any kind of investigation, civil or criminal, related to federally insured financial institutions; pursue any person manufacturing, trafficking in, or possessing counterfeit U.S. currency abroad as if the act occurred within the United States; and investigate any fraud or attempts to commit fraud involving tele-marketing (Secret Service History, 2011). Like numerous other federal agencies, the terrorist attacks of September 11, 2001 impacted the Secret Service.

The Secret Service had been housed in the U.S. Department of Treasury since its inception, however after 9/11 and the passage of the Homeland Security Act in 2002 the agency was transferred to the newly created Department of Homeland Security (DHS) effective March, 2003. It was an interesting move as the Secret Service and U.S. Department of the Treasury already had the mandate to ensure the safety and security of financial institutions and to conduct investigations and counterintelligence operations involving crimes such as money laundering and counterfeiting that may support terrorism. Nonetheless there are specific responsibilities outlined in the Homeland Security Act that are directly connected to the activities the Secret Service. The DHS mission of preventing terrorist acts within the United States involved concerns over potential threats to top government officials, and protecting the nation's currency, which is viewed as a critical infrastructure. Locating the Secret Service within DHS would settle jurisdictional battles between the Secret Service and agencies such as the FBI and ATF and ensure that the nation's lead agency on protecting elected officials, heads of state, and currency could now operate under the authority of the DHS (Reese, 2010).

Organization and Personnel

The United States Secret Service has a fascinating and lengthy history. It is a story that has reflected some of the darkest periods of the United States. It is also an agency that has a complex internal structure to carry out its dual missions of presidential protection and anti-counterfeiting. The Secret Service is headquartered in Washington, D.C. and has more than 150 field offices in the United States and abroad. The President of the United States appoints a director of the Secret Service. Directors have historically not been outside political appointees but are selected from the ranks of distinguished career agents (Melanson & Stevens, 2002). The United States Secret Service's internal structure has been fluid over the last few years and only select information is made public by the agency. The following represents the best assessment of the organization at this time.

Under the Director of the Secret Service are eight assistant directors who head up distinct divisions critical to the operations of the agency:

- The Office of Protective Operations—Is the core of Secret Service operations and may be viewed as the heart of the agency. The office oversees and coordinates the protection and security details for current and former presidents and their spouses. Protective Operations also protects presidential candidates and visiting foreign dignitaries (Melanson, 2002).

- The Office of Strategic Intelligence & Information—Is a recent addition to the Secret Service, created in October of 2010. SII plans and coordinates all efforts involving collecting, evaluating and distributing operational intelligence impacting the protective mission of the Secret Service as well as risk assessment and behavioral research (United States Secret Service, 2010).

- The Office of Human Resources and Training—Provides the critical specialized training for agents at the James T. Rowley Training Center (RTC), and instructs the Uniformed Division in the latest techniques of profiling and investigations, as well as maintaining a library of reports and studies on protective operations and counterfeiting technology. In addition the HRT also engages in recruitment efforts to attract a diverse work force for the agency (Melanson & Stevens, 2002).

- The Office of Professional Responsibility—Was created in 2008 to combine the existing Inspection and Management and Organization Divisions and serves as the internal affairs investigator for the agency in addition to handling complaints and issues of compliance (United States Secret Service, 2008).

- The Office of Administration — Is responsible for the day-to-day operations of the Secret Service and enables the various divisions to carry out their missions. The office performs management analysis, handles budgets, and conducts key administrative housekeeping functions (Melanson, 2005).

- The Office of Technical Development & Mission Support — Actively participates in the investigative and the protective missions of the Secret Service by providing technical personnel, information technology, and protective countermeasures such as communications, access control systems, and state of the art surveillance and detection equipment employed in the White House, hotel rooms and other sites (United States Secret Service, 2010).

- The Office of Investigations — Carries out the other primary mission of the Secret Service, investigating counterfeiting and protecting the nation's paper and coin currency as well as threats against protectees. The Office of Investigations also conducts background checks on government employees, scrutinizes documents, and conducts forensic analysis (Melanson & Stevens, 2002).

- The Office of Government & Public Affairs — Establishes and maintains effective working relationships with members of the news media, and groups interested in the agency's programs and field offices. The office also responds to information requests from the news media; prepares and edits speeches, press releases, and television scripts for senior management officials and advises staff on the impact of news stories. The office also serves as editor of internal publications and authors articles on the Secret Service (United States Secret Service, 2010).

In addition to the eight major offices headed by assistant directors there are several subdivisions within each major office, all with specialized task to carry out the office's mission. One division that stands out is the Secret Service Uniformed Division. Most Americans are familiar with the special agents dressed in suits, overcoats, and wearing hidden communication gear who accompany the president. The Secret Service Uniformed Division has a lengthy history as well. The Uniformed Division began as the White House Police Force in 1922 at the request of President Harding to provide security on the grounds. The White House Police Force was placed under the supervision of the Secret Service in 1930 (Bumgarner, 2006). In 1970 the White House Police Force was renamed the Executive Protective Service, and was officially renamed the Secret Service Uniformed Division in 1977. Its responsibilities now include the protection of diplomatic missions throughout the United States (Secret Service History, 2011). Despite its relatively small size, the Secret Service has an intricate structure, and operates on a budget of nearly $2 billion a year, with several career paths for personnel (Department of Homeland Security, 2011).

The United States Secret Service is one of the smaller federal law enforcement agencies within the Department of Homeland Security and operates with fewer than 7,000 employees. There are three categories of personnel in the Secret Service: special agents, Uniformed Division, and administrative/support. Currently there are 3,200 special agents, 1,300 Uniformed Division officers, and more than 2,000 technical, professional, and administrative support personnel including accountants, attorneys, and intelligence analysts among other positions (Frequently Asked Questions, 2012). The entry requirements and career path for special agents is unique from other positions in the Secret Service. It is a high profile position undertaking the dual missions of protection and investigation.

Becoming a Secret Service Agent

In general an applicant for the position of special agent must be at least 21 and no more than 37 years of age at the time of appointment, and must be in excellent physical condition. In accordance with the agency's public image, agents must have weight proportionate to their height (Melanson & Stevens, 2002). Special agent applicants must also possess a bachelor's degree from an accredited college, although the agency may make exceptions in some cases for experience in law enforcement. Applicants undergo an arduous pre-employment screening and selection process. Candidates must qualify for a top secret security clearance, give a full disclosure of past drug use, write a series of mini-essays about their abilities and experiences, pass the Treasury Enforcement Agent Exam, undergo several interviews with a hiring panel, pass a physical fitness exam and undergo a thorough background investigation (Special Agents, 2012). After this initial process and screening, applicants will undergo 27 weeks of rigorous training. The training begins at the Federal Law Enforcement Center (FLETC) in Glynco, Georgia where agents are enrolled in the Criminal Investigator Training Program (CITP). This ten-week course trains new federal investigators in areas such as criminal law and investigative techniques, and provides a general foundation for the agency-specific training. This training is followed by an additional 17 weeks at the James J. Rowley Training Center for instruction on specific Secret Service policies and procedures associated with the dual responsibilities of investigation and protection (Frequently Asked Questions, 2012).

Once training is complete, agents will be assigned to a major city field office for their first six to eight years to begin investigative work. After their field experience, agents usually are transferred to a protective detail where they will stay for three to five years. After protective details agents may return to their field office, or headquarters. There is also an opportunity to be transferred overseas (Frequently Asked Questions, 2012). The work of a special agent in the Secret Service can be difficult. The agency informs potential hires that the job has risk and requires stamina and sacrificing personal life. Agents frequently move, travel, train extensively, must be highly professional at all times and work demanding hours. It is a challenging career that must be discussed thoroughly with family before accepting the position (Melanson & Stevens, 2002).

Applicants for a position in the Uniformed Division must be at least 21 years of age and younger than 40 at the time of appointment, and have a high school diploma or equivalent. The requirements are less rigid than those for a special agent, however candidates for a position in the Uniformed Division must undergo a thorough background check and obtain a top-secret clearance, pass a written exam, polygraph, fitness test, and medical exam. The tasks of a Uniformed Division officer do not involve investigations like those of a special agent. New appointees also attend the Federal Law Enforcement Training Center in Glynco, Georgia for 12 weeks followed by a 12-week specialized training session at the Secret Service's training facilities outside Washington, D.C. (Frequently Asked Questions, 2012). The Uniformed Division is often referred to as a specialized police force charged with protecting the grounds of the White House main complex, the residence of the vice president, and the U.S. Treasury Building among other designated facilities. The Uniformed Division employs the use of specialized teams such as Countersniper, Canine Explosive Detection Team, and Emergency Response Team (Frequently Asked Questions, 2012).

The third career path within the Secret Service is in Administrative, Professional, and Technical. The basic requirements for applicants for each position is being a U.S. citizen, passing a drug test, qualifying for a top-secret clearance, and undergoing a complete background investigation. The experience and educational requirements vary by the specific position category. For example, within the administrative category there are accounting technicians, human resources, secretarial, and investigative assistants. Professional and scientific positions for the Secret Service such as accountant, architect, attorney, chemist, and research psychologist requires knowledge in the appropriate professional or scientific field and applicants must possess a bachelor's degree or higher depending on the position. Finally, there are technical positions within the Secret Service that provide direct support to professional or administrative personnel through a variety of fields. Individuals working in technical positions typically possess practical knowledge or have specialized skills developed from work experience, and include photographers, fingerprint and document analysts, and telecommunications specialists (Employment Opportunities, 2012).

Functions

The United States Secret Service began with a straightforward mandate to pursue counterfeiters and protect the nation's currency. While these functions remain, the agency took on more responsibilities and directives that would require an evolving structure and expand the number of specialist and support personnel, most notably in the wake of the terrorist attacks on 9/11. Within these challenging times, the basic functions of the Secret Service have revolved around two areas to carry out their missions — criminal investigation and protection.

Criminal Investigation

As discussed earlier, the original mission of the Secret Service was to investigate counterfeiting in the United States. Yet, throughout the agency's early history agents would probe crimes outside of the financial system including investigations of the Ku Klux Klan in the 1860s, and engage in counter-espionage activities in the United States during World War I (Reese, 2011). Since 1984, Secret Service investigative responsibilities have been increased to include financial institution fraud, computer and telecommunications fraud, false identification documents, ATM access fraud, and money laundering. The Secret Service has jurisdiction over violations involving the counterfeiting of United States currency and coins, but also investigates fraud and counterfeiting revolving around treasury checks, food coupons including Electronic Benefit Transfer, postage stamps, and savings bonds. This wide range of protected items requires cooperation with local law enforcement and other federal agencies (Investigative Missions, 2011).

After the attacks on 9/11, President Bush signed into law the USA PATRIOT Act, in which the U.S. Secret Service was mandated to establish a nationwide network of Electronic Crimes Task Forces (ECTFs). These task forces bring together federal, state, and local law enforcement, as well as legal professionals, private industry, and academicians for the common purposes of prevention, detection, mitigation and aggressive investigation of electronic attacks on the nation's financial and critical infrastructures. Examples of these actions would be unauthorized access to protected computers, theft of data such as personal identification for the purpose of committing identity theft, the denial of service attacks used for extortion or disruption of e-commerce, and malware and viruses used for monetary gain (Investigative Missions, 2011).

The Secret Service also maintains an accredited advanced forensic laboratory, which includes the world's largest ink library and advanced fingerprint identification center. The agency also has one of the premiere polygraph programs in the country with highly trained personnel who are experts in the psychology of deception and employ cutting edge technology to assist investigations. The laboratory also examines questioned documents, performs voice identification, conducts forensic photography, provides audio/image enhancement, and uses 3-D modeling and simulation. These services have all become extremely important as the majority (63%) of counterfeit currency is produced digitally today as compared to less than 1% fifteen years ago (United States Secret Service, 2010).

These proactive approaches to prevention and investigation have led to notable national and international apprehensions of criminals and the dismantling of organizations that threaten the financial security and safety of the United States. In FY 2010, the Secret Service made 3,028 total domestic and foreign arrests for counterfeiting offenses and helped to remove more than $261 million in counterfeit U.S. currency from circulation. The Secret Service is also involved in international operations such as Vetted Anti-Counterfeiting Forces (VACF) in Colombia. Columbia is one of the largest producers of counterfeit U.S. currency in the world, and the operation has seized approximately $263 million in counterfeit U.S. currency, made nearly 700 arrests, suppressed more than 110 counterfeit printing plants, and reduced the amount of Colombia-origin fake currency by 72% (United States Secret Service, 2010).

The agency has also conducted successful investigations outside of their traditional mandate of anti-counterfeiting. In February 2012, government anti-fraud software alerted Secret Service investigators of possible illegal use of the food stamp benefits. A Santa Fe Dollar Discount Store sold non-food items to food stamp customers while overcharging their Electronic Benefit Transfer (EBT) cards and taking a large cut of the cash proceeds. The alert resulted in the Secret Service dispatching an undercover agent who conducted multiple EBT cash transactions totaling hundreds of dollars. The store would typically take a $50 fee for providing a food stamp customer with $100 in cash racking up more than $2 million in illegal sales between 2009 and the first quarter of 2011. A civil suit was filed and the storeowner's bank account was liquidated as restitution (Warren, 2012).

In August 2010 an investigation led by the Secret Service's Cyber Intelligence Section, with key assistance from international authorities led to the arrest of Vladislav Anatolieviech Horohorin, of Moscow, Russia, as an alleged co-founder of one of the most sophisticated carding forums, and the first and only fully-automated card information online vending site. Horohorin was one of the founders of CarderPlanet, one of several websites taken down in 2004 as part of the Secret Service's Operation Firewall investigation, and operated by cyber criminal organizations to traffic counterfeit credit cards, false identification information, and documents (Press Releases, 2012).

For more than fifteen years the United States Secret Service has been investigating mortgage fraud under their most recent task force "Operation Stolen Dreams." Mortgage fraud is viewed as a threat to the financial security of the United States and its citizens. To date Operation Stolen Dreams resulted in the arrests of 485 individuals associated with fraud totaling $2.3 billion. The USSS continues to enhance their investigations in creative ways. For example, the agency has formed the Electronic Crimes Special Agent Program (ECSAP) to deal with more threats from cyber-criminals. The program provides 1,300 special agents with specialized training to conduct forensic examinations on electronic evidence obtained from computers and other devices (United States Secret Service, 2010).

Protection Details

While the mandated mission of securing the nation's currency provided the impetus for creating the United States Secret Service, it is the secondary mission of protection that has made the agency one of the most respected in the world. From part-time protection of President Grover Cleveland in 1894 to constant protection of the current president, the protection mission of the Secret Service has expanded to cover a diverse group of individuals, and evolved to face new threats for more than a century.

Currently the Secret Service is authorized to provide protection for:

- The president, the vice president (or other individuals next in order of succession to the Office of the President).
- The president-elect and vice president-elect.
- The immediate families of the above individuals.
- Former presidents and their spouses for their lifetimes, except when the spouse remarries (presidents, elected after 1997, and their spouses are given protection for a period of not more than 10 years from the date the former president leaves office).
- Children of former presidents until age 16.
- Visiting heads of foreign states or governments and their spouses traveling with them.
- Other distinguished foreign visitors to the United States and official representatives of the United States performing special missions abroad as directed by the president.
- Major presidential and vice presidential candidates and their spouses within 120 days of a general presidential election.
- Other individuals as designated by the president (United States Secret Service, 2010).

Protection missions today have moved beyond what could be viewed as simply bodyguard details and now include advanced security visits, intelligence analysis, and threat assessments that employ skilled agents working in coordination with numerous agencies. Protection is a mission that is complex and commands most of the agency's resources. In fiscal year 2010 the protection mission of the Secret Service received 58% of the agency's funding and employed 73% of its full-time equivalents (Reese, 2011). Consider the following highlights of the agency's activities during 2010. The Secret Service:

- Provided protection for former presidents and spouses for a combined total of 1,674 stops and 2,964 calendar days;
- Provided protection during 3,926 travel stops for domestic protectees and 2,492 travel stops for visiting foreign dignitaries;
- Coordinated protective measures for 1,167 visits of foreign heads of state/governments and spouses to the U.S.;
- Screened approximately 2.2 million pieces of mail (letters, flats, and parcels) at the White House Mail Screening Facility; and
- Provided protection in more than 460 visits to various foreign locations and conducted protective security advances and other protection-related support for 482 overseas surveys (United States Secret Service, 2010).

Protective details are comprised of special agents who have paid their dues through investigative fieldwork and have risen through the ranks. Special agents are assigned protective duty on a three-to-five year rotation in an effort to reduce stress and prevent burnout. While there are many protective details, it is the presidential detail that has fascinated the public. Agents typically work eight-hour shifts to provide around the clock protection for permanent protectees like the United States president and vice president. Agents assigned to protect the president must strike a balance between security and sensitivity to the needs of the first family. Agents must allow some freedoms, but reminding the parties that security and safety is the Secret Service's primary mission, and the agency can overrule a president.

The Secret Service does not publically describe specific details of protection operations and methods. However, some basic information exists on how a detail operates in the field. There are typically four to five advance teams that work for the president, vice president, and their wives. Advanced site visits are critical for protection details and the Secret Service wants at least a week to conduct reconnaissance and plan the event. Nonetheless, the reality of politics sometimes results in short notices and changes requiring a frenzy of activity from the agency. Presidential travel presents much more of a challenge to the Secret Service than protection at the White House. When the president or other permanent protectees are on the move in limousines, helicopters, or Air Force One, planning is of the utmost importance. Agents also spend time reviewing photos and reports of dangerous persons in the area. The trip file may contain up to 100 names (Melanson & Stevens, 2002).

All routes the presidential limousine may take must be assessed, entry points controlled, traffic restricted, alternate routes chosen, and local hospitals and emergency medical sites must be selected. Agents survey all buildings along the route and deploy counter-sniper teams. Every room in a building the president will occupy is searched for electronic devices, bombs, toxins and fire hazards. After John Hinckley's attempted assassination of President Reagan, special agents have paid close attention to rope-lines where the president meets and greets the public often staying right by the president's side with a hand ready to pull them to safety. Secret Service agents also spend a great deal of time checking the credentials of reporters, and scrutinizing everyone who may come into close contact with the president at events.

Special Agents typically try to maintain an area surrounding the protectee known as a zone of security. While agents prefer to maintain a zone the size of a football field, realistically the zone may only be several feet given the nature of politics and the president's desire to meet and greet citizens. This 360-degree zone gives agents a chance to prevent an attack or in Secret Service terms absorb the shock so the results will not be tragic (Melanson, 2002). In the wake of the terrorist attacks of 9/11 the mission of protecting the president and other designated individuals has become even more complex. New threats have emerged that Secret Service agents must now consider. The use of toxic gases, biological weapons, rocket propelled grenades, and improvised explosive devices are all real weapons that may be in the arsenal of a would-be attacker. Although protection details cannot realistically prepare for every contingency, these are real possibilities for an assassination attempt and have created significant changes to protection details and White House security.

High profile approaches and attempted attacks on the president have been studied and serve as training tools for Secret Service agents. Within the context of this heightened awareness and security after 9/11 even the smallest written, spoken, or published possible threat against the president may come under the investigation of the Secret Service. For example, in 2012 seven teenagers in Arizona posed for a photo in which they were holding a bullet-riddled T-shirt featuring President Obama's face. The photo was then posted on a local police officer's Facebook page. The officer did not feel this was a threat against the president, but the Secret Service chose to investigate the incident after several blogs and posts about the picture surfaced (Newcomb, 2012). In 2011, a Carson, California city councilman posted racists comments and a call to assassinate President Obama on his Facebook page after Obama signed the National Defense Authorization Act. News spread and three Secret Service agents visited the councilman, searched his home and vehicle, and interviewed his family to assess his potential to carry out the act (Mazza, 2011). In short, no matter how large or small a threat may appear to be, the Secret Service considers all possible actions against any of its protectees, and every one must be investigated to determine the validity and ability of the individual or group to carry out an attack.

Protecting the infrastructure of a country requires addressing numerous risks. Attacks on physical targets in a nation can be devastating, and threats against a country's currency and leadership may have equally disastrous consequences. The United States Secret Service began with a single mission of protecting the currency of the nation from counterfeiters nearly 150 years ago. This mission expanded to include one of the agency's most high profile and critical duties — protection of the president. While the public has become accustomed to seeing special agents surrounding the president, direct information on protective duties are kept confidential. In general, the United States Secret Service does not publish trends nor absolute numbers of threats against its protectees, in part because doing so may reveal the agency's investigative network and techniques, and there is a concern that publishing the nature of threats may give ideas to individuals and terrorist groups. As the agency points out, the public is often aware of their failures because they are so shocking and out of their control. However, they have numerous successes that the public will never know about. Stopping major counterfeiters is newsworthy, yet major threats are assessed and stopped nearly every day without public notice. The United States Secret Service is an agency unlike any other federal law enforcement organization. At its headquarters in Washington, D.C., uniformed guards protect the entrances, there are no tours, and public access is virtually non-existent for outsiders. It is an agency that values secrecy and security and is willing to evolve to take on new missions in some of the most challenging times the country has faced.

References

Bumgarner, J. (2006). *Federal agents: the growth of federal law enforcement in America.* Westport, CT: Greenwood Publishing Group.

Bureau of Engraving and Printing (2011). Annual production figures. Retrieved from http://moneyfactory.gov/uscurrency/annualproductionfigures.html.

Department of Homeland Security (2011). *FY 2012 budget in brief.* Washington, D.C. Employment Opportunities. (2012). Retrieved from http://www.secretservice.gov/join/index.shtml.

Frequently Asked Questions (2012). Retrieved from http://www.secretservice.gov/faq.shtml.

Gaines, A. (2001). *The U.S. Secret Service.* New York: Infobase Publishing.

Holden, H. (2006). *To be a U.S. Secret Service agent.* Minneapolis, MN: Zenith Press.

Investigative Missions (2011). Retrieved from http://www.secretservice.gov/investigations.shtml.

Jones, M. (2011). *History of criminal justice.* New York: Elsevier.

Kessler, R. (2010). *In the President's secret service: Behind the scenes with agents in the line of fire and the presidents they protect.* New York: Random House Inc.

McPherson, J. (2003). *Battle cry of freedom: the Civil War era.* New York: Oxford University Press.

Mazza, S. (2011). Secret Service investigating Carson man for making threats against Obama on Facebook. Retrieved from http://www.dailybreeze.com/news/ci_19586022.

Melanson, P., and Stevens, P. (2002). *The Secret Service: The hidden history of an enigmatic agency.* New York: Carrol & Graf Publishers.

Melanson, P. (2005). *The Secret Service: The hidden history of an enigmatic agency 2nd Ed.* New York: Basic Books.

Newcomb, A. (2012). Bullet-ridden Obama shirt sparks investigation. Retrieved from http://abcnews.go.com/blogs/headlines/2012/01/bullet-ridden-obama-shirt-sparks-investigation/.

Oliver, W., and Marion, N. (2010). *Killing the President: assassinations, attempts, and rumored attempts on U.S. commanders-in-chief.* Santa Barbara, CA: ABC-CLIO.

Press Releases (2012). Retrieved from http://www.secretservice.gov/press_release.shtml.

Reese, S. (2011). The United States Secret Service: An examination and analysis of its evolving missions. In K. Sayers (Ed.) *The U.S. Secret Service: Background, missions, and issues.* New York: Nova Sciences Publishers Inc.

Secret Service History (2011). Retrieved from http://www.secretservice.gov/history.shtml.

Special Agents (2012). Retrieved from http://www.secretservice.gov/whoweare_sa.shtml.

United States Secret Service (2008). *Fiscal year 2008 annual report.* Washington, D.C.

United States Secret Service (2010). *Fiscal year 2010 annual report.* Washington, D.C.

Warren, G. (2012). Small market racked up $2 million in food stamp charges. Retrieved from http://www.news10.net/news/local/article/179253/2/Food-stamp-fraud-probe-targets-Modesto-area-market.

Chapter Ten

Federal Air Marshal Service

Air transportation, like any other critical piece of infrastructure in a nation, is vital for the free movement of citizens, commerce, and government. In a country like the United States, air travel is no longer a luxury for the elite; it is a heavily utilized mode of transportation. According to the Bureau of Transportation Statistics, in 2011 more than 600 million Americans boarded domestic flights, averaging more than 1.7 million passengers day, in addition to nearly 20 billion pounds of freight and mail (Transtats, 2012). The sheer volume and importance of air travel in the United States combined with the complex mechanics and vulnerable nature of an aircraft makes safety and security of passengers and cargo of the utmost importance. As commercial air travel expanded in America and abroad, acts of sabotage and hijackings were soon to follow proving that attacks on airlines could be proportionally more deadly than other forms of violence.

History

Airport and airline security are facts of life for travel in America today and most modern nations across the globe. While these procedures may feel like nuisances at times, the use of these techniques were born out of the realities and tragedies in the history of commercial flight. The heavy demand for the use of air travel and increased criminal activity and terrorist attacks on air space have all pointed to the need for additional airline security. The first recorded airplane hijacking took place in 1931 in Peru, as rebels attempted to take command of a mail plane in order to distribute propaganda fliers. Although the pilot refused, he was later forced to fly one of the rebels to the city of Lima (Price & Forrest, 2009).

While hijackings were relatively rare events, the pace of such actions would increase during the Cold War as citizens from Eastern European nations viewed seizing an airplane as a means to escape oppression (Elias, 2010). Between 1947 and 1953 there were 23 hijackings worldwide, most involved Europeans seeking political asylum. By 1967, there were 12 attempted, and seven successful hijackings in the United States (Price & Forrest, 2009). These events would give impetus for adding a new level of security to airlines. However, security procedures were already in place for aircraft carrying U.S. mail. Regulations required couriers and pilots to be armed. In 1954, a 15-year old boy stormed the cockpit of an American Airlines flight demanding to be flown to Mexico City, and the captain drew his regulation required .380 pistol from his flight bag and killed the teenager (Moore, 2001).

Prior to the 1960s hijackings were rare events in the United States, but the late 1960s and 1970s would lead the country in a new direction. This time period may be viewed as the dawn of the age of terrorist attacks on airlines. Hijackings were becoming standard operating procedure for radical groups in the Middle East who were using this tactic as a bargaining tool to gain the release of their compatriots from prisons or to bring attention to their causes. Hijacking was becoming a dangerous gambit as confrontations often resulted in shootouts between the hijackers and local police, the FBI, and military. While few in number, some hijackings did end with negotiation and safe passage of the hijackers to a country that would not let them be extradited. In 1961, the first hijacking from the United States to Cuba took place as Antuilo Ortiz used a gun and forced a plane to divert from Miami to Havana (Price & Forrest, 2009).

Hijackings as a New International Threat

During the 1960s there was tension between the United States and Cuba, and Cubans began hijacking planes to escape from Castro's regime and seek asylum in America. By the late 1960s and early 1970s, the trend had reversed and hijackers in the United States were forcing pilots to take them to Cuba to seek asylum. This trend peaked in 1969 at a rate of more than one every two weeks. By 1973 over 100 hijackers were believed to be in Cuba (Elias, 2010). Hijacking a plane to escape oppression or to reach freedom was a dominant motive during this time period. However in the 1970s a frightening shift in attacks against aircraft during the jet age began.

On March 17, 1970 a passenger aboard an Eastern Airlines flight from Newark, New Jersey to Boston, Massachusetts entered the cockpit of the aircraft with a firearm and shot First Officer James Hartley in the chest, then ordered the crew to continue flying over the ocean until fuel no longer remained and the plane crashed. Despite suffering a mortal gunshot First Officer James Hartley managed to disarm John DiVivo and shot him. Captain Robert Wilbur Jr. was also shot by the suicide hijacker, yet still managed to land the plane safely (Moore, 1976).

In 1972, three desperate men armed with guns and a hand grenade hijacked a Memphis-to-Miami-flight during a layover in Birmingham Alabama. The hijackers had an apparent grudge against the city of the Detroit in which they had pending criminal charges, and they demanded $10 million ransom from the city, 10 parachutes, 10 bulletproof vests, and told the pilots to fly north. The hijackers set a deadline of 1 pm and told the pilot to begin circling the site of the Y-12 nuclear weapons plant and nuclear research reactor at the Oak Ridge National Laboratory. The hijackers threatened to crash the plane into the nuclear facility. The airline offered $2 million in ransom to the hijackers. The threat to the Oak Ridge Facility was over, and the plane landed for the money exchange. The plane was forced to Orlando, Florida to refuel, and was surrounded by the FBI who shot out the plane's tires. The hijackers forced the pilot to take them to Cuba. Upon landing in Havana, Fidel Castro promptly had the hijackers imprisoned and ultimately returned to the United States for lengthy prison terms. The 31 hostages were held for 29 hours and were unharmed, with the exception of the first officer who suffered a gunshot wound to his arm (Mansfield, 2001).

In 1974, Samuel Byck, a manic-depressive who had once been arrested for threatening President Nixon, attempted to board a Delta Airlines flight out of the Baltimore-Washington airport bound for Atlanta. An airport security guard was checking passengers with a metal detector. As Byck walked past him, he turned and fired three rounds from his .38 caliber revolver into the guard's back. Byck stormed the plane and entered the cockpit, demanding that the pilots take off. When the pilots refused, Byck held his gun to the head of a female passenger. The pilots refused again, and Byck shot both the pilot and co-pilot. He took another female hostage and forced her to watch while he shot the pilots several more times. An off-duty police officer in the terminal pulled his firearm and fired two shots through the terminal windows into the cockpit striking Byck in the chest. Byck then took his own life. Upon further investigation authorities discovered Byck's briefcase contained a gas bomb and his notes on the operation he planned to carryout. The purpose of his hijacking was to take command of the plane while in flight and crash it into the White House (Piszkiewicz, 2003).

This particular hijacking represented a scenario that had been considered by security experts, that is the use of an airplane as a weapon. Byck clearly understood that a fully fueled jet plane was a powerful missile and could be directed at any target. There were some critical lessons learned during the wave of hijackings in the 1960s and 1970s as the purpose and conditions of the crimes changed. Hijackers were typically small in numbers and used firearms, explosives, or threats of explosives to take over an aircraft. Hijackings were often handled by law enforcement in a direct manner such as shooting out the plane's tires or firing on the hijackers. Another important lesson was that once airborne, a plane was a moving crime scene with lethal potential to destroy land targets, other aircraft, or leave the jurisdiction of the United States.

Emerging Threats to Airline Security

While hijackings were prolific during the 1960s and early 1970s, and were clearly terrifying events, other threats to airline safety were also major concerns, particularly the use of explosives against an aircraft in flight. In 1933 the first reported bombing of a mid-air flight in the United States occurred on a United Airlines flight between Cleveland Ohio and Chicago Illinois. A nitroglycerin explosive device with a timer destroyed the Boeing 247 aircraft killing all seven on board. A motive was never uncovered and there were no arrests or prosecutions for the murders (Price & Forrest, 2009).

The 1950s and 1960s also contained a rash of bombings for insurance fraud, murder, and suicide. For example, in 1955 a bomb destroyed a United Airlines plane shortly after departing Denver Colorado, killing all 38 passengers and five crew members. John Gilbert Graham was later convicted and executed for the crime—his motive was to kill his mother who was a passenger. In 1962, a Continental Airlines flight in route to Kansas City was destroyed over the state of Missouri. An investigation revealed that a bomb had been detonated in the rear lavatory. Evidence pointed to a passenger named Thomas Doty. Federal Aviation Investigators and the FBI surmised that Doty had studied books on the use of explosives and purchased dynamite. He carried the bomb in his briefcase, and detonated it causing the rear tail section to break away and the crash that killed all 45 on board.

Doty was a married man with a young child. He was facing criminal prosecution and had purchased a large life insurance policy to cover his family's expenses—essentially committing suicide and mass murder for profit (Felt & Connor, 2006). As shocking as these incidents were there would not be changes in security procedures in airports and on aircraft until years later. Passengers entered airports and boarded planes without any security screening, and baggage remained vulnerable. However these hard learned lessons would eventually lead to action.

The Temporary Federal Response to Airline Security and Lessons Learned From Dawson's Field

The many high profile attacks on aircraft in the United States would lead to several important responses from the federal government. The roots of the Federal Air Marshals

Program would begin in 1961 under President Kennedy in partial response to Antuilo Ortiz's use of a gun to force the National Airlines jet to fly to Cuba. President Kennedy ordered armed law enforcement officers to accompany key flights at the request of airlines or the FBI. Kennedy's administration insisted that all airplane cockpit doors be locked, and the U.S. Congress approved legislation mandating a 20-year prison sentence or the death penalty for hijacking an aircraft (Price & Forrest, 2009).

These responses, including the informal and occasional sky marshal force, would prove inadequate in the light of the Dawson's Field hijackings that would soon unsettle numerous nations and usher in the modern era of armed airline security. In the late 1960s one of the leading terrorist groups targeting airlines was the Popular Front for the Liberation of Palestine (PFLP). The PFLP felt as though their cause and grievances were being ignored on the global stage and found that hijackings and taking hostages would gain immediate media exposure. On September 6, 1970 PFLP teams attempted five separate hijackings, two of which were outbound from European cities to New York: TWA Flight 741 and Swissair Flight 100. Each was hijacked and forced to land at an abandoned British airbase known as Dawson's Field in Jordan (O'Connell & Williams, 2011).

One of the five hijackings, the Pan Am Flight was taken to Cairo, Egypt and moments after the plane landed and passengers were removed, the aircraft was destroyed with a bomb. One of the other attempted hijackings—on an Israeli airline—was thwarted by crew, passengers, and an armed Israeli guard on board who shot and killed one of the hijackers and subdued his accomplice Leila Khaled. Three days later a fifth aircraft was hijacked out of Bahrain and forced to land at Dawson's Field for use in bargaining for the release of Khaled. The hijackers issued ultimatums demanding their comrade's freedom in exchange for the more than 300 hostages. By September 12, most hostages had been released with the exception of Jewish passengers, airline crew, military personnel, and government officials. The hostages were taken to secret locations and PFLP explosives destroyed the airplanes. All of the hostages were later released in exchange for Khaled and other PFLP compatriots (Price & Forrest, 2009).

The Dawson's Field hijackings were viewed worldwide, transfixed Americans, and revealed several important facts and lessons for the future of airline security:

- Hijackings may no longer be just one or two fringe individuals, but could involve a coordinated effort from groups working in teams.
- Hijackings could involve multiple airlines, countries of origin, and destinations.
- The hazard to aviation was not restricted to one country but represented a worldwide threat—no one and no country was safe.
- Groups learned that hijackings as a tactic for extortion or political ends were extremely effective.

From these key observations and painful lessons, the United States would now have to revisit the security of aircraft, airports, and passengers in earnest as the stakes were simply too high to have an informal approach.

The Creation of the Air Marshals Program

During the midst of the PFLP hijackings President Nixon held a brief press conference outlining the U.S. government's plan to combat hijackings. Nixon pointed out that piracy is not a new challenge to countries of the world, and as the nations dealt with piracy on the seas, they must also deal with piracy in the skies today (Smith, 1970). The plan outlined by the president was based on establishing armed guards on high-risk flights, increased inspections and screenings of passengers, tougher penalties for hijackings, and extradition treaties to bring hijackers to justice (291—Statement Announcing, 1970). In 1968 a temporary force of Federal Aviation sky marshals was already in place while plans for the new sky marshals program were being developed. Congress authorized temporary funding for two years, and by the fall of 1970 the U.S. Customs Air Security Officers Program—better known as the Sky Marshals—was launched.

The new program was estimated to cost $50 million per year, and in late fall of 1970 nearly 1,800 recruits for the new Sky Marshals Program began training at Fort Belvoir Virginia in a four week course taught by the United States Secret Service (U.S. To Train, 1971). These new sky marshals were to be the first line of defense and protection on key flights. The exact coverage of flights by armed officers was never made public, and shortly after the announcement of both the temporary and new permanent sky marshal force, hijackings in the United States decreased. At the outset of the Sky Marshal Program there were questions about the effectiveness of this force. While hijackings did decrease after their creation it was difficult to determine to what degree the marshals were a deterrent. Landes (1978) provided an early quantitative assessment of the reduction of hijackings during the 1970s and found that three factors were the most influential—passenger screening created the largest reduction at 45%, the sky marshals contributed to a 28% decline, and the extradition treaty with Cuba created a 9% decline in hijackings.

This reduction of hijackings led to feelings of safety and complacency. However, criticisms of the program remained. The newly appointed Assistant Secretary of Transportation Lt. General Benjamin Davis (ret.) referred to the sky marshal force as a costly and ambitious program with some results. Davis pointed out there were roughly 1,500 sky marshals to provide protection for 500,000 passengers each day on 15,000 flights out of 500 airports. He argued that this was a program that couldn't work and couldn't last. Davis felt that the program was risky and at best a stopgap measure until better procedures and approaches could be developed such as behavioral profiling (Mason, 1972). Ultimately, the decreased number of hijackings, federal aviation laws that increased airport security, and increased passenger screening procedures all led to scaling back the number of sky marshals, a trend that would continue through the 1980s (Elias, 2010).

While the number of sky marshals was declining from the 1970s through the early 1980s, a number of devastating airline attacks and exploitations of security lapses occurred. A new era of hijackings emerged in the 1980s with new techniques and objectives. One new technique was passengers stating they possessed explosives and would destroy the aircraft when in fact they did not have actually have them. Others moved away from explosives like dynamite and began using flammable liquids such as rubbing alcohol and gasoline, spreading the chemicals and threatening to ignite them (Price & Forrest, 2009). Interestingly, hijackings to Cuba returned during the 1980s in partial response the Mariel Boatlift, with a total of 17 between 1983 and 1985. Hijackers during this period employed some of these new methods including the use of flare guns, starter pistols, and knives (U.S. Congress, 2004).

Terrorism and Airline Security

Despite the creation of the Sky Marshals Program and enhanced penalties for hijackings, terrorist organizations realized the vulnerable nature of aircraft and airport security and more high profile incidents began to occur, ushering in a new wave of violence. On June

14, 1985 Lebanese terrorists hijacked TWA Flight 847 en route from Athens to Rome and held 153 passengers and the crew hostage. The aircraft was diverted to Beirut where an unprecedented level of violence unfolded. The terrorists demanded fuel and began beating several of the passengers so their cries could be heard over the radio to force officials to comply. The terrorist demanded the release of hundreds of Shia Muslims being held by Israel. To prove the seriousness of their intentions, passenger and U.S. Navy Petty Officer Robert Stethem was tortured, publicly executed, and his body thrown onto the tarmac.

Jewish passengers were handed over to members of Hezbollah while ten additional gunmen boarded the plane. The plane departed for Algiers and returned to Beirut, staying on the move and making a military assault nearly impossible. By June 16th the terrorists had fled the plane and transferred the remaining hostages to the Amal militia where they would remain for more than two weeks in several locations around Beirut. International negotiations involving several countries would eventually secure the hostages' release (Teitelbaum, 1987). Only one of the terrorists was captured and sentenced to life in prison in Germany. Mohammed Ali Hamadei would eventually be paroled and allowed to enter Lebanon; he remains on the FBI's most wanted list (Elias, 2010).

The immediate response from the United States government to this international incident was to pass the International Security and Development Cooperation Act of 1985. The Act outlined treaties and policies for handling terrorism and assisting foreign nations. However, the most relevant part of the act for this discussion was the mandate for the FAA to study options for an expanded air marshals program on international flights of U.S. airlines. The act provided the statutory basis for the FAA Air Marshal Program and authorized air marshals to carry firearms aboard planes, make arrests without warrants for crimes against the United States committed in their presence and for felonies they reasonably believed had been committed. Furthermore, the act created new regulations requiring all scheduled carriers and public charter operators to carry air marshals on a priority basis, provide seating selected by the marshals, and do so without charge (Wells & Rodriquez, 2004).

Security did improve during the 1980s, most notably with international flights. However, there were incidents that pointed out the flaws in domestic flight security, including lapses in control of airport access credentials that would allow individuals to bypass screening, and several high profile aircraft bombings. The federal government conducted additional evaluations, and passed acts related to airline security mainly focusing on screening cargo, airport personnel, and increased detection technology. The spending on airport and aircraft security increased tremendously and while these would add to the safety of air travel, the 1990s proved to be a decade of failure and inadequate preparation all leading up to the events of September 11, 2001 (when hijackings were essentially forgotten and viewed as an issue of the past).

Four teams of al-Qaeda trained hijackers carried out the 9/11 attacks. Each team consisted of five hijackers including one trained in basic piloting. The hijackers killed the crew of American Airlines Flight 11 and flew the jet plane into the north tower of the World Trade Center (WTC) in New York City. Fifteen minutes later hijackers crashed United Airlines Flight 175 into the south tower of the WTC. Hijackers aboard the third aircraft, American Airlines Flight 77, crashed into the Pentagon. The fourth airplane, United Airline Flight 93 only had a team of four hijackers aboard. As the reality of the situation was revealed to the passengers aboard the flight, they fought back resulting in the aircraft crashing into a field in Pennsylvania rather than the intended target of the White House. Nearly 3,000 people lost their lives in this coordinated hijacking. The United States was completely unprepared on numerous fronts (Price & Forrest, 2009).

The tragic events brought about a new round of evaluations and changes to the federal government and airline security. Among the many changes and improvements was a closer look at the Federal Air Marshal Service. The FAMS had been slowly whittled down over the years with the shift towards technology and screening. According to the 9/11 Commission Report, at the time of the September 11th hijackings there were only 33 armed and trained air marshals, none of whom were deployed on domestic flights except when they were international departures from the United States. The lack of additional marshals reflected the view that hijackings where not a domestic concern (National Commission on Terrorism, 2004).

One of the key government responses to the 9/11 attacks was the passage of the Aviation and Transportation Security Act of 2001 (ATSA). The act focused on preventing another attack of this magnitude through a multilayered approach to airline security including increasing the size of the Federal Air Marshal Service. The actions aboard the hijacked aircraft during 9/11 demonstrated the need for an armed law enforcement presence, and President George W. Bush ordered the rapid expansion of the FAMS. After the passage of the ATSA more than 200,000 applications were received by the FAMS and several thousand qualified recruits were hired (Our Mission, 2012). The ATSA also created the Transportation Security Administration, which was moved in 2003 to the newly created Department of Homeland Security subsequent to the Homeland Security Act of 2002. In 2003 the FAMS was moved to Immigration and Customs Enforcement (ICE) for what was viewed as a multi-front approach to anti-terrorism. There was a surge in personnel to secure the borders and air space of the United States. The FAMS was moved back to TSA in 2005. Today the revamped Federal Air Marshal Service serves as the primary law enforcement entity within the Transportation Security Administration and is deployed on flights in the United States and around the world.

Organization and Personnel

The Federal Air Marshal Service is a critical component within the overall mission of the Transportation Security Administration and the Department of Homeland Security. The FAMS headquarters is in the TSA Freedom Center in Herndon, Virginia and is housed within the Office of Law Enforcement, which is headed by an assistant administrator who also serves as the director of the FAMS. The deputy director of the FAMS also serves as the deputy assistant administrator of the Office of Law Enforcement. Since 9/11 the Federal Air Marshal Service has grown from one office to 25 separate field offices. Field office locations and staffing are based on intelligence, concept of operations (the approach the FAMS uses to determine which flights will receive air marshal coverage), and proximity to airports (Department of Homeland Security, 2012). Each field office is managed by a supervisory agent in charge (SAC) who oversees planning, direction, and coordination of operations and is aided by an assistant supervisory agent in charge (ASAC).

The Federal Air Marshal Service has been in the process of streamlining its organization and has moved from five separate directorates to three with all remaining functions from the former Administrative and Technical Services, and Training and Workforce Programs directorates transferred to the appropriate TSA divisions. All supporting elements transferred to the Business Management Office. The remaining FAMS directorates are:

- Security Services and Assessments Division—Oversees and engages in critical tasks for the Federal Air Marshal Service such as the National Explosives Detection Canine Team Program (NEDCTP), mitigating man-portable air defense systems (MANPADS), conducting airport security and vulnerability assessments, and giving attention to emerging missions such as the Insider Threat Section that will enable TSA to better identify and mitigate risks posed by individuals with inside knowledge or access to the transportation system.

- Field Operations Division—Contains four distinct branches with unique operations, three of the branches are responsible for overseeing supervisory air marshals in charge (SACs) for the 25 Field Offices and the fourth manages all other field-related law enforcement programs. The Law Enforcement Programs Branch contains three sections—Visible Intermodal Prevention and Response (VIPR)/Joint Co-ordination Center, Tactical Support, and Law Enforcement Information Coordination. Finally, the newly created Tactical Support Section is composed of operational elements that sustain Field Office operational functions.

This recent streamlining and restructuring of the FAMS in 2011 was done for several purposes: (1) to be consistent and work in coordination with other TSA operational components, (2) to have a field centered approach so field offices and supervisors can focus on emerging threats and trends, and (3) to promote professionalism. The emphasis on promoting professionalism came to light after accusations of racism, sexism, and homophobia within the FAMS. The hope is that this new structure will lay the foundation for greater oversight and direction from headquarters and positive change in the workplace (Testimony of Robert Bray, 2012).

The Transportation Security Administration has more than 50,000 employees working in a variety of positions including security officers, inspectors, directors, managers, and air marshals. The Federal Air Marshal Service operates on a budget of nearly $1 billion and contains several key positions to help carry out their mission. Within the FAMS there are intelligence, information technology, instructor, and mission support positions, and federal air marshals. FAMS intelligence positions involve the collection, analysis, evaluation and dissemination of foreign and domestic intelligence as well as threat warning information. FAMS information technology personnel focus on the development, deployment, and maintenance of cutting edge technology for federal law enforcement agencies and the aviation industry. Civilian instructors in the FAMS provide specialized law enforcement training to federal air marshals.

Mission support personnel covers a wide range of professional and technical positions that operate in a variety of areas, such as intelligence research, mission operations, medical records, and human resources. Other positions include attorneys, management analysts, and medical professional as well as secretarial and administrative. Finally, there is the critical frontline and best-known position of Federal Air Marshal Service—air marshals. The exact number of federal air marshals is classified information, but the best estimates from different sources reveal there are between 2,500 and 4,000 air marshals (Meuller & Stewart, 2011). Air marshals are armed federal law enforcement officers who are deployed on American passenger flights worldwide to protect airline passengers and crew against the risk of criminal and terrorist violence (Federal Air Marshal Service Careers, 2012).

Becoming a Federal Air Marshal

Applicants for the position of air marshal must be between the ages of 21 and 37. Waivers can be made for the upper age limit if the applicant can show prior service in federal law enforcement. Applicants must be able to obtain a top-secret security clearance and complete a comprehensive background. Background reviews are conducted every five years. Applicants must pass drug and alcohol screenings and are subject to random tests throughout their career. Applicants must possess a degree from a four-year accredited university, or three years of responsible general experience in the federal or private service, or any combination of experience and education. Federal air marshals are required to carry a firearm and must be proficient and accurate as their duties may require the use of deadly force. Applicants then undergo a screening process that includes a suitability assessment, mental health/psycho-social screening, a panel interview, and a supervisory air marshal evaluation and recommendation (Today's Federal Air Marshal, 2012).

Upon finishing the screening process applicants must complete a two-stage, fifteen-week training program. The first stage of the training takes place at the Federal Law Enforcement Training Center in Artesia, New Mexico where recruits receive basic instruction in federal law, arrest procedure, survival, marksmanship, and tactics. The second half of training takes place at the FAMS Training Academy in Atlantic City, New Jersey, which includes a five-story simulated control tower, three outdoor shooting ranges with moving targets, and two donated aircrafts for training and aircraft familiarity (Harr & Hess, 2010). It is at the Atlantic City Training Center where recruits learn mission specific tactics and advanced marksmanship as firearm skills are critical for air marshals and the agency has stringent requirements.

After completing the second phase of training air marshal recruits are assigned to one of the 25 field offices to begin a standardized Field Training Program where they will be assessed, monitored, and evaluated through several training exercises for three 28-day roster periods. A team leader provides guidance and critical feedback for the trainee. If the field office supervisor deems it necessary an additional 28-day cycle may be required (Aviation Jobs, 2012).

Functions

The mission of the Federal Air Marshal Service is essentially making air travel safe for the public. This is accomplished through investigation, deterrence, and defeating hostile acts targeting U.S. air carriers, airports, passengers, and crews. Federal air marshals essentially work undercover and only the flight crew knows their identities. The appearance of an air marshal has been controversial as the GAO in 2003 reported that there was no formal policy addressing what is appropriate attire. The military haircuts and business attire marshals were required to wear made them easy to identify as they simply did not blend in with the rest of the traveling public. Other concerns over identifying air marshals have been raised such as the policy that allowed them to bypass airport security by showing credentials in full view of passengers. The consequences of having an air marshal team identified are tremendous as they could be targeted, overpowered, and their weapons taken and used to commandeer the plane (Elias 2010). In 2006, the FAMS changed their policy to allow marshals more flexibility in choosing clothing and other procedures that would make it easier for them to remain inconspicuous.

Air marshals are typically armed with a Sig P229 with .357 hollow point rounds designed to stop when it hits a suspect and not continue through the target. Air marshals are authorized to use deadly force to protect the flight deck from hijackings or a terrorist takeover. Air marshals tend to work in pairs or a small team. Typically one air marshal sits in the front of the airplane to guard the cockpit and another in the rear to watch the coach area. Marshals must use their training and instincts to determine when they should identify themselves and engage a potential threat (Seidenstat & Splane, 2009).

An air marshal's task begins before boarding the plane. There are air marshals present in airport terminals in plain clothes to observe travelers for suspicious behavior. They can employ their agency issued Personal Digital Assistants to send photos and alerts to TSA officials and other marshals about potential threats (Price & Forrest, 2009). Air marshals typically travel four days a week for an average of 181 days a year, and may have to travel internationally to high-risk destinations. The working environment can be demanding and has dangers. Air marshals operate independently and without the ability to call additional backup beyond a partner on the plane and may have to deal with several potential threats in a contained space, 35,000 feet in the sky, and moving more than 400 miles per hour.

Due to the demanding conditions of the job, air marshals once had an attrition rate of around 10% in the few years after 9/11. Today it is 6.5%, which is comparable to other federal agencies. There are tens of thousands of commercial flights each day making it impossible to deploy air marshals on each plane. The number of flights covered by the FAMS is considered classified information and the agency does not want to provide information that may allow terrorists to engage in a statistical guessing game. The FAMS essentially uses a risk model to determine which flights will have air marshals aboard based on intelligence, airline request, or specific information. Seidenstat and Splane provide an estimate of air marshal coverage. If a typical work-week is considered, roughly 70% of air marshals are on duty. Assuming there are 3,000 air marshals, and 25,000–30,000 flights a day, the FAMS covers only 3 to 4% of all commercial flights (2009, p. 156).

Recent Federal Air Marshal Cases

Federal air marshals respond to dozens of security incidents each day. Such incidents include disruptive passengers and potential security threats on board. In the first two years after 9/11 the FAMS made 28 arrests, used less than lethal force 16 times, and discharged their weapons 3 times (Elias, 2010). For example, in 2008 a federal air marshal broke cover and arrested a 25-year-old Slovenian passport holder on a Delta Airlines international flight from Atlanta to Vienna, Austria. The passenger appeared to be intoxicated and struck a flight attendant. The marshal then observed the man attempt to set fire to curtains in the crew area and one of the marshals immediately identified himself and arrested the suspect. The suspect was turned over to Austrian authorities who agreed to prosecute him (Federal Air Marshals Make Arrest on International Flight, 2012).

The use of deadly force is rare by air marshals, and the most recent deadly force incident occurred in 2005. Rigoberto Alpizar, a passenger aboard American Airlines Flight 924, left his seat next to his wife and ran towards the airline door saying he had to get off the plane. Alpizar was heard uttering threatening words suggesting he had a bomb. His wife ran after him stating Alpizar is bipolar and had not taken his medication. Two air marshals confronted Alpizar and ordered him to the ground. The marshals stated Alpizar did not comply and reached for his bag. They drew their weapons, fired, and killed him. No bomb was found, and the two air marshals involved were found to be justified in their use of deadly force. Alpizar was the first shooting since 9/11 by the FAMS (Air Marshals 'Had To Stop Threat,' 2012).

The Federal Air Marshal Service is an agency created out of crisis. The hijackings and interruption of safe travel and commerce had become major problems in the United States and for numerous countries around the world during the 1960s and 1970s. As the stakes were raised and violence began to fall upon passengers and crews the federal government responded by creating the first Sky Marshals Program to provide an armed presence on the nation's airlines to restore confidence in a critical section of infrastructure. The Sky Marshals Program would evolve into the Federal Air Marshal Service with the same vital mission of protecting the nation's air transport systems. Hijackings have always been a threat and the use of this tactic by terrorists is not new in the United States and around the world. However, the need to address this potential danger would become vital after the terrorists attacks of September 11th. The attacks would fundamentally change the FAMS through increasing their ranks by thousands and changing their organization.

Interestingly, air marshals have been largely untested when it comes to preventing terrorist attacks or hijackings and it is an agency that does not have enough personnel to realistically cover every flight in the country. The Federal Air Marshal Service remains a low profile agency, keeping its procedures and exact numbers classified. Despite unclear evidence of the effectiveness of an armed force to act as frontline defenders of the airlines, the FAMS provides security, psychological deterrence, and is viewed as a critical component of the layered approach to protection within TSA and the Department of Homeland Security.

References

291-Statement Announcing a Program To Deal With Airplane Hijacking (1970). Retrieved from http://www.presidency.ucsb.edu/ws/index.php?pid=2659#axzz1wJosumTB.

Aviation Jobs (2012). Retrieved from http://www.avianation.com/aviation_jobs/jobDetail.cfm?jobid=11074633997.

Air Marshals 'Had To Stop Threat' (2012). Retrieved from http://www.cbsnews.com/stories/2005/12/08/national/main1107653.shtml.

Bureau of Transportation Statistics (2012). Retrieved from http://www.transtats.bts.gov/.

Department of Homeland Security (2012). Allegations of misconduct and illegal discrimination and retaliation in the federal air marshal service. Washington, D.C.: U.S. Department of Homeland Security.

Elias, B. (2010). *Airport and aviation security: U.S. policy and strategy in the age of global terrorism*. Boca Raton, FL: Taylor & Francis Group.

Federal Air Marshals Make Arrest on International Flight (2012). Retrieved from http://www.tsa.gov/press/happenings/federal_arrest_international_flight.shtm.

Federal Air Marshal Service Careers. (2012). Retrieved from http://www.tsa.gov/lawenforcement/people/fams_join.shtm.

Felt, W. and O'Connor, J. (2006). *A G-Man's life: The FBI, being "Deep Throat," and the struggle for honor in Washington*. Cambridge, MA: Perseus Book Group.

Harr, J. and Hess, K. (2010). *Careers in criminal justice and related fields: From internship to promotion* (6th ed.) Belmont, CA: Cengage Learning.

Landes, W. (1978). An economic study of U.S. aircraft hijacking, 1961–1976. *Journal of Law and Economics.* 21:1–32.

Mansfield, D. (2001). Tennessee narrowly dodged bullet in tense '72 hijack episode. Retrieved from http://articles.latimes.com/2001/sep/23/news/mn-48746.

Mason, B. (1972, November). Grounding the skyjacker. *Ebony*, 48–52.

Moore, E. (2001). Hero in the cockpit / Pistol served pilot well in '54. Retrieved from http://www.chron.com/CDA/archives/archive.mpl/2001_3341305/hero-in-the-cockpit-pistol-served-pilot-well-in-54.html.

Moore, K. (1976). *Airport, aircraft, and airline security.* Los Angeles: Security World.

National Commission on Terrorist Attacks Upon the United States (2004). *Nine/eleven commission report, final report of the National Commission on Terrorist Attacks Upon the United States.* New York City: W. W. Norton & Company.

O'Connell, W. and Williams, G. (2011). *Air transport in the 21st century: Key strategic developments.* Surrey, England: Ashgate Publishing, Ltd.

Our Mission (2012). Retrieved from http://www.tsa.gov/lawenforcement/mission/index.shtm.

Piszkiewicz, D. (2003). *Terrorism's war with America: A history.* Westport, CT: Greenwood Publishing Group.

Price, J. and Forrest, J. (2009*). Practical aviation security: Predicting and preventing future threats.* Burlington, MA: Butterworth-Heinmann.

Seidenstat, P. and Splane, F. (2009). *Protecting airline passengers in the age of terrorism.* Santa Barbara, CA: ABC-CLIO, LLC.

Smith, R. (1970, September 12). President asks wider use of electronic surveillance. *The New York Times*, p. 11.

Stewart, M. and Mueller, J. (2011). Cost-benefit analysis of advanced imaging technology full body scanners for airline passenger security screening. *Journal of Homeland Security and Emergency Management,* 8(1): 1–17.

Teitelbaum, J. (1987). Armed operations. In Rabinovich, I. and Shaked, (Eds.) *Middle East Contemporary Survey*, Volume 9, 1984–85 (pp. 86–105). Boulder, CO: Westview Press Inc.

Testimony of Robert Bray (2012). Retrieved from http://www.dhs.gov/ynews/testimony/20120216-2a-tsa-fams.shtm.

Today's Federal Air Marshal (2012). Retrieved from http://www.tsa.gov/press/happenings/todays_fams.shtm.

U.S. Congress (2004). Congressional record: Proceedings and debates of the 108th Congress. United States Government Printing Office.

U.S. To Train Permanent Airplane Security Guard (1971). Retrieved from http://news.google.com/newspapers?id=mytSAAAAIBAJ&sjid=pHUDAAAAIBAJ&pg=6992,5555243&dq=sky+marshals&hl=en.

Wells, A. and Rodriquez, C. (2004). *Commercial aviation safety.* New York: McGraw Hill.

Part IV
Federal Law Enforcement Agencies

Department of Interior

Chapter Eleven

National Park Service

The National Park Service (NPS) is a bureau of the U.S. Department of the Interior, and has consistently been rated by the general public as one of the most popular federal agencies (Mackintosh, 1999). It manages nearly 400 units of the *National Park System*, a title used to refer to all of the units managed by the NPS. The NPS oversees sites other than those with the term "park" in their title, and helps administer many other affiliated sites, including the National Register of Historic Places, National Heritage Areas, National Wild and Scenic Rivers, National Historic Landmarks, and National Trails.

The 396 units, or areas managed by the NPS, comprise 84 million acres across every state except Delaware, and include 123 historical parks or sites, 74 monuments, 58 national parks, 25 battlefields or military parks, 18 preserves, 18 recreation areas, 10 seashores, four parkways, four lakeshores, two reserves, and the White House (National Park Service, 2010b, 2011). Most of the units within the NPS were created by acts of Congress and confirmation by the President. The exception occurs under the Antiquities Act of 1906, which allows the president to deem and protect areas as National Monuments by executive order.

Controlling, managing, and preserving the vast areas and landmarks, and nature and wildlife within the national parks provides several unique challenges for the NPS. Law enforcement within the NPS is primarily performed by two groups: Park rangers and Park Police. Park rangers are primarily located in national parks and typically provide a variety of services (both law enforcement and non-law enforcement) to park visitors. U.S. Park Police more closely resemble local police departments and are tasked with law enforcement responsibilities in specific sites across the U.S.

In commenting on the law enforcement component of the National Park Service, Lucas (1999, 1) noted: "Law enforcement is an essential tool used in the accomplishment of the National Park Service's mission. The primary and proactive goal of the National Park Service is the prevention of criminal activities through resource education, public safety efforts, and deterrence." This statement provides an overview of the many important responsibilities of the federal law enforcement personnel employed by the NPS.

History

Historical accounts of law enforcement within the NPS typically focus on the creation of the NPS and ultimately the hiring of park rangers. However, many of these accounts overlook the fact that the U.S. Park Police trace their history to 1791; long before many other federal law enforcement agencies existed and many years prior to the creation of the NPS. President George Washington created the Park Watchmen in 1791 to protect designated areas and buildings in the District of Columbia, including the Capitol and the White House (Farabee, 2003). Management of the Park Watchmen moved to the

Department of the Interior in 1849, and in 1867 relocated to the U.S. Army Corps of Engineers. In 1919, the Park Watchmen received a new name: "United States Park Police." The agency was ultimately placed under the guidance of the NPS in 1933 (Farabee, 2003).

The historical development of park rangers and the NPS differ from the history surrounding the Park Police. Particularly, the history of the NPS and park rangers largely begins with Congress' designation of Yellowstone National Park as the nation's (and the world's) first national park in 1872. The establishment of Yellowstone as a national park set the precedent for locating other natural reserves under federal jurisdiction (U.S. Park Service). The first superintendent of Yellowstone was Nathaniel Langford, who was directed to protect and preserve the park. However, he received no funding from Congress to do so, and was ultimately powerless to protect against the harms being done to the park. The harms included the disappearance of game from the park and vandalism. Langford resigned from his position largely due to frustration from the lack of Congressional support. Congress would, in 1877, appropriate $10,000 to protect the park, which the new superintendent Philetus Norris used to hire an assistant superintendent and the nation's first park ranger.

Norris later encouraged the Secretary of Interior to allocate additional funding, and soon there were ten rangers to protect the park. The rangers were heavily armed "rough and tough wilderness men" who typically worked alone in the parks (Bytnar, 2010, p. 59). However, they were not overly effective as they were political appointees and had no experience with regard to poaching and vandalism. Congress later appointed the protection of Yellowstone to the Department of War, and the U.S. Army enforced the regulations in Yellowstone. The overall administration of the park remained under the direction of the Department of the Interior. The U.S. Army was instrumental in providing protection and administration in the first four national parks: Yellowstone, Sequoia, General Grant, and Yosemite (Farabee, 2003), although the military personnel tasked with protecting the parks were somewhat harsh in their enforcement practices (Lucas, 1999).

As of 1916 the Interior Department was accountable for 14 national parks and 21 national monuments, but no designated agency or centralized group managed them. What existed was largely a compilation of Army troops in some locations enforcing regulations against hunting, grazing, timber cutting, and vandalism. Civilian appointees oversaw the other parks, and monuments received little supervision (Mackintosh, 1999). Prior to the establishment of the NPS in 1916, the U.S. Army secured national parks, and they assumed a predominantly law-enforcement approach targeted to prevent and address poaching, illegal grazing, and vandalism (Runte, 1979). Each park was managed independently as there was no federal agency that directly oversaw park operations and protection.

The National Park Ranger Service (NPRS) was created in 1915, one year prior to the creation of the National Park Service, by the Secretary of the Interior. The NPRS was created to bring under one agency the existing eleven national parks, eighteen national monuments, the Casa Grande Ruins, and the Hot Springs Reservation (Farabee, 2003). On August 25, 1916 President Woodrow Wilson signed the "Organic Act" which created the NPS and located all of the existing national parks under its management. The act, which brought together 37 separate and diverse areas (Farabee, 2003), stated that the primary purpose of the NPS was "to conserve the scenery and the natural and historic objects and the wildlife therein and to provide for the enjoyment of the same in such manner and by such means as will leave them unimpaired for the enjoyment of future generations" (National Park Service, 2010b). The Act provided a basis for the "fundamental mission, philosophy, and policies of the National Park Service" (National Park Service).

The creation of the NPS did not come swiftly, as there was some resistance and apprehension regarding the development of an agency that was proposed to regulate national treasures. Among the obstacles that needed to be overcome for the creation of the NPS was a highly politicized Congress which resisted the creation of the NPS; fears of regulation by ranchers and miners in the western portion of the U.S., and; resistance on behalf of the well-established U.S. Forest Service (Farabee, 2003). The first director of the NPS, Stephen T. Mather feared that political interference could hamper the overall functioning and utility of the parks (Kiernan, 2005). Despite these challenges, the NPS was created and continues to serve the U.S.

The early history (through the 1920s) of the NPS was largely impacted by what was a "western park system," as only Acadia National Park in Maine was east of the Mississippi. During the 1930s the Park Service became involved with areas intended for mass recreation, including several Depression-era relief projects. Notable reorganization within President Franklin Roosevelt's Executive Branch in 1933 had several impacts on the NPS. Two executive orders transferred the War Department's parks and monuments to the NPS, and the agency received all the national monuments held by the Forest Service. The NPS would become responsible for mostly all monuments created thereafter. The NPS also assumed responsibility for the parks in Washington, D.C., which had previously been managed by a separate office. This reorganization notably impacted the NPS, as its holdings were vastly expanded and it created a single, national system of parklands. The reorganization and new responsibilities resulted in historic preservation becoming a primary mission of the NPS (National Park Service).

Following World War II, national parks became increasingly prominent as the nation's energies were redirected to domestic pursuits. The NPS and the amount of lands and materials it was designated to protect continued to increase (Mackintosh, 1999). During the early 1950s, Park Rangers were the primary employees in the NPS, and they performed most of what was needed in the parks. Among their charges were cleaning the parks, fighting fires, managing traffic, investigating crime, and assisting visitors (Colby, 1955). They still perform many of these services.

Several acts passed during the 1980s impacted the NPS. For instance, the Alaska National Interest Lands Conservation Act of 1980 more than doubled the size of the national park system by adding over 47 million wilderness acres (Mackintosh, 1999), and the National Park Omnibus Management Act of 1988, among other contributions, provided for improved management and increased accountability for particular NPS programs. The Act permitted the NPS to retain concessions franchise fees in parks in which they were collected (National Park Service).

Recently, the NPS and park rangers have had to address the complexity of their position and issues pertaining to terrorist threats and homeland security (Welch, 2012). For instance, Park Rangers have had to increasingly confront a wide array of challenges, ranging from poaching; traditional crimes; drug use, smuggling, and production; wildfires; terrorist threats; immigration, and; related issues. Security and law enforcement efforts were notably increased following the 2001 terrorist attacks against the U.S., resulting in park rangers assuming expanded roles in securing national landmarks and parks. Immediately following the attacks, law enforcement personnel from the NPS were instrumental in a variety of capacities, including securing national parks, protecting U.S. symbols of freedom and critical structures (e.g., the Liberty Bell, Mount Rushmore, the Statue of Liberty, nuclear power plants, various large-scale dams, etc.), assisting in recovery efforts at various sites, and protecting high-profile political figures (Farabee, 2003). NPS law enforcement personnel continue to perform many of these and related functions as the focus of the agency shifted to some extent with the beginning of the 21st century.

Organization and Personnel

The NPS employs roughly 20,000 permanent, temporary, and seasonal workers, who are assisted by over 221,000 volunteers who help in the parks. The NPS maintains 909 visitor centers and contact stations (National Park Service, 2010b) for the many people who use the parks, including the estimated 281,303,769 visitors who attended national parks in 2010 (National Park Service, 2011). Park rangers comprise a small percentage of the individuals employed by the NPS. For instance, a Bureau of Justice Statistics report noted that as of 2008, the NPS employed 1,951 full-time officers with authority to carry firearms and make arrests. This total included 1,404 Park Rangers and 547 U.S. Park Police. The number of Park Rangers decreased 9% from 2004, while the number of Park Police officers decreased 11% (Reaves, 2012). Additional part-time rangers were employed by the NPS.

Annually, NPS sites generate 246,000 jobs for local economies and provide $12 billion in economic impacts (National Park Service, 2010b). The NPS is headed by a director who works out of the Department of Interior building in Washington, D.C. The director is a presidential appointee who oversees the administration and management of the NPS. The units within the NPS are divided into seven areas which are overseen by regional offices. Each NPS unit is managed by a superintendent, and the size, complexity, and level of staffing within each unit determines the organization and distribution of jobs (Bytnar, 2010). The NPS headquarters organization is depicted in Figure 11.1.

The NPS is not a particularly diverse agency in terms of race, ethnicity, and gender. For instance, only 15% of the full-time sworn officer positions in the Ranger Division were filled by females in 1998, although this percentage increased to about 19% by 2008. Females held 9% of the full-time sworn officer positions with the U.S. Park Police in 1998, although this percentage increased to 13% by 2008 (Langton, 2010). Historically, females have been underrepresented as rangers with the NPS despite the many contributions that women have provided to the service and national parks in general. Part of the early apprehension in hiring females to become rangers was the belief that females were unsuited for the rugged and dangerous nature of a ranger's job (Farabee, 2003). This perception has decreased over time, as noted in the increased presence of female rangers.

With regard to race and ethnicity, only 12.7% of full-time NPS Rangers with arrest and firearm authority within the NPS were members of a racial or ethnic minority group in 2008. African-Americans constituted 2.1% of the rangers, while 4.8% were Hispanic/ Latino. Roughly 22% of the Park Police were from a racial or ethnic minority group (Reaves, 2012). Akin to many other federal law enforcement groups, the NPS has become more diversified as females and racial and ethnic minorities are more frequently employed at all levels of the agency compared to years past.

Individuals choose to become a park ranger for various personal reasons. Pay is not primary among the reasons, as park rangers are "notoriously underpaid" (Lucas, 1999, p. 207). Individuals are often attracted to the position by their love of the outdoors, concern for keeping national parks scenic, love of wildlife, desire to serve and protect the public, interest in natural processes, and concern for keeping the parks free of crime (Lucas, 1999).

Individuals applying for full-time national park employment face competition from the large number of individuals who apply for openings. Most park rangers begin their careers as temporary seasonal employees, and are often required to move around the country based on agency staffing needs and funding. Relocation can be difficult for some

Figure 11.1 NPS Headquarters Organization

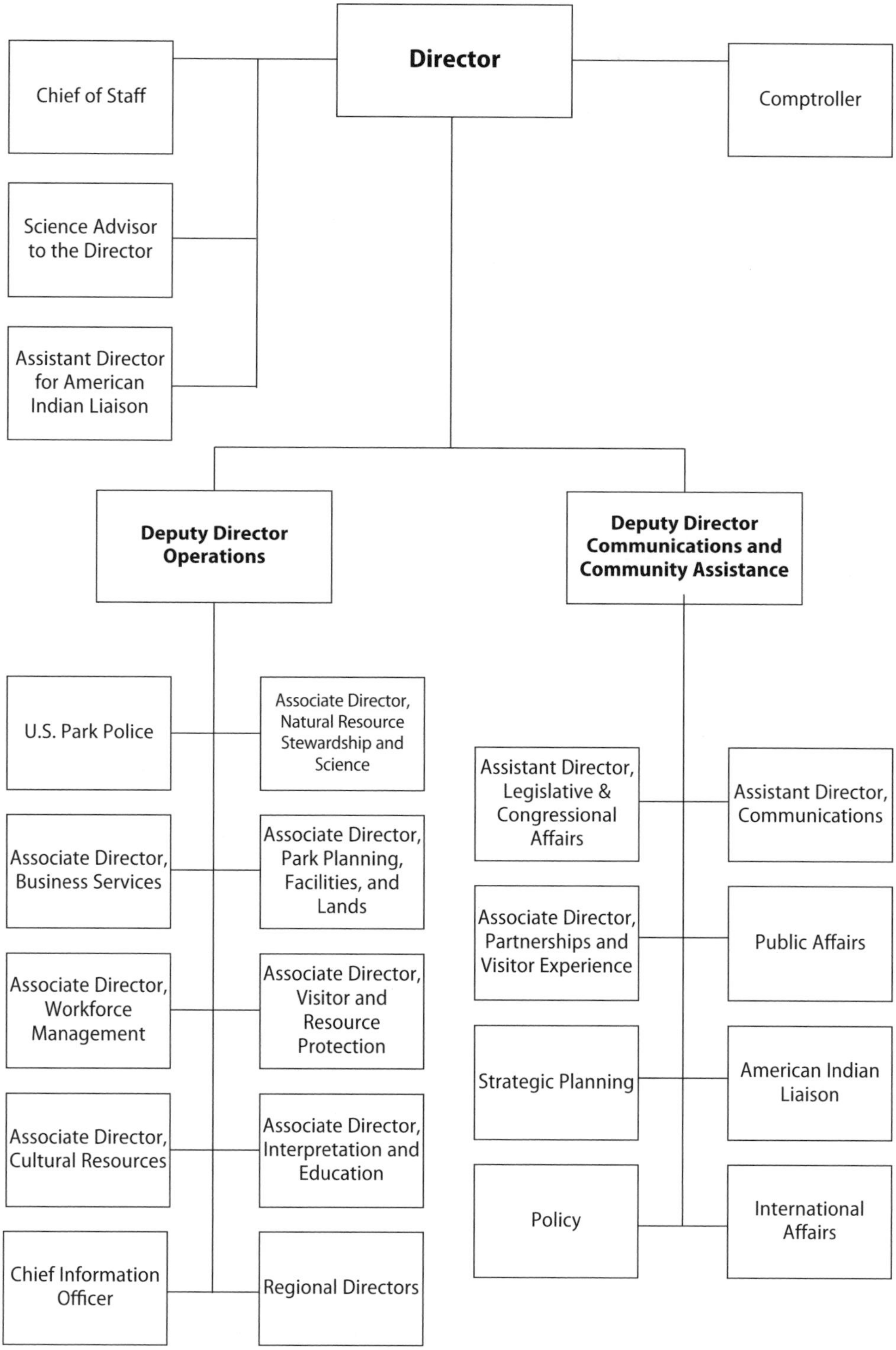

```
                                    ┌──────────────┐
                                    │   Director   │
                                    └──────────────┘
┌─────────────┐                                              ┌─────────────┐
│Chief of Staff│                                             │ Comptroller │
└─────────────┘                                              └─────────────┘

┌─────────────┐
│Science Advisor│
│to the Director│
└─────────────┘

┌─────────────┐
│Assistant Director│
│for American│
│Indian Liaison│
└─────────────┘


        ┌──────────────────┐              ┌──────────────────────┐
        │ Deputy Director  │              │   Deputy Director    │
        │   Operations     │              │ Communications and   │
        └──────────────────┘              │ Community Assistance │
                                          └──────────────────────┘
```

U.S. Park Police	Associate Director, Natural Resource Stewardship and Science
Associate Director, Business Services	Associate Director, Park Planning, Facilities, and Lands
Associate Director, Workforce Management	Associate Director, Visitor and Resource Protection
Associate Director, Cultural Resources	Associate Director, Interpretation and Education
Chief Information Officer	Regional Directors

Assistant Director, Legislative & Congressional Affairs	Assistant Director, Communications
Associate Director, Partnerships and Visitor Experience	Public Affairs
Strategic Planning	American Indian Liaison
Policy	International Affairs

Source: http://www.nps.gov/news/upload/WASO_Org-Chart.pdf.

individuals, particularly those with a family. The willingness to relocate and the experience gathered from seasonal work, however, contribute much toward gaining full-time employment (Bytnar, 2010). Attaining permanent status in the civilian federal government is also helpful in securing a permanent ranger position, as is having a college degree, particularly an advanced degree (Farabee, 2003).

Some parks offer employee housing with the intent to have individuals be on-site in case of emergencies and to deter criminal activity. Some positions require individuals to live in park housing. Such housing is sometimes dilapidated and outdated, and rent is charged based on what local rents are being paid in the area, which can be problematic when local rents are costly. Living on-site can be somewhat burdensome for employees in the sense that they are essentially on-duty at all times (Bytnar, 2010). Park housing may be isolated and remote, which can pose problems for rangers with families. As of 2004, NPS full-time personnel with arrest and firearm authority most often worked in Washington, D.C. (19%), California (11%), New York, and Arizona (each at 7%). Most of the NPS officers who worked in D.C. and New York were part of the U.S. Park Police (Reaves, 2006).

NPS Rangers remain the most visible employee within the Park Service. They are primarily tasked with interpreting and explaining park resources to visitors, facilitating visitor enjoyment of the parks and their resources, helping to ensure that visitors abide by the law when using the parks, and encouraging park stewardship among visitors to the parks. In its description of the Position Classification Standards for the "Park Ranger Series" (GS-0025), the United States Office of Personnel Management (United States Office . . . , 1985) noted that:

> This series includes positions the duties of which are to supervise, manage, and/or perform work in the conservation and use of Federal park resources. This involves functions such as park conservation; natural, historical, and cultural resource management; and the development and operation of interpretive and recreational programs for the benefit of the visiting public.

There are two types of U.S. Park Rangers within the NPS: interpretive and law enforcement. The former provide educational and informational services to park guests in the form of tours, demonstrations, and historical re-enactments. This group generally promotes education and stewardship in the parks. The latter consist of commissioned federal law enforcement officers who are primarily responsible for enforcing the laws and are expected to perform a variety of public safety responsibilities such firefighting, search and rescue operations, and emergency medical tasks. Rangers are often certified as paramedics, Wilderness First Responders, or Emergency Medical Technicians. In some parks, special operations are performed by non-commissioned personnel. The NPS also employs some special agents who engage in more complex criminal investigations. U.S. Park Rangers and Park Police work cooperatively with local, state, and other federal law enforcement agencies to address crime in National Parks (Grinols, Mustard, and Staha, 2011).

The NPS's budget for fiscal year 2010 was $3.16 billion to help support the 21,574 employees within the agency. These numbers reflect an increase from 2009 when the agency's budget was $2.92 billion and it consisted of 20,876 employees. The NPS's budget is supplemented by other sources of income, including recreation fees (which amount to approximately $190 million annually), park concessions franchise fees (approximately $60 million), and filming and photography special use fees (approximately $1.2 million) (National Park Service, 2010a). It is argued that the NPS has historically lacked the funding required to effectively meet the expectations of both the public and Congress, largely

Figure 11.2 NPS Arrowhead

Source: http://www.nps.gov/glac/parknews/history-of-the-nps-arrowhead.htm.

because funding was based on political—as opposed to practical objectives. Politically-based decisions made instead of best-choice decisions have long challenged the NPS (Bytnar, 2010).

Shortly prior to the September 11, 2001 attacks, rangers were battling several severe wildfires. Following the attacks and the relocation of some rangers to designated areas, protection in the parks was limited. Around this time, the Park Service's field staff was at its lowest level in 20 years after adjusting for notable increases in park acreage and visitation ("Security, Fire Duties...," 2002). Funding shortfalls and an administration whose environmental policies often differ with from the preservation ethic of the Park Service have provided notable challenges for park rangers (Kiernan, 2005). The NPS budget has increased over the years, however the added responsibilities associated with homeland security concerns, mandatory pay increases, and other expenses have absorbed much of the funding increases (Kiernan, 2005). A report by the National Parks Conservation Association (NPCA) highlighted the notable shortage of staff in national parks, with low budgets resulting in fewer rangers and fewer programs. Such a shortage could result in increased poaching, park and artifact degradation, and limited monitoring of endangered species (Dougherty, 2004). One could argue that a limited number of park rangers would lead to increased levels of other types of crime as well.

NPS Rangers are known for their distinguished uniform and appearance. Several symbolic aspects of the rangers' uniform include the ranger badge, the Stetson hat with the accompanying hatband, and the NPS Arrowhead. These and other features help distinguish NPS rangers from other law enforcement agents. Each of these features contains symbols that speak to the functions and responsibilities of the NPS. For instance, the NPS Arrowhead, depicted in Figure 11.2, was authorized as the official NPS emblem by the Secretary of the Interior in 1951. The arrowhead is a symbol of land management professionalism and represents various aspects of the missions of the NPS. The Sequoia tree and bison represent vegetation and wildlife, respectively. The water and mountains represent scenic and recreational values. The arrowhead shape reflects historical and archeological values (Farabee, 2003).

Advocacy for park rangers is largely provided by the Association of National Park Rangers (ANPR), which was created to represent the interests of park rangers. Its mission is to communicate for, about, and with NPS employees to promote and enhance the professions, spirit, and mission of the NPS and the National Park System (Association of National Park Rangers). Other advocacy groups exist to promote awareness and protection with regard to the national parks. For instance, the NPCA protects the interests of the parks and has been a leader in protecting and enhancing the National Park System. The NPCA is the only national independent membership organization that focuses directly on preserving the park system (Kiernan, 2005).

United States Park Police

The U.S. Park Police, a full-service police organization, provides traditional police protection for designated National Park areas. These areas are primarily located in Washington, D.C., although they are also located in San Francisco (CA) and New York City. the U.S. Park Police is authorized to provide law enforcement services within the entire NPS, and they use a variety of patrol methods including automobiles, horses, motorcycles, helicopters, watercraft, and bicycles. The U.S. Park Police also use detectives to investigate crimes that occur on lands under the police protection of the agency, including national monuments, forested preserves, and large vehicular parkways (Bumgarner, 2006).

The mission statement for the U.S. Park Police (2011) summarizes the charges and responsibilities of this important component of the NPS: "We, the United States Park Police, support and further the mission and goals of the Department of the Interior and the National Park Service by providing quality law enforcement to safeguard lives, protect our national treasures and symbols of democracy, and preserve the natural and cultural resources entrusted to us." Table 11.1 depicts the personnel employed and related information pertaining to the Park Police in 2009 and 2010.

As noted in the table, the Park Police saw a four percent increase in personnel from 2009–2010, resulting in a total of 649 officers on staff. This reversed a trend of declining Park Police officer employment from 2004–2008. The Park Police made 68,287 incident

Table 11.1 Performance and Personnel Statistics CY 2010

	CY 2009	CY 2010	% Change
Sworn Officers	624	649	4.0%
Security Guards	28	25	−10.7%
Full-Time Civilian Personnel	87	97	11.5%
Service Incidents	35,957	42,229	17.4%
Incident Reports	59,125	68,287	15.5%
Vehicle Accident Response	3,371	3,276	−2.8%
Citizen Complaints Against Officers	43	53	23.3%
Law Enforcement Officers Assaulted	42	44	4.8%
Resulting in Death of Officer	0	0	0.0%
Resulting in Injury to Officer	14	4	−71.4%

Source: U.S. Park Police, 2011.

reports in 2010, and 44 officers were assaulted, although assaults against officers resulting in an injury notably decreased.

Functions

The safety and well-being of national park visitors are largely ensured by NPS uniformed rangers and criminal investigators (special agents). Both park rangers and special agents maintain law enforcement authority, including the right to carry firearms, make arrests, and execute search warrants. They provide general policing services to visitors of the parks and conduct investigations of criminal offenses committed against the NPS or inside national parks. In addition to park rangers and special agents, U.S. Park Police personnel maintain the same powers and provide law enforcement services at select sites.

The primary functions of each national park staff generally include protection, interpretation, maintenance, administration, and resource management. The protective function includes law enforcement, firefighting, public safety, medical services and related duties. With regard to this function, park rangers are tasked with protecting park visitors from interacting with wildlife; a responsibility that has been deemed "... the toughest part of (their) job" (Bytnar, 2010, 131). Fighting fires is also an important responsibility for park rangers. The NPS, as part of the Interagency Wildfire Coordinating Group, may be required to send specially trained rangers to assist in fighting fires in areas where help is needed beyond what is immediately available.

Interpretation involves educating national park visitors, for instance through guided walks, visitor centers, outreach programs, and websites. Maintenance involves keeping the parks safe, clean, and ready for visitors, while the administrative functions are similar to what is found in the administrative ranks of most other agencies, including budgeting, staffing, purchasing, and general facilitation of the parks. Resource management includes scientists and historians monitoring, researching, and generally helping to document and preserve the treasures located in national parks. The existence, organization, and emphasis placed on each of these functions vary by park (Bytnar, 2010).

In 2007, park rangers in 16 national parks were awarded grants to fund the development of public health-focused programs for individuals who visit the parks. Rangers led programs that focused on a variety of public health topics, including infectious disease, environmental health, injury prevention, and chronic disease/wellness. The focus on public health differed from the traditional programming in national parks that focuses on natural and cultural resources. An assessment of the program found that almost 12,000 visitors attended the programs, the programs were supported by park management, and NPS units appeared to be excellent settings for delivering the public health messages. Further, 87% of park rangers believed that the visitors enjoyed the public health program (Wong & Higgins, 2010).

The NPS, like all other law enforcement agencies, was impacted by the terrorist attacks against the United States on September 11, 2001. For instance, rangers provided extra security within the parks and stepped up their crime prevention and surveillance practices, particularly as they pertained to national monuments. Following the attacks, the Department of Interior reassigned law enforcement rangers to secure several specific areas of the country, including the Liberty Bell and Pearl Harbor ("Security, fire duties...," 2002). Rangers worked with the Department of Homeland Security, for example by training in areas such as biochemical response, and have taken many other steps to better secure federal parks and forests (Wilkinson, 2002).

Individuals attend national parks for various reasons. Particularly, they go to parks for their commercial and scientific utility; social and recreational pursuits; environmental management and preservation; individual subsistence; spiritual development and religious ceremony, and; criminal pursuits (Pendleton, 1996). Accordingly, park rangers, akin to local street cops, must be prepared to interact with and confront a wide array of individuals, including the mentally ill and emotionally unstable. National parks have been the site of numerous suicides and suicide attempts (Lucas, 1999) as some individuals seek to end their lives in the serenity of the parks and/or utilize the natural landscapes as part of the process.

Accordingly, national parks are the site of many different types of crime. Aside from experiencing the traditional crimes most often recognized in the larger society (e.g., burglary, theft, assaults), national parks more often experience non-traditional crimes such poaching, timber theft, and related wildlife and agricultural crimes. Specific features of national parks often provide apt opportunities for these types of non-traditional crimes, as the parks are large and often remote geographical areas which extend police response time and hamper backup efforts for law enforcement intervention. Rangers are often isolated from their colleagues, and thus must be notably cautious when encountering dangerous activities. The general lack of immediate backup support for park rangers arguably results in suspects feeling more confident engaging in violence against rangers (Bytnar, 2010).

Poaching by both individuals and organized crime groups has become notably problematic for park rangers and parks in general. In 2005, Toops (2005, p. 25) noted that in the previous two decades trade in reptiles and amphibians had emerged "into a multi-million-dollar enterprise." Plants and other forms of wildlife such as snakes, cacti, black bear, ginseng, and scorpions are also increasingly being sought by poachers, who are motivated to illegally seize wildlife and plants by profit and/or trophies denoting their accomplishments (Bytnar, 2010).

Economic factors have influenced poaching and responses to it in national parks in several ways. For instance, budget cuts and the increasing responsibilities of park rangers persuaded park rangers to adopt new enforcement approaches, including the use of cutting edge technology and savvy strategies, such as tagging plants and animals with electronic codes. Park rangers have also sought the assistance of other groups, including law enforcement personnel at various levels (Toops, 2005). Economics appears to impact poaching in the parks as it is suggested that economic declines in society are related to increases in plants being poached for profit (Bytnar, 2010).

Since its inception, the NPS has used a low key philosophical approach to law enforcement even though the parks have been, and remain subject to overuse and degradation (Lucas, 1999). The lack of emphasis on law enforcement stems, in part, from most national park managers and superintendents typically lacking experience in law enforcement positions and having a "negative mindset about law enforcement in their attitudes and decision making" (Bytnar, 2010, 59). The lack of support for the law enforcement function of park rangers was particularly evident in the early 1970s, when many park managers were largely liberal-minded and lacked law enforcement experience. Among other effects, this has contributed to debate concerning the primary roles of park rangers, including whether or not they should carry firearms (Bytnar, 2010).

The functions of park rangers have changed over time. Initially, park rangers were generalists who were firefighters, naturalists, managers, interpreters, trail blazers, game wardens, trail builders, and biologists. More recently, rangers have become specialists and the trend is toward greater specialization. The NPS is divided into many divisions, and rangers primarily engage in law enforcement, resource management, and interpretation (Lucas, 1999). Whether or not park rangers should be generalists or specialists has been a topic of discussion within the NPS (Meadows & Soden, 1988). Currently, there is a mix of rangers who are specialists and generalists, as some focus specifically on tasks such as emergency response, environmental education, wilderness protection, or the like, while others perform a wide array of tasks (Farabee, 2003).

NPS rangers provide various types of law enforcement functions and services. Primary among these functions are natural resource management and enforcing laws in national parks. The balance between these two primary functions has varied across time, as national parks have historically been viewed as preserved lands for recreation and a place of refuge from the outside world. Accordingly, it is argued that park rangers should be well-versed in law enforcement, wildlife management, recreation, and biological and physical sciences. Finding appropriate individuals to become rangers can be challenging. Aside from their law enforcement services, park rangers act as guides, naturalists, and educators (Lowry, 1997). Recently, however, there has been a shift toward increased law enforcement duties, as crime in national parks has increased. Among the types of crimes that appear to be increasing in national parks are drug and alcohol-related offenses, vandalism, natural resources violations, traffic offenses, and off-road vehicle violations (Lucas, 1999).

The dangers associated with policing national parks remains constant. Recent data suggest that in 2010 injuries occurred in 14% of the 98 assaults against law enforcement agents from the NPS, and there were no deaths (FBI, 2011a). These incidents most often occurred when NPS personnel were on patrol or guard duty (37.8%); making an arrest or issuing a summons (28.6%); or conducting an investigation or search (21.4%) (FBI, 2011b). The number of NPS personnel assaulted in 2010 constituted 5.2% of assaults against federal law enforcement officers. The increasingly dangerous nature of a park ranger's job is evidenced in the finding that prior to 2012, eight park rangers had been killed in the line of duty since the NPS was created in 1916. Five of those deaths have occurred since 1990. In comparison, eight FBI agents were killed in the line of duty since 1990, even though the FBI is a much larger agency than the NPS (Welch, 2012). The eight rangers who were killed do not include the death of ranger Margaret Anderson who was shot to death by a man she stopped after he ran through a winter tire checkpoint at Mount Rainier on January 1, 2012. Despite the many unique aspects of law enforcement within the NPS, it is argued that "the job of park ranger is generally safer than law enforcement positions in urban and more heavily populated areas" (Farabee, 2003, p. 95).

Results from several research studies shed light on Park Rangers and their responsibilities. Earlier research found that older park rangers and those with the greatest number of years of service had high levels of negative feelings about law enforcement activities. These findings may be indicative of the shift that has occurred in national parks as more law enforcement activities have been incorporated into rangers' daily activities (e.g., Soden and Hester, 1989; Meadows & Soden, 1988). One study found that law enforcement activities may be perceived as an intrusion on the professional domain of some rangers who believe law enforcement is negatively impacting their chosen careers (Soden and Hester, 1989). A different study found that Rangers perceive a high degree of professionalism within the NPS, and a college degree would result in Rangers providing more efficient service (Meadows & Soden, 1988).

Other research focused on the nature of crime in federal forests and parks, the offenders who commit the crimes, and the nature of guns and law enforcement in those settings. Pendleton (1996) found that the belief that national parks and forests are pristine places safe from criminal behavior is inaccurate. Instead, he found that crime was common in these areas; however, the types of crime did not directly reflect the types of crimes found in major cities. He noted that the crimes that most often occurred reflected "the unique physical, legal and social characteristics of the environment," and included tree theft and animal poaching (Pendleton, 1996, p. 22).

Lucas (1999) examined the law enforcement problems that occurred in 29 national parks over the course of a year and found that poaching (66%) was the most commonly reported offense. Most parks included in the study also experienced off-road vehicle (e.g., motorcycles, snowmobiles, recreational campers) violations (55%), and nearly half (48%) experienced violent crime. Less than half of the respondents noted that drugs (38%) and archaeological resource (e.g., any material remains of past human life or activities which are of archeological interests and are at least 100 years of age) violations (28%) occurred in their park.

More recent research tested the assumption that visitors to national parks increase crime and have similar crime-inducing characteristics. Using a large-scale data set of national park visitors, Grinols and colleagues (2011) found that national park visitors did not affect crime, either for FBI Index I violent crimes or for property crimes. These results held consistent across various measures of park visitors and for different ways of estimating the effect.

The aforementioned studies focus on crime and law enforcement as they pertain to park rangers, however the services provided by the Park Police have also undergone evaluation. Park Police perform more traditional police practices compared to park rangers. Table 11.2 depicts the types of crimes encountered by the Park Police from 2005–2010.

Table 11.2 Crimes Encountered by the U.S. Park Police, 2005–2010

Crime Category	CY 2005	2006	2007	2008	2009	2010	% Change from Previous Year	5-Year Average
Homicide	5	3	0	0	0	1	100%	0.8
Rape/Sodomy	3	18	19	14	13	22	69%	17.2
Robbery	56	46	44	56	43	43	0%	46.4
Aggravated Assault	99	138	112	114	107	143	34%	122.8
Burglary	26	57	32	32	31	42	35%	38.8
Larceny/Theft	538	505	471	540	426	461	8%	480.6
Vehicle Theft	42	28	36	31	17	21	24%	26.6
Arson	4	11	2	4	3	6	100%	5.2
Totals	773	806	716	791	640	739	4%	787.3

Source: U.S. Park Police, 2011.

As noted in the table, most of the crimes to which the Park Police responded were generally less serious in nature, akin to the types of crimes encountered by local law enforcement agencies. Annually, most of the incidents involved larceny/theft, however the Park Police do encounter a notable number of aggravated assaults. Table 11.3 provides greater context to the types of crimes encountered by the Park Police, and the various types of personnel involved in the incidents.

Lowry (1997) argued that to better assist the NPS and the national parks in general: 1) park management must receive additional funds; 2) Congress, along with NPS personnel and the public, should seek to clarify the conflicting goals of law enforcement and natural resources advocate within the agency's mandate; and 3) the organizational structure of the NPS should be revised to make it more responsive and effective. He also called for the better use of mass transit within the parks. These and similar suggestions highlight the need for increased funding and outside support to better enable the NPS to best protect national treasures.

Law enforcement personnel in national parks and those protecting national treasures face many atypical challenges compared to other law enforcement agents. National parks provide several unique settings for individuals to commit crime and to be victimized. Park rangers must provide guidance, education, law enforcement, and emergency medical service, which generates numerous challenges that require a wealth of skills and a

Table 11.3 Calendar Year 2010 Performance Measures

Aviation Calls for service	1,041
Communication Dispatched calls for service	178,595
Criminal Investigations Assigned investigations Closure rate on assigned cases	407 52%
Horse-Mounted Patrol Incidents handled	3,782
K-9 Unit (Bomb and Patrol) Incident handled	15,939
Marine Patrol Unit Incident responses	1,555
National Icon Protection Incidents that pose serious threats to Icons Prohibited items confiscated Incidents documented by camera (CCTV) operator	224 17,283 659
Patrol Environmental/resource crimes Drug cases DWI/DUI arrests	955 1,209 678
Special Events/Crowd Control Special events handled by the Force	9,296

Source: U.S. Park Police, 2011.

commitment to public safety and well-being. Many park visitors remain unaware that park rangers are indeed law enforcement agents (Welch, 2012), nevertheless rangers serve many important functions and face many difficult tasks in facilitating safety in the parks. The same can certainly be said for the Park Police.

References

Association of National Park Rangers (nd). *About ANPR: 34 Years of Advocacy*. Accessed online November 11, 2011 at: www.anpr.org/anprwho.htm.

Bumgarner, J. B. (2006). *Federal agents: The growth of federal law enforcement in America*. Westport, CT: Praeger.

Bytnar, B.W. (2010). *A Park ranger's life: Thirty-two years protecting our national parks*. Tucson, AZ: Wheatmark.

Colby, C.B. (1955). *Park ranger: The work, thrills and equipment of the national park rangers*. NY: Coward-McCann.

Dougherty, R. (2004). The endangered park ranger. *National Parks*, 78(3): 7.

Farabee, Jr., C.R. (2003). *National Park Ranger: An American Icon*. Lanham, MD: Roberts Rinehart.

Federal Bureau of Investigation (2011a). *Uniform Crime Reports: Law enforcement officers killed & assaulted, 2010*. Table 76: Federal Law Enforcement Officers Killed and Assaulted. Accessed online December 2, 2011 at: http://www.fbi.gov/about-us/cjis/ucr/leoka/leoka-2010/tables/table76-federal-leoka-department-agency-by-extent-of-injury-06-10.xls.

Federal Bureau of Investigation (2011b). *Uniform Crime Reports: Law enforcement officers killed & assaulted, 2010*. Table 81: Federal Law Enforcement Officers Killed and Assaulted. Accessed online December 2, 2011 at: http://www.fbi.gov/about-us/cjis/ucr/leoka/leoka-2010/tables/table81-federal-leoka-department-agency-by-activity-10.xls.

Grinols, E.L., Mustard, D.B., and Staha, M. (2011). How do visitors affect crime? *Journal of Quantitative Criminology*, 27: 363–378.

Kiernan, T.C. (2005). A salute to the park stewards. *National Parks*, 79(3): 3.

Langton, L. (2010). *Women in law enforcement, 1987–2008*. Washington, D.C.: U.S. Department of Justice, Bureau of Justice Statistics. NCJ 230521.

Lowry, W.R. (1997). Paradise lost in U.S. parks? *Forum for Applied Research and Public Policy*, 12: 6–14.

Lukas, L. (1999). *National Park Service law enforcement: To conserve and protect*. Incline Village, NV: Copperhouse.

Mackintosh, B. (1999). The National Park Service: A brief history. Accessed online, November 4, 2011 at: http://www.cr.nps.gov/history/hisnps/NPShistory/brief history.htm.

Meadows, R. & Soden, D.L. (1988). National Park ranger attitudes and perceptions regarding law enforcement issues. *Justice Professional*, 3(1): 70–93.

National Park Service (n.d.). *History E-Library.* Accessed online, November 7, 2011 at: http://www.nps.gov/history/history/hisnps/NPSHistory/timeline_annotated.htm.

National Park Service. (2010a). *Budget.* Accessed online, November 4, 2011 at: http://www.nps.gov/aboutus/budget.htm.

National Park Service. (2010b). *NPS overview.* Accessed online, October 31, 2011 at: http://www.nps.gov/news/loader.cfm?csModule=security/getfile&PageID=387483.

National Park Service. (2011). *Frequently asked questions.* Accessed online, November 4, 2011 at: http://www.nps.gov/faqs.htm.

Pendleton, M.R. (1996). Crime, criminals and guns in "natural settings": Exploring the basis for disarming federal rangers. *American Journal of Police,* 15(4): 3–25.

Reaves, B. A. (2006). *Federal law enforcement officers, 2004.* Washington, D.C.: U.S. Department of Justice, Bureau of Justice Statistics. NCJ 212750.

Reaves, B.A. (2012). *Federal law enforcement officers, 2008.* U.S. Department of Justice, Bureau of Justice Statistics. NCJ 238250.

Runte, A. (1979). *National parks: The American experience.* Lincoln, NE: University of Nebraska Press.

Security, Fire Duties Strain Park Rangers. (2002). *National Parks,* 76(7/8).

Soden, D.L. & Hester, W.H. (1989). Law enforcement in the National Park Service: The rangers' perspective. *Criminal Justice Review,* 14(1), 63–73.

Toops, C. (2005). Raiders of the last parks. *National Parks,* 79(1).

United States Office of Personnel Management. (1985). *Position classification standard for park ranger series, GS-0025.* Accessed online December 5, 2011 at: http://www.opm.gov/fedclass/gs0025.pdf.

United States Park Police (2011). *2010 Annual report.* U.S. Department of the Interior, National Park Service. Accessed online November 7, 2011 at http://www.nps.gov/uspp/210anrt5411a.pdf.

Welch, C. (January 4, 2012). Park rangers' jobs increasingly dangerous. *Seattle Times,* accessed online January 12, 2012 at: http://seattletimes.nwsource.com/text/2017147696.html.

Wilkinson, T. (2002). On the homefront. *National Parks,* 76 (3/4): 34–39.

Wong, D., & Higgins, C.L. (2010). Park rangers as public health educators: The Public Health in the Parks grants initiative. *American Journal of Public Health,* 100(8): 1370–1373.

Chapter Twelve

The Bureau of Indian Affairs

The relationship between the federal government of the United States and the hundreds of American Indian tribes has been contentious at best. It is a relationship that mirrors American history in many ways, from partnerships, treaties and trusts, to fraud, forced relocation, and cultural destruction with experiences differing depending on the tribe and area of the country. This relationship has impacted the lives of millions of citizens and acres of land in the United States. Furthermore, this intricate history and relationship has led to the creation of a federal agency to manage the multitude of issues surrounding American Indians and law, and provide a police presence and service to some of the most needy populations in the country.

History

The association between the federal government and American Indian people has a long and detailed history from the first foray of settlers to land on the shores of America, through the Revolutionary War, to the current state of tribes reestablishing traditional governments and new business opportunities. By 1780, the United States was a fledgling nation recovering from war and trying to manage treaties that were in place with the British and French, both of whom still had a stake in America and were forces to be reckoned with. This meant a time period of mutual respect emerged from the federal government in the United States in an effort to not antagonize American Indians by encroachment onto their lands. The Proclamation of the Continental Congress in 1783 would forbid and prohibit all persons making a settlement on land claimed or inhabited by Indians (Johannsen, 2004).

There was also a push for trade and cooperation with American Indian tribes as evident by President George Washington's proposed government controlled and operated trading houses. The Government Trading Act of April 18, 1796 was established for conducting liberal trade with Indian nations within the limits of the United States (Prucha, 1990, 16). Treaties and doctrines with American Indians during this time were complex and dealt with each nation separately. There was also a concern about the cultural differences, and many acts were passed along with funding allotted to bring education, Christianity, and White civilization to American Indians (Rockwell, 2010). While this time period may have reflected some benevolence and paternalism towards independent American Indian nations, there was still a level of animosity among some settlers and government officials that would soon change the nature of the relationship for decades and usher in a new federal agency.

By 1786 Congress placed the Secretary of War in charge of all Indian affairs, with little administrative structure for the mission (Utter, 2001). By the end of the War of 1812 there was considerable pressure and demands in Congress to remove American Indians from their lands in the east and to revisit the treaties that were in place. The view within the east was that Indians were in the way of White men and progress. Although some early groundwork had been laid for the relocation of American Indians by Thomas Jefferson's administration, two presidents would lead the way in federally supported removal programs: Presidents James Monroe and Andrew Jackson. President Monroe's view was that assimilation and citizenship were the only just long-term approach to dealing with American Indians. During Monroe's administration Congress would appropriate funds to "civilize" American Indians, and in 1824 the Secretary of War John C. Calhoun created the Office of Indian Affairs within the War Department. The purpose of the newly created Office was to oversee appropriations for treaty annuities, funds for "civilizing" Indians, mediating disputes, and handling all correspondence involving Indians (Utter, 2001).

Removal of American Indians

By the mid-1820s the view of American Indians had changed, and removal was becoming a highly contested issue. Most of the White population in America now viewed natives as a major roadblock, and land was needed to grow the economy. In March 1824, President Monroe addressed Congress with an ominous message that the process for removal of American Indians would be for their benefit and best interests. By December of the same year, Monroe would again speak to Congress stating the process of changing the conditions necessary for survival of the Indian population was moving too slowly, and Indians simply could not remain in their homeland. Monroe would carry out the plans laid by Jefferson, as they both believed Indians would not survive if they remained in the east. Secretary of War Calhoun vowed to move 97,000 Indians from 11 states and territories (Marder et al., 2005). Voluntary removal continued under President John Quincy Adams, however removal would take on a new urgency and intensity under President Andrew Jackson (Littlefield & Parins, 2011).

The 1830s were marked by Jackson's forced removals through the Indian Removal Act, creating some of the most tragic events in the nation such as the "Trail of Tears" wreaking destruction on numerous tribes as more than 100,000 natives were removed (Hämäläinen, 2009). Congress would purchase lands in the west and pay for the cost of removals. As the tribes were removed, an onslaught of paperwork and accounting issues for the War Department and the Office of Indian Affairs. There were numerous renegotiations of treaties, purchases, and contracts with private companies that supplied provisions during the removal. These actions were not met passively and American Indian tribes used both traditional warfare and the courtroom to try and end the forced removals, often to little avail. The Office of Indian Affairs would oversee both voluntary and forced removals, and as these actions grew more complex there was a need for reorganization.

In 1832 Congress would finally acknowledge the Office of Indian Affairs and create a presidential appointed position of commissioner of Indian Affairs. The reorganization would also include superintendents of Indian Affairs who were assigned to territories to oversee all issues involving Indians. Also within this new structure were Indian agents. Indian agents were appointed by the president and reported directly to the Superintendent of Indian Affairs in most cases. Agents worked directly with the tribes as mediators, suppliers, and served as the local representative of the federal government. Furthermore, arrests of Indians could not occur without the Indian agents approval (Hämäläinen, 2009). In some instances Indian agents were assigned a specific tribe, while others were assigned a territory. Soon, the Office of Indian Affairs was supervising trade, land, and numerous issues involving American Indians all as the United States began to expand westward encountering new tribes. The early history of the Office of Indian Affairs to this point was a complex mix of diplomacy, land purchases, trade, and coercion as the federal government attempted to avoid a costly drawn out war with native populations.

The Creation of the Bureau of Indian Affairs

By the 1840s the expansion west brought settlers into contact with numerous tribes, and many territories were becoming states. This added to the complexities of the Office of Indian Affairs and the War Department. William Medill was appointed as the new Indian commissioner. Facing the problems of adding Texas and Southwest California to the Office of Indian Affairs management, Medill called for reform within the agency through better supervision, hiring more qualified personnel, and tighter control over trade between Whites and American Indians. In 1847, the Office of Indian Affairs would be renamed the Bureau of Indian Affairs with nearly $1 million a year being paid out to various tribes. In 1849, Congress created the Department of the Interior that was responsible for the migration out west and the distribution of public lands. The Bureau of Indian Affairs was moved to the newly created Department of the Interior, essentially changing from military to civil control.

This move was not without controversy as there were different opinions in Congress on how the country should respond to its indigenous populations—whether through civilian commissioners or the military. Most felt that civilian control was best and cost effective as warfare between American Indian tribes and Whites on the Great Plains was destructive. Congress came to the conclusion that creating a reservation system to be maintained by the Department of the Interior was the best solution for peace and survival of the Indians. Nonetheless, there was still conflict between the parties that advocated what was to be known as the Peace Policy, and those in the military and western settlers that wanted extermination of Indians. During President Ulysses S. Grant's administration, negotiations with tribes and the Peace Policy faltered, there were allegations of corruption in the Bureau of Indian Affairs, and resistance was felt from Indian tribes who refused to give up their homelands and way of life. This all culminated in the Indian Wars (1865–1890) and included all major battles and skirmishes between the United States Army and the Indian tribes of the west (Heidler & Heidler, 2007).

Early BIA Policing

The creation of the reservation system was complicated and fraught with a mix of many issues such as forced assimilation, oppression, military control, education, and deculturalization (Cuyjet, Howard-Hamilton, & Cooper, 2010). The reservation system also created a need for a law enforcement presence within Indian territory. The first federal experiment with law enforcement on an Indian reservation began in 1872 with the Navajo Nation. The primary problems on the reservation were cattle rustling and theft. Special Indian Commissioner Howard recruited a force of 100 young Navajos representing the 13 bands and gave them the duties of apprehending livestock thieves. He placed them under the control of Chief Manuelito. The force proved to be highly successful. By 1874, a permanent 200-person force was established without funding.

The second early federal experiment took place in the San Carlos territory. The territory in Arizona contained several bands of Apaches who were in conflict with one another. Indian Agent John Clum arrived in 1874 and appointed four Apaches as a police force.

Their duties included guarding prisoners, enforcing alcohol regulations, and arresting insubordinate Indians. Within six months the force was expanded to 60 members and was viewed as a highly effective operation by Indians and non-Indian settlers. By 1875 all law enforcement duties were handed over to this new Apache police force and they would go on to be a part of the territory militia and patrol off the reservation in southeastern Arizona. Indian police agents at this time period made several high profile arrests such as the peaceful apprehension of Geronimo in 1877, and the violent arrest of Sitting Bull in 1890 (BIA, 2012). By 1880, nearly two-thirds of reservations had a police force varying in size from 2 to 50 officers. What these experiments in native policing proved was that having a tribal force to police American Indians was successful and set the tone for the Bureau of Indian Affairs and law enforcement for the future (Luna-Firebaugh, 2007).

During the 1880s, this system of reservation policing was slowly whittled away and placed under control of the Bureau of Indian Affairs. This move towards federal control of Indian police would create animosity between tribal citizens and the new force as they were viewed as progressives rather than traditionalists who wore modern clothing, were given land allotments for their families, and were to report on citizens who fell below a set moral standard. However, there were instances in which Indian police officers refused to act against members of their community and would draw the line at using force against tribal members which in turn was unsettling to federal authorities (Hagan, 1966).

This federally controlled Indian police force was issued uniforms, horses, and rifles. Issuing rifles was abandoned due to fears of arming Indians, but was returned after a few years. Under federal control the Indian police force carried out a variety of law enforcement duties such as removing squatters, protecting agency property, arresting drunks, and guarding rations. Outside of law enforcement tasks, Indian police also conducted a census and built roads. However, one of the most unsettling duties was collecting Indian children for removal and relocation to Indian schools and apprehending those that ran away (Luna-Firebaugh, 2007). The expansion of federal control over Indian police would continue into the 1920s.

After the 1920s, federal concerns over policing on Indian reservations were being redirected and the budget for the forces was being reduced, from nearly 1,000 officers in 1880 to fewer than 200 by 1925 (BIA, 2012). This time period was impacted by the Indian Reorganization Act, which reversed the policies of allotment and assimilation, and mandated a transfer of federal law enforcement authority within certain tribal nations to state governments. While this move would allow self-policing for some tribes it also meant a major reduction in funding and personnel. By World War II, the federal budget would only allow for less than 50 Indian police officers nationwide (BIA, 2012). By the early 1950s, the Termination Era had begun with several attempts to end trust agreements.

Public Law 83-280 (1953) transferred legal jurisdiction over Indian tribes in 15 states from federal to state governments. For tribes in the affected states these changes put them under local justice and police authority ending all federal support and funding for tribal law enforcement. This reduction in funding and officers resulted in spikes in the crime rate within Indian territory (Wells & Falcone, 2008). The Civil Rights Movement of the 1960s would have an impact on numerous institutions and social relations in the United States, and American Indian tribes were no different. This was also a time period of Indian self-determination. The Indian Self-Determination and Education Assistance Act of 1975 (Public Law 93-638) authorized federal funding for tribal courts and police in addition to other services. During the 1960s more than 100 police officers were added to the BIA payroll and in 1969 the first Indian police academy was established in Roswell, New Mexico (Luna-Firebaugh, 2007).

Prior to the creation of this academy, training for Indian law enforcement personnel was sporadic and recruits often had to wait for openings in either state or federal police academies resulting in officers receiving only in-service training. The Indian Police Academy program was designed for the training of both Bureau of Indian Affairs (BIA) and tribal law enforcement officers. The academy would change locations several times over the years, moving to Brigham City, Utah in 1973, to Marana, Arizona in 1985, until finally moving to its current location at the Federal Law Enforcement Training Center in Artesia, New Mexico in 1992 (Indian Police Academy, 2012). The Indian Law Enforcement Reform Act of 1990 established the Division of Law Enforcement Services within the Bureau of Indian Affairs in an effort to centralize administration, and shift BIA based policing forces to federal control which would allow the FBI to train local police at the academy (Wells & Falcone, 2008).

Today there are 208 police departments operating in Indian territory, 43 of which are directly controlled by the BIA. The officers in these departments are federal employees. The majority of the remaining 165 departments are contracted under Public Law 93-638, which allows tribes to establish their own government functions by contracting with the BIA's Division of Law Enforcement Services. There are also departments that are completely funded with tribal money. The officers and staff in these departments cover nearly 56 million acres of Tribal land and provide policing services to over 1 million Indians in the United States (Tribal Law Enforcement, 2012) in what may be one of the most unique tasks in federal law enforcement.

Organization and Personnel

The Bureau of Indian Affairs has a history extending nearly 200 years and is nearly as old as the United States itself. The BIA's headquarters is in Washington, D.C within the Department of the Interior, and has been the primary agency involved in negotiations between the United States and the numerous Indian tribes within the country. Consequently, the BIA has a complex organization as it covers nearly the entire range of programs and government services for American Indian tribes. Programs include an educational system covering primary schools, secondary schools, and colleges, gaming, social services, natural resource management, housing, disaster relief, justice services including courts, detention, and most important for this chapter, law enforcement (Regional Offices, 2012).

The Director of the Bureau of Indian Affairs is the main leadership position of the BIA and reports to the assistant secretary of Indian Affairs. The Director of BIA is responsible for managing the day-to-day operations through the following offices that are headed by Deputy Directors:

- The Office of Indian Services—Facilitates support for tribal people and governments by promoting safe and quality living environments, strong communities, individual rights, and enhancing the lives, prosperity and well being of American Indians and Alaskan Natives. Within the Office of Indian Services there are four divisions: Human Services, Tribal Government Services, Transportation, and Self-Determination (Office of Indian Services, 2012).

- The Office of Field Operations—Oversees the delivery of program services to federally recognized tribes, individual Indians and Alaskan Natives. The 12 regional offices report directly to the deputy director of field operations in Washington,

D.C. Each regional office is headed by a regional director who is responsible for all bureau activities within a defined geographical area with the exception of education and law enforcement (Fixico, 2012).

- The Office of Trust Services—Handles all Indian Affairs' trust responsibilities to tribes and individuals, and oversees all headquarter activities associated with management and protection of trust and restricted lands, natural resources, and real estate. The Office of Trust Services contains six divisions: Real Estate Services, Land Titles and Records, Probate, Natural Resources, Forestry and Wildland Fire Management, and Irrigation, Power and Safety of Dams (Office of Trust Services, 2012).

- The Office of Justice Services—Is responsible for the overall management of the BIA's law enforcement programs, and protects the lives and property of Indian communities. The Office of Justice Services contains five divisions: Corrections, Drug Enforcement, Training (which includes the Indian Police Academy), Professional Standards, Tribal Justice Support, and Law Enforcement (Office of Justice Services, 2012).

The Law Enforcement Division of the Office of Justice Services is comprised of six separate regional districts, and supervised by a Special Agent in Charge. The districts are located in Aberdeen, South Dakota (District I); Muskogee, Oklahoma (District II); Phoenix, Arizona (District III); Albuquerque, New Mexico (District IV); Billings, Montana (District V); and Nashville, Tennessee (District VI). The Law Enforcement Division operates on a budget of more than $300 million and engages in some of the most challenging work in federal law enforcement (Division of Law Enforcement, 2012).

The Bureau of Indian Affairs Law Enforcement Division is one of the smaller federal agencies. The BIA employs less than 300 full-time sworn officers operating in 43 agencies nationwide. These are typically smaller departments serving small populations. All together there are more than 4,000 employees in tribal policing including 3,000 sworn officers providing service in Indian country. The largest employer of tribal officers is the Navajo Police Department with nearly 400 officers.

Becoming a BIA Police Officer

The maximum entry age for a BIA police officer is 37. The educational and experience requirements for police officers in the BIA vary depending on the grade-level the applicant is seeking. For the position of police officer, the grade-levels range from GL-4 to GL-8. GL-4 applicants must have completed two years of education beyond high school and GL-5 applicants must possess a bachelor's degree in police science or a related field. For grade levels beyond GL-5, applicants must have increasing levels of specialized police experience including stakeouts, terrorists investigations, handling hostages situations, and undercover work (USAJOBS, 2012).

Applicants must pass drug, medical, psychological, and written tests, in addition to a background investigation. One of the more unique qualifications for working in the Bureau of Indian Affairs, including all law enforcement positions, is Indian preference. In accordance with the Indian Preference Act of 1934, preference is given to applicants of Indian descent who have the appropriate verification forms to show membership in a federally recognized tribe. The BIA is the only federal law enforcement agency permitted to have a racial preference in hiring.

Once the applicants have completed the initial screening process, they attend a 16-week training session at the Indian Police Academy located at the Federal Law Enforcement

Training Center (FLETC) in Artesia, New Mexico. The rigorous training covers critical aspects of working in law enforcement including officer safety and survival, criminalistics, search and seizure, detention and arrest, Indian country law, and BIA specialized training (Basic Police Officer Training Program, 2012). Upon successful completion of the academy, officers may take their assignment as a uniformed police officer on a reservation. In addition to uniformed police officers within the BIA, individuals may be hired or promoted to special agent and other supervisory and administrative positions.

Functions

Policing in Indian territory may be one of the most challenging operations in federal law enforcement. The crime rates on some reservations are alarmingly high in the United States, with some tribes experiencing violent crime rates two to ten times higher than the national average (Secretary Salazar, 2010). The BIA Law Enforcement division has a direct mission of protecting lives, property, and resources through criminal investigation and police services (Summary of the BIA, 2012). This mission is carried out in the face of several challenges. The first major challenge in providing police services in Indian country is jurisdiction. Tribal jurisdiction stems from a complex maze of treaties, agreements, and negotiations that have been expanded and interpreted through law over the decades. Inside Indian country, tribal departments and BIA police officers have the full authority of federal law. Outside of Indian territory, tribal law enforcement is subject to state certification or cross agency agreements or deputization. Both areas of jurisdiction may be further complicated by situational factors, such as if the parties involved are Indian or non-Indian, or if they involve actions exclusive of state and federal authority (Luna-Firebaugh, 2007).

Policing in Indian territory also has challenges stemming from organization and geography. In many cases Indian country is rural with a population that may be widely dispersed throughout the area and connected with unpaved roads. Officers in some departments may have to cover hundreds of square miles in rugged mountainous terrain without backup, and departments frequently deal with the problems of understaffing and underfunding. Despite these challenges both tribal police officers and BIA police officers provide general law enforcement services to more than 300 reservations in the United States (Summary of the BIA, 2012).

Notable BIA Law Enforcement Cases

As illustrated above, geographic dispersion and organizational issues are problematic for BIA police officers. Further exacerbating the problem are the under-developed economies and severe unemployment on reservations making some of these spaces highly conducive to drug crimes and methamphetamine distribution. Given the jurisdictional issues and the various levels of laws and codes involved, BIA police officers and agents often work in multi-agency taskforces. For example, in January of 2012, the BIA Law Enforcement division along with dozens of other federal law enforcement agencies arrested 24 members of the notorious Native Mob, a roughly 200-member gang operating out Minneapolis. The Native Mob is a violent criminal organization that originated in the 1990s in Minnesota; the gang is highly active with prison counterparts and a criminal influence on reservations in Minnesota, North Dakota, South Dakota, and Wisconsin. The long-term investigation resulted in indictments covering firearms possession, drug trafficking, racketeering, assault, and attempted murder (Sweeping Racketeering Indictment, 2012).

BIA police officers have also been involved in the investigation of a variety of offenses against Indians and tribal lands and they play a key role in the tribal court system, such as by executing arrest warrants, enforcing protection orders, and providing court security. In 2009 the FBI, BIA Law Enforcement Division, and tribal police officers created a joint investigation into an act of arson, which led to the arrest of a 20 year-old offender in Nett Lake Minnesota who maliciously set fire to the Bois Forte Tribal Headquarters (Arson Suspect Arrested, 2009). Another key function of both tribal police and BIA police officers is providing public safety services. According to a 2008 survey, more than 40% of BIA police departments and tribal agencies engaged in emergency search and rescue operations, and more than 20% provided tactical support, fire fighting, and emergency medical services (Reaves, 2008).

These operations, investigations, and arrests are important functions for BIA police officers and other tribal agencies. However, drugs and drug trafficking has had a major impact on law enforcement in Indian country. More specifically, methamphetamine use and dealing has spread rapidly on reservations, causing a new level of concern among law enforcement in the BIA. A 2006 report from the BIA Law Enforcement Division presented the results from their survey of tribal police departments and found that nearly 75% indicated methamphetamine was the greatest drug threat they were facing, 40–50% of all violent crime on reservations was methamphetamine related, and nearly half of all tribal law enforcement officials reported an increase in child neglect cases due to the increase in methamphetamine use (Methamphetamine in Indian Country, 2006).

Due to these concerns, increases in violence, and the methamphetamine supply coming from Mexican drug cartels (with notable trafficking activity on the Tohono O'Odham Indian Reservation in Arizona) there has been a rapid expansion in drug enforcement by the BIA Law Enforcement Division on Indian reservations. In 2006, the BIA Law Enforcement Division was a part of a joint operation named "700 Ranch Round Up" along with Chickasaw Nation Lighthorse Police, the Drug Enforcement Administration, the Bureau of Alcohol, Tobacco, Firearms and Explosives, and state/local law enforcement agencies in both Oklahoma and Texas. The operation targeted a methamphetamine ring that included a Chicago based gang which distributed the drug in southern Oklahoma and Northern Texas. The operation led to the arrest and indictment of 108 defendants, and the seizure of 15 pounds of methamphetamine, 49 guns, and more than $160,000 in cash (Testimony of William P. Ragsdale, 2006).

In 2010 the BIA Law Enforcement Division was involved in a joint operation with the Navajo Nation Division of Public Safety, the FBI, and the Flagstaff Police Department targeting one of the largest methamphetamine distribution networks in the Navajo Nation (the largest reservation in the United States). The year-long undercover investigation resulted in the arrests of 16 suspects on 47 separate charges including conspiracy, aiding and abetting, and possession with the intent to distribute various quantities of methamphetamine (Sixteen Arrested, 2010). The success of these operations illustrates not only the seriousness of the methamphetamine problem within Indian territory, but the importance of joint task force and interagency cooperation with the Bureau of Indian Affairs Law Enforcement Division. The function of protecting lives, property, and resources is at the core of the BIA Law Enforcement Division. It is a task that is central to the BIA's main goal of upholding the constitutional sovereignty of the federally recognized tribes in the United States and preserving peace within Indian country.

The Bureau of Indian Affairs encompasses several different offices that handle a wide range of issues connected to the complex relationship between American Indians and the United States government. As the oldest bureau of the United States Department of the Interior, the BIA has been at the center of American history, from the contested issues of land ownership and forced migration to culture conflict and warfare. The Office of Justice Services within the BIA contains the Law Enforcement Division that provides policing services, training, and support to dozens of agencies as well as the operation 43 police departments.

Enforcing federal, state, local and tribal laws within the shifting context of jurisdiction and heritage of the individuals involved is a complex task. Law enforcement in Indian country must be carried out in the context of the vast geographic dispersion of people, rugged terrain, understaffed departments, and working unassisted while facing dangerous suspects and hostile encounters. Despites these daunting challenges the BIA Law Enforcement Division officers and tribal departments have established themselves as capable of providing justice and safety to residents and visitors to American Indian territory.

References

Arson Suspect Arrested (2009). Retrieved from http://www.boisforte.com/divisions/Arsonsuspectedarrested.htm.

Basic Police Officer Training Program (2012). Retrieved from http://www.fletc.gov/training/programs/artesia-fletc/bureau-of-indian-affairs-training-program-biatp-indian-police-academy.

BIA (2012). Retrieved from http://www.bia.gov/WhoWeAre/BIA/index.htm.

Cuyjet, M., Howard-Hamilton, M., and Cooper, D. (2010). *Multiculturalism on campus: Theory, models, and practices for understanding diversity and creating inclusion.* Sterling, VA: Stylus Publishing.

Division of Law Enforcement (2012). Retrieved from http://www.bia.gov/WhoWeAre/BIA/OJS/DOLE/index.htm.

Fixico, D. (2012). *Bureau of Indian Affairs.* Santa Barbara, CA: ABC-CLIO.

Hagan, W. (1966). *Indian police and judges: experiments in acculturation and control.* New Haven, CT: Yale University Press.

Hämäläinen, P. (2009). *The Comanche empire.* New Haven, CT.: Yale University Press.

Heidler, D., and Heidler, J. (2007). *Daily lives of civilians in wartime modern America: From the Indian Wars to the Vietnam War.* Santa Barbara, CA: ABC-CLIO.

Indian Police Academy (2012). Retrieved from http://www.bia.gov/WhoWeAre/BIA/OJS/IPA/index.htm.

Johansen, B. (2004). *Enduring legacies: Native American treaties and contemporary controversies.* Westport, CT: Greenwood Publishing Group.

Littlefield, D., and Parins, J. (2011). *Encyclopedia of American Indian removal.* Santa Barbara, CA: ABC-CLIO.

Luna-Firebaugh, E. (2007). *Tribal policing: Asserting sovereignty, seeking justice.* Tucson: University of Arizona Press.

Marder, W, Tice, P., and Sando, J. (2005). *Indians in the Americas: The untold story*. San Diego, CA: Book Tree.

Methamphetamine in Indian Country (2006). Retrieved from www.justice.gov/tribal/docs/fv_tjs/session ... /Meth_Overview.pdf.

Office of Indian Services (2012). Retrieved from http://www.bia.gov/WhoWeAre/BIA/OIS/index.htm.

Office of Justice Services (2012). Retrieved from http://www.bia.gov/WhoWeAre/BIA/OJS/index.htm.

Office of Trust Services (2012). Retrieved from http://www.bia.gov/WhoWeAre/BIA/OTS/index.htm.

Prucha, F. (1990). *Atlas of American Indian affairs*. Lincoln, NE: University of Nebraska Press.

Regional Officers (2012). Retrieved from http://www.tribal-institute.org/lists/enforcement.htm.

Reaves, B. (2008). *Tribal law enforcement*. Washington, D.C.: Bureau of Justice Statistics.

Rockwell, S (2010). *Indian affairs and the administrative State in the nineteenth century*. New York: Cambridge University Press.

Secretary Salizar (2010). Retrieved from http://www.doi.gov/news/pressreleases/Secretary-Salazar-Assistant-Secretary-Echo-Hawk-Laud-Presidents-Signing-of-Tribal-Law-and-Order-Act.cfm.

Sixteen Arrested (2010). Retrieved from http://www.fbi.gov/phoenix/press-releases/2010/px042210.htm.

Sweeping Racketeering Indictment (2012). Retrieved from http://www.justice.gov/usao/mn/nativemobindictment.html.

Summary of the BIA Office of Justice Services (2012). Retrieved from http://www.bia.gov/WhoWeAre/BIA/OJS/index.htm.

Testimony of William P. Ragsdale (2006). Retrieved from http://www.doi.gov/ocl/2006/MethamphetamineUseInIndianCountry.htm.

Tribal Law Enforcement (2012). Retrieved from http://www.tribal-institute.org/lists/enforcement.htm.

USAJOBS (2012). Retrieved from http://www.usajobs.gov/GetJob/ViewDetails/313298200.

Utter, J. (2001). *American Indians: Answers to today's questions*. Norman, OK: University of Oklahoma Press.

Wells, L., and Falcone, D. (2008) Tribal policing on American Indian reservations. *Policing: An International Journal of Police Strategies & Management*, 31(4), pp. 648–673.

Part V
Federal Law Enforcement Agencies

Other Agencies

Chapter Thirteen

Internal Revenue Service

Taxes have existed as long as there have been organized nations, with ancient examples being traced back to the Egyptians. There has been an equally long history of resistance to taxation. Taxes play a significant role in a developed economy such as the United States, as well as numerous other nations around the world. On the individual level nearly everyone sees the impact of federal taxes in the differences between their gross earnings and net income. On the national scale, federal taxes touch nearly every aspect of our society as they are used to finance government programs, stabilize the economy, and balance the federal budget. Furthermore, as the activities of the federal government expand so the does the demand for greater taxation to generate funds for programs and defense of the nation.

While the issue of taxation can often result in divisive political and legal battles, their importance is clear, and the collection efforts represent a monumental logistical task. During fiscal year 2011, the Internal Revenue Service (IRS) processed more than 234 million returns, collected $2.4 trillion in federal revenue, and provided $416 billion in refunds (Internal Revenue Service, 2011). From the early days of the first authorized taxes in the United States fraud and evasion have been problems for the federal government and American citizens. Today these actions are not only a threat to the economy of the United States, but also pose a potential national security risk in the wake of the terrorist attacks of 9/11 demonstrating the importance of the enforcement of tax laws and criminal investigation.

History

Taxes have been a contentious issue in nearly every society, with disputes over the amount collected, the use of money, or redistribution of wealth. Taxation in the modern era can be traced back to the outbreak of the Civil War, which created a financial emergency for Congress and President Abraham Lincoln. Millions of dollars were needed to support and supply troops in this conflict and the decision was made to levy a tax on certain properties while excluding others, creating a heavy burden on some territories. This would not provide enough revenue, so the controversial decision was made to institute a tax on personal income. Congress introduced the Revenue Act of 1861, "to provide increased Revenue from Imports, to pay Interest on the Public Debt, and for other Purposes" (Lincoln, 2010, 292).

The act was replaced the next year with the Revenue Tax Act of 1862 and signed into law by President Lincoln. This act created the first personal federal income tax in the history of the United States levying a flat rate of 3% for individuals making over $600 a year and a 5% rate on those earning more than $10,000 a year (Owensby, 2010). The act would established the Bureau of Internal Revenue within the Department of the Treasury, and the position of Commissioner of Internal Revenue who would collect the payments being withheld by employers.

The Constitution grants Congress the authority to lay and collect taxes as well as duties, excises, and imports to pay national debts, provide defense, and general welfare. The Constitution also places limits on taxation stating that all direct taxes shall be laid uniformly throughout the United States and in proportion to the population. These concepts of uniformity and proportionally would lay the foundation for numerous cases that would challenge the constitutionality of federal taxes prior to the 1900s. For example, *Pollock v. Farmer's Loan and Trust* would challenge the Income Tax Law of 1894—the first federal income tax since the Civil War. The law levied a 2% tax on gains on income over $4,000 derived from property, rents, dividends, or salaries. The argument was that the new tax was discriminatory, targeted certain groups, and was essentially a direct tax (Smith et al., 2008).

In a five to four vote the Supreme Court declared the law unconstitutional due to violating the uniformity test. The decision was controversial and appeared to go against previous rulings that supported a federal income tax. Conservatives in the country were pleased as they viewed the tax as a socialist attack, while other Americans, most notably farmers, viewed the decision as a win for the rich and powerful to the detriment of common people (Jayfox, 2005). The *Pollock* decision would also make the source of income relevant for taxation and challenges.

Taxation in the Twentieth Century

Near the turn of the century, the growth of the federal government was becoming costly and revenues were now needed to fund the Spanish-American War all resulting in growing support for a new income tax despite the *Pollock* case. It was also clear that passing a Constitutional Amendment giving the federal government the power to impose income taxes would be the most expedient method. However, passing a Constitutional Amendment is a time-consuming process, and due to the need for immediate revenue, Congress simultaneously passed the Sixteenth Amendment and the Tax Act of 1909. The Tax Act of 1909 would impose a 1% tax on corporate profits over $5,000. Prior to this act, corporation profits were not subject taxation. This new act was met with immediate resistance by highly influential citizens and within one year 15 cases challenged the act in front of the Supreme Court. In a unanimous decision the Supreme Court upheld the act in *Flint v. Stone Tracey Co.* (1911) ruling that it was not a direct tax, but an indirect one or an excise for the privilege of doing business as a corporation (Smith et al., 2009).

The Sixteenth Amendment profoundly changed funding of the federal government giving Congress the power to levy and collect taxes on any income no matter the source and without regard to any census or enumeration. The context of the amendment was the Progressive Era (1900–1920) under the presidencies of Roosevelt, Taft, and Wilson. Americans were growing increasingly wary of the disparities in wealth and were challenging the social issues of the time. Tariffs were the primary source of funding for the federal government at this point, but they simply could not keep pace with federal growth and were perceived as damaging to the poor and protecting large businesses. President Taft supported the proposed amendment and the tax on income, despite heavy resistance from those who felt the taxing of income would turn America into a socialist state. Many in Congress felt the amendment was doomed and would never pass.

To the surprise of many of those in politics, 36 states ratified the controversial Sixteenth Amendment in 1913 that would create a progressive tax system on individuals and corporations earning more than $4,000 per year at a rate of 1%, and up to 6% for those making more than $500,000. The new income tax was used to fund military efforts in World War I and rates would be raised as high as 70% over time (Wayne, 2011). The Sixteenth Amendment gave Congress nearly unlimited funds to create programs, deal with insolvency, encourage citizens to rely on the federal government in times of need, and expand the federal government to levels beyond the scope of the Constitution (Bloom & Johnson, 2001). The Sixteenth Amendment revitalized the Bureau of Revenue, which had a reduced burden as many taxes had been relaxed after the Civil War.

The passage of the Sixteenth Amendment and the War Revenue Act of 1917 also revealed the limits of Bureau of Internal Revenue to carry out the collection and management of large sums of cash and navigate the complex laws that were in place. The existing bureau was realigned with new offices and divisions to assist with the heavier workload. The number of field forces operating under the supervision of internal-revenue collectors, administrative, and executive officers were all increased, and the number of personnel at the bureau in Washington, D.C. increased more than four-fold (United States Department of the Treasury, 1919). With a Constitutional Amendment that withstood the scrutiny of the Supreme Court there was now a legal foundation for a federal income tax. Income tax was now a part of life in America and created a host of new problems, most notably tax evasion and fraud.

The Creation of Special Agents

Under the new tax laws, there were numerous deductions and exemptions to tax liability including home mortgages, interests paid on state bonds, and charitable giving. Because of these personal exemptions only individuals with high incomes paid taxes, making compliance a serious issue. By 1914, the total number of returns filed was less than .5% of the U.S. population and up until 1939, the number of returns filed never exceeded 7% of the total population (Slemrod & Bakija, 2004). In addition to the problems of citizens failing to file, the Bureau of Internal Revenue was also facing issues of internal misconduct by employees. By 1917, Bureau Commissioner Daniel Roper, who also served as assistant postmaster general, created a new division within the Bureau of Internal Revenue, the Intelligence Unit. Commissioner Roper envisioned the Intelligence Unit performing a similar role to that of postal inspectors as they frequently dealt with fraud and internal misconduct. On July 1, 1919, the commissioner of the Bureau of Internal Revenue gained approval from the Secretary of the Treasury to transfer six experienced postal inspectors to the Bureau of Internal Revenue to become a part of the new unit.

Commissioner Roper was allowed to choose the six men he wanted for the Intelligence Unit, and he selected individuals with excellent records of investigation, determination, and honesty. These six men would become the first Bureau of Internal Revenue special agents. Based on their experience as postal inspectors the new special agents were able to quickly develop procedures for conducting fair investigations. The tasks of these initial special agents were serious as they made recommendations for assessing tax fraud penalties, liens on property, and prosecution of tax evaders and bureau personnel involved in conspiracies. Specials agents wielded a tremendous amount of power; their recommendations or errors could ruin a business, a reputation, or possibly result in criminal prosecution of a taxpayer or a bureau employee.

Because of the dire consequences of an investigation, supervisors in the Intelligence Unit carefully reviewed all reports. The compliance rate for filing taxes increased considerably after the formation of the Intelligence Unit. The initial mandates of the Intelligence Unit were to investigate attempts to defraud the government of taxes that were due. However, the mission would expand to background checks of applicants, attorneys and accountants who represented taxpayers, and any special investigation called for by the commissioner or the Secretary of the Treasury (Internal Revenue Service, 1996).

The federal government and specifically the Bureau of Internal Revenue would soon wrestle with an interesting question. Were criminals or others obtaining an illegal income required to file a tax return? Several high profile cases involving taxes, criminal activity, and the law would answer this question. In 1921 Manny Sullivan, a bootlegger, was arrested and charged with income tax evasion. Sullivan took a stand against the charges and offered a unique defense that income from illegal activities should not be taxable, as filing a tax return would amount to self-incrimination and a violation of his Fifth Amendment rights. In 1927 the Supreme Court ruled against Sullivan. The issue was now resolved and the Bureau of Internal Revenue would start aggressively pursuing bootleggers during Prohibition. One remarkable approach the Intelligence Unit undertook was to attempt to get mobsters to report their income. A young inexperienced special agent named Eddie Waters was dispatched to Chicago and began pestering Ralph Capone, the older brother of Al Capone.

Targeting Al Capone

Ralph Capone eventually complied and filed a tax return covering income for the four years of his profession as a gambler. However, the older Capone failed to pay income taxes on his reported legal income and subsequently had $11,000 in liens placed on his property. After the success of targeting Ralph Capone, the Intelligence Unit began to focus on what would become one of the most important income tax investigations in the Bureau of Internal Revenue Service and American history — the case against the infamous gangster Al Capone. Al Capone arrived in Chicago around 1920 and quickly rose in the Colosimo mob and with prohibition in place his profits were enormous. Capone made a citywide grab for power culminating in the St. Valentine's Day massacre in 1929. Once in power, Capone expanded his empire into bootlegging, extortion, vice crimes, and unions (Internal Revenue Service, 1996).

As the high profile gangster continued to operate, the government was unable to convict Capone of any murders despite his reputation as a feared killer, and the fact that eyewitnesses were present at his crimes. Liquor laws were hardly enforceable and the penalties were minimal. The federal government finally concluded that the use of a tax evasion investigation would be the best strategy to bring down Capone. Using a tax evasion investigation strategy is not direct. Because illegal income is undeclared and hard to assess, investigators essentially had two available approaches: a net worth approach in which the expenditures of an individual are compared to their declared income (the difference would show the evasion), or track an individual's expenditures to show there is income being earned (Eghigian & Nitti, 2006).

Al Capone was astute at hiding his wealth. He showed no income, did not own property in his name, had no bank account and never signed a check. The Bureau of Internal Revenue chose the expenditure strategy since Capone did not have an income trail. The difficulty was in being able to prove to a grand jury that Capone led a lifestyle that was well beyond the means he claimed (Iorizzo, 2003). Investigators were able to show that Capone led an extravagant lifestyle and spent large sums of money, hundreds of dollars a week on meat, thousands of dollars on suits and parties, and more than $3,000 in phone bills in 1929. By 1931, the Intelligence Unit had compiled enough evidence to apprehend Al Capone and during his trial contractors and store merchants were brought to the stand to testify about Capone's excessive spending. Bureau agents estimated Capone's bootlegging revenue to be $70 million per year (Eghigian & Nitti, 2006). Capone was found guilty of three counts of felony tax evasion and two counts of failing to file a tax return. He was sentenced to 11 years in federal prison and assessed fines of over $50,000. In addition, he owed more than $200,000 in back taxes and interest (Internal Revenue Service, 1996).

IRS Special Agents over the Decades

The Intelligence Unit was praised after the conviction of Al Capone, and press coverage suggested their success proved that law enforcement could make inroads against organized crime. Observers also felt the prosecution and conviction of Al Capone prompted delinquent tax filers of both legal and illegal income to immediately file their returns. Throughout the 1930s and 1940s the Bureau of Internal Revenue would go on to successfully pursue other organized crime leaders, drug smugglers, movie stars, and business leaders for tax evasion. By 1950, the Intelligence Unit had over 1,600 special agents and was engaging in high profile investigations. In 1952, the Bureau of Internal Revenue underwent a comprehensive reorganization. As a part of this change the Intelligence Unit was renamed the Intelligence Division and its criminal investigation functions were decentralized. On July 9, 1953 the Bureau of Internal Revenue was renamed the Internal Revenue Service (IRS) to emphasize service on the behalf of taxpayers (Internal Revenue Service, 1996).

The ensuing decades introduced major changes to the IRS and Intelligence Division including automated data processing that would make fraud detection easier during the 1960s. One of the most notable changes revolved around the training of IRS special agents during this decade. Prior to the 1960s, there was no formalized classroom training of special agents. Special agents took correspondence courses on accounting and income tax laws and then worked under a seasoned special agent for six weeks. In May of 1960, the first Special Agent Basic School was opened in Washington, D.C. By the 1970s, the number of special agents increased to over 1,800 and the Intelligence Division was loaning agents to the Sky Marshals Program.

By 1975, the Intelligence Unit was coming under public scrutiny for allegations of gathering non-tax related personal information on individuals that led to substantial changes in procedures and the use of sensitive information. During this same year the Federal Law Enforcement Training Center in Glynco, Georgia created a training program for IRS special agents. In July 1978, the Intelligence Division was renamed the Criminal Investigation Division (CID) after a review suggested it was a more fitting title. The CID began to focus on new tax violations — tax protestors, unethical tax return preparers, and tax shelters. By 1980 the CID had increased to nearly 3,000 special agents, expanded the use of computers to detect fraud, and was participating in interagency drug task forces (Internal Revenue Service, 1996).

The 1990s would see further reorganization and assessment of the CID including two reports that recommended regulating overtime and official vehicle and firearm use by special agents. During this time period IRS special agents also uncovered one of the largest drug-related money laundering schemes in the United States involving more than $400 million from New York cocaine sales that was being funneled to Cali Cartel members in

Colombia (Internal Revenue Service, 1996). The terrorist attacks of September 11, 2001 would also have an impact on the Internal Revenue Service and the Criminal Investigation Division, as it resulted in nations becoming more concerned over the means by which terrorist organizations raise funds.

Because financial crimes may be used to fund terrorism, the Criminal Investigation Division of the IRS has played a critical role in exposing schemes involving tax exempt fund raising and money laundering. For example, special agents participate in what are termed "jump teams" that are sent to the Middle East, Europe, and the Caribbean to conduct financial investigations and analyze financial data. CID special agents have also taken on special assignments such as being a part of interagency efforts to trace and recover Iraqi assets, including both the official and illicit assets of Saddam Hussein, his associates, their families, and front companies (Criminal Investigation Responds to Terrorism, 2012). The unique skills of IRS special agents combine accounting and law enforcement, and agents have proven to be very useful assets in dealing with a wide array financial crimes connected to organized crime, drug trafficking, identity theft, and terrorism in a post-9/11 United States.

Organization and Personnel

The Internal Revenue Service plays a critical role within the Department of the Treasury and the financial health of the United States. The IRS was restructured in 1998 to modernize the agency and to reflect the private sector model of customer service. The modern day IRS is divided into three commissioner-level organizations. The commissioner of the IRS is appointed by the President of the United States and confirmed by the Senate for a five-year term and is responsible for planning, directing, and evaluating IRS policies, programs, and performance. The commissioner of the IRS is supported by other offices and special staff members.

- Office of the Deputy Commissioner for Services and Enforcement—The IRS commissioner's first assistant and aids in establishing and enforcing tax policy. The Office of the Deputy Commissioner for Services and Enforcement helps in carrying out the IRS' mission of providing top quality service to America's taxpayers by helping them understand and meet their tax responsibilities. Several of the IRS divisions and sub offices report to the Deputy Commissioner for Services and Enforcement such as the Wage and Investment Division, Large and Mid-Size Business Division, and the Office of Professional Responsibility. Most relevant for this chapter, the Criminal Investigation Division reports to the Deputy Commissioner for Services and Enforcement.

- Office of the Deputy Commissioner for Operations Support—Responsible for overseeing IRS operations, and providing executive leadership on policies, programs, and activities. The Deputy Commissioner for Operations Support assists the IRS commissioner in establishing tax administration policy, and developing strategic issues and objectives for IRS management.

- Office of the Chief of Staff—Reviews and appraises major policy issues and questions with implications for the IRS' position on a wide variety of issues.

- The Chief Counsel—Appointed by the President of the United States and serves as the primary legal advisor to the commissioner of the IRS on all matters related to interpreting policy and enforcement of IRS laws. Chief Counsel reports directly to the IRS commissioner and the Treasury Counsel on certain matters.

- Special Assistant to the Commissioner — Serves as the commissioner's principal advisor on general management and administration of the IRS. The Special Assistant to the Commissioner works closely with the commissioner, deputy commissioners and other members of the commissioner's office on overall policy, operations, and management of the IRS (Organization, Finance and Management, 2012).

In fiscal year 2011 the Internal Revenue Service had nearly 105,000 employees including full-time, part-time, and seasonal personnel. Most employees work in one of the three core areas within the IRS: taxpayer's services, enforcement, or operations support. The IRS operates on a budget of more than $12 billion which breaks down to roughly $2.5 billion for taxpayer services, $5 billion for enforcement, and $4 billion for operations support (Internal Revenue Service, 2011). The agency has numerous career opportunities and positions within each of its core areas such as tax law specialists, tax examiners, internal revenue officers, and research analysts. Each of these positions has its own education and experience requirements. However, it is the law enforcement branch of the IRS that serves the American public by investigating criminal violations of the Internal Revenue Code and related financial crimes.

The Criminal Investigation Division houses IRS special agents. As of fiscal year 2011 there were 4,100 employees in the CID including 2,730 special agents (Internal Revenue Service, 2011). IRS special agents are a key component in larger federal law enforcement efforts and often work closely with the Department of Justice, U.S. Attorneys, the FBI, the Department of Homeland Security, Drug Enforcement Administration, U.S. Postal Inspection Service, and the U.S. Marshals Service (IRS Criminal Investigation Special Agent, 2012).

Becoming an IRS Special Agent

Applicants for the position of special agent in the IRS must not have reached their 37th birthday at the time of certification, and they must be available to work anywhere in the United States. The upper age limit can be waived in cases of applicants with prior federal law enforcement experience seeking veteran positions. Applicants must possess a valid driver's license and are required to carry a firearm. The educational requirements for applicants for the position of special agent are specific and demanding. For the entry level position applicants must have a four-year degree in any field of study that includes, or was supplemented by at least 15 semester hours or 23 quarter hours in accounting, plus an additional 9 semester hours or 14 quarter hours from among the following closely related fields: finance, economics, business law, tax law, or money and banking. Applicants may also meet the requirement through possessing a Certified Public Accountant (CPA) Certificate, or demonstrating three years of successful, responsible accounting, business experience, and auditing principles. Entry positions at a higher grade require a masters or law degree (IRS Criminal Investigation Special Agent, 2012).

Candidates are rated based on their education and experience and are required to demonstrate their abilities at a skills assessment center. At the assessment center applicants undergo interviews, written exercises, and are scored on benchmarks. Applicants must also submit to a drug test, medical examination, background investigation, and undergo and successfully complete a pre-appointment income tax audit. After successfully completing pre-employment screening, candidates attend a nine-week Criminal Investigation Training Program (CITP) at the Federal Law Enforcement Training Center (FLETC) in Glynco, GA. The program covers basic federal criminal investigation techniques, federal criminal law, courtroom procedures, enforcement operations, interviewing, physical training, firearms and vehicle handling (Criminal Investigator Training Program, 2012).

Once the CITP training is complete, recruits move on to a 16-week Criminal Investigator specialized training program including instruction in tax law, criminal tax fraud, money laundering and other financial schemes. Trainees are also introduced to IRS specific undercover operations, forensics, and trial preparation. Trainees may also further specialize and receive computer investigative training and become a Computer Investigative Specialist (CIS) in which they receive five weeks of additional training at the FLETC on computer evidence recovery. Once this phase is complete, CIS agents attend a three-week Computer Evidence Analysis Training course at the University of North Texas followed by additional advanced training after one year. Once all training has been completed special agents are assigned to a field office with opportunities to receive an international assignment (IRS Criminal Investigation Special Agent, 2012).

Functions

The mission of the Internal Revenue Service is to provide American taxpayers with top quality service by helping them understand and meet their tax obligations as well as enforcing the law with fairness. However, the mission of the Criminal Investigation Division is more specific as it is to serve the American public by investigating potential criminal violations of the Internal Revenue Code and related financial crimes in a manner that fosters confidence in the tax system and compliance with the law. The CID strategic plan is comprised of three programs: Legal Source Tax Crimes, Illegal Source Financial Crimes, and Narcotics Related and Counterterrorism Financial Crimes (Criminal Investigation At-a-Glance, 2012).

The American tax system is voluntary and self-assessed and all income is taxable (legal or illegal). However, when an individual or corporation intentionally tries to conceal income from the federal government or take an active part in criminal activity involving money laundering or fraud, IRS special agents may investigate. The CID classifies its investigations into 18 program and emphasis areas. A few examples are bankruptcy fraud, corporate fraud, gaming, healthcare fraud, identity theft, nonfiler enforcement, and public corruption crimes (Program and Emphasis Areas, 2012).

IRS Criminal Investigation Procedures and Recent Cases

IRS special agents have strict procedures and codes guiding their investigations. Special agents may begin an investigation if they obtain information from within the IRS, a revenue collection officer, investigations from other law enforcement agencies, or a private citizen. Special agents conduct a preliminary investigation to evaluate information to determine if a financial crime has taken place. From this point, the agent's supervisor reviews the preliminary information. If approved, the case goes forward to be reviewed by a special agent in charge. After two levels of review the special agent may open a criminal investigation employing various techniques to obtain evidence, including interviews of third party witnesses, conducting surveillance, executing search warrants, and reviewing financial information. After all the evidence is gathered and analyzed, the special agent and his or her supervisor either make the determination that evidence does not substantiate criminal activity or there is sufficient evidence to support the recommendation of prosecution. If there is sufficient evidence of criminal activity the special agent prepares a written report detailing the findings of the violation and recommends prosecution (How Criminal Investigations Are Initiated, 2012).

In fiscal year 2011, the Criminal Investigation Division initiated 4,700 criminal investigations and assessed almost $31 billion in civil penalties. The division referred more than 3,000 illegal income and narcotics-related financial crime cases for prosecution. More than 80% of those sentenced received a prison term (Internal Revenue Service, 2011). The Criminal Investigation Division is often involved in numerous interagency investigations to protect the American public and taxpayers. For example, in 2011 the Criminal Investigation Division along with the FBI and the Securities and Exchange Commission Enforcement Division staff in Fort Worth, Texas initiated an investigation against Robert David Watson of Spring, Texas for his illegal activities in a foreign currency investment strategy he termed Alpha One. Between 2003 and 2009, Watson raised tens of millions of dollars from scores of investors, did not trade in currency as he led the investors to believe, earned few profits, and sent out false statements. Based in part on the investigative skills of IRS special agents, Watson pled guilty and was sentenced to 20 years in federal prison and ordered to pay more than $22 million in restitution to his victims (Examples of International Investigations, 2012).

Not unlike the role the IRS investigators played in bringing down Al Capone during prohibition, IRS special agents can be key law enforcement assets in fighting drug trafficking. Special agents are typically brought in to trace and find the money connected to illegal activities, money laundering, and tax evasion. For example, in February 2012, Jimmie Goodgame was sentenced to 70 months in prison for laundering more than $1.5 million in drug proceeds from a large-scale heroin trafficking ring that brought the drug into Ohio. Goodgame deposited more than $1.5 million in cash into accounts he controlled between 2008 and 2010, and had more than 50 automobiles titled to three companies he controlled, which were actually driven and controlled by drug dealers. Goodgame presented false representations to car dealerships and salespeople to obtain vehicles for the dealers and in turn charged them a fee using multiple bank accounts to disguise his illegal income.

In April 2012 Benjamin Arellano-Felix, the former leader of the Tijuana Cartel/Arellano-Felix Organization (AFO), was sentenced to 300 months in prison and ordered to forfeit $100 million in criminal proceeds. Arellano-Felix and other AFO members brought in tons of cocaine and marijuana into the United States and then conspired with other members of the AFO to launder the proceeds by having associates transport, transmit, and transfer hundreds of millions in U.S. dollars from the United States to Mexico (Examples of Money Laundering, 2012).

Occasionally IRS special agents must target individuals who are or have been connected to the agency itself. For example, March 2012 George Tannous, a former revenue agent with the Internal Revenue Service, was sentenced to 33 months in prison for his role in a securities fraud scheme that took more than $8 million from hundreds of victims across the country. Tannous and three co-conspirators solicited victims to purchase unregistered stock in Bidbay.com, Inc. and several related companies under the pretense the companies would be bought out by eBay. Tannous personally received nearly $3 million from investor funds that he failed to report to the IRS (Examples of General Fraud, 2012).

In 2011, former IRS Revenue Agent Steven Martinez was arrested by IRS agents following the return of a 49 count indictment of mail fraud, procuring false tax returns, social security fraud, aggravated identity theft, making false tax returns, money laundering, and criminal forfeiture. Martinez prepared tax returns for wealthy taxpayers and informed clients they owed substantial amounts of money and needed to write a check for the amount. He then deposited the funds in accounts he controlled under fictitious names, profiting nearly $11 million, and filed false tax returns to the IRS. Once facing federal tax fraud charges, Martinez attempted to hire a contract killer to murder two key witnesses in the trial against him. Martinez provided $100,000 and the photos of the two witnesses to a former employee who contacted the FBI and then recorded a meeting between Martinez and the informant (Former IRS Agent Accused, 2012).

Taxation in nearly every society has been the source of not only protest but also outright rebellion. While unpopular, taxes are necessary in modern society particularly in one such as the United States where the government has expanded to provide numerous services to its citizens. The imposition of taxes in the United States has been an interesting mix of law and political debate with challenges to nearly every facet of taxation. With a tax law in place, evasion and fraud soon followed demonstrating a need for an agency to oversee the collection of taxes in the United States. The Criminal Investigation Division of the IRS had humble beginnings with just six special agents, but would expand its personnel and roles considerably over the years. The Criminal Investigation Division represents the law enforcement branch of the IRS and has provided a critical law enforcement service not only to the federal government but also to all American taxpayers.

Today the Criminal Investigation Division's role is more complex than just enforcement of tax laws and codes. Special agents are one of the most unique investigative tools in the federal government, often working with multiple federal, state and local agencies to find the money trail in a wide range of cases including abusive return preparers, identity theft, public corruption, narcotics and organized crime. The Internal Revenue Service Criminal Investigation Division has an enviable success rate with their investigations, recommendations, and collection of billions of dollars in penalties and owed taxes. The special agents of the Criminal Investigation Division have played significant roles in dismantling nationwide fraudulent schemes, toppling organized crime leaders, and detecting the funding of extremist groups in a post-9/11 United States, proving themselves to be the premier financial investigators in the federal government.

References

Bloom, S., and Johnson, L. (2001). *The story of the Constitution, Second Edition.* Arlington Heights, IL: Christian Liberty Press.

Criminal Investigation At-a-Glance (2012). Retrieved from http://www.irs.gov/irs/article/0,,id=98398,00.html.

Criminal Investigation Responds to Terrorism (2012). Retrieved from http://www.irs.gov/compliance/enforcement/article/0,,id=107510,00.html.

Criminal Investigator Training Program (2012). Retrieved from http://www.fletc.gov/training/training-management/training-management-division/center-basic-programs-branch/criminal-investigator-training-program-citp/.

Eghigian, M., and Nitti, F. Jr. (2006). *After Capone: The life and world of Chicago mob boss Frank "the Enforcer" Nitti.* Nashville, TN: Cumberland House Publishing.

Examples of General Fraud Investigations—Fiscal Year 2012 (2012). Retrieved from http://www.irs.gov/compliance/enforcement/article/0,,id=246534,00.html.

Examples of International Investigations—Fiscal Year 2012 (2012). Retrieved from http://www.irs.gov/compliance/enforcement/article/0,,id=252338,00.html.

Examples of Money Laundering Investigations—Fiscal Year 2012 (2012). Retrieved from http://www.irs.gov/compliance/enforcement/article/0,,id=246537,00.html.

Former IRS Agent Accused of Ordering Hits on Customers (2012). Retrieved from http://www.nctimes.com/news/local/ramona/region-former-irs-agent-accused-of-ordering-hits-on-customers/article_215ce240-857a-5bd7-b87f-07972855b4f8.html.

How Criminal Investigations Are Initiated (2012). Retrieved from http://www.irs.gov/compliance/enforcement/article/0,,id=175752,00.html.

Internal Revenue Service (1996). *75 years of IRS criminal investigation history, 1919–1994.* Ann Arbor, MI: University of Michigan Library.

Internal Revenue Service (2011). *Data book 2011.* Washington, D.C.

Iorrizo, L. (2003). *Al Capone: A biography.* Santa Barbara, CA: Greenwood Publishing.

IRS Criminal Investigation Special Agent (2012). Retrieved from http://jobs.irs.gov/midcareer/criminal-investigation-special-agent.html.

Jayfox, F. (2005). *The Progressive era.* Facts on File Inc.: New York.

Lincoln, A. (2010). *Works of Abraham Lincoln: Includes inaugural addresses, state of the union addresses, Cooper's union speech, Gettysburg address, house divided speech, proclamation of amnesty, the emancipation proclamation and more.* MobileReference.

Organization, Finance and Management (2012). Retrieved from http://www.irs.gov/irm/part1/irm_01-001-005.html.

Owensby, J. (2010). *The United States Constitution (Revisited).* Kernersville, N.C.: A-argus Books.

Program and Emphasis Areas (2012). Retrieved from http://www.irs.gov/compliance/enforcement/article/0,,id=130611,00.html.

Slemrod, J., and Bakija, J. (2004). *Taxing ourselves: A citizen's guide to the debate over taxes.* Cambridge, MA: MIT Press.

Smith, E., Harmelink, P., and Hasselback, J. (2009). *Federal taxation: Comprehensive topics 2009.* Chicago: CCH.

United States Department of the Treasury. (1919). *Report of the Secretary of the Treasury on the state of the finances.* Washington, D.C.: Government Printing Office.

Wayne, B. (2011). The Sixteenth Amendment (1913). In C. Clark (ed.) *The American Economy: A Historical Encyclopedia*, Volume 1. ABC-CLIO LLC: Santa Barbara, CA.

Chapter Fourteen

U.S. Postal Inspection Service

The U.S. Postal Inspection Service (USPIS) is the law enforcement, crime prevention, and security arm of the U.S. Postal Service (USPS). The mission of the USPIS is to secure the nation's mail system and ensure public trust in the mail. Addressing this mission is no easy task, given that the USPS maintains about 37,000 postal facilities, employs over 696,000 workers, delivers mail to over 148 million households and businesses in the U.S., and moves roughly 212 billion pieces of mail per year (U.S. Postal Inspection Service, 2008; U.S. Postal Inspection Service, 2009).

Akin to the U.S. Marshals, the USPIS has been called the "silent service," (Bern, 2007; Heath, 2005) and its agents have been deemed "America's Silent Investigators" (Denniston, 1964) or "The Silent Investigators" (Phinazee, 2003). The agency is purported to be one of the oldest federal law enforcement agencies (e.g., Bumgarner, 2006) and for much of its history sought to avoid publicity and didn't desire credit for great achievements (Denniston, 1964). Phinazee (2003, p. xiv) noted: "Although the Inspection Service had never shunned publicity, neither had it deliberately sought it." Recently, however, the agency has sought to garner the public's attention, although it seeks to do so for crime prevention purposes; not self-promotion. For instance, the Service has increasingly provided crime prevention tips for those who use the U.S. mail. Much of the work provided by the USPIS is overlooked by the public, yet the impact and importance of their efforts are notably valuable to the success of mail services.

Early Postal Inspector investigations were conducted without much publicity and notoriety, despite the fact that their work impacts the lives of all postal consumers on a regular basis (U.S. Postal Inspection Service, 2009). Recently, the agency has made special efforts to generate consumer safety and promote the services of the agency. For instance, the agency recently sent a brochure to nearly every home in the U.S. to alert postal customers regarding how they can recognize the warning signs of fraud. The initiative was financially supported by money collected in fines and damages from offenders convicted of fraudulent schemes. Among the benefits of shifting from a silent service toward one that publicizes its accomplishments are promoting knowledge and compliance among those who use and rely on mail services, and promoting public safety, for instance as individuals who may be victimized through the mail can understand that their interests are protected by an agency devoted specifically toward ensuring the safe and legal distribution of the mail.

Aside from being one of, if not the oldest federal law enforcement agency, the USPIS is considered one of the "premier federal law enforcement agencies" in the federal government (Bumgarner, 2006, p. 135; Denniston, 1964). The "Posties," as Postal Inspectors are known in law enforcement circles, are recognized for their "professionalism and being competent, fiercely proud and hard-nosed" (Sweeney, 2006, p. 28). In commenting on the effectiveness of the USPIS, Phinazee (2003, p. xiii) noted that "Although the Inspection Service is small in number as compared with other highly organized federal investigative agencies, it has consistently had the highest conviction rate of any of the federal agencies."

History

The U.S. Constitution provides the federal government exclusive permission to establish and regulate a national postal system. The first postal system in the U.S., however, pre-dates the Constitution. Benjamin Franklin, who is often recognized as the first U.S. Postal Inspector largely for his efforts directed toward auditing the accounts of post offices (Denniston, 1964), was appointed Postmaster General of the postal system in 1753 during colonial times. Franklin expanded the involvement and number of Postal Surveyors as he attempted to protect the mail and establish new mail routes (Phinazee, 2003).

In 1772, Postal Surveyors, precursors to the current Postal Inspectors, were required by the British Crown to protect the mail as there was concern that Colonial Revolutionaries would disrupt the mail service (Phinazee, 2003). Surveyors were expected to assist with regulating and auditing postal functions. Their title would change to "special agents" in 1801, and their name would continue to change throughout history. The creation of these positions was the precursor to the current Postal Inspection Service (Bumgarner, 2006).

Congress temporarily created a national post office in 1789 (after the adoption of the Constitution) and formally created the Office of Postmaster General. At that time, there were 75 existing post offices and roughly 2,000 miles of post roads that had earlier existed under the postal systems of colonial and confederation governments. The Postal Service became a permanent agency in the U.S. government by 1792, at which time postal employees included a Postmaster General, several surveyors, an Inspector of Dead Letters, and several dozen post riders.

In 1830, the Postal Service created the Office of Instructions and Mail Depredations which served as the investigative and inspection/audit branch of the Postal Service. The special agents within the agency, and the surveyors who preceded them, had a notable law enforcement role. "From colonial times in the early 1770s until the middle part of the 1800s, postal officials pursued those who would rob mail riders and mail stagecoaches, steamboats, and trains" (Bumgarner, 2006, p. 26). There were 18 special agents working for the Post Office by 1853, each of whom was assigned to specific territories. The agents possessed firearms and were provided law enforcement powers as representatives of the federal government (Bumgarner, 2006).

The Mail Fraud Act dates back to 1872 and is the nation's first consumer protection law. The legislation was passed largely in response to an outbreak of swindles involving the mail that occurred following the Civil War (U.S. Postal Inspection Service, 2009). The need for legislation pertaining to the use of the mail for fraudulent purposes remains over 140 years later as Postal Inspectors in FY 2010 initiated 589 new fraud cases, arrested 1,007 mail fraud suspects, and reported 964 convictions as a result of fraud investigations conducted in FY 2010 and previous years (U.S. Postal Inspection Service, 2011). Mail fraud charges stem from a variety of offenses, including illegal sweepstakes schemes, travel and vacation scams, rebate fraud, foreign lottery schemes, merchandise misrepresentations, and a host of other practices.

Other pieces of early legislation affecting the current Postal Inspection Service include the 1873 Postal Obscenity Statute, referred to as the Comstock Act, which is the federal postal obscenity law. The legislation was named after Postal Inspector Anthony Comstock, whose investigations into obscenity distributed via the mail persuaded him to actively solicit the legislation (Postal Inspection Service, 2009).

In 1880 an act of Congress resulted in a name change for those tasked with ensuring the protection of the mail. Particularly, special agents were thereafter referred to "Post

Office Inspectors." The title would remain until 1954 when such personnel were renamed "Postal Inspectors," which remains the current title. The change to "Postal Inspector" was designed to reflect the Inspectors' relationship to all phases of postal services, instead of restricting their title to only post offices (U.S. Postal Inspection Service, 2009).

The responsibilities of Postal Inspectors and their predecessors have shifted to some extent over the years, however the ultimate responsibility of ensuring the safety and legal use of mail services has remained constant. Denniston (1964) noted that Postal Inspectors in the early 1960s were tasked with two primary responsibilities. First, they were accountable for ensuring that post offices were efficient, competent, and honest. Inspectors were tasked with overseeing the effectiveness and integrity of post offices, and in this capacity they acted akin to the current U.S. Postal Service Office of Inspector General.

Criminal investigations was the second primary responsibility of the earlier Postal Inspectors (Denniston, 1964), and this task remains prominent today within the agency. Postal Inspectors were and are responsible for conducting investigations, gathering evidence, and generally supporting the prosecution of those who use the U.S. mail for illegal purposes. In discussing the challenges and responsibilities faced by Postal Inspectors in the 1960s, Denniston (1964, p. 79) noted: "Their investigations cover theft of the mails, fraud in countless forms, forgery of stolen money-order forms, the use of threats and blackmail or poison-pen letters, and many forms of violence by mail." Postal Inspectors today face the same and additional issues, albeit often in more advanced forms, for instance as technology has increasingly altered the nature of crime.

The Postal Reorganization Act of 1970 resulted in additional changes for the individuals responsible for protecting the mail service in the U.S. Specifically, the Bureau of the Chief Postal Inspector would be renamed to the "United States Postal Inspection Service," and a uniformed security force was added to assist in carrying out the agency's mission. Around the same time (1971), the U.S. Postal Inspection Service became one of the first federal law enforcement agencies to hire female agents.

The beginning of the 21st century brought about new challenges for the Postal Inspection Service. Concerns regarding homeland security, mail bombings, Anthrax and ricin-tainted mailings, child pornography being distributed through the mail, and technology-based crimes and related offenses became increasingly prominent among the agency's areas of focus. The Service has become increasingly international, more involved in consumer safety promotions, and has had to confront a changing society and increased public concern regarding the use of mail services.

Personnel and Organization

Unlike most other federal law enforcement agencies, the USPIS does not refer to the investigators within the agency as special agents. Instead, they are referred to as "Postal Inspectors." Postal inspectors have full federal law enforcement authority and are permitted to make warrantless arrests based on probable cause, carry firearms, execute search warrants, serve subpoenas, and seize property. They investigate a wide range of federal offenses as they pertain to the mail. Among the types of crimes they investigate are letter bombs, fraud, embezzlement, extortion, homicide, robbery, burglary, child exploitation and pornography, and any other offense that involves the use of mail. They work closely with U.S. attorneys, local prosecutors, and other law enforcement personnel to investigate postal cases, and are stationed throughout the U.S. They enforce about 200 federal laws pertaining crimes involving the U.S. mail and the postal system. The Chief Postal Inspector leads the Postal Inspection Service and is appointed by and reports to the Postmaster General of the U.S. He or she is accountable for providing direction and issuing regulations regarding security and enforcement services.

The USPIS employs roughly 1,600 Postal Inspectors and another roughly 800 Postal Police Officers nationwide. The Postal Inspection Service employed 2,288 full-time officers with authority to carry firearms and make arrests in 2008, which was 23.1% fewer than in 2004. This was the largest decrease in the number of officers at any federal law enforcement agency during this period (Reaves, 2012). The recent decline in the number of Postal Inspectors is largely explained through passage of the Omnibus Consolidated Appropriations Act of 1997, which resulted in many oversight functions traditionally performed by Postal Inspectors being transferred to the U.S. Postal Service's Office of Inspector General. Among the responsibilities transferred was the oversight of internal fraud, waste, and abuse activities. The general lack of public recognition of the services provided by the USPIS is largely attributable to the relatively small number of Postal Inspectors nationwide (Sweeney, 2006).

A Bureau of Justice Statistics report noted that the greatest number of Postal Inspectors were located in New York, California, Pennsylvania, and Maryland (Reaves, 2006), although Postal Inspectors were and are located in all states, Puerto Rico, Guam, Germany, and England. They are also located at the Interpol headquarters in Lyon, France; The Hague, in the Netherlands, and; at the Universal Postal Union which is headquartered in Berne, Switzerland (U.S. Postal Inspection Service, 2009). The internationalization of the Postal Inspection Service is due in large part to the increasing frequency with which international communication, crimes, commerce, and travel are occurring.

Recently, females have been slightly overrepresented in the USPIS relative to other federal law enforcement agencies. For instance in 2004, 19.6% of full-time individuals with arrest and firearm authority in the agency were female, compared to the average of 16.1% among all federal law enforcement groups (Reaves, 2006). In 2008, females comprised about 22% of the Postal Inspection Service sworn force, compared to the average of 15.5% of females in other federal law enforcement agencies (Langton, 2010; Reaves, 2012). Racial and ethnic minorities were also slightly overrepresented, accounting for 36.5% of full-time individuals with arrest and firearm authority, compared to the average among all federal agencies of 34.3%. Blacks/African Americans were notably overrepresented in the agency (20.4% in the Postal Inspection Service; 10.4% among other federal law enforcement agencies; Reeves, 2012).

The USPIS maintains a uniformed police force of roughly 800 Postal Police Officers and hires other contract security guards who secure postal facilities at specific locations around the U.S. The uniformed staff was created with the Postal Reorganization Act of 1970, and the officers on staff provide physical security for postal facilities and employees who work in high-risk postal facilities in large metropolitan areas around the U.S. The officers "provide perimeter security, escort high-value mail shipments, and perform other essential protective functions" at these locations (U.S. Postal Inspection Service, 2011).

Recently, the USPIS sought individuals for specific employment tracks to help meet agency needs and address changes in society. Particularly, the Service sought individuals with advanced competency in a foreign language, especially Spanish, Arabic, Armenian, Czech, Urdu, Thai, and Serbo-Croatian. The Service also sought individuals with recent experience as a USPS employee, contractor, or intern. The third track sought personnel with specific non-postal experience and/or particular types of degrees. Specifically, the agency sought individuals with military experience, a law degree, an auditing or investigative background, computer knowledge, law enforcement experience, and experience with bioterrorism investigations. Further, the Service sought individuals with high academic achievement, including a combination of degrees, work experience, and a 3.0 or higher grade-point average for a bachelor's or graduate degree (Perin, 2011).

Unlike many other federal law enforcement agents, Postal Inspectors do not undergo basic training at the Federal Law Enforcement Training Center (FLETC). Instead, newly hired postal inspectors attend basic training at the Inspection Service's Career Development Division (CDD) located in Potomac, MD. The CDD is a fully accredited federal law enforcement academy that lasts about 12 weeks and is designated specifically for the USPIS (Perin, 2011). Upon completion of the academy recruits are located to areas throughout the U.S. largely depending on the needs of the Service, which maintains eighteen divisions throughout the country, with each division containing several domiciles (Perin, 2011).

The selection and training practices of today's Postal Inspectors somewhat differ from those that existed in the 1960s. For instance, candidates who were selected as investigators for the USPIS during the early 1960s were expected to pass a rigorous physical exam; be between the ages of twenty-five and thirty-eight; pass a Civil Service exam, and; undergo a seven-month program involving academic and on-the-job training (Denniston, 1964). The first month of the program involved classwork in Washington, D.C., followed by five months accompanying an experienced investigator. The final month involved a return to Washington, D.C. to complete the academic component. The seven-month training program was followed by two and a half years of supervision by a training counselor (Denniston, 1964).

Postal Inspectors may work in a number of teams maintained by the Service. Agency need and Inspector qualifications and interests are considered when locating new Inspector on a team. Among the different teams are those that focus on violent crimes and child exploitation. Those who work with violent crimes may investigate cases involving violence in the workplace (including internal and external acts of violence), while those working on child exploitation cases may partner with the Department of Justice and the National Center for Missing and Exploited Children to identify and arrest individuals who use the mail to exploit children. Other teams focus on specific types of offenses and offenders as they pertain to the agency's legal jurisdiction.

Functions

The USPIS serves three primary purposes. First, the Service seeks to assure businesses that they can safely use the mail to dispatch funds, securities, and information. Second, the Service helps ensure that postal customers can safely use mail services and generally maintain confidence in the USPS. The Service also helps provide a safe environment for postal employees (Perin, 2011).

Primary among these responsibilities is investigating cases involving dangerous mail, which may contain explosives or biological, chemical, or radiological substances. Inspectors have been specially trained and use advanced equipment to detect and respond to dangerous mail. The agency's Dangerous Mail Investigations Program works closely with the U.S. Department of Homeland Security and others to ensure the safety and well-being of those who use the mail and postal employees (Perin, 2011). Further, inspectors are also tasked with identifying and responding to drugs, fraudulent schemes, child pornography, and various other prohibited materials that are sometimes transported via the mail. Postal inspectors are responsible for regulating and investigating the materials shipped through the U.S. mail and protecting the individuals who facilitate the delivery of mail. With regard to the former, postal inspectors use tested protocols for and coordinated responses to reports of known and suspected dangerous items in the mail or at mail facilities.

Although the USPIS is deemed the "silent service," its jurisdiction over the U.S. mail results in the agency's involvement in many high-profile investigations. For instance, postal inspectors apprehended John J. Rigas, the head of Adelphia Communications Corporation who was sentenced to fifteen years in prison for bank fraud, securities fraud, and conspiracy. Other top executives from the company also received prison sentences. The national media mis-credited both the FBI and U.S. Marshals with the arrests, which demonstrates the lack of attention and credit attributed to the Postal Inspection Service (Sweeney, 2006).

The USPIS uses both human checks and screening machines to identify suspicious mail. Postal inspectors investigate claims and have responded to over 52,000 calls regarding suspicious mail since 2001, with inspectors responding to roughly 10 calls daily. Most calls are false alarms (O'Keefe, 2011). Historically, calls regarding dangerous mail pertained to disputes between individuals, although there have been several high-profile criminal cases involving the use of the mail, including the series of mail bombings by Theodore Kaczynski (aka "the Unabomber") who was arrested in 1996. Kaczynski sent a series of bombs via the mail over a span of almost 20 years, killing three people and injuring 23 others.

More recent concerns regarding Anthrax and ricin-tainted mailing, Internet crime, and various homeland security issues have resulted in the USPIS becoming increasingly active and diligent in securing mail services. With regard to Internet crime, postal inspectors become involved when crimes involve the use of the USPS. For instance, the Service will become involved when offenders from other countries use stolen payment cards to purchase goods and have the items mailed to accomplices in the United States, who then forward the goods to the fraudster in the other country.

Examination of recent efforts of the USPIS sheds greater light on the agency's responsibilities. In FY 2010, postal inspectors responded to 2,269 incidents in the U.S. which involved unidentified suspicious powders and liquids as reported by postal employees, customers, or representatives from other federal agencies. During the same time period, inspectors responded to 1,085 incidents involving "explosive devices placed in mail receptacles, hoax bombs, suspicious items found in postal facilities or equipment, and mailed explosive devices." Most of the incidents were false alarms or involved goods inadvertently left behind by customers. Inspectors also responded to 187 incidents involving restricted, hazardous or other types of non-mailable material found in the mail or at postal facilities (U.S. Postal Inspection Service, 2011).

In FY 2010, postal inspectors arrested 2,775 suspects for mail theft, and 3,031 suspects of mail theft from this and preceding years were convicted in court. Of particular interest to the USPIS is the increasing number of mail thefts termed "volume attacks," which are thefts of large volumes of mail by gangs. Also of concern are the increasing amount of mail theft at domestic and international airports and the proliferation of identity theft, which is often conducted through violations involving the mail (U.S. Postal Inspection Service, 2009).

Among the many functions of the USPIS is the protection of employees in the workplace. Postal inspectors investigated 508 postal-related assaults and credible threats during FY

2010, which was a 4.7% decrease from the 533 cases investigated in FY 2009. They arrested 229 suspects as part of their investigations. Postal inspectors must also address robberies and attempted robberies of postal employees. In FY 2010, postal inspectors arrested 61 suspected robbers and reported 43 convictions, some of which resulted from earlier reporting periods. In FY 2010 Postal Inspectors reported 129 burglaries at postal facilities across the U.S., and arrested 62 suspected burglars (U.S. Postal Inspection Service, 2011). Table 14.1 notes the Postal Inspection Service's enforcement-oriented actions for FY 2010.

Postal inspectors face relatively little physical threat compared to some other federal law enforcement agents. For instance, in 2008 no Postal Inspection Service personnel were assaulted or killed (Reaves, 2012), and in 2010 only six inspectors were assaulted in the line of duty, and there were no deaths. The large majority (83.3%) of those assaults occurred while inspectors were conducting investigations or searches. The small number of postal inspectors assaulted in 2010 constituted 0.4% of assaults against all federal law enforcement officers (FBI, 2011a, 2011b).

The USPIS, akin to other federal law enforcement agencies, works cooperatively with other groups including law enforcement agencies at all levels. They also work with international law enforcement agencies, for instance as they are members of task forces with Canadian police and regulatory agencies in the fight against international telemarketing fraud (Heath, 2005). In FY 2010, postal inspectors conducted roughly 40 international investigations pertaining to cross-border partnerships (U.S. Postal Inspection Service, 2011). Postal inspectors are assigned to the U.S. National Central Bureau, which serves as the national point of contact for Interpol matters and results in postal inspectors responding to various international investigative requests and responsibilities.

The first USPIS forensic laboratory was created in 1940, and the use of forensic science in protecting mail services has since proliferated. Currently, forensic scientists and administrative staff at the National Forensic Laboratory in Dulles, VA provide scientific analyses of evidence collected by the Postal Inspection Service. The lab is fully accredited by the American Society of Crime Laboratory Directors Laboratory Accreditation Board and consists of latent fingerprints, physical science, questioned document, and imaging sections (Perin, 2011). In FY 2010, forensic examinations identified 479 suspects in criminal cases and matched 90 of them to subjects in the Automated Fingerprint Identification System. Laboratory personnel gave expert testimony pertaining to such cases on 17 occasions during the same year. Lab analysts completed over 1,700 requests from postal inspectors and examined roughly 45,000 exhibits, including various types of evidence (U.S. Postal Inspection Service, 2011).

The laboratory services provided by the USPIS are separated into different units. The Questioned Documents Unit primarily processes requests from Inspectors to assess the authenticity of questioned or disputed documents. For instance, they may compare questioned and known handwriting or printing impressions, or analyze paper and ink. The Fingerprint Unit helps identify suspects who have handled items of evidence, and often interfaces with automated fingerprint identification systems across the U.S. to assist in matching fingerprints found on evidence with those in the system. Among other services, the Physical Sciences Unit, which includes a Physical Evidence and a Chemistry section, helps process crime scenes; performs physical examinations and comparisons of evidence such as bomb debris, firearms, and tire impressions, and; conducts chemical analyses. The unit also analyzes material suspected of being controlled substances, primarily drugs. The Digital Evidence Unit has analysts throughout the U.S. and is the primary group responsible for gathering, preserving, and examining computer digital evidence in support of all Postal Inspection Service investigations. Such evidence may include cell phones, computers, digital cameras and recorders, and related items.

Table 14.1 U.S. Postal Inspection Service 2010 Statistics

Criminal Statistics > FY 2010				
	Investigations Initiated	Arrests	Indictments	Convictions*
Mail Theft by Non-employees and Contractors (includes theft, possession of stolen mail, and identity theft)	1,702	2,775	994	3,031
Suspicious Substances (includes non-threatening, hazardous, and hoax CBRN**)	33	18	11	14
Suspicious Items (includes non-threatening items, bombs, threats, hoaxes, and explosive material)	31	35	12	35
Nonmailable, Restricted, and Perishable Matter (includes firearms, weapons, intoxicants, extortion threats, and miscellaneous matter)	105	75	36	66
Assaults and Threats (includes threats and assaults against on-duty postal employees and homicide)	508	229	40	187
Robbery	75	61	37	43
Burglary	129	62	24	51
Mailing of Controlled Substances (includes narcotics, steroids, drug-related proceeds, and drug paraphernalia)	1,075	1,322	481	1,083
Mail Fraud	589	1,007	903	964
Child Exploitation, Mailing of Obscene Matter, and Sexually Oriented Advertisements	118	115	70	157
Revenue Fraud	334	68	39	65
Money Laundering (includes postal money orders)	154	203	71	170
Vandalism and Arson	68	42	2	44
Workers' Compensation Fraud	1,091	1	0	0
Total	**6,012**	**6,013**	**2,720**	**5,910**

* Convictions include pretrial diversions and may be related to cases from prior reporting periods.
** CBRN refers to chemical, biological, radiological, and nuclear.

Source: U.S. Postal Inspection Service, 2011, p. 87.

The USPIS works cooperatively with most federal law enforcement agencies, and has done so historically. Overlapping jurisdiction often requires postal inspectors to work closely with law enforcement authorities at all levels. The agency has historically cooperated with other law enforcement and non-law enforcement groups in meeting its charges, including for instance the Criminal Investigation Division of the Internal Revenue Service (then known as the Bureau of Internal Revenue), which was created in 1919 with the goal of investigating serious incidents of tax fraud and evasion. The creation of the unit was facilitated by the transfer of six U.S. postal inspectors to the Bureau (Bumgarner, 2006). More recently, the Service, often in conjunction with other federal law enforcement agencies, arrested 1,322 suspects for drug trafficking via the mail in FY 2010, and their investigations resulted in the seizure of roughly $7.6 million in cash and goods, and 37,759 pounds of illegal drugs found in the mail (U.S. Postal Inspection Service, 2011).

The USPIS is part of the Department of Homeland Security's Special Events Working Group and provides subject-matter expertise, and has provided mail screening at large-scale events such as Super Bowls, the Olympic Games, and political and presidential events. The Dangerous Mail Investigators Team is deployed to National Special Security Events at which they screen mail using a transportable mobile Mail Screening Station and vans equipped with X-ray units and field-screening devices (Perin, 2011).

Similar to many other law enforcement agencies, the USPIS regularly engages in directed crackdowns on particular types of crimes. For instance, the agency participated in Operation Stolen Dreams, which was the federal government's largest-ever mortgage fraud crackdown. The operation was launched in March 2010 and was a multi-agency initiative that resulted in 485 arrests, over 330 convictions, and nearly $11 million in seizures. As members of President Obama's Financial Fraud Enforcement Task Force, the USPIS and many other law enforcement agencies at all levels share intelligence and work together cooperatively in other capacities to identify illegal mortgage activities nationwide (U.S. Postal Inspection Service, 2011). The agency also participated in Operation Broken Trust, which targeted fraud against the investing public in 2010. The four-month effort resulted in enforcement actions against 340 criminal defendants and 189 civil defendants for scams. Investigators identified 31,195 victims of financial schemes in which victims lost a combined $602.1 million (U.S. Postal Inspection Service, 2011).

Using the mail to traffic in child pornography or to otherwise sexually exploit children remains a significant problem in society and a challenge for postal inspectors. In response, the agency has become a leader in the fight against child exploitation, and has investigated thousands of these types of cases since the passage of the Child Protection Act of 1984. The act gave postal inspectors additional powers to target individuals peddling child pornography. Addressing harms against children is not new to the Service, as it has investigated cases involving the use of the mail to exploit children for over a century, and "was the first federal law enforcement agency to aggressively identify, target, and arrest those who produce and traffic-in child pornography" (Perin, 2011, pp. 14–15). As evidence of their success, inspectors identified and rescued 60 children who were victims of exploitation and sexual abuse, and initiated 214 new investigations in 2009. They arrested 187 suspects and identified 39 child molesters (Perin, 2011).

In August 2001, Attorney General John Ashcroft and Chief Postal Inspector Kenneth Weaver announced the successful conclusion of a two-year investigation which dismantled the largest-known commercial child pornography enterprise ever identified. Thirty federally funded groups comprised the Internet Crimes Against Children Task Force, which partnered with Postal Inspectors to launch Operation Avalanche. The undercover operation targeted child pornography distributed through the mail and via the Internet. Funded through the Office of Juvenile Justice and Delinquency Prevention, the operation provided grants to state and local law enforcement groups for the development of regional task forces that addressed Internet-related crimes against children (U.S. Postal Inspection Service, 2002).

These are by no means the only issue-focused efforts of the USPIS. For instance, in 2006 the agency and the National Center for Missing & Exploited Children began the 2 SMRT 4U campaign, which was an effort to encourage teens to practice safe, smart habits when sharing personal information on social networking websites and blogs. The campaign was recognized by the U.S. Department of Justice, which honored the agency with its Internet Safety Award (U.S. Postal Inspection Service, 2009). The USPIS has increasingly utilized public service campaigns to encourage citizens to protect themselves from harms committed through the mail. These and related efforts toward reaching the public differ from the earlier practices of the agency when it seemingly didn't seek much public attention.

In discussing the charges of the Postal Inspection Service and the need to better inform the public, Denniston (1964, p. 151) earlier noted:

> From the time when the United States Government began to function we have had a small and devoted group of men whose job it has been to protect the mails from theft, from fraud, from violence. They have had an even harder job than that, trying to protect the American people from their own gullibility.

The USPIS remains a vital component of the USPS and serves several unique functions within law enforcement. The agency is generally tasked with investigating and preventing the illegal use of mail services, and protecting those who facilitate mail delivery. These are by all means important, yet often overlooked and underappreciated contributions to law enforcement and society in general. The extensive amount of mail that must be safely delivered daily provides many challenges for an agency that is relatively small in size. The agency has made strides in keeping pace with a changing society, for instance through the use of high-technology to detect harmful or illegal mailings, and continues to address issues pertaining to terrorism and homeland security.

References

Bern, D. (2007). Postal Inspectors: Not Secret, No Longer Silent. *The Police Chief*, 74 (12). Accessed online October 17, 2011 at http://www.policechiefmagazine.org/magazine/index.cfm?fuseaction=display_arch&article_id=1341&issue_id=122007.

Bumgarner, J. B. (2006). *Federal agents: The growth of federal law enforcement in America*. Westport, CT: Praeger.

Denniston, E. (1964). *America's silent investigators: The story of the postal inspectors who protect the United States mail*. NY: Dodd, Mead & Company.

Federal Bureau of Investigation. (2011a). *Uniform Crime Reports: Law enforcement officers killed & assaulted, 2010*. Table 81: Federal Law Enforcement Officers Killed and Assaulted. Accessed online December 2, 2011 at: http://www.fbi.gov/about-us/cjis/.ucr/leoka/leoka-2010/tables/table81-federal-leoka-department-agency-by-activity-10.xls.

Federal Bureau of Investigation. (2011b). *Uniform Crime Reports: Law enforcement officers killed & assaulted, 2010*. Table 80: Federal Law Enforcement Officers Killed and Assaulted. Accessed online December 2, 2011 at: http://www.fbi.gov/about-us/cjis/

ucr/leoka/leoka-2010/tables/table80-federal-leoka-department-agency-by-type-weapon-10.xls.

Heath, L.R. (2005). U.S. Postal Inspectors: Partners in the investigation of identity theft and crimes involving the U.S. Mail. *The Police Chief*, 72(3): 44.

Langton, L. (2010). *Women in law enforcement, 1987–2008*. Washington, D.C.: U.S. Department of Justice, Bureau of Justice Statistics. NCJ 230521.

O'Keefe, E. (2011, November 9). Postal Service remains diligent on mail safety. *Washington Post*, A6.

Perin, M. (2011). More than mailmen with guns. *Law Enforcement Technology*, October. pp. 11, 12, 14–16.

Reaves, B.A. (2012). *Federal law enforcement officers, 2008*. U.S. Department of Justice, Bureau of Justice Statistics. NCJ 238250.

Reaves, B. A. (2006). *Federal law enforcement officers, 2004*. Washington, D.C.: U.S. Department of Justice, Bureau of Justice Statistics. NCJ 212750.

Sweeney, P. (2006). Delivering evidence: Not just the mail. *Financial Executive*, 22 (10): 27–30.

U.S. Postal Inspection Service (2002). *2001 Annual report of investigations of the United States Postal Inspection Service*. Accessed online October 31, 2011 at: https://postalinspectors.uspis.gov/radDocs/pubs/ar01_04.pdf.

U.S. Postal Inspection Service (2008, February). *A guide for the U.S. Congress*. Publication 278.

U.S. Postal Inspection Service (2009, February). *Because the mail matters*. Publication 162.

U.S. Postal Inspection Service (2011). *Annual report FY 2010*. Accessed online October 17, 2011 at: http://www.postalinspectorsvideo.com/uspis/AnnualReport2010.pdf.

Chapter Fifteen

Uniformed Police Services

It is sometimes said among federal law enforcement officers that every other person in Washington, D.C. has a badge. It stands to reason that the nation's capital city would be heavily policed—not only because most federal law enforcement agencies are headquartered there, but because there are so many high-profile targets for those wishing to protest, or violently strike out, against the United States and its government.

Most Americans associate with federal law enforcement the criminal investigative functions of the FBI and other agencies. As noted in Chapter 2, approximately 37% of all federal law enforcement officers are engaged in criminal investigative duties—the largest category of federal law enforcement responsibilities. But the second largest category is police response and patrol. Approximately 28,000 federal law enforcement officers fall into this category, or 23% of the federal law enforcement community. In Washington, D.C. there is no more visible element of the federal law enforcement community than the uniformed police organizations of several federal departments and agencies patrolling federal lands and facilities (Reaves, 2012).

There are dozens of federal uniformed police agencies, many with a presence throughout the country. But most federal police officers are located in Washington, D.C. and the metropolitan area. The federal police patrol agencies with significant numbers of officers stationed in the Washington, D.C. metropolitan area include the Pentagon Force Protection Agency (Department of Defense), the U.S. Park Police (Department of Interior), the FBI Police (Department of Justice), the Bureau of Engraving and Printing Police (Department of the Treasury), the U.S. Mint Police (Department of the Treasury), the U.S. Secret Service Uniformed Division (Department of Homeland Security), the Federal Protective Service (Department of Homeland Security), the National Institutes of Health Police (Department of Health and Human Services), the U.S. Postal Police (Postal Service), the Government Printing Office Police, the U.S. Capitol Police, and the U.S. Supreme Court Police (GAO, 2003; GAO, 2012). These departments collectively employ thousands of police officers.

From the abbreviated list above, it is apparent that the uniformed police services of the federal government span across the landscape of Executive Branch departments, and also exist within the Legislative and Judicial Branches of government as well. In this chapter, three of these police agencies will be highlighted—one from each branch of government. The three agencies are the U.S. Capitol Police, the U.S. Supreme Court Police, and the Federal Protective Service. Although these agencies have their own policies, modern histories, and culture, they are fairly representative in their missions and responsibilities of those many other federal uniformed police agencies not highlighted here.

U.S. Capitol Police

As noted in Chapter 1, the U.S. Capitol Police was formally established by Congress in 1828. The early history of the U.S. Capitol Police is explored fully in Chapter 1 as the protection of federal property was one of the early responsibilities of federal law enforcement in the United States. Of course, it is not just the U.S. Capitol Police, but other federal uniformed police patrol agencies as well that can trace their lineage to the appointment of six night watchmen in 1790 to patrol the grounds of federal real property as government buildings in the District of Columbia were under construction (see Chapter 1).

But in 1828, the U.S. Capitol Police came into its own, having been formally created by statute as the police organization with exclusive jurisdiction to protect the Capitol grounds, the members of Congress and their staff who work there, and the multitude of visitors who frequent the properties.

Today, the U.S. Capitol Police is a modern police department employing approximately 1,800 police officers, making it the largest federal police department in the Washington, D.C. metropolitan area. The department employs an additional 500 non-sworn employees who occupy support roles (Spochart, 2005). Its mission is similar to that of any other police department. The U.S. Capitol Police exists to protect life and property, prevent and detect crime, and enforce traffic laws in and around the U.S. Capitol grounds. To accomplish this mission, the U.S. Capitol Police relies on uniformed patrol officers, detectives, and specialized police units, such as K-9 officers, tactical response teams, and HAZMAT response teams. Uniformed officers might be assigned fixed posts to man, foot patrol duty, or vehicular patrol.

Organizationally, the U.S. Capitol Police answers to a Capitol Police Board. The board consists of three individuals: the Sergeant at Arms of the U.S. House of Representatives, the Sergeant at Arms of the U.S. Senate, and the Architect of the Capitol. The U.S. Capitol Police is headed by a police chief who also sits on the Capitol Police Board as a non-voting *ex officio* member.

The U.S. Capitol Police derives its mission and authority as a law enforcement agency from Title 2 of the United States Code. According to 2 USC 1961, they are responsible for patrolling the "Capitol Buildings and Grounds," which include not only the Capitol building itself, but also any other buildings or facilities used by the House of Representatives or the Senate, and their staffs. Additionally, the statute includes the authority to police Library of Congress buildings and grounds, as the Library of Congress Police was absorbed into the U.S. Capitol Police in 2003 (H.J. Res 2, 2003).

U.S. Capitol Police officers are authorized to make arrests on Capitol grounds for any criminal violations of federal, state, or District of Columbia laws. Additionally, 2 USC 1966 provides for the protection of members of Congress and their families on or off Capitol grounds. The law reads:

> Subject to the direction of the Capitol Police Board, the United States Capitol Police is authorized to protect, in any area of the United States, the person of any Member of Congress, officer of the Congress..., and any member of the immediate family of any such Member or officer, if the Capitol Police Board determines such protection is necessary.

Customarily, House and Senate leaders, such as the Speaker of the House and the Majority Leader in the Senate, are afforded such protection automatically. However, other members of Congress may request protective services of the U.S. Capitol Police. Members of Congress in the media spotlight due to controversial legislation they may have sponsored, or having taken unpopular positions on hot-button issues, can result in threats from members of the public. If the threats are deemed credible, the U.S. Capitol Police will assign a protection detail to that member and his or her family.

The law enforcement authority of the U.S. Capitol Police extends throughout the District of Columbia under certain circumstances. U.S. Capitol Police officers are authorized to make arrests and enforce the laws of the Unites States and the District of Columbia (2 USC 1967):

- within the District of Columbia for any crimes of violence committed within the U.S. Capitol grounds;

- within the District of Columbia for any crimes committed in the presence of the officer;

- within the District of Columbia to prevent imminent loss of life or injury to person or property; and

- within a defined portion of the District of Columbia surrounding the Capitol grounds (which amounts to dozens of city blocks).

The geographic jurisdiction — both exclusive and concurrent — of the U.S. Capitol Police is depicted in Figure 15.1.

The U.S. Capitol Police has also been called upon to assist with law enforcement missions outside of Washington, D.C., and unrelated to the protection of members of Congress. Typically, providing law enforcement assistance to agencies outside of Washington, D.C. requires the advance notification and tacit approval of the House and Senate Appropriations Committees. However, in emergencies, such assistance can be provided at

Figure 15.1 Geographic Jurisdiction of the U.S. Capitol Police

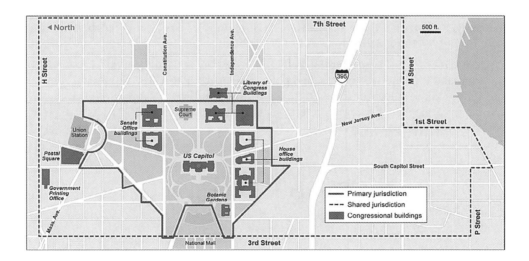

Source: GAO-12-58 (January 2012).

the discretion of the U.S. Capitol Police Chief without Congressional notification up front. For example, the U.S. Capitol Police provided law enforcement assistance to local and state agencies in the Gulf region in the aftermath of Hurricane Katrina and Hurricane Ike in 2005 and 2008, respectively (GAO, 2009).

The U.S. Capitol Police has been involved in a few high profile incidents in the past several years. In July of 1998, two Capitol Police officers were killed when Russell Eugene Weston, a paranoid schizophrenic, entered the Capitol Building and immediately opened fire with a .38 caliber revolver, killing Officer Jacob Chestnut who was manning a metal detector at the building entrance. Weston then proceeded into the office of Representative Tom Delay of Texas, which happened to be near the security checkpoint that Weston breached. Capitol Police Detective John Gibson was assigned to Representative Delay's protection detail and was in Delay's office at the time of the first shooting. When Weston entered Delay's office, he and Detective Gibson exchanged gunfire. The battle mortally wounded Gibson and seriously wounded Weston, who was then captured and treated for his injuries. A third Capitol Police Officer, Douglas McMillian, was also injured in the firefight.

In March of 2006, the U.S. Capitol Police was again in the national news when Representative Cynthia McKinney of Texas got into an altercation with Capitol Police officer Paul McKenna. Representative McKinney had walked around the metal detector. Members of Congress are not required to go through the metal detectors at the U.S. Capitol. However, this waiver is predicated on the officers at security checkpoint recognizing members of Congress. In this case, Officer McKenna did not recognize Representative McKinney and proceeded after her. Upon stopping her, according to the police report, Representative McKinney struck the officer in his chest with a closed fist (Todd, 2006). The facts of the case were presented to a federal grand jury which declined to indict Representative McKinney for lack of evidence.

The U.S. Capitol Police has also experienced some budget woes in recent years. The U.S. Capitol Police Office of Inspector General released a report in 2010 highlighting a number of errors which occurred in the department's budget formulation and requests for Fiscal Years 2010 and 2011. The Inspector General found that the department failed to have adequate controls in place to ensure the proper collection of budget data, resulting in a budget shortfall in Fiscal Year 2010 of $6.8 million and a projected shortfall in Fiscal Year 2011 of $9.4 million (Capitol Police OIG, 2010).

Despite occasional controversy, the U.S. Capitol Police is an agency with a storied tradition and known for a professional police workforce. Regardless of previous budget shortfalls, Congress has continued to fund and support through appropriations the organization from which it receives protection, authorizing the hiring of 50 additional police officers in 2012 (USAJOBS, 2011).

U.S. Supreme Court Police

The U.S. Supreme Court Police possesses responsibilities similar to the U.S. Capitol Police, except that the objects of the former's protective responsibilities are the Supreme Court Building, the Supreme Court Justices, their staffs, and visitors to the Supreme Court. The U.S. Supreme Court Police is a relatively small uniformed police agency, consisting of approximately 150 police officers.

Although its ancestry can be linked with the U.S. Capitol Police and other agencies to the early night watchmen appointed by Congress in the late 18th Century to look over and patrol federal property, the U.S. Supreme Court Police organizationally didn't come into existence until after the U.S. Supreme Court got its own building in 1935. From 1800 until 1935, the U.S. Supreme Court convened at various locations on the U.S. Capitol grounds. The exception to this was in 1812 when the British, with whom America was at war, set fire to the Capitol building (U.S. Supreme Court, n.d.).

In 1932, construction began on a new building for the U.S. Supreme Court. It was completed in 1935. That same year, 33 police officers were transferred from the U.S. Capitol Police to form a Supreme Court security force. The U.S. Supreme Court Police was formally established as a police agency in 1949.

The U.S. Supreme Court Police derives its authority as the sole law enforcement organization of the Judicial Branch via Title 28 and Title 40 of the United States Code. The U.S. Supreme Court Police fall under the Supreme Court Marshal, who is the chief administrative officer for the Supreme Court. The Marshal is appointed by the Court and directly supervised by the Chief Justice of the Supreme Court. Among the Marshal's many responsibilities articulated in 28 USC 672, oversight of the Supreme Court Police is expressly listed.

Additionally, the Marshal's authority includes the promulgation of regulations which are necessary for "the adequate protection of the Supreme Court Building and grounds and of individuals and property in the Building and grounds; and the maintenance of suitable order and decorum within the Building and grounds" (40 USC 6102). Pursuant to the Marshal's responsibility for keeping safety and order at the U.S. Supreme Court, the Supreme Court Police is given the following authority under 40 USC 6121:

- to police the Supreme Court Building and grounds and adjacent streets to protect individuals and property;
- in any State, to protect—(A) the Chief Justice, any Associate Justice of the Supreme Court, and any official guest of the Supreme Court; and (B) any officer or employee of the Supreme Court while that officer or employee is performing official duties;
- while performing duties necessary to carry out paragraph (1) or (2), to make arrests for any violation of federal or state law and any regulation under federal or state law; and
- to carry firearms as may be required while performing duties.

As with the U.S. Capitol Police, the U.S. Supreme Court Police maintains a number of units within the organization to perform generalized and specialized law enforcement functions. This includes a uniformed patrol division which provides police officers to conduct foot and vehicle patrols, as well as manning fixed posts. Some officers of the U.S. Supreme Court Police are assigned to protective details for the justices. Still other officers are assigned to specialized units such as the Threat Assessment Unit, the Tactical Response Team, the HAZMAT/Bomb squad, the Supreme Court Police Honor Guard, and other units.

Occasionally, large-scale protests are held at the Supreme Court. In January of 2012, members of the Occupy Movement gathered at the Supreme Court steps to protest the second anniversary of the Citizens United case, which struck down parts of the federal campaign financing law known as McCain-Feingold. Protesters had pushed past police barricades intended to keep them clear of Supreme Court property. The U.S. Supreme Court Police moved in and arrested 11 protesters (Sacks and Levy, 2012).

Federal Protective Service

The Federal Protective Service (FPS) is a uniformed and criminal investigative law enforcement agency within the U.S. Department of Homeland Security and is charged with the mission of securing most of the nation's federal civilian public properties. In total the Federal Protective Service provides law enforcement and security services to the government employees, public officials, and visitors in over 9,000 federal buildings around the United States, including the large concentration of federal buildings in Washington, D.C.

Just as with the U.S. Capitol Police, the Federal Protective Service identifies its origin as the federal government's hiring of six night watchmen in 1790, discussed earlier in this chapter and in Chapter 1. However, its modern history as a distinct organization began in 1949, coinciding with the creation of the U.S. General Services Administration (GSA). The GSA was created to be the manager of real property and supply purchaser for the entire civilian federal government. The hope and expectation of Congress in creating the GSA was to realize standardization of quality and economies of scale in the construction of federal buildings and the purchase of federal supplies, such as fleet vehicles, office supplies, technology, and other needed goods. Additionally, GSA, through its Public Building Service, served as the property manager for all civilian federal buildings and courthouses of the Executive Branch. GSA's clients were and are the federal agencies occupying GSA-owned or leased buildings. GSA's funding was primarily secured by tenant fees paid from the other federal agencies. Part of GSA's responsibility as property manager was to provide for law enforcement and security services at its buildings.

Consequently, in 1949, Congress extended to GSA the authority to hire and employ uniformed police officers and "non-uniformed special policemen" to provide police patrol and criminal investigative services on federal property. This included the power to carry firearms and make arrests. The uniformed police officers were called upon, by statute, "to enforce the laws enacted for the protection of persons and property, ... to prevent breaches of the peace, to suppress affrays or unlawful assemblies, and to enforce any rules and regulations made and promulgated by the Administrator [of the General Services Administration]" (40 USC 318).

Additionally, the criminal investigators had limited law enforcement authority off federal property for crimes that occurred on federal property or affected the operations of GSA (40 USC 318 and 318d). These officers and investigators worked as a part of a unit known as the Protection Division within the Public Building Service of GSA. In 1971, the GSA Protection Division was renamed and reorganized into the Federal Protective Service.

In the wake of the terror attacks perpetrated on September 11, 2001, Congress passed the Homeland Security Act of 2002. This resulted in the creation of a new federal cabinet level department—the Department of Homeland Security. A total of 22 existing federal agencies were transferred into the new Department of Homeland Security (DHS). Among these were the U.S. Customs Service, the Immigration and Naturalization Service (INS), the U.S. Secret Service, the U.S. Coast Guard, and others—including the Federal Protective Service.

The Homeland Security Act of 2002 removed the FPS from the organizational control of the GSA (a client-oriented, customer-service driven agency) and placed it under the newly created Bureau of Immigration and Customs Enforcement (ICE) within DHS, along with what had been the criminal investigative divisions of U.S. Customs and the INS. The transfer to DHS formally occurred in March of 2003.

From the beginning, the FPS was something of an odd-man out within ICE. Officially, ICE is the primary criminal investigative arm of the Department of Homeland Security. Its mission is to focus on criminal customs- and immigration-related investigations. The FPS role of protecting and policing federal property never seemed like a proper fit.

In October of 2009, Homeland Security Secretary Janet Napolitano announced the transfer of the FPS from ICE into the National Protection and Programs Directorate (NPPD) of Homeland Security (DHS Press Release, 2009). The NPPD includes several offices related to the protection of America's critical infrastructure, including:

- Federal Protective Service
- Office of Cybersecurity and Communications
- Office of Infrastructure Protection
- Office of Intergovernmental Programs
- Office of Risk Management and Analysis

The FPS received expanded law enforcement authority as a result of the Homeland Security Act of 2002. That authority carried over with the FPS upon transfer to the NPPD. Title 40, Section 1315 reads in part:

OFFICERS AND AGENTS—

(1) DESIGNATION—The Secretary may designate employees of the Department of Homeland Security, including employees transferred to the Department from the Office of the Federal Protective Service of the General Services Administration pursuant to the Homeland Security Act of 2002, as officers and agents for duty in connection with the protection of property owned or occupied by the Federal Government and persons on the property, including duty in areas outside the property to the extent necessary to protect the property and persons on the property.

(2) POWERS—While engaged in the performance of official duties, an officer or agent designated under this subsection may—

(A) enforce Federal laws and regulations for the protection of persons and property;

(B) carry firearms;

(C) make arrests without a warrant for any offense against the United States committed in the presence of the officer or agent or for any felony cognizable under the laws of the United States if the officer or agent has reasonable grounds to believe that the person to be arrested has committed or is committing a felony;

(D) serve warrants and subpoenas issued under the authority of the United States;

(E) conduct investigations, on and off the property in question, of offenses that may have been committed against property owned or occupied by the Federal Government or persons on the property; and

(F) carry out such other activities for the promotion of homeland security as the Secretary may prescribe.

The law enforcement authority articulated above is considerably stronger and broader than had been conferred through 40 USC 318 and 318d. Today, FPS police officers, inspectors, and special agents have full law enforcement authority on and off of federal property while engaged in the performance of their duties. Additionally, Section 1315 (2)(F) states that officers of the FPS can be utilized in any other law enforcement or protective capacity as deemed necessary by the Secretary of Homeland Security.

According to the Department of Homeland Security, the Federal Protective Service exists to "protect and serve." This mantra, borrowed from common use associated with traditional local-level police departments, highlights the policing nature of the FPS. But the FPS certainly possesses a wider range of responsibilities than the traditional police department. The protective services provided by the FPS include (DHS, n.d.):

- Conducting Facility Security Assessments
- Designing countermeasures for tenant agencies
- Maintaining uniformed law enforcement presence
- Maintaining armed contract security guards
- Performing background suitability checks for contract employees
- Monitoring security alarms via centralized communication centers
- Conducting criminal investigations
- Sharing intelligence among local/state/federal
- Protecting special events
- Working with FEMA to respond to natural disasters
- Offering special operations including K-9 explosive detection
- Training federal tenants in crime prevention and Occupant Emergency Planning

Today, the Federal Protective Service has a budget of approximately $1 billion and employs 1,200 employees, 900 of whom are law enforcement officers (GAO, 2011). There are three types of law enforcement officers within the FPS: police officers, law enforcement security officers (LESOs), and criminal investigators (special agents). FPS police officers are responsible for general patrol duties on and around federal property. Because of the concentration of federal property in Washington, D.C., a significant FPS police officer contingent is stationed there. FPS police officers conduct patrols on foot and in vehicles. In Washington, D.C., as a result of memoranda of agreements with the DC Metropolitan Police, FPS police officers have concurrent jurisdiction with local law enforcement in many areas of the city apart from federal property. It is not uncommon for an FPS police officer to back up a DC Metro police officer or a Metro Transit police officer on a matter entirely unrelated to protecting federal property (Bumgarner, 2006).

The largest share of the FPS law enforcement contingent is the Law Enforcement Security Officers, also known as inspectors. These officers have the same law enforcement authority as other FPS officers. However, traditional police activities, such as patrol or crowd control, are a small portion of the LESO's workload. LESOs are certified physical security specialists. As such, they conduct physical security assessments of federal building and facilities. LESOs then make recommendations concerning security improvements, such as how to harden a federal building as a potential target. They also oversee the implementation of security recommendations if adopted by GSA or other client agencies.

Special agents make up the smallest group within FPS, numbering in the dozens nationwide. FPS special agents constitute the detective branch of the FPS. They conduct criminal investigations relating to offenses which occur on or near federal property, including assaults, sexual assaults, thefts, robberies, burglaries, narcotics violations, and other "general crimes" types of offenses. They also investigate threats made against public officials who occupy federal property under the jurisdiction of FPS. In fact, as a part of the FPS Protective Investigations Program, initiated in 2004, FPS has entered into an agreement with the U.S. Capitol Police to respond to, and investigate, threats made against members of Congress, their staffs, and their families when outside of the Washington, D.C. metropolitan area (DHS, 2010). Criminal investigators of the FPS also serve on various federal task forces, including FBI Joint Terrorism Task Forces (JTTFs) in several major cities throughout the United States.

In addition to enforcing federal criminal laws on federal property, FPS officers frequently enforce state laws on federal property when no applicable federal law exists. The authority to treat state laws as a federal matter is found in the Assimilated Crimes Act (18 USC 13). The law reads in part:

> Whoever within or upon any of the places now existing or hereafter reserved or acquired as provided in section 7 of this title, or on, above, or below any portion of the territorial sea of the United States not within the jurisdiction of any State, Commonwealth, territory, possession, or district is guilty of any act or omission which, although not made punishable by any enactment of Congress, would be punishable if committed or omitted within the jurisdiction of the State, Territory, Possession, or District in which such place is situated, by the laws thereof in force at the time of such act or omission, shall be guilty of a like offense and subject to a like punishment.

The Assimilated Crimes Act provides federal police agencies such as the FPS a significant tool pursuant to their mission of providing police patrol services on federal property, lands, and reservations. By way of the Assimilated Crimes Act, behavior which is illegal in the areas adjacent to federal property is also illegal within that federal building or on that federal land, without regard for the lack of federally-codified laws specifically outlawing the same acts (Bumgarner, 2006).

While FPS has seen enhancement of its authorities and refinement of its organizational position since the passage of the Homeland Security Act of 2002, the agency has been plagued by a number of problems in recent years. These problems have typically boiled down to questions of resources.

The FPS is responsible for policing and securing over 9,000 federal buildings nationwide. And yet, the agency only employs 900 law enforcement officers. Consequently, FPS relies heavily on a contract security guard force. Armed private security guards can be found in federally-owned and leased buildings and offices across the country. In total, FPS contracts with several security companies who provide a total contract force of approximately 15,000 security guards nationally. FPS is responsible for administering these contracts and ensuring that the security guard force is properly trained and has been properly vetted through background checks.

FPS contract security guards are primarily used in performing routine patrol in and around federal buildings and manning fixed security posts, such as at building and parking lot controlled entrances. FPS reports two primary benefits of utilizing contract security guards at federal facilities: the potential cost savings of using contract staff to perform routine duties over salaried and benefited federal employees and the flexibility that comes with annual contracts — allowing the FPS to increase or decrease security staff in given locations as the needs shift (GAO, 2011). However, the FPS's lack of quality control and poor management of some of the security contracts, resulting in unqualified or ineligible security guards working in many federal buildings around the country (including armed guards with prior felony convictions), has brought down on FPS considerable criticism from client federal agencies, the GSA, and from Congress. Indeed, the FPS has been the subject of many critical evaluative reports by the Government Accountability Office. The GAO noted in 2011 that none of the 28 recommendations it had previously made to the FPS for improving organization efficiency and quality control in the contract guard program had been fully implemented. However, GAO struck an optimistic tone that the transfer of FPS from ICE to the NPPD would likely result in a greater emphasis on addressing infrastructure-protection related issues.

The U.S. Capitol Police, the U.S. Supreme Court Police, and the Federal Protective Service all serve as examples of the larger community of federal police departments located primarily in Washington, D.C. and surrounding communities. These agencies operate in similar ways, and perform similar duties, as uniformed police organizations found at the state and local level. Many individuals interested in traditional police patrol careers, but desiring to work at the federal level, will find precisely that blend in departments such as these. Given the emphasis on infrastructure protection that emerged after 9/11 and has continued to this day, there is every reason to believe that opportunities for employment and advancement in federal uniformed police service agencies will be relatively robust in the foreseeable future.

References

Consolidated Appropriations Resolution, 2003. H.J. Res.2 (2003).

General Accounting Office (2003). *Federal uniformed police: Selected data on pay, recruitment, and retention at 13 police forces in Washington, D.C., metropolitan area.* GAO-03-658.

Government Accountability Office (2012). *Capitol Police: Retirement benefits, pay, duties, and attrition compared to other federal police forces.* GAO-12-58.

Government Accountability Office (2011). *Homeland security: Protecting federal facilities remains a challenge for the Department of Homeland Security's Federal Protective Service.* GAO-11-813T.

Government Accountability Office (2011). *Federal facility security: Staffing approaches used by selected agencies.* GAO-11-601.

Government Accountability Office (2009). *United States Capitol Police—deployment of personnel.* B-317252.

Reaves, B. (2012). *Federal law enforcement officers, 2008.* Washington, D.C.: Bureau of Justice Statistics.

Sacks, M. and Edwards-Levy, A. (2012, January 21). United protest. Retrieved from http://huffingtonpost.com/2012/01/20.

Spochart, M. (2005, May 10). Inside the U.S. Capitol Police: Q & A with Lt. Spochart. Retrieved from http://blog.discoverpolicing.org.

Todd, B. (2006, April 20). Police report: McKinney hit officer with fist. *CNN Politics.* Retrieved from http://articles.cnn.com/2006-04-19/politics/mckinney.report_1_mckinney-police-officer-metal-detector?_s=PM:POLITICS.

USAJOBS (2011, October 1). United States Capitol Police Officer. Retrieved from http://www.usajobs.gov/GetJob/ViewDetails/2408093.

U.S. Capitol Police Office of Inspector General (2010). *Audit of USCP budget formulation process.* OIG 2010-03.

U.S. Department of Homeland Security (n.d.). *About the Federal Protective Service.* Retrieved from http://www.dhs.gov/xabout/structure/gc_1253889058003.shtm.

U.S. Department of Homeland Security (2010, May 11). *Protective Investigations Program.* Retrieved from http://www.dhs.gov/files/programs/gc_1253819254180.shtm.

U.S. Department of Homeland Security (2009, October 29). Press Release: Secretary Napolitano Announces Transfer of Federal Protective Service to National Protection and Programs Directorate. Washington, D.C.: DHS.

U.S. Supreme Court (n.d.). *The Court building.* Retrieved from http://www.supremecourt.gov/about/courtbuilding.aspx.

Chapter Sixteen

Military Criminal Investigative Agencies

The United States has five war-fighting branches of the military. These include the U.S. Army, U.S. Navy, U.S. Air Force, U.S. Marines, and U.S. Coast Guard. The latter branch, the Coast Guard, is the smallest of the military services. It is the only branch of the military not permanently housed under the Department of Defense. Instead, it operates as an agency of the Department of Homeland Security. However, during times of war, or pursuant to particular combat missions, the U.S. Coast Guard or its sea-faring elements move under the command of the U.S. Navy.

Collectively, the United States military includes nearly 1.5 million active duty officers and enlisted personnel. Reservists account for an additional cadre of over 850,000. Further, the five branches employ nearly 700,000 civilians in support roles. The U.S. Department of Defense employs an additional 108,000 civilians (DOD, 2010). Although the United States does not have the largest military in terms of personnel, it spends more on its military than any other country in the world. The annual base budget for defense spending is in excess of $500 billion. The Department of Defense receives additional appropriations to fund ongoing war-fighting missions. Indeed, U.S. military spending totaled 41% of all military spending around the world in 2011. The next highest military spender, China, was responsible for 8.2% of the world's military spending (SIPRI, 2011).

With well over 2 million people under its charge, and hundreds of military installations in the United States and worldwide, law enforcement—and in particular, criminal investigation—is a significant ancillary responsibility which must be attended to by the military branches. Pursuant to this responsibility, each of the five military branches field criminal investigative law enforcement organizations which employ both military and civilian personnel. These agencies are:

   Criminal Investigation Division (Army)

   Naval Criminal Investigative Service (Navy)

   Criminal Investigation Division (Marines)

   Office of Special Investigations (Air Force)

   Coast Guard Investigative Service (Coast Guard)

Additionally, the Department of Defense possesses a criminal investigative agency of its own (the Defense Criminal Investigative Service) made up entirely of civilian employees. The military criminal investigative organizations are responsible for investigating crimes affecting their respective military branches and personnel.

Most of the crimes investigated by these agencies fall under the Uniform Code of Military Justice (UCMJ) found in Title 10 of the United States Code. The UCMJ amounts to a parallel criminal code to the civilian criminal codes found in Title 18 and in the states around the country. Only members of the military are subject to prosecution (known as courts-martial) under the UCMJ. Civilians who commit crimes against the military community are prosecuted under civilian law at the state or federal level. The UCMJ also specifies unique procedures for handling criminal cases within the military. Although many of the crimes and processes are unique to the military, the UCMJ is federal law and still must pass constitutional muster in areas of due process and other protections.

The military's criminal investigative agencies have received considerable attention in the popular media in recent years. Thus, many Americans — even those who have never served in the military — are not completely unaware of these agencies' existence.

Undoubtedly, the most notable popular portrayal of military law enforcement is the long-running CBS television series *NCIS* starring Mark Harmon as Supervisory Special Agent Jethro Gibbs. The show follows a team of Naval Criminal Investigative Service special agents as they solve one homicide after another from week to week. The show began in 2003 as a spin-off from the CBS show *JAG* (short for Judge Advocate General). There has since been an additional spin-off from *NCIS* called *NCIS: Los Angeles*, which follows the same format but features a different team of agents, this time operating on the West Coast.

Although the Coast Guard Investigative Service has not been profiled with its own television series or cinematic production, it has been featured on a couple of episodes of *NCIS*. CGIS special agent Abigail Borin, played by Diane Neal, is an occasional recurring character who teams up with NCIS's Gibbs when Navy and Coast Guard jurisdiction overlap.

The Army CID has also been introduced to the public via entertainment productions. The 1999 movie *The General's Daughter* featured John Travolta as CID special agent Paul Brenner and Madeleine Stowe as CID special agent Sara Sunhill; the CID pair were teamed-up to investigate the murder of an Army captain, who also happened to be the daughter of a high-ranking Army general. The movie was based on the popular 1992 novel of the same title by author Nelson DeMille.

The Air Force OSI was also featured in film. The 2008 movie *Eagle Eye* is a counter-terrorism yarn that features Rosario Dawson as AFOSI Special Agent Zoe Perez. Actual special agents of the AFOSI worked with Dawson, providing her with an orientation to the agency and even limited firearms and tactics training as she researched her role.

The history of the military investigative agencies parallels the unique histories of each of the branches. Likewise, the organization, personnel and functions of each of these agencies is unique. Consequently, the history, organization, and function of each of these agencies will be considered in turn.

Army Criminal Investigation Division

The United States Army Criminal Investigation Division (Army CID), formally known as the Army Criminal Investigation Command, is a general crimes federal investigative agency headquartered in Quantico, Virginia. Army CID constitutes a major command of the U.S. Army and is headed by a major general, who also serves as the Provost Marshal General of the Army, and head of the Army Corrections Command. Army CID has been called the "Army's FBI." It investigates all crimes against persons and property in which the Army has an interest or is a victim.

The history of the Army CID and army law enforcement generally can be traced back to the U.S. Civil War. Congress passed a law which provided for the drafting of conscripts into the Union Army. Forced conscription was not well received and riots and protests often broke out among draftees. In March of 1863, Secretary of War Edwin Stanton established the Provost Marshal General's Bureau to enforce the conscription law and to arrest army deserters (U.S. Army, n.d.).

The Army further developed within itself a law enforcement function during World War I. The Army created the Military Police Corps in October of 1917 to help police the hundreds of thousands of soldiers that made up the American Expeditionary Force in France. The Military Police Corps essentially served as a uniformed police service wherever American soldiers were garrisoned. However, as with any large police force, the need for criminal investigative specialists became apparent as the uniformed patrol officers were ill-equipped and ill-trained for detective work. In November 1918, the Army established the Criminal Investigation Division within the Military Police Corps to investigate criminal activity within the territories occupied by the U.S. Army. The CID at that time was headed by a division chief who served as an advisor to the Provost Marshal General. However, operational control of CID fell under the local provost marshals at various bases and camps. CID investigators were selected from among military police officers and were truly a detective augmentation to localized police services provided by the Military Police Corps under individual provost marshals (U.S. Army, n.d.). As such, there was no central command for CID operations Army-wide, nor was there a standardized training program beyond the general law enforcement training CID investigators received when they had served as military policemen.

The lack of coordination in CID changed with World War II. In January of 1944, the Office of the Provost Marshal General created within itself the Criminal Investigation Division. CID no longer would merely advise the Provost Marshal General; it would now answer to the Provost Marshal General directly. At this time, training and policies for criminal investigators began to be standardized. Organizational reforms ebbed and flowed after World War II. In the 1950s, the Army loosened centralized control of CID in deference to local commands, only to tighten it up again in the 1960s. Finally, in September of 1971, at the direction of Secretary of Defense Melvin Laird, the Army formed the U.S. Army Criminal Investigation Command, which exercised control over all CID assets and activities Army-wide (U.S. Army, n.d.).

Today, Army CID is staffed by approximately 2,000 military and civilian personnel, including over 900 special agents. The Army Criminal Investigation Command is organized into six major groups:

202nd MP Group (CID) — headquartered in Seckenheim, Germany

3rd MP Group (CID) — headquartered at Ft. Gillem, GA

6th MP Group (CID) — headquartered at Ft. Lewis, WA

701st MP Group (CID) — headquartered in Quantico, VA

U.S. Army Criminal Investigation Laboratory — located at Ft. Gillem, GA

U.S. Army Crime Records Center — located in Quantico, VA

Within the MP Groups above there are multiple CID battalions and units which are organized to cover geographic and functional areas. The 701st MP Group is home to several specialized units, including the Major Procurement Fraud Unit, the Computer Crime Investigative Unit, and the Army Protective Services Battalion.

The Army Criminal Investigation Command (CID) employs both military and civilian special agents. Special agents from within the ranks of the Army can be non-commissioned officers (i.e. army sergeants) or warrant officers. There are no CID special agents holding the rank of a commissioned officer (i.e. 2nd Lieutenant or higher). Special agents can also be active duty or reservists in the Army Reserve or Army National Guard. Special agents in the Army Reserve and National Guard have a very high operations tempo and are routinely called up into active duty—sometimes for extended tours of a year or more, and sometimes for just a couple of days (such as for a protective detail or for a quick investigation). Many CID agents who are reservists are employed in civilian law enforcement agencies while not on active duty.

As noted above, Army CID also employs civilian special agents. Civilian CID agents are not general crimes investigators like their enlisted and warrant officer counterparts. Rather, civilian agents are confined to specializations, such as procurement fraud or computer crimes, and work those types of cases exclusively.

Army Regulation 195-2 defines the parameters of criminal investigative activities by the Army CID, as well as CID's authorities. Army CID is responsible for investigating all felonies in which the Army is believed to have an interest. The Army asserts that it generally has an investigative interest when (AR195-2, 2009, p. 5):

(1) The crime is committed on a military installation or facility, or in an area under Army control;

(2) There is a reasonable basis to believe that a suspect may be subject to the UCMJ;

(3) There is a reasonable basis to believe that a suspect may be a civilian employee of the Department of Defense (DOD) or DOD contractor who has committed an offense in connection with his or her assigned contractual duties which adversely affects the Army;

(4) The Army is the victim of the crime; for example, the offense involves the loss or destruction of Government property or allegations of fraud (as defined in DOD/DOJ instructions concerning the criminal investigation of fraud offenses) relating to Army programs or personnel;

(5) There is a need to protect personnel, property, or activities on Army installations from criminal conduct on, or directed against, military installations that has a direct adverse effect on the Army's ability to accomplish its mission; for example, the introduction of controlled substances onto Army installations, acts of terrorism, and logistical security;

(6) In contingency operations there is a need to investigate crimes to establish law and order as identified by senior mission commander.

Crimes investigated by Army CID commonly include robbery, sexual assault, homicides, burglaries, espionage, acts of terrorism, and contract fraud. Army CID special agents also provide force protection support to Army personnel in the field and serve on personal protection details for high ranking Army and Defense Department officials.

Army CID special agents possess full law enforcement authority while on duty on military bases and in areas controlled by the Army. Warrant officer CID special agents have broader authority than enlisted CID agents in that the latter are not permitted to arrest civilians, even while on a military base. Civilian CID special agents have traditional federal law enforcement authority granted to them under 10 USC 4027. This authority is broader than that of their military counterparts. Civilian CID special agents may execute search and arrest warrant both on and off Army installations. Additionally, they may make arrests for violations of federal crimes under Title 18 as well as crimes under the UCMJ. All CID special agents (military and civilian) may carry firearms on and off of military installations in the performance of their official duties (Bumgarner, 2006).

U.S. Marine Corps Criminal Investigation Division

The Marine Corps Criminal Investigation Division (CID) is responsible for investigating misdemeanor and certain minor felony offenses that occur on Marine bases or that involve U.S. Marines. The caveat is that the NCIS has primary jurisdiction over all criminal offenses of both Naval and Marine personnel. However, the NCIS waives its jurisdiction and defers to Marine Corps CID for criminal offenses which fall below NCIS investigative thresholds. Effectively, this relegates the Marine Corps CID primarily to the investigation of misdemeanor offenses, such as minor theft and minor assaults, including domestic assaults.

Marine Corps CID operates under the command of the local provost marshal for a given Marine Corps base. In addition to investigating minor crimes not investigated by NCIS, the Marine Corps CID also investigates felony drug violations which are declined for investigation by NCIS. Further, the Marine Corps CID is responsible for receiving and maintaining criminal evidence in the Provost Marshal's evidence repository on each base and for liaising with various agencies on and off base regarding domestic violence issues (MCB Quantico, n.d.). Finally, criminal investigators of the Marines Corps CID also compile criminal intelligence that relates to force protection and military readiness (MCB 29 Palms, n.d.).

Most Marine Corps CID special agents are chosen from the enlisted ranks of Marine Corps military police officers. Marine Corps MPs must successfully complete the Army's CID Apprentice Special Agent training in order to become a Marine Corps special agent. Indeed, due to the uniform training received by Army and Marine Corps CID agents, the Army has at times sought to fill its own CID ranks by recruiting Marine Corps CID agents. This is tempting for many Marines who are special agents as they have limited opportunities in the Marine Corps to investigate serious violent and other traditional crimes given NCIS's investigative jurisdiction.

Another option for Marine Corps special agents is to apply for a tour of duty with NCIS. Tours usually last 2–3 years. Navy policy permits the temporary transfer of Marine Special Agents into the NCIS. Secretary of the Navy Instruction 5430.107, issued in 2005, reads in part (SECNAV 5430.107, 2005, p. 9):

> NCIS may seek to have agents from Marine Corps Criminal Investigation Division assigned to NCIS for duty as Special Agents. Marine Special Agents so assigned will carry NCIS credentials and badges, conduct criminal investigations under the authority of NCIS, and fall under the operational control of NCIS. While assigned duties with NCIS, Marine Special Agents may be authorized to undertake official duties in a manner that disassociates them from identification as a military member. Given their military status, Marine Special Agents may not exercise the arrest authorities extended to NCIS civilian Special Agents ....

In the late 1990s, there were approximately 300 Marine Corps CID special agents worldwide. None of these agents were civilians. However, in 1999, CID offices were shut down and merged with NCIS. By 2004, only dozens of Marine Corps CID agents were still on active duty—and those were working directly for NCIS. Smaller crimes and unsung felonies on Marine Corps bases were not attended to properly. Incidents requiring investigation were only producing cursory reports from the uniformed MPs (Tilghman, 2008).

In 2004, a decision was made by Marine Corps leadership to reinvigorate the CID program. From 2004 to 2008, the CID agent cadre grew from a little over 50 to 128, with a total authorized strength of 235 special agents worldwide (Tilghman, 2008). Additionally, the hiring of civilian special agents was authorized. The goal was to develop continuity between Marine Corps CID and other law enforcement agencies. Civilian CID agents can (and are encouraged to) spend their entire career on a single Marine base (Tilghman, 2008).

Naval Criminal Investigative Service

The Naval Criminal Investigative Service (NCIS) is the criminal investigative branch of the United States Navy. Its investigative jurisdiction includes crimes perpetrated by personnel of, or committed against, the U.S. Navy and U.S. Marine Corps. The NCIS originates from the Office of Naval Intelligence (ONI), which was created by the Secretary of the Navy William Hunt in 1882. ONI initially possessed only an information-gathering mission. However, during World War I, it expanded its mission to include counterespionage and preventing sabotage. Thwarting espionage and sabotage was an inherently criminal investigative mission in nature. The investigative mission of the ONI continued to mature and develop alongside the intelligence mission in the years following World War I and through World War II. By 1945, the ONI was officially responsible for investigating a wide range of criminality, as well as conducting security investigations (NCIS, n.d.).

In 1966, the criminal investigative mission of ONI was officially partitioned from the rest of the organization by the creation within ONI of the Naval Investigative Service (NIS). NIS continued to operate under the Director of Naval Intelligence, but was exclusively an investigative organization. In 1972, the function of security clearance investigations was transferred out of NIS to the newly created civilian Defense Investigative Service. Although many NIS special agents transferred to DIS, the remaining agents in NIS were permitted to focus all of their attention on investigating crimes and spying.

Like the Army CID, the NIS was designated as a command of its own. In 1985, NIS became the Naval Security and Investigative Command. The command changed its name to the Naval Investigative Service Command in 1988.

During the 1990s, the NIS transitioned further into a federal law enforcement agency distinct from its military oversight. In 1992, the Naval Investigative Service Command was changed to the Naval Criminal Investigative Service and was eliminated as a standalone command headed by a naval officer. That year, Roy Nedrow became the first civilian director of the NCIS, which was realigned under the Secretary of the Navy—also a civilian. Director Nedrow moved quickly to replace regional offices with field offices. By 1996, NCIS had 165 field offices and resident agencies worldwide (NCIS, n.d.).

Despite NCIS's move toward a traditional federal law enforcement organization, it was still encumbered by the limitations of its military jurisdiction. As late as 2000, it was legally only authorized to make arrests of military personnel. If civilians were to be prosecuted as a result of an NCIS investigation, other agencies (such as the FBI, the U.S. Marshals, or the Defense Criminal Investigative Service) had to be brought into the case and relied upon to cover the civilian arrests. But in the year 2000, the transition to a full-fledged federal law enforcement organization was made complete when Congress passed legislation authorizing civilian special agents of NCIS (as well as civilian special agents of the Army and the Air Force) the authority to execute federal warrants on and off military installations and to make arrests of civilians. The legislation designated to civilian criminal investigators of military agencies the same authorities granted to Defense Criminal Investigative Service special agents in 10 USC 1585a (P.L. 106-398, Sec 554).

Today, the NCIS has 16 field offices and dozens of resident agencies in the United States and in other countries. In total, NCIS has a presence in 140 locations globally. NCIS special agents number approximately 1,200; additionally, there are over 900 civilian and 200 military support staff who are not special agents. These include computer specialists, forensic analysts, physical security specialists, and crime analysts (Bumgarner, 2006). Among the special agents, well over half are civilians. The remaining active duty special agents come from both enlisted and officer ranks.

The mission of the NCIS is multi-pronged (SECNAV 5430.107, 2005):

- to protect and defend the Department of the Navy against terrorism and foreign intelligence threats;
- to investigate major criminal offenses;
- to enforce the criminal laws of the United States and the UCMJ;
- to assist commands in maintaining good order and discipline; and
- to provide law enforcement and security services to the Navy and Marine Corps globally.

In particular, NCIS criminal investigations are routinely initiated, until such time as criminality can be excluded, when Navy and Marine Corps personnel succumb to non-combat related deaths that aren't attributable to disease or natural causes; fires or explosions of unknown origin affecting Navy property; incidents of theft of ordinance; controlled substance violations; missing command members when foul play cannot be excluded; fraud against the Navy; and acts or attempted acts of terrorism, sabotage, espionage, and assassination (SECNAV 5430.107, 2005).

In addition to the significant criminal investigative responsibilities of NCIS, the agency has a major role in counterintelligence. NCIS is a close partner with agencies such as the Federal Bureau of Investigation, the Central Intelligence Agency, the National Security Agency, and the Defense Intelligence Agency (Bumgarner, 2006). Counterintelligence, in support of American Naval forces around the world, is identified as the first of its strategic imperatives in its 2010 Strategic Plan, even ahead of crime fighting (NCIS, 2010).

NCIS special agents operate worldwide, as do criminal investigators from the other military investigative agencies. However, NCIS has a unique operational challenge in that many of the Navy's service members and assets can be found at sea. The need to conduct investigations of crimes committed aboard naval vessels at sea gave birth to the Agent Afloat program in 1970. The program assigns NCIS special agents to all aircraft carriers, whether they are deployed at sea or not. From the aircraft carriers, agents can fly by way of helicopter to other ships in the carrier group, such as a cruiser or destroyer, to investigate serious criminal offenses. Agents afloat generally serve in that capacity for 6 months to a year.

Air Force Office of Special Investigations

The United States Air Force is the youngest of America's military branches. It was separated from the Army Air Corps as a stand-alone military service in 1947. It stands to reason, then, that the Air Force Office of Special Investigations (AFOSI) must be the youngest of military investigative agencies. And it is. The AFOSI was established in August of 1948.

Organizationally, AFOSI reports to the Air Force Inspector General, which is a part of the Office of the Secretary of the Air Force. Like its sister agencies in the other branches of the military, the AFOSI possesses a dual mission: criminal investigation and counter-intelligence. It pursues its mission with a little over 2,700 active-duty, reserve, and civilian personnel, approximately 2,000 of whom are special agents. Of the 2,738 who work at AFOSI, 311 are active-duty officers, 1,253 are active-duty enlisted personnel, 389 are Air Force reservists, and 785 are civilians (AFOSI, 2011).

The Air Force OSI headquarters is located in Quantico, Virginia. Additionally, there are eight field investigations regions. Seven of the eight regions are aligned with other Air Force commands:

Region 1—Air Force Material Command

Region 2—Air Combat Command

Region 3—Air Mobility Command

Region 4—Air Education and Training Command

Region 5—U.S. Air Forces in Europe

Region 6—Pacific Air Forces

Region 8—Air Force Space Command

Region 7 provides investigative support to the other regions. Through these regions, the AFOSI operates a total of 144 offices in the United States and 63 offices abroad (AFOSI, 2011).

The AFOSI breaks its activities down into five operational areas: threat detection, criminal investigation (general crimes), economic crime investigations, specialized services, and cyber crime detection and prevention. Threat detection primarily relates to investigating and preventing acts of terrorism, espionage, technology transfers, and other force protection activities. Criminal investigation of general crimes includes the investigation of felonies, including homicide, sexual assault, robbery, assault, burglary, arson, and serious controlled substance violations. Special agents working in the area of economic crimes focus primarily on procurement fraud, bribery, and embezzlement. Specialized services include AFOSI personnel involved in administering polygraphs, forensic laboratory analysts, and even behavioral scientists and profilers. Finally, the cyber crime activities of the AFOSI are concentrated on operating the Defense Cyber Crime Center. The Center consists of two major parts: the Defense Computer Forensics Laboratory and the Defense Computer Investigations Training Program. Although the AFOSI is the custodian of the Defense Cyber

Crime Center, its services and training are made available to the entire Department of Defense criminal investigative community (AFOSI, 2011).

AFOSI special agents on active duty, or reserve agents called up to active duty, possess full law enforcement authority, including the power to carry firearms and make arrests, on Air Force and other military installations. However, as with Army CID and NCIS, only civilian special agents of the AFOSI have full federal law enforcement authority off military reservations, including the power to execute search warrants and to arrest civilians off base.

AFOSI special agents also engage in dignitary protection details for high ranking Air Force and Department of Defense officials. From time to time, AFOSI agents might also be called upon to serve on protective details for other dignitaries, up to and including the President of the United States.

The AFOSI, like other military investigative agencies, is aggressive in its counterterrorism and counterespionage mission. Pursuant to that mission, the AFOSI initiated the Eagle Eyes program, which is an Air Force-wide anti-terrorism effort relying on the informed observations of Air Force personnel. In other words, the program raises awareness among personnel throughout the Air Force community of the need to be watchful for tell-tale signs of potential terrorism or espionage activity. Examples of suspicious activity include individuals conducting surveillance of Air Force facilities, elicitation of information about military operations or facilities, tests of Air Force security measures, the acquiring of supplies (such as explosives or ammunition), and suspicious persons simply "out of place" (AFOSI, n.d.). The hope is that the entire Air Force community, when taught to identify behavior that is suspicious, and when encouraged to report such activity, will help prevent acts of terror and sabotage before they can ever be consummated.

United States Coast Guard Investigative Service

The United States Coast Guard is in the unique position of being able to claim status as one of the oldest federal law enforcement agencies and one of the oldest branches of the military. As noted in Chapter 1, the U.S. Coast Guard finds its ancestry in the Revenue Cutter Service, which not only collected tariffs and fought piracy, but also constituted our nation's only naval force until the early 19th Century.

The U.S. Coast Guard possesses both military and civilian responsibilities. The Coast Guard is organizationally a part of the U.S. Department of Homeland Security. However, it is nonetheless a uniformed military service. Active-duty members of the Coast Guard are subject to the UCMJ just as other military personnel are. In times of war, assets of the Coast Guard are transferred to the command of the United States Navy. During wartime, the Coast Guard is primarily used for port security, both in the United States and overseas. When not engaged in a war-time mission, the Coast Guard is a maritime law enforcement, regulatory, and emergency services agency (Bumgarner, 2006).

The U.S. Coast Guard has been housed in several cabinet level departments. For most of its history, it was a part of the U.S. Treasury Department. In 1915, the Revenue Cutter Service and the United States Life Saving Service combined to form the U.S. Coast Guard. Even with a broadening of its responsibilities into rescues at sea and maintaining navigational aids, the organization remained a U.S. Treasury agency. Like other branches within the Treasury Department around the turn of the 20th Century, the Coast Guard established an intelligence unit. The Coast Guard Intelligence Unit was especially robust during the years of Prohibition, employing as many as 45 criminal investigators (USCG, 2002). The Coast Guard Intelligence Unit engaged in counterespionage and security investigations during World War II. After the war, agents with the Intelligence Unit expanded their investigative responsibilities to cover all criminal and personnel security investigations relating to or impacting the U.S. Coast Guard (Bumgarner, 2006).

In 1967, the U.S. Department of Transportation was established. Reflecting the Coast Guard's modern role as a nautical services organization rather than a tax and tariff collecting organization, the Coast Guard was relocated under the Department of Transportation. Criminal investigators within the Coast Guard continued to focus on maritime law enforcement activities, customs violations, and personnel violations of the UCMJ. In 1996, the criminal investigative, counterintelligence, and protective service function of the Coast Guard were all consolidated under the newly named Coast Guard Investigative Service (CGIS).

In March of 2003, the U.S. Coast Guard, along with the Coast Guard Investigative Service, was transferred yet again ... this time to the Department of Homeland Security as an outcome of the Homeland Security Act of 2002. CGIS special agents are part of the U.S. Department of Homeland Security criminal investigative community, which includes special agents of the Bureau of Immigration and Customs Enforcement (ICE), the U.S. Secret Service, the Federal Protective Service, and Federal Air Marshals.

The CGIS structure consists of eight regions, with each region led by a CGIS special agent-in-charge (SAC). Not surprisingly, each region includes shoreline and navigable bodies of water. Each SAC reports to the Deputy Director of CGIS, who in turn reports to the director. CGIS headquarters is located in Arlington, Virginia. In addition to the eight regional offices, CGIS has over 30 resident agent offices spread across the United States (primarily, but not exclusively, in coastal areas). Organizationally, CGIS falls under the Office of the Vice Commandant of the Coast Guard (USCG, n.d.).

The CGIS is made up of over 110 active duty special agents, over 150 Coast Guard Reserve special agents, and over 120 civilian special agents. Active duty CGIS special agents are not hampered by the restrictions of their active-duty counterparts in other military investigative agencies. While the Posse Comitatus Act of 1878 precludes (generally) the engagement of military personnel in civilian law enforcement, Coast Guard personnel are exempt from this act. What's more, 14 USC 95 specifically grants special agents of the CGIS, without regard for active-duty or civilian status, full law enforcement authority, including the power to execute federal warrants, make arrests, and carry firearms. Additionally, the law provides that CGIS special agents may be called upon to engage in law enforcement activities outside the scope of the Coast Guard's normal jurisdiction at the direction of the Secretary of Homeland Security.

The CGIS has several law enforcement responsibilities. These include (USCG, n.d.):

- criminal investigations for crimes relating to the maritime realm and Coast Guard mission;
- law enforcement task force participation and liaison;
- investigations into felony violations of the UCMJ;
- protective service operations for dignitaries and facilities; and
- law enforcement intelligence collection and dissemination.

Although special agents of CGIS have broad investigative authority, a large share of its investigative activities focuses on smuggling, narcotics violations, and human trafficking on the high seas.

Defense Criminal Investigative Service

The last criminal investigative organization associated with the United States military is an agency made up entirely of civilian criminal investigators, employing more than 340 special agents nationwide. The Defense Criminal Investigative Service (DCIS) is the investigative arm of the Department of Defense, Office of Inspector General. Although the Inspector General community will be explored in greater detail in the next chapter, it is appropriate to introduce the DCIS here in the context of military criminal investigative law enforcement.

The DCIS works in close partnership with the investigative agencies of the various military branches. Many of the law enforcement authorities attached to those agencies—particularly their civilian special agents—flow from the authority bestowed by Congress on DCIS special agents. DCIS exercises oversight over all other military criminal investigations by DOD investigative agencies. The DCIS may assert its jurisdiction over the military investigative agencies on any cases affecting the operations of any DOD element (Bumgarner, 2006).

However, DCIS special agents generally do not involve themselves in general crimes investigations. Rather, the focus of most DCIS criminal investigations is on fraud (primarily contract fraud), embezzlement, and public integrity. These types of cases are consistent with the general mission of all Offices of Inspector General, which is to combat fraud, waste, and abuse in government programs. DCIS special agents routinely work jointly with Army CID, NCIS, and AFOSI on large-scale procurement fraud schemes. These crimes are particularly serious as they can impact the war-fighting readiness and safety of troops, airmen, and sailors in battle.

In addition to allegations of fraud, DCIS special agents regularly investigate cases of misconduct among high-ranking DOD civilian and military officials. DCIS was the lead agency in the Tailhook investigation in 1991. The investigation explored allegations of dozens of sexual assaults committed against both men and women during a naval aviation convention in Las Vegas. The case garnered considerable national and international media attention. Since then, the DCIS has been called upon to investigate other high profile cases of sexual misconduct in the military, including charges of criminal sexual harassment committed by Sergeant Major of the Army Gene McKinney (the Army's highest ranking enlisted soldier) in 1996.

While popular media portrayals have introduced the American public to NCIS, and to Army CID and Air Force OSI to a lesser extent, the fact is that all five military services, as well as the Department of Defense, possess criminal investigators in place to police and protect the operations and personnel of the United States military. The community of military special agents, made up of active duty, reserve, and civilian personnel, fulfill an important mission in preserving America's war- and terror-fighting readiness and securing the nation's superiority among the world's militaries.

References

Air Force Office of Special Investigations (2011). *Air Force OSI fact sheet.* Retrieved from http://www.osi.andrews.af.mil/library/factsheets/factsheet.asp?id=4848.

Air Force Office of Special Investigations (n.d.). *Eagle eyes.* Retrieved from http://www.osi.andrews.af.mil/eagleeyes/index.asp.

Army Regulation 195-2 (2009). *Criminal investigation activities.* Washington, D.C.: Department of the Army.

Bumgarner, J. (2006). *Federal agents: The growth of federal law enforcement in America.* Westport, CT: Praeger Publishers.

Marine Corps Base 29 Palms (n.d.). *Provost Marshal's Office: Criminal Investigation Division.* Retrieved from http://www.marines.mil/unit/29palms/G7/PMO/pages/cid.aspx.

Marine Corps Base Quantico (n.d.). *Criminal Investigation Division (CID).* Retrieved from http://www.quantico.usmc.mil/activities/display.aspx?PID=587&Section=SECBN.

National Defense Authorization, Fiscal Year 2001. Public Law 106-398 (2001).

Naval Criminal Investigative Service (n.d.). *History of the Naval Criminal Investigative Service.* Retrieved from http://www.ncis.navy.mil/AboutNCIS/History/Pages/default.aspx.

Naval Criminal Investigative Service (2010). *The Naval Criminal Investigative Service strategic vision: Global support to global challenges.* Quantico, VA: NCIS.

Secretary of the Navy (2005, December 28). *Mission and functions of the Naval Criminal Investigative Service* (SECNAV Instruction 5430.107). Washington, D.C.: Department of the Navy.

Stockholm International Peace Research Institute (2011). *Recent trends in military expenditure.* Retrieved from http://www.sipri.org/research/armaments/milex/resultoutput/trends.

Tilghman, A. (2008, May 17). Corps to boost criminal investigator numbers. *Marine Corps Times.*

U.S. Army Criminal Investigation Command (n.d.). *CID history.* Retrieved from http://www.cid.army.mil/history.html.

U.S. Coast Guard (2002). *U.S. Coast Guard: An historical overview.* Washington, D.C.: USCG Historian's Office.

U.S. Coast Guard (n.d.). *Coast Guard Investigative Service: Organization.* Retrieved from http://www.uscg.mil/hq/cg2/cgis/organization.asp.

U.S. Coast Guard (n.d.). *Coast Guard Investigative Service: Personnel.* Retrieved from http://www.uscg.mil/hq/cg2/cgis/personnel.asp.

U.S. Department of Defense (2010). *Population representation in military services.* Washington, D.C.: Office of the Under Secretary of Defense, Personnel, and Readiness.

Chapter Seventeen

Offices of Inspector General

In June of 2011, a Florida man was sentenced in federal court to over 19 years in prison. The man was not a bank robber or kidnapper. He hadn't conspired to commit acts of terrorism or to smuggle narcotics or drugs. The man was a medical doctor. He was convicted of perpetrating a $23 million fraud against the Medicare program. Prosecutors demonstrated that the doctor had intentionally misdiagnosed multiple patients with a rare blood disorder and then prescribed to them very expensive medication for the purpose of receiving Medicare payments. Other individuals working at the doctor's clinic who also participated in the fraud were convicted and sentenced on lesser charges (HHS OIG, 2012).

This investigation was led by special agents of the U.S. Health and Human Services (HHS) Office of Inspector General (OIG). In Fiscal Year 2011, HHS OIG opened 1,110 health care fraud criminal investigations involving over 2,500 suspects. That same year, federal health care fraud charges were brought in 489 cases against 1,430 defendants (HHS OIG, 2012). In an average year, HHS OIG recovers over $3 billion for the U.S. Treasury from criminal and civil penalties. This is an impressive tally for an organization with 1,700 employees, which include both criminal investigators and auditors.

The Office of Inspector General for the HHS is one of 73 federal offices of inspector general established by federal statute. These OIGs are found in every cabinet level federal department and major independent agency, as well as in several smaller federal agencies. Collectively, the federal OIG community recovered over $7 billion in penalties and over $80 billion in cost savings through audit recommendations regarding wasteful spending and programmatic inefficiencies in fiscal year 2010. Federal OIG investigations were also responsible for over 5,000 criminal indictments and 5,600 convictions in fiscal year 2010 (CIGIE, 2011).

Although they permeate the entire federal executive branch today, civilian inspectors general offices are a relatively new creation as federal law enforcement agencies go.

History

There have long been inspectors general in government set in their places to ensure operational efficiency and effectiveness—particularly in military organizations. During the American Revolutionary War, General George Washington appointed Frederick William Augustus von Steuben as the Continental Army's Inspector General in 1778. As the Army's inspector general, von Steuben ensured that proper tactics, training, and discipline were observed among the ranks. General von Steuben is credited with being the father of the military inspector general system in the United States (Clary and Whitehorne, 1987).

However, it wasn't until the 1960s that the notion of having an inspector general oversee the operations of a civilian agency in the federal government gained traction. The impetus for establishing offices of inspector general in the federal civilian realm has roots in a scandal born out of the U.S. Department of Agriculture (USDA), known generally as the Billy Sol Estes scandal.

Billy Sol Estes was a businessman with political connections who sold agricultural supplies to cotton farmers in Texas during the 1950s. However, his business began to decline as fewer farmers were planting and harvesting cotton because of USDA efforts to regulate cotton production. Estes then conspired with individuals inside and outside of the USDA to secure agricultural subsidies through fraudulent means. An investigation ensued and in April of 1962, a multi-count indictment was handed down against Estes for defrauding the federal government. After his trial and conviction in 1963, he was sentenced to eight years in prison.

In the wake of the Billy Sol Estes scandal, Congress held hearings on corruption in government programs and began to develop an intense interest in pushing governmental reform. However, Orville Freeman, the Secretary of Agriculture, hadn't waited for Congress to act; in fact, he didn't even wait for the Billy Sol Estes scandal to be completely resolved. In 1962, Freeman signed an administrative order to create the USDA Office of Inspector General. The USDA OIG possessed no statutory authority other than general executive authorities vested in the Secretary of Agriculture and delegated to the OIG. Freeman's OIG was organized around two primary functions: audits and investigations. The USDA OIG created under Freeman is regarded as the first modern Office of Inspector General in the United States civilian government. Its dual-track structure, possessing both audit and criminal investigation units, served as a model for statutorily-created OIGs with the Inspector General Act of 1978 (Bumgarner, 2006).

The 1970s turned out to be a bad decade for the prestige of the U.S. Government and the trust that Americans afforded it. Corruption scandals and examples of government ineptitude seemed to abound. The shootings of war protesters at Kent State University in Ohio by members of the National Guard (ostensibly, the Army), the environmental disaster at Love Canal, the nuclear accident and near catastrophe at Three Mile Island, and the Watergate scandal resulting in President Richard Nixon's resignation, all undermined the faith Americans placed in their government (Nowolinski, 2001).

Against that backdrop in the 1970s, and the Billy Sol Estes scandal from the decade before, Congress continued to examine the operations of government with an eye for reform. Of particular concern to Congress was the potential for fraud, waste, and abuse in the Medicaid Program, which provided needed healthcare coverage for the poor. This program was administered by the Department of Health, Education, and Welfare (HEW). According to one Congressional report, the fraud and waste in the Medicaid program cost the government nearly $2 billion per year.

Reports of fraud, waste, bribery, and other scandals soured the American people on the federal government. According to Paul Light of the Brookings Institute, the erosion of confidence in the trustworthiness of government declined precipitously from the 1950s to the 1970s. Citing a University of Michigan study, Light notes that Americans' agreement with the statement "quite a few people running the government are a little crooked" increased from 24% in 1958 to 42% in 1976. Americans who agreed with the statement that they "could not trust the government to do right most of the time" increased from 23% in 1958 to 63% in 1976. Americans believing that "government is run by a few big interests looking out for themselves" went from 29% in 1964 to 66% in 1976. And finally, the percentage of Americans who believed that government wastes a lot of taxpayer money rose increased from 43% in 1958 to 74% in 1976 (Light, 1993).

With a crisis of confidence in government looming, Congress began to act by establishing statutory Offices of Inspector General, first in 1976 with HEW, and then in 1977 with the Department of Energy. Against the backdrop of the public's growing disdain for government, a majority in Congress bought into the expected 4-pronged benefits of the IG concept (Light, 1993):

- guaranteed high rates of return, both political and budgetary;
- creation of a new legislative arena in an age of fiscal restraint;
- some protection for Congress against the lack of public confidence in government;
- an opportunity for Congress to take a more aggressive role in the management of the federal government and programs.

The HEW Inspector General Act of 1976 was the first statutorily-established OIG in the American civilian federal government. Its structure was patterned after the USDA OIG, including both audit and investigative divisions. However, by statute, the Inspector General for HEW, and later for the Department of Energy, would be a presidential appointee rather than serving at the pleasure of the cabinet secretary—in this case, the Secretary of Health, Education, and Welfare. The goal was to appoint an individual to the position of Inspector General who would be independent of the leadership within the Department being overseen and could only be removed by the President. Further, the HEW Inspector General was given the charge in the statute to report periodically to Congress on the findings and recommendations of the OIG as a result of its audits and investigations. While some politicians were concerned with the report requirement because of the possible blurring of executive and legislative responsibilities of the OIG, the reporting requirement was passed nonetheless under the logic that it was an extension of Congress' oversight responsibilities toward the federal bureaucracy, something for which Congress paid the bills.

As already noted, similar legislation was passed in 1977 creating an Office of Inspector General at the Department of Energy. However, Congress decided soon thereafter that creating OIGs in a piecemeal, agency-by-agency fashion as the need arose was an inefficient approach to the problem. Besides, Congress was convinced that all the major departments of the federal government were vulnerable to fraud, waste, and abuse in their respective programs. So, in 1978, Congress passed the Inspector General Act of 1978 which established OIGs in 12 additional departments and agencies (besides HEW and Energy), including all Cabinet-level departments. These inspectors general for the OIGs were to be presidential appointees and confirmed by the Senate. This included the USDA OIG, which became a statutory agency (rather than administratively created).

Just as with the OIGs at USDA, HEW, and Energy, the OIGs established by statute in the Inspector General Act of 1978 were organized around the two primary functions of audits and investigations. Within each OIG, there existed (and still exists) both an Office of Audit and an Office of Investigation. The overall mission of the OIGs to combat fraud, waste, and abuse in government programs under their purview is fulfilled through conducting both criminal investigations and audits of the various programs, funds, contractors, and expenditures of the parent department or agency.

The mission and structure of the OIGs was clearly articulated in the 1978 statute, which reads in part:

Sec. 2. Purpose and establishment of Offices of Inspector General; departments and agencies involved

In order to create independent and objective units—

(1) to conduct and supervise audits and investigations relating to the programs and operations of the establishments listed in section 11(2);

(2) to provide leadership and coordination and recommend policies for activities designed

    (A) to promote economy, efficiency, and effectiveness in the administration of, and

    (B) to prevent and detect fraud and abuse in such programs and operations; and

(3) to provide a means for keeping the head of the establishment and the Congress fully and currently informed about problems and deficiencies relating to the administration of such programs and operations and the necessity for and progress of corrective action;

In addition to the OIGs at HEW and Energy, which were statutorily created in 1976 and 1977, the 1978 legislation established permanent OIGs in 12 federal agencies, including the Departments of Agriculture, Commerce, Housing and Urban Development, Interior, Labor, Transportation, the Community Services Administration, the General Services Administration, the Small Business Administration, the Veterans Administration, the National Aeronautics and Space Administration, and the Environmental Protection Agency.

The statute makes clear that the OIGs were to be independent and would have a free hand to report findings without political considerations or consequences. The goals of the OIGs are outlined in Section 2(2) of the statute. The goals include:

- promoting economy, efficiency, and effectiveness in the administration of department or agency programs (largely achieved by the audit function of the OIG);

- detecting and prevent fraud, waste, and abuse within the parent department and their respective programs (achieved through both audits and investigations); and

- keeping Congress informed about problems uncovered within the departments or agencies to which the OIGs belong—whether they are problems of management, ethics, crimes, or vulnerabilities to fraud, waste, and abuse.

Organization and Personnel

According to the U.S. Department of Justice's Bureau of Justice Statistics, in 2008 there were 33 Offices of Inspector General (OIG) in the federal government that employed full-time criminal investigators with arrest and firearms authority. In total, these 33 OIGs employed 3,501 special agents. The OIG with the largest cadre of special agents belonged to the U.S. Postal Service with 508 special agents in 2008. The Library of Congress OIG possessed the fewest sworn criminal investigators with only two special agents. Eleven of the OIGs employed over 100 agents. Five OIGs employed fewer than 10 special agents (Reaves, 2012). The total number of special agents for each of the 33 OIGs is provided in Figure 17.1.

There were an additional 36 statutorily-established OIGs operating in the federal government. While those 36 OIGs possessed criminal investigative units, they did not, however, actually employ criminal investigators vested with law enforcement

Figure 17.1 Offices of Inspector General Special Agents

Offices of Inspector General	Number of Full-Time Officers
Total	3,501
U.S. Postal Service	508
Dept. of Health and Human Services	389
Dept. of Defense	345
Treasury IG for Tax Administration	302
Social Security Administration	272
Dept. of Housing and Urban	228
Dept. of Agriculture	164
Dept. of Labor	164
Dept. of Homeland Security	157
Dept. of Veterans Affairs	132
Dept. of Justice	122
Dept. of Transportation	94
Dept. of Education	85
General Services Administration	67
Dept. of the Interior	66
National Aeronautics and Space Admin	52
Dept. of Energy	48
Environmental Protection Agency	40
Federal Deposit Insurance Corporation	35
Small Business Administration	34
Dept. of State	32
Office of Personnel Management	28
Dept. of the Treasury	21
Tennessee Valley Authority	20
Dept. of Commerce	16
U.S. Railroad Retirement Board	16
Agency for International Development	13
Nuclear Regulatory Commission	13
Corp. for National and Community Service	9
National Science Foundation	6
National Archives and Records Administration	6
Government Printing Office	5
Library of Congress	2

Source: Reaves, B. (2012). Census of Federal Law Enforcement Officers, 2008. Bureau of Justice Statistics.

powers—namely, firearms and arrest authority. The overlapping existence of OIGs possessing law enforcement authority and OIGs having no such authority highlights a long-standing issue in the OIG community. The question of just what police powers an OIG special agent should have, even as agents were given badges and told to conduct criminal investigations, has been wrestled with by Congress, other federal law enforcement agencies, and the OIGs themselves since the very establishments of OIGs by statute.

From their beginnings, OIGs were unique in the federal law enforcement community. They were not created exclusively for federal law enforcement purposes, as audits and program evaluations were a significant responsibility of the OIGs. But they did possess investigative responsibilities and employed criminal investigators. Under the Inspector General Act of 1978, OIG special agents possessed the authority to investigate criminal offenses relating to the government department or agency to which their respective OIGs were attached. Generally, OIG criminal investigations related to program fraud and corruption involving federal employees (such as bribery or embezzlement).

In 1988, Congress passed legislation to amend the Inspector General Act of 1978. In the 10 years that had transpired since the passage of the 1978 law, many federal agencies which were not among the original 14 to be given statutory OIGs nonetheless saw wisdom in possessing such an office and went on to administratively create their own—much like USDA had done in 1962. The 1988 amendment to the 1978 act established 28 additional OIGs.

To aid them in their investigations, the Inspector General Act of 1978 gave OIG criminal investigators the power to issue administrative subpoenas for the production of documentary evidence related to an OIG investigation. Administrative subpoenas are easier and faster to secure than seeking a subpoena from the federal courts through the U.S. Attorney's Office. Administrative subpoenas could be challenged in court by those receiving them, at which time a judge would either uphold the subpoena and enforce it, or throw it out. Administrative subpoenas are a particularly useful tool in securing documents from organizations not unwilling to help the government (such as banks, utilities, or communications companies), but needing some authority to do so because of customer privacy laws.

Although the Inspector General Act of 1978 created OIGs with criminal investigative units statutorily built into their structure, the Act did not explicitly grant law enforcement powers to OIG special agents. In fact, the Act made no mention of such powers. The result was the creation of OIG criminal investigative units within the federal government employing special agents who possessed no statutory power to make arrests or carry firearms. Further, when Congress amended the 1978 Act in 1988, the gap in law enforcement authority remained unaddressed.

Opposition to OIG special agents possessing law enforcement authority—especially firearms authority—was linked to a broader concern about the federal government's ever-expanding law enforcement role in American society. In the 1980s and 1990s when OIGs were coming of age as efficacious organizations for combating fraud and abuse in federal government programs, many in Congress were concerned about police powers which had already accrued to other federal agencies. In the early 1990s, Congress witnessed along with the rest of the country two high-profile botched law enforcement operations carried out by federal agencies and found them to be very disconcerting.

In 1992, deputy U.S. Marshals attempted to arrest Randy Weaver of Ruby Ridge, Idaho, for a gun-related charge resulting from a Bureau of Alcohol, Tobacco, and Firearms (ATF) investigation. During the initial operation, a gun battle ensued between the deputy marshals and Weaver, his 13 year old son, and a family friend named Kevin Harris. In the gun battle, Deputy Marshal William Deagan and 13-year-old Sammy Weaver were killed. Because a federal officer had been murdered, the FBI took over jurisdiction and manned the standoff with Weaver and the rest his family. During the stand-off, an FBI sniper accidentally shot and killed Weaver's wife, Vicki, while she was holding the Weaver's baby daughter. Days later, Weaver finally gave up. The FBI received considerable criticism for its handling of the stand-off, and especially for the unintentional killing of Vicki Weaver.

Only a year later, in 1993, over 70 ATF agents attempted to execute search and arrest warrants for gun violations at a religious sect's compound outside of Waco, Texas. The religious group was an offshoot of the Seventh Day Adventists and was led by David Koresh. The group was known collectively as the Branch Davidians. During the warrant attempt, a large gun battle took place. Four ATF agents and six Branch Davidians died in the gunfire. Again, the FBI took over jurisdiction as federal agents had been killed. At the conclusion of a 51-day standoff, the FBI inserted tear gas and used armored vehicles as battering rams against the building walls. In response, Branch Davidians set fires throughout the compound in an apparent attempt commit mass suicide. When the fire subsided, 75 Branch Davidians were confirmed dead, including 20 young children.

Many in Congress viewed these two incidents — Ruby Ridge and Waco — as examples of federal overreach and heavy-handedness. And with these incidents in the backdrop, there wasn't much appetite for giving additional federal agencies the power to wield weapons and deny freedoms.

Despite Congress' reluctance to bestow on OIG criminal investigators statutory law enforcement authority, a couple of OIGs possessed that authority by other means. Criminal investigators of the Defense Criminal Investigative Service (DCIS), which is the investigative arm of the Department of Defense OIG, exercised firearms authority under Title 10, Section 1585. This statute permitted the Secretary of Defense to authorize civilian employees of the Defense Department to carry firearms in the course of their duties. However, it wasn't until Section 1585 was amended (10 USC 1585a) in 1997 that arrest and search warrant powers were also given to DCIS agents.

Additionally, OIG special agents of the U.S. General Services Administration (GSA) also possessed limited law enforcement authorities. These agents were authorized to carry firearms, execute warrants, and make arrests as "non-uniformed special policemen" under Title 40, Section 318d. The purpose of this statute was to authorize uniformed and non-uniformed law enforcement officers of the GSA to police federal property. Most federal buildings and courthouses are managed and operated by the GSA. Although the 1947 statute was crafted to authorize federal detectives investigating traditional street crimes occurring on federal property, the GSA OIG also made use of the statute's empowering language.

In 1988, the U.S. Department of Agriculture OIG became the first to be given specific statutory law enforcement authority intended for carrying out its responsibilities as an OIG. U.S. Department of Agriculture special agents received firearms, search warrant, and arrest authority under Title 7, Section 2207. The primary driver behind this authority was the fact that USDA OIG agents routinely conducted food stamp trafficking investigations in dangerous inner-city neighborhoods. What's more, the food stamp trafficking often coincided with other crimes, such as drug trafficking and other forms of vice.

During the 1990s, while OIGs at Defense, GSA, and Agriculture could rely on statutory law enforcement authority to one degree or another, most OIGs possessed no statutory police power. As an alternative, OIG special agents could be deputized by the U.S. Marshals Service. The deputizing of OIG special agents was done on an agent-by-agent, case-by-case basis (Light, 1993). In other words, an OIG agent might be granted firearms and arrest authority as "special deputy U.S. Marshal" when working on one case, but then would need to stow his or her weapon and handcuffs when he or she began to work on another case (for which police powers were not authorized).

The deputation process was also very time-consuming, not just for the OIG agents, but for the U.S. Marshals Service. It often took several weeks for the deputation requests to be vetted and granted. In many cases, the need for the law enforcement authority (e.g., to conduct a search warrant) would be gone by the time the authorization was received by the OIG case agent.

As former Justice Department Inspector General Glenn Fine noted, the various OIGs grew tired of the deputation process and began to press Congress for statutory law enforcement powers. Many OIGs began to document instances in which the lack of law enforcement authority put investigations and the agents themselves at risk due to delays in receiving deputation. There were many examples presented to Congress of unarmed special agents presenting their badges and credentials to subjects who believed them to be armed officers and then assaulted them in quick and violent fashion to get the jump on them (Fine, 2003).

The U.S. Marshals Service also grew tired of the deputation process and decided to wait no longer for Congress to act. In 1995, the U.S. Marshals began to grant blanket deputation to most OIG special agents. OIG investigators received annual deputation from the U.S. Marshals and no longer were required to demonstrate a case-by-case need for police powers. In 2001, the U.S. Marshals revised the process further and granted special deputy U.S. marshal status to OIG agents on a 3-year term, rather than annually.

While Congress was still unwilling to pass legislation granting OIGs universal law enforcement authority, they did not move to intervene with the U.S. Marshals' permissive approach to extending deputation. Congress did pass legislation that gave law enforcement authority to additional specific OIGs. For example, in 1995, Congress reorganized the Social Security Administration (SSA) into an independent agency apart from the Department of Health and Human Services. A part of the corresponding legislation was to create an OIG for the SSA. In doing so, Congress also granted special agents of the new SSA OIG statutory law enforcement authority. Then in 1996, Congress established an OIG for the U.S. Postal Service as a separate agency from the U.S. Postal Inspectors (which remained focused on violent/street crime rather than program fraud). This OIG too was given statutory law enforcement authority. In 1998, Congress reorganized the Internal Revenue Service's Inspection Division into the Treasury Inspector General for Tax Administration (TIGTA). Special agents with TIGTA, which is effectively the OIG for the IRS, were given full federal law enforcement powers by Congress.

In 2000, the U.S. Justice Department, which had opposed law enforcement authority for the OIGs as unnecessary in prior years, went on the record in support of full law enforcement authority for the OIGs. At that time, there were six OIGs with some sort of statutory law enforcement authority. The OIGs and the Justice Department emphasized to Congress not only the utility of having statutory police powers while conducting criminal investigations, but also the personnel downsides in not having those powers. OIG agents in agencies without statutory authority would often seek to transfer to OIGs and other federal agencies which did possess statutory law enforcement authority, thus creating turnover problems in the agencies lacking authority. For the agents remaining behind, there was often diminished morale as they perceived their agencies and themselves as second-class citizens within the federal law enforcement community.

However, despite the Attorney General's support for OIG statutory law enforcement authority, the FBI still opposed such legislation and prevailed upon Congress to kill the idea. Any enhancement of OIG law enforcement powers was perceived by FBI leadership as a blow against the FBI's authority and influence in government fraud and corruption investigations. The FBI viewed the issue of OIG law enforcement authority as a zero-sum game (Bumgarner, 2006).

But then the terror attacks of September 11, 2001, came. In the wake of the 9/11 attacks, Congress lost its reluctance to grant federal law enforcement powers to agencies, including the OIGs. With a war on terror looming, the mantra for federal law enforcement was "all hands on deck." Congress couldn't permit some of those law enforcement hands to man their battle stations unarmed. Indeed, in the weeks and months after 9/11, most federal law enforcement agencies, including most OIGs, loaned special agents to the Transportation Security Administration (TSA) to serve as temporary air marshals until TSA could stand up a permanent cadre of air marshals in sufficient numbers to perform its mission.

The FBI also lost interest in opposing OIG police powers. The FBI's leadership knew that the Bureau would be consumed with the war against terrorism for the foreseeable future. It would have considerably less time and fewer resources to commit to mundane crimes such as government program fraud and low level corruption. In light of the FBI's emerging priorities regarding counter-terrorism abroad and at home, the OIGs were no longer viewed as a threat to the FBI's turf (Fine, 2003; Bumgarner, 2006). On October 4, 2002, FBI Director Robert Mueller wrote a letter to Congress which expressed the FBI's official support for the granting to OIGs statutory law enforcement authority (Fine, 2003). Congress concurred. In the Homeland Security Act of 2002, Section, 812, Congress amended the Inspector General Act of 1978 and granted explicit law enforcement authority to 25 OIGs. The statute reads in part:

SEC. 812. LAW ENFORCEMENT POWERS OF INSPECTOR GENERAL AGENTS.

(a) IN GENERAL — Section 6 of the Inspector General Act of 1978 (5 U.S.C. App.) is amended by adding at the end the following:

(e)(1) In addition to the authority otherwise provided by this Act, each Inspector General appointed under section 3, any Assistant Inspector General for Investigations under such an Inspector General, and any special agent supervised by such an Assistant Inspector General may be authorized by the Attorney General to—

(A) carry a firearm while engaged in official duties as authorized under this Act or other statute, or as expressly authorized by the Attorney General;

(B) make an arrest without a warrant while engaged in official duties as authorized under this Act or other statute, or as expressly authorized by the Attorney General, for any offense against the United States committed in the presence of such Inspector General, Assistant Inspector General, or agent, or for any felony cognizable under the laws of the United States if such Inspector General, Assistant Inspector General, or agent has reasonable grounds to believe that the person to be arrested has committed or is committing such felony; and

(C) seek and execute warrants for arrest, search of a premises, or seizure of evidence issued under the authority of the United States upon probable cause to believe that a violation has been committed.

(2) The Attorney General may authorize exercise of the powers under this subsection only upon an initial determination that—

(A) the affected Office of Inspector General is significantly hampered in the performance of responsibilities established by this Act as a result of the lack of such powers;

(B) available assistance from other law enforcement agencies is insufficient to meet the need for such powers; and

(C) adequate internal safeguards and management procedures exist to ensure proper exercise of such powers.

The statute went on to specifically grant this law enforcement authority to the following OIGs, exempting them from the initial determination requirement by the Attorney General under (e)(2):

Department of Commerce

Department of Education

Department of Energy

Department of Health and Human Services

Department of Homeland Security

Department of Housing and Urban Development

Department of the Interior

Department of Justice

Department of Labor

Department of State

Department of Transportation

Department of the Treasury

Department of Veterans Affairs

Agency for International Development

Environmental Protection Agency

Federal Deposit Insurance Corporation

Federal Emergency Management Agency

General Services Administration

National Aeronautics and Space Administration

Nuclear Regulatory Commission

Office of Personnel Management

Railroad Retirement Board

Small Business Administration

Social Security Administration

Tennessee Valley Authority

By exempting the above OIGs from the provisions of (e)(2), the Justice Department has no authority to take away law enforcement powers away from these OIGs. The statute did not specifically include the USDA OIG, DCIS, TIGTA, or the Postal Service

OIG as their pre-existing statutory authority was sufficient. On the other hand, the GSA OIG and the SSA OIG were included by name in the Homeland Security Act of 2002 because the act expanded their existing authorities under other statutes. The law also gives the Attorney General the power to delegate full law enforcement authority to any other OIG not listed in the statute if the Attorney General decides such authority is needed.

Like most federal law enforcement officers, OIG special agents receive the basic law enforcement training from the Federal Law Enforcement Training Center (FLETC) in Glynco, GA. FLETC was once operated by the U.S. Department of the Treasury but transferred over to the Department of Homeland Security with passage of the Homeland Security Act of 2002. New OIG special agents must attend the Basic Criminal Investigator School, as well as an advanced OIG course at FLETC. The Basic Criminal Investigator School is also attended by new special agents of the U.S. Secret Service, U.S. Immigration and Customs Enforcement (ICE), the Internal Revenue Service (IRS), new deputy U.S. Marshals, and investigators from many other agencies (Bumgarner, 2006).

Functions

OIG special agents investigate a wide range of federal offenses. Common federal crimes investigated by OIG agents and charged by U.S. Attorneys offices include conversion (theft) of government property, bribery, mail fraud, collusion, contract fraud, false statements, and others. But modern OIG agents also engage in considerable law enforcement activities apart from traditional program fraud. OIG criminal investigators routinely serve on federal and local task forces, including FBI Joint Terrorism Task Forces (JTTFs) in major cities around the country. OIG special agents also provide dignitary protection for cabinet secretaries, undersecretaries, and other VIPs within a given OIG's parent organization.

While all OIGs are in existence to confront fraud, waste, and abuse in the federal government, the manifestations of this confrontation looks different from one OIG to another because the programs are obviously different across government agencies and departments. Fraud committed against the U.S. Department of Agriculture might involve a scheme to traffic in food stamps, or to claim damages for crop insurance when in fact the crops were fine and sold on the market. Fraud committed against the Department of Defense might involve using substandard materials, or different (cheaper) materials than contractually agreed upon, when building a tank or a helicopter, and then billing the government for the more expensive materials that were expected. Fraud against programs of the Department of Housing and Urban Development might involve unscrupulous landlords receiving Section 8 housing subsidies to rent to the poor, when in fact no tenants are actually located in the building (or perhaps the building itself doesn't actually exist).

The U.S. Department of Labor (DOL) OIG is unique among the Inspectors General. The crimes investigated by every other OIG implicate, in some way, the programs, money, personnel, or integrity of the parent federal department. However, one of the primary investigative responsibilities of DOL's OIG is completely external to the operations of the Department of Labor. The DOL OIG has concurrent jurisdiction with the FBI to investigate labor racketeering. The DOL OIG is the only OIG to have a clear nexus to the investigation of organized crime. Labor racketeering cases commonly involve allegations of embezzlement of funds from union pension plans and dues, loan sharking, money laundering, extortion, and violence committed against union members and union opponents (Bumgarner, 2006).

Despite unique agency responsibilities, the various Offices of Inspector General have far more in common with each other than dissimilarities. Given the shared, broad mission of confronting fraud, waste, and abuse in government programs, and given the overlapping programmatic concerns about fraud across departments (e.g., food stamp fraud, social security fraud, Medicaid fraud, and subsidized housing fraud might all occur simultaneously with the same offender), the Inspectors General have a history of cooperating and collaborating with one another. Congress codified this collaboration formally with the Inspector General Reform Act of 2008. This law established the Council of Inspectors General on Integrity and Efficiency (CIGIE) as an independent entity of the Executive Branch. The CIGIE is made up of 69 statutory federal Inspectors General, as well as four Inspectors General from intelligence agencies, and exercises oversight of the inspector general community. The CIGIE exists to advance the efforts of OIGs government-wide through standardization of professional practices and training, identification of best practices in OIG investigations, audits, and evaluations, and to promote the accomplishments of the OIGs before Congress, the President, the federal law enforcement community, and other constituencies.

References

Bumgarner, J. (2006). *Federal agents: The growth of federal law enforcement in America.* Westport, CT: Praeger Publishers.

Clary, D. and Whitehorne, J. (1987). *The inspectors general of the United States Army 1777–1903.* Washington, D.C.: Government Printing Office.

Council of the Inspectors General on Integrity and Efficiency (2011). *A progress report to the President, fiscal year 2010.* Washington, D.C.: CIGIE.

Fine, G. (2003). The new statutory law enforcement authority for OIG criminal investigators. *The Journal of Public Inquiry.* Spring/Summer.

Health and Human Services Office of Inspector General (2011). *Semiannual report to Congress: April 1, 2011–September 30, 2011.* Retrieved from http://oig.hhs.gov/reports-and-publications/archives/semiannual/2011/fall/HHS-OIG-SAR-Fall2011.pdf.

Light, P. (1993). *Monitoring government: Inspectors general and the search for accountability.* Washington, D.C.: The Brookings Institution.

Nowolinski, G. (2001). *A brief history of the HHS Office of Inspector General.* Retrieved from http://www.kinneyassoc.com/MedEdHistory/historyhhsoig.pdf.

Reaves, B. (2012). *Federal law enforcement officers, 2008.* Washington, D.C.: Bureau of Justice Statistics.

Part VI
Careers and Trends

Chapter Eighteen

Careers in Federal Law Enforcement

Careers in law enforcement can be rewarding, dangerous, exciting, prestigious, and a host of other adjectives, and there are law enforcement agencies at various levels of government. Individuals become interested in law enforcement careers for a variety of reasons, for instance to help others, to protect society, because of the excitement and unpredictability, and/or perhaps to apply their specialization in a law enforcement capacity (e.g., accountants who work on white collar crime cases). One of the most prestigious law enforcement positions involves working as a federal law enforcement agent.

There are numerous employment opportunities that exist within a wide array of agencies within federal law enforcement, which is fitting in the sense that criminal justice majors regularly demonstrate notable levels of interest in careers in federal law enforcement (Bumgarner, 2006). One particular concern with regard to student interest in federal law enforcement is that students, and the general public, are often only aware of the more popular federal law enforcement agencies such as the FBI, the ATF, the DEA, and the Marshals. Part of the disconnect between student interest and familiarity with federal law enforcement is due to criminal justice academic programs being largely focused on local level crime and justice (Walker, et al., 2008).

Federal law enforcement personnel work in over 100 agencies and sub-agencies in the federal government, perform many different tasks, and assume many wide-ranging responsibilities. The numbers of federal agents and agencies are relatively small compared to the number of local level law enforcement personnel and agencies, and roughly one out of every 100 felony arrests in the U.S. was made by a federal agency in 2009 (Motivans, 2011). Nevertheless, federal agents have played an integral role in law enforcement in the U.S. throughout history and continue to do so.

Federal law enforcement agencies have become increasingly active in providing law enforcement services. For instance, from 2000 to 2006, the rate of arrests made by federal law enforcement personnel increased at roughly eight times the rate of arrests by state and local law enforcement. Further, the number of suspects arrested for a federal offense reached a record level of 183,986 in 2009; up from 140,200 in 2005. The number of suspects arrested by federal law enforcement has more than doubled since 1995, and growth in federal law enforcement has increased at a faster pace than later stages of the federal justice process (e.g., courts and corrections; Motivans, 2011). The notable increase in federal law enforcement involvement in justice-related practices in the U.S. suggests that greater career opportunities exist and will continue to exist in this area of law enforcement.

Generally, federal law enforcement agents and officers are expected to investigate potential and recognized federal offenses, and enforce the laws pertaining to federal crimes. In doing so, federal agents work with a variety of groups both within and outside of law enforcement and government in general. The prestige, benefits, training, pay, and resources provided to federal agents are generally superior to those provided to law enforcement personnel at the state and local levels (e.g., Harr & Hess, 2010).

Popular culture has largely contributed to the general public's notable level of interest in federal law enforcement. Depictions of FBI agents, U.S. Marshals, Border Patrol agents, and other federal law enforcement personnel on television and in movies have generated many different societal perceptions of federal law enforcement, leading Bumgarner (2006, p. ix) to note that "Americans are fascinated with federal law enforcement." However, the public's fascination typically involves limited awareness of the many different types of federal law enforcement agencies and opportunities for employment, and the public often has a skewed, media-generated view of what federal agents actually do. In attempt to address the uncertainty regarding the opportunities for careers in federal law enforcement, Walker and colleagues (Walker, et al., 2008) earlier provided descriptions of the opportunities, qualifications, and requirements of federal law enforcement positions. Their focus was primarily on Series 1811 *Criminal Investigator* positions, and the researchers briefly described federal-level careers in forensic science and criminal profiling. The following revisits and adds to that and other accounts of careers in federal law enforcement through focusing on the history, organization, personnel, and functions of federal law enforcement agents and agencies in general.

History

Federal law enforcement careers throughout history have largely been shaped by the histories of each federal law enforcement agency, which in turn have largely been shaped by societal developments and the history of criminal justice in general. Many of the preceding chapters in this book have commented on the historical development of federal law enforcement agencies, often including discussion of how societal events have shaped federal law enforcement and careers within the field. A brief look at the historical evolution of criminal justice in the United States, with an emphasis on career developments at the federal level, supplements the material addressed in preceding chapters.

Criminal justice in the U.S. has historically been impacted by technological advances, societal changes and events, politics, economics, and a host of other factors. These same factors have influenced careers in federal law enforcement. Consider and compare, for example, the organization and responsibilities of federal law enforcement prior to the 2001 terrorist attacks against the U.S. with what currently exists. The nature and organization of federal law enforcement appears much different than it did prior to the attacks. Other factors such as Prohibition, gun laws, the Civil War, the Civil Rights Movement, and the drug war have also significantly impacted careers in federal law enforcement.

Earlier research suggested that a notable percentage of undergraduate criminal justice students felt that the study of historical criminal justice practices was not significant to their current studies (Duffee & Bailey, 1991). Nevertheless, examination of the history of criminal justice and federal law enforcement careers lays the groundwork for understanding how agencies, departments, careers, and responsibilities evolved. Observing history also helps prevent repeating mistakes. Jones (1994) earlier commented on the importance of teaching criminal justice history in suggesting that doing so facilitates understanding of current criminal justice systems; highlights the impactful social, political, economic, and philosophical forces that have contributed to current justice-based practices; enables comparisons of criminal justice practices with those of years past, and; permits an understanding of how current practices fit within historical context. The benefits of studying the history of criminal justice in general also apply to studying the history of federal law enforcement.

Careers in federal law enforcement did not evolve in a vacuum. Simply, the historical evolution of each agency, and agency and personnel responsibilities emerged throughout the history of the U.S. Some agencies (e.g., the U.S. Marshals) have existed for quite some time, while others have existed for a relatively short period (e.g., the DEA). Agencies have existed in some form or fashion under different names, were located in different departments, and were tasked with various responsibilities. Accordingly, careers in federal law enforcement have changed as society and federal law enforcement agencies have changed.

There is a great deal of history to the criminal justice system, much like there is a vast history associated with careers in federal law enforcement. Criminal justice practices in the U.S. generally originated from the English model, as colonists settled and constructed much of the same legal structure that existed in the country they left (primarily England). Throughout history, the criminal justice system has been altered and continues to be tweaked according to what was and is believed to be best practices. Several authors have addressed the history and evolution of criminal justice in the U.S., including Oliver and Hilgenberg (2006) who noted several periods of criminal justice development in the U.S. Other works denote similar although slightly different periods of development (e.g., Walker, 1998; Roth, 2005; Shelden, 2001). The following account of the history of criminal justice in the U.S. is mostly based on the work of Oliver and Hilgenberg, and provides insight regarding the development of careers in federal law enforcement.

The Colonial Era (1607–1775) of criminal justice consists of two periods: the village period (1607–1699) and the town period (1700–1775). The era is characterized by informal social control efforts on behalf of colonists and the notable lack of formal criminal justice practices. Survival and retaining independence from England were primary considerations, and religion heavily influenced justice-based practices. Common law emerged and legal procedures adopted from England were implemented. This period is characterized by low crime rates, although crime would increase in frequency as communal living increased. The severity of punishments for offenders increased throughout this period, particularly as the punishments were applied to slaves. Informal social control practices would become less effective throughout the era, as social, political, and economic changes impacted the country. There was a significant lack of law enforcement careers and agencies at this time at any level of government, as again, formal law enforcement in general didn't exist.

Oliver and Hilgenberg deem the period from 1776–1828 "A New Nation" as the United States gained its independence from England and began to formalize many practices, including criminal justice. Crime was increasing, and the lack of established law enforcement agencies in many areas left individuals vulnerable to victimization. The federal government provided protection in some form, for instance as the U.S. Marshals began serving the country in 1789, the Attorney General's position was created during the 1790s, and the first federal statute emerged and noted which crimes constituted a federal offense during this period (Roth, 2005). Nevertheless, there were not nearly enough law enforcement agents or agencies to effectively address growing crime concerns, and settlers and colonists remained skeptical of government intervention in their lives; the primary reason why many left England.

The Jacksonian Era (1829–1855) was characterized by concerns for several social issues, including slavery, economics, and the relocation of, and confrontations with, Native

Americans. Tensions between the industrialized North, which sought to end slavery, and the largely agrarian South, which relied heavily on slavery, would increase during this period and lead to much social unrest. Federal agents (e.g., U.S. Marshals) were often caught in the difficult position of enforcing unpopular laws or failing to respond to what were perceived as social injustices. For instance, Marshals were expected to help enforce the Fugitive Slave Act (enacted in 1850), which meant that they were responsible for capturing and returning fugitive slaves to their owners. Federal agents were also tasked with providing protection to groups that chose to relocate and settle the western portion of the U.S. Criminal justice practices in general began to increasingly resemble what currently exists, although much reform, development, and professionalism was needed.

The tensions evident during the Jacksonian Era would largely contribute to what Oliver and Hilgenberg termed "The Civil War Era" (1856–1878). The era is characterized by social, political, and economic instability, and of course much violence in the form of war. Progress in relation to criminal justice practices during the Jacksonian Era ceased with the beginning of the Civil War, although the situation would improve following the war; largely toward the end of Reconstruction. Federal agents assisted with war time efforts in various capacities, and some federal officers left their positions to fight in the war. Additional federal law enforcement agencies would emerge during this time, for instance as the Secret Service was formally established in 1865 and assumed the responsibility of investigating counterfeiting, and the U.S. Department of Justice was created in 1870 (Roth, 2005).

"The Gilded Age" (1879–1899) of the historical evolution of criminal justice in the U.S. conjured much hope in the U.S. as the country recovered from the Civil War. Criminal justice was becoming increasingly institutionalized in the U.S., as increased numbers of individuals were employed in all components of the system. Nevertheless, the country faced increased levels of poverty, immigration, and discrimination. Culture clashes provided many challenges for law enforcement. The expansion of criminal justice practices led to a need for much reform, which came about during "The Progressive Era" (1900–1919). President Theodore Roosevelt was instrumental in reforming criminal justice practices and social reform during this time, for instance through providing assistance to poor and/or disadvantaged individuals. Crime continued to rise during the period, and new laws and law enforcement agencies emerged. Among the agencies created during this time was the FBI, which was formally created in 1908. Criminal justice practices were increasingly distanced from political influences during this period of reform, although reform efforts received less attention with the beginning of World War I (1914–1918). The war not only brought about a redirected focus among government leaders, it also reshaped the responsibilities of some federal law enforcement agents, for instance as U.S. Marshals helped protect the U.S. from enemy aliens, spies, and saboteurs during the war.

Passage of the 18th Amendment in 1919, also known as Prohibition, brought about new changes for criminal justice practices and federal law enforcement agents. It would lead to the beginning of what Oliver and Hilgenberg termed "The Crisis Era" (1920–1939), which also included the 1929 stock market crash and the Great Depression. The increase in crime resulting from Prohibition and the Depression generated increased levels of crime, including a substantial amount of organized crime. Federal agents continued to play important roles during this period, for instance as U.S. Marshals helped arrest bootleggers during Prohibition, and the origins of the modern day ATF are largely traced to the Prohibition Unit of the U.S. Treasury Department.

The repeal of Prohibition in 1933 and the end of the Depression in the late 1930s and early 1940s helped address many of the crime-related problems associated with these events, however a second world war provided new challenges. "The War Years" (1940–1959), as termed by Oliver and Hilgenberg, resulted in little criminal justice reform. The U.S. remained troubled by inequalities with regard to race and class, however there was strong solidarity in efforts to fight the war. Economic prosperity followed World War II, although the criminal justice system and federal law enforcement would become heavily involved in the social unrest that would emerge during the 1960s and 1970s. The Supreme Court's decision to integrate schooling in the 1954 case *Brown v. Board of Education* helped set the stage for a series of controversial Court decisions and notably impacted federal law enforcement. With regard to the latter, Marshals helped ensure the safe integration of African-Americans into public schools in the South following the Court's decision, and would later be required to assist with law and order efforts in response to the many civil rights demonstrations that occurred during the 1960s and 1970s.

Oliver and Hilgenberg deemed the years 1960–1979 "The Nationalization Era" with regard to the history of criminal justice. The period is characterized by civil unrest, a baby boom, and political and economic instability. These and related issues contributed to much social unrest and collective violence during the years. Generational differences and a counterculture that lacked confidence or trust in governments and other institutions contributed to the problems faced by federal agents and others within the criminal justice system. Economic and energy crises, rising crime rates, and criticism directed at the criminal justice system perpetuated much of society's discontent. The inability of local-level justice agencies to address social problems led to society increasingly requesting that all levels of government respond, which impacted careers in federal law enforcement. Also during this time, several Supreme Court decisions under Chief Justice Earl Warren led to greater restrictions on law enforcement personnel and more protections for citizens. Several of the Court's decisions continue to regularly impact federal law enforcement agents. The turbulent 1960s and 1970s contributed to a substantial portion of society supporting the proposition that the criminal justice system should become more punitive in nature (Hindelang, Gottfredson, & Flanagan, 1981). One response to such claims was the notable expansion of the criminal justice system and a more punitive approach to criminal behavior.

The "Post-Modern Era" (1980–September 11, 2001) of criminal justice began with much promise as many of the problems experienced in the previous period were largely quelled, including the economic concerns. The economy stabilized during the 1980s and there was an economic boom in the 1990s. The crime rate dropped and continued to do so beginning in the early 1990s, and incarceration rates increased. The war on drugs became a high priority for the federal government (and other levels of government), which contributed to enhanced efforts on behalf of many federal agents (and other law enforcement personnel) to more intensely focus on drug crimes. Community policing was being implemented in many departments across the U.S., and there was a sense that the justice system had become particularly effective. Such optimism, however, was tempered by the September 11, 2001 terrorist attacks against the U.S., which led to many changes in all levels of law enforcement. Included within those changes was a major restructuring of federal law enforcement agencies, added responsibilities for law enforcement personnel, and increased career opportunities for individuals interested in the field.

Oliver and Hilgenberg's insightful account of the history of criminal justice concludes with the "Post-Modern Era," however the history of criminal justice and federal law enforcement continues to be written. In his account of the recent developments within criminal justice, Oliver (2006) noted that we are currently in the "Homeland Security Era," which is characterized by strong efforts directed toward anti-terrorism and general homeland safety. Similarly, criminal justice historian Mitchell Roth (2005, p. 351) stated: "The criminal justice system is changing more quickly than ever before." This statement is particularly obvious in the changes that have taken place within federal law enforcement. For instance, the creation of the Department of Homeland Security and the accompanying restructuring of the organization of federal law enforcement were designed to generate greater cooperation and coordination among federal law enforcement agencies, and are only part of the major transformations in federal law enforcement that have taken place since the attacks.

Organization and Personnel

The terrorist attacks against the United States in 2001 generated numerous changes in federal law enforcement, particularly in response to the need for greater information sharing and cooperative efforts among law enforcement groups (e.g., Hutton and Mydlarz, 2003; Spielman, 2002). For instance, there was major organizational restructuring which included the creation of the cabinet-level Department of Homeland Security (DHS) and all or part of 22 existing federal agencies being transferred to the DHS following passage of the Homeland Security Act, the legislation responsible for creating the DHS. The efforts constituted the largest government reorganization in 50 years. New positions and/or responsibilities emerged in most, if not all federal law enforcement agencies following the attacks.

The attacks also perpetuated notable efforts on behalf of the federal government to increase cooperation between agencies and to increase the number of individuals working in federal law enforcement. For instance, between 1982 and 2002, federal justice system employment increased by 115%. Federal-level justice-based employment increased from 7% to 11% of total justice employment between 1982 and 2007. In 1982 only 8% of law enforcement personnel worked at the federal level; that percentage increased to 14% in 2007 (Kyckelhahn, 2011). These numbers suggest that there has been a directed focus on enhancing the federal law enforcement ranks, which in turn suggests greater career opportunities for individuals interested in a career in federal law enforcement.

Additional evidence of the expansion of federal law enforcement is reflected in Department of Justice reports, which noted that between 2002 and 2004 there was an increase of 13% in the number of full-time federal agents authorized to make arrests and carry firearms. Between 2004 and 2008 the number of federal officers increased by roughly 15,000, or 14% (Reaves, 2006, 2012). Among the larger agencies most recently expanding (between 2004 and 2008) in size with regard to the number of federal law enforcement officers were the U.S. Customs and Border Protection (33.1%), the Veterans Health Administration (29.1%), and the U.S. Immigration and Customs Enforcement (19.7%; Reaves, 2012). Continued concerns for homeland security, immigration, high-technology crime, and international crime will likely contribute to the continued expansion of the federal law enforcement ranks and generate additional career opportunities for individuals interested in working in the field.

Historically, federal agents primarily consisted of white males, although federal law enforcement agencies have become increasingly diverse in terms of race, ethnicity, and gender. For instance, until 1971 women were not considered for agent positions in any major federal law enforcement agency (Vizzard, 1997). Recently, however, the percentage of female federal law enforcement officers increased from about 14.0% (in 1998) to 15.5%

(2008). The percentage of female federal officers in 2008, however, is lower than the percentage of female officers in 2004 (which was 16.1%; Reaves, 2012). As previously noted in Chapter 2, federal law enforcement agencies generally have been slightly more progressive than their law enforcement counterparts at the local level, as data suggest that ethnic and racial minorities and females are more represented in federal law enforcement.

An exploratory study of female Special Agents in Charge suggested that women were moving up through the ranks of federal agencies, although the percentages of females in federal law enforcement were becoming somewhat static. Most subjects in the study had been promoted in the only agency in which they were employed. Females in the study who made at least one career change largely came from other federal agencies instead of other levels of law enforcement (Schulz, 2009).

A few historical limitations to employment in federal law enforcement include the need for relocation and the bureaucracy often associated with employment in the federal government. Federal agents have jurisdiction over the entire U.S., thus agents are spread out as needed, which may require relocation. Five judicial districts along the U.S.-Mexico border accounted for over half (56%) of all federal arrests in 2009 (Motivans, 2011). These numbers suggest that many federal agents are located to this part of the U.S.

Federal law enforcement officers are sometimes expected to relocate several times during the course of their career, and their work responsibilities may also involve extensive travel and/or extended periods away from home (Hutton and Mydlarz, 2003). Such disruptions can be welcomed by agents, and they can also be disruptive, particular in relation to one's family life (Harr & Hess, 2010). Some agencies and employment positions are more likely than others to require relocation.

The bureaucratic nature of working for the federal government can be a deterrent for some individuals interested in working for a federal law enforcement agency. Bureaucracy sometimes hampers work effectiveness and may lead individuals to feel a notably limited connection with the agency with which they work. Careers in the federal government in general have long been impacted by bureaucratic constraints.

Federal law enforcement agents undergo much training throughout their career. The majority of federal agents are trained at the Federal Law Enforcement Training Center (FLETC), which conducts basic and in-service training. The FLETC is the largest training operation for federal law enforcement agents and graduates approximately 50,000 students annually ("Federal Law Enforcement...," 2005). Most federal law enforcement agencies supplement the training provided by FLETC with in-house training programs and training opportunities provided by other groups, including state and local law enforcement, private industry groups, and colleges and universities.

FLETC provides law enforcement training to over 80 partner organizations, and also trains state, local, tribal, campus, and international law enforcement agents. It was established in 1970 as a bureau within the Department of the Treasury largely in response to the need for a consolidated training center that could avoid redundancy and provide a high-quality, cost-effective approach to training federal law enforcement agents. In March 2003, FLETC was transferred to the Department of Homeland Security.

The original FLETC headquarters facility was located in Washington, D.C. and later moved to Glynco, Georgia. The FLETC has expanded to other areas of the U.S. and abroad. In 1989, the FLETC opened operations in Artesia, NM, and in 2001 the former Naval Communications Detachment facility in Cheltenham, MD was transferred to the FLETC. In 2003, the FLETC formally expanded into Charleston, SC. In 2001, the FLETC opened an International Law Enforcement Academy (ILEA) in Gaborone, Botswana, which provides training for middle managers in criminal justice from countries in the Sub-Saharan African Region ("Federal Law Enforcement...," 2007). Each facility provides specialized training in various areas for law enforcement personnel at all levels, and overall the FLETC provides over 100 different agency-specific training programs (Reaves, 2004).

In FY 2004, the FLETC provided roughly 150,000 student weeks of training to roughly 45,000 personnel. Most weeks spent (74%) were in basic programs, and the FLETC Glynco facility provided most (71%) of all training measured in student weeks. The FLETC Artesia Training Division accounted for 13% of the student training weeks, followed by the FLETC facility in Charleston (10%). The U.S. Customs and Border Protection recorded the most student weeks trained through FLETC in FY 2004 (about 49,000 weeks), which included a substantial amount of training for Border Patrol agents (19,000 weeks). ICE had the second most training weeks (21,000; Reaves, 2004).

It would seem that the organization of federal law enforcement would be easily understood given that there is only one federal government. However, federal law enforcement personnel are spread out among different departments and agencies within the federal government. Accordingly, employment opportunities and careers in federal law enforcement exist in many different areas. Most federal agents, other than those who are employed by the Armed Forces, are housed within the Department of Justice (DOJ) or the DHS. Combined, these departments housed roughly 79% of all federal officers with arrest and firearm authority in 2008 (Reaves, 2012).

Individuals seeking a career within the DHS should expect to plan, coordinate, and integrate activities directed toward securing the homeland; a broad description of the many varied tasks and responsibilities associated with agencies in this department. As of 2008, the DHS employed 46% of all federal law enforcement officers and housed the largest federal law enforcement agency, the U.S. Customs and Border Protection (which had 36,863 full-time officers). The DHS also houses several other large agencies, including Immigration and Customs Enforcement (12,446 officers) and the Secret Service (5,213; Reaves, 2012). The increasingly prominent role of the DHS is evident in a report which suggested that DHS agencies accounted for 35% of all case referrals to U.S. attorneys in 2005 and 54% of all referrals in 2009; most of which pertained to immigration cases (Motivans, 2011). The impact of the DHS on other departments is evidenced, for instance, in the Department of Treasury. Suspects referred to U.S. attorneys by the Treasury decreased to 1% of the total referrals in 2009, compared with 43% of referrals in 2005 and 58% of referrals in 2000 (Motivans, 2011).

The largest federal law enforcement agencies within the DOJ are the Federal Bureau of Prisons (16,835 federal officers), the FBI (12,760), the DEA (4,308), the U.S. Marshals Service (3,313), and the ATF (2,541; Reaves, 2012). Career opportunities within the DOJ generally include being a(n): attorney, special agent, engineer, auditor, information technology specialist, criminal investigator, scientist, correctional officer, budget and management specialist, accountant, research specialist, and related positions. Law enforcement agencies within the DOJ referred 30% of suspects to U.S. attorneys in 2009, compared to 43% of referrals in 2005 and 58% of referrals in 2000 (Motivans, 2011). The decreased numbers of referrals by the DOJ is largely attributable to the creation of the DHS and its enhanced focus on enforcing immigration laws.

The DHS and DOJ are not the only departments that house federal law enforcement personnel. Many other federal law enforcement agencies exist outside of the DOJ and DHS, including but not limited to the U.S. Postal Inspection Service, the Internal Revenue

Service (IRS), the National Park Service, and the U.S. Fish and Wildlife Service. Further, various regulatory agencies such as the Environmental Protection Agency and the Food and Drug Administration employ personnel who maintain law enforcement powers, and the federal offices of inspector general also maintain law enforcement positions. Ultimately, there are numerous career opportunities in a variety of areas for individuals interested in careers in federal law enforcement.

Responsibilities

The wide range of responsibilities maintained by the various federal law enforcement agencies result in federal agents being required to provide many different types of services. The Bureau of Justice Statistics (Reaves, 2012) recently noted that in 2008 federal law enforcement personnel most often engaged in criminal investigation (37.3%), police response and patrol (23.4%), inspections (15.3%), corrections and detention (14.2%), security and protection (5.1%), and court operations (4.7%). To be sure, these responsibilities varied by agency and positions within those agencies. For instance, the wide range of employment opportunities with the DHS involve securing borders, airports, seaports, waterways, and related areas; researching and creating new security technology and techniques; responding to natural disasters and threats to homeland security; generating, analyzing, and implementing data, and; other activities focused on securing the U.S.

Thomas Ackerman (2006) identified ten categories of federal law enforcement positions including criminal investigators; intelligence analysts; uniformed law enforcement officers; law enforcement technicians and specialists; general and compliance investigators; compliance inspectors and specialists; security specialists; correctional officers and specialists; federal court personnel and prosecutors, and; communications and electronics personnel. An overview of the responsibilities of each category sheds light on the wide array of responsibilities and related career opportunities maintained by federal law enforcement personnel.

Criminal investigators primarily collect and examine evidence pertaining to federal offenses, serve subpoenas, conduct surveillance operations, interrogate suspects, assist U.S. attorneys with prosecuting crimes, assist law enforcement agencies at all levels, and provide security for high-ranking government personnel and foreign dignitaries.

Intelligence analysts compare, assess, and share crime and related information pertaining to national security, while uniformed law enforcement personnel perform functions quite similar to local law enforcement personnel. They protect various federal locations including courthouses, national borders, airports, hospitals, historical sites, national parks, power plants, and related federal areas that require law enforcement protection. Federal law enforcement technicians and specialists maintain and apply their expertise in specific areas, including evidence analysis, aircraft operation, photography, and other areas.

General and compliance investigators inspect and investigate incident potential and recognized violations of various federal laws and regulations. They primarily regulate specified areas (e.g., food safety, the environment, labor laws), and their efforts may result in the imposition of administrative sanctions, judgments, or penalties. The duties and responsibilities of compliance inspectors and specialists are similar to those of general and compliance investigators, although the former primarily conduct inspections instead of investigations. The inspections may involve a wide array of areas regulated by the federal government, including mining procedures, tobacco and alcohol production, or marine safety regulations.

Federal security specialists primarily protect federal government assets and employees. Their responsibilities generally include the protection of physical assets (e.g., forests, buildings, etc.) and personnel. Communications and technology personnel, including telecommunications specialists, dispatchers, and computer database systems operators, provide valuable support for field law enforcement agents (Ackerman, 2006).

Several helpful books, journal articles, and websites are suggested for individuals interested in additional information on careers in federal law enforcement. Appendix A provides an account of some of the more recent, helpful resources. One particularly helpful resource is the U.S. Office of Personnel Management's (OPM) website USAJOBS.gov. It is the federal government's website that lists all employment position openings and enables users to search for positions in a variety of ways. Users can search by keywords (e.g., "law enforcement," "investigation," or "police"), job titles, series numbers, salary ranges, pay grades, locations, agencies, occupational series, type of work, work schedule, and applicant eligibility (e.g., veteran's preferences). For instance, individuals interested in a career as a criminal investigator can easily use the website by entering a Series Number (which is 1811) or by simply accessing the "Criminal Investigation" box provided in the Occupational Series area of the website. The resultant information depicts the available openings in the series; not all of the job opportunities. Each job opening is described via the link, and includes information such as an overview of the position, the salary range, the promotion potential, the duty locations, a job summary, the duties of the position, qualifications for the job, a description of the benefits and related information, and explicit instructions for applying. Each listing also notes the grade series for which candidates may be eligible and the qualifications for each series.

Many employment positions within the federal government, including most white-collar positions, conform to the General Schedule (GS) pay system, which consists of 15 grades (GS-1 through GS-15) based on the difficulty and responsibility of the work and the qualifications required for its performance. A salary range of 10 steps exists within each grade. Federal employees covered under the GS system receive locality pay in addition to their regular salary. Locality pay helps adjust for the discrepancies in the costs of living that exist throughout the U.S. Criminal investigators, through Law Enforcement Availability Pay (LEAP), may also be eligible for an additional 25% of their salary if they are expected to work or be available to work a specified number of unscheduled hours.

Federal agencies, like many non-government employers, require individuals interested in an employment position opening to contact the agency directly for application processing and job information. There are, however, a few exceptions that pertain to federal agencies, primarily in relation to particular laws, executive orders, and regulations that regulate employment in the federal government. In years past, individuals interested in working for the federal government were required to pass a civil service test, after which their name was placed on standing registers of candidates. The registers were maintained by OPM. Applicants also had to submit a completed Federal employment application form, the SF-171, to apply for a position. Currently, OPM no long maintains a list of eligible candidates, and applicants can submit their materials using USAJOBS.gov. Civil service exams are no longer needed for many positions within the federal government.

The federal government maintains two classes of jobs: competitive and excepted service. Competitive service jobs fall under the jurisdiction of OPM and the jobs are subject to civil service laws enacted by Congress. The laws ensure that individuals both applying and employed are treated fairly in the hiring process. Agencies can generally choose from different groups of candidates when filling competitive service positions. For instance, they may choose from a competitive list of eligibles, which consists of candidates who meet the requirements for a position opening. Further, they may choose from a list of eligibles who have civil service status and are presently or have previously served under career-type appointments in the competitive service. Such individuals are chosen by agency merit promotion procedures, and fill the opening through promotion, reassignment, transfer, or reinstatement. Agencies within the competitive service are required by law and OPM regulations to post vacancies with the OPM when seeking candidates from outside their own workforce for positions lasting more than 120 days.

Agencies within the excepted service set their own qualification requirements, and are not subject to the appointment, pay and classification requirements enacted by law, although they are subject to veteran's preference. Some federal agencies (e.g., the FBI) have only excepted service positions, while others may have divisions or positions that are excepted from civil service requirements. Positions are excepted by law, executive order, or by the OPM. Excepted agencies are not required to post their announcements to USAJOBS.gov. Individuals interested in employment openings with excepted agencies are encouraged to visit the respective agency's website.

Experience in law enforcement is particularly important for many careers in federal law enforcement, however many different types of experience are considered with regard to hiring practices. Federal law enforcement agencies consider both general and specialized experience, and note in their job advertisements the types of experience required for various series levels of employment. General experience requirements do not necessarily require candidates to have specialized skills or knowledge; instead, such experience should demonstrate one's ability to acquire the knowledge and skills required for the position. Specialized experience demonstrates one's knowledge and/or skills directly required to perform the duties associated with the position (Ackerman, 2006). Candidates lacking experience, either specialized or general, may be hired; however they will begin their appointment at a lower series level (e.g., GS-5). Individuals with experience and/or higher levels of education generally qualify for higher grade levels.

Candidates for careers in federal law enforcement are generally expected to have field experience and an impressive academic record. Students lacking field experience are encouraged to seek full- or part-time employment in the field and/or secure an internship. Students are also encouraged to regularly peruse the OPM website to become familiar with the qualifications for various federal law enforcement positions, to learn about employment openings, and to view the special opportunities available to students and newly graduated students. Among other contributions, StudentJobs.gov enables visitors to easily prepare a resume, search job openings, and become familiar with the federal government hiring process.

Students interested in a career in federal law enforcement are encouraged to earn high grades, network as much as possible, productively use internships, remain active in their communities, assume leadership roles in groups and organizations, and use the student resources available to them via the federal government. For instance, the USAJOBS website has a link to student resources which describes in detail several government hiring programs for students. The information includes descriptions of opportunities for part-time or seasonal work under the Student Temporary Employment Program (STEP), and encourages students to engage in internships, volunteer activities, and summer jobs with the federal government. There is also information regarding the Student Career Experience Program (SCEP), the Federal Career Intern Program (FCIP), and the Presidential Management

Fellows Program (PMFP). The SCEP permits appointment of students to positions that are related to their academic field of study, which enables agencies to develop potential employees. The FCIP helps agencies recruit exceptional individuals into a variety of occupations at the GS-5, 7, and 9 grade levels. It allows individuals to be appointed to a 2-year internship. The PMFP helps agencies meet their workforce and succession planning needs by attracting outstanding graduate, law, and doctoral-level students to federal employment. Fellows are groomed for leadership positions within the organization.

The federal government offers several provisions designed to recruit a qualified, diverse, and deserving workforce. For instance, under the Superior/Academic Achievement provision, students who meet specific requirements are provided enhanced opportunities for advancement and can be hired at a higher series level. Eligibility for the provision is based on class standing, grade-point average, and honor society membership. There are also conditional provisions for veterans, Native Americans, and other groups.

Candidates who meet the initial employment requirements should be prepared for a series of evaluations that agencies use to determine the suitability of candidates. Those who progress through the selection process should expect to undergo a polygraph examination, a personal interview, a medical exam, a drug test, a psychological evaluation, a physical agility test, a written aptitude test, and a personality inventory. Not all agencies or positions require each of these evaluations and the emphasis placed on each varies. Nevertheless, candidates should be prepared to fully demonstrate their suitability for the position in a variety of means.

Ultimately, federal law enforcement positions are generally competitive and the process of becoming a federal agent can be time-consuming and tedious. The bureaucracy involved in the federal government and the sometimes highly-sensitive aspects of federal law enforcement result in the hiring process sometimes lasting an extended period of time. Individuals interested in careers in federal law enforcement are strongly encouraged to be patient and seek alternative employment options while waiting for their application to be considered.

References

Ackerman, T. A. (2006). *Federal law enforcement careers* (2nd ed.). Indianapolis, IN: JIST Works.

Bowman, M. D., Carlson, P. M., & Colvin, R. E. (2006). The loss of talent: Why local and state law enforcement officers resign to become FBI agents and what agencies can do about it. *Public Personnel Management*, 35(2): 121–136.

Boylan, R. T. (2004). Salaries, turnover, and performance in the federal criminal justice system. *Journal of Law and Economics*, 47: 75–92.

Bumgarner, J. B. (2006). *Federal agents: The growth of federal law enforcement in America.* Westport, CT: Praeger.

Courtright, K. E., & Mackey, D.A. (2004). Job desirability among criminal justice majors: Exploring relationships between personal characteristics and occupational attractiveness. *Journal of Criminal Justice Education*, 15(2): 311–326.

Duffee, D. E. and F. Y. Bailey. (1991). A Criminal justice contribution to a general education diversity requirement. *Journal of Criminal Justice Education*, 2: 141–157.

Federal Law Enforcement Training Center Director Honored with Presidential Rank Award for Federal Service (2005). Federal Law Enforcement Training Center, Department of Homeland Security. Accessed online December 27, 2011 at: http://www.fletc.gov/ news/press-releases/federal-law-enforcement-training-center-director-honored-with-presidential-rank-award-for-federal-service.html.

Federal Law Enforcement Training Center. (2007). *Federal Law Enforcement Training Center strategic plan FY 2008–2013*. U.S. Department of Homeland Security. Accessed online December 27, 2011 at: www.fletc.gov/about-fletc/strategicplan.pdf/download.

Fuller, J. (2001, December 7). So you want to be a serial-murderer profiler … *The Chronicle of Higher Education*, p. B5.

Hindelang, M. J., Gottfredson, M.R. and T.J. Flanagan, eds. (1981). *Sourcebook of criminal justice statistics — 1980*. Washington, D.C.: U.S. Government Printing Office.

Harr, J. S., & Hess, K. M. (2010). *Careers in criminal justice and related fields: From internship to promotion* (6th ed.). Belmont, CA: Wadsworth.

Hutton, D. B., & Mydlarz, A. (2003). *Guide to homeland security careers*. Hauppauge, NY: Barron's Educational Series.

Jones, M. (1994). Reflections on historical study in criminal justice curricula. *Journal of Criminal Justice Education*, 5 (2): 167–187.

Kyckelhahn, T. (2011). *Justice expenditures and employment, FY 1982–2007 — Statistical tables*. U.S. Department of Justice, Bureau of Justice Statistics. NCJ 236218.

Motivans, M. (2011). *Federal justice statistics, 2009*. U.S. Department of Justice, Bureau of Justice Statistics, NCJ 234184.

Oliver, W.M. (2006). The fourth era of policing: Homeland security. *International Review of Law, Computers & Technology*, 20(1/2): 49–62.

Oliver, W.M. & Hilgenberg, J. F., Jr. (2006). *A History of crime and criminal justice in America*. Boston, MA: Allyn & Bacon.

Reaves, B. A. (2006). *Federal law enforcement officers, 2004*. U.S. Department of Justice, Bureau of Justice Statistics. NCJ 212750.

Reaves, B. A. (2012). *Federal law enforcement officers, 2008*. U.S. Department of Justice, Bureau of Justice Statistics. NCJ 238250.

Roth, M. P. (2005). *Crime and punishment: A history of the criminal justice system*. Belmont, CA.

Schulz, D. M. (2009). Women special agents in charge: The first generation. *Policing: An International Journal of Police Strategies & Management*, *32*(4), 675–693.

Shelden, R. G. (2001). *Controlling the dangerous classes: A critical introduction to the history of criminal justice*. Needham Heights, MA: Allyn & Bacon.

Spielman, F. (2002, August 23). Law enforcement agencies tout new unity. *Chicago Sun-Times*, p. 6.

Walker, J. T., Burns, R. G., Bumgarner, J., & Bratina, M. P. (2008). Federal law enforcement careers: Laying the groundwork. *Journal of Criminal Justice Education*, *19*, 110–135.

Walker, S. (1998). *Popular justice: A history of American criminal justice, 2nd ed*. NY: Oxford University Press.

Appendix A

Ackerman, T. H. (2006). *Federal law enforcement careers* (2nd edition). Indianapolis, IN: JIST Works.

Ackerman, T. H. (2006). *FBI careers: The ultimate guide to landing a job as one of America's finest.* Indianapolis, IN: JIST Works.

FedJobs — www.fedjobs.com.

Federal Government Jobs — www.dcjobsource.com/fed.html.

Federal Job Search — www.federaljobsearch.com.

Hutton, D.B. & Mydlarz, A. (2003). *Guide to homeland security careers.* Hauppauge, NY: Barron's Educational Series.

Lambert, S. & Regan, D. (2007). *Great jobs for criminal justice majors.* NY: McGraw-Hill.

LexisNexis — Gould Publications (2005). *Homeland security and federal law enforcement: career guide* (2nd ed.). Charlottesville, VA.

Troutman, K. K., & Troutman, E. K. (2004). *The student's federal career guide: 10 steps to find and win top government jobs and internships.* Baltimore, MD: The Resume Place.

USAJobs — www.usajobs.gov/.

Walker, J. T., Burns, R. G., Bumgarner, J. & Bratina, M. P. (2008). Federal law enforcement careers: Laying the groundwork. *Journal of Criminal Justice Education*, 19: 110–135.

Chapter Nineteen

The Future of Federal Law Enforcement

Careful thought, substantial knowledge, and familiarity with forecasting research methods are necessary for projecting the future. However, even expert futurists are subject to mis-projecting the future, and forecasters typically expect that their projections will not be completely accurate. Nevertheless, individuals who offer input regarding what they believe the future holds hope to project the future as accurately as possible.

Similar to forecasting the future in any field, forecasting the future of federal law enforcement is filled with uncertainty. Several specific drivers of federal law enforcement, such as the economy, globalism, legal issues, technology, politics, and various related social issues will undoubtedly impact the field in the future, although there are certainly other factors to consider. The varied responsibilities of federal law enforcement agents must be considered in forecasting the future of federal law enforcement, and the decentralized organizational structure of federal law enforcement results in any generalizations regarding the field and personnel perhaps being applicable to some, yet not others. Specificity with regard to agency and personnel are noted as warranted in this chapter; however the bulk of the content that follows refers to the federal law enforcement field in general.

This chapter provides an examination of how the federal law enforcement field may appear in the future. The discussion is largely based upon recent trends and developments both internal and external to federal law enforcement, general expectations regarding law enforcement, the existing federal law enforcement research literature, and other projections of the future of federal law enforcement. To be sure, many of the projections offered in this chapter are positive in nature. Such an optimistic look is largely based on the great deal of progress and the increased levels of professionalism recently recognized in federal law enforcement. It is certainly possible that federal law enforcement may take a step backward with regard to progress, particularly in light of the many societal changes that are currently occurring and will occur in the future.

Generally, law enforcement must become increasingly proactive and rely less on reactive techniques and approaches. In doing so, agents and agencies must always consider individual rights and protections, and protect against existing and anticipated domestic and international threats and harms. Further, law enforcement must embrace change and further strive toward incorporating changes that permit and facilitate increased professionalism within the field.

Many of the same issues anticipated to impact federal law enforcement are expected to affect local policing. For instance, futurist Gene Stephens (2005) assembled a group of police experts to gain their insight regarding the future direction of policing. Generally, the panel agreed that more education and refocused training will be needed to best address emerging and high-technology crime and disorder. The panelists also felt that law enforcement was "taking a back seat to pressures from homeland security and similar non-neighborhood or off-site threats" (p. 54), and greater intelligence gathering and sharing would be necessary. Improved technology and better community ties were viewed as areas where there is much promise for police in the future, although there was concern that the police may not be able to keep pace with rapid technological advances. Further, the panel noted that the police may be criticized for imposing on civil liberties, and the paramilitary model of police will persist in countries ruled by dictators or military force, while more democratic countries will experience a consensus model of policing that is largely based at the community level. These anticipated developments could certainly have notable impacts on federal law enforcement.

In a similar study, Crank, Kadleck, and Koski (2010) surveyed 14 police scholars regarding the issues that are likely to impact policing in the future, and identified the issues for which the police should be prepared. The authors found that the police are generally unprepared for the changes coming their way, and that a return to the professional model of policing using technology-driven, information-based approaches is likely ahead for policing. They found that police practices are expected to become more militaristic in nature, with a focus on counter-terrorism and intelligence, and departments will largely abandon the vestiges of community policing. The researchers also found that computer crimes will increasingly trouble police departments, and changing demographics in society will pose additional challenges. Again, many of the same challenges faced by local policing will effect federal law enforcement, although there are some anticipated forthcoming issues that are more directly applicable to federal law enforcement than to local law enforcement.

This chapter is organized differently from most others in this book given the nature of the topic. Particularly, the chapter addresses several areas anticipated to notably affect federal law enforcement, including: the organization of federal law enforcement; entering federal law enforcement careers; the functions and responsibilities of federal law enforcement; interagency and intergroup relations; legal aspects; misconduct, corruption, and ethical issues; administration; the drug war; technology and criminalistics, and; homeland security and international threats. To be sure, this is not a comprehensive account of all issues projected to impact federal law enforcement. However, these are believed to be primary among the concerns.

Organizational Issues

The history of federal law enforcement is rife with organizational changes, agency name changes, and agency restructuring. Such changes occur due to emerging societal developments (e.g., an enhanced concern for homeland security), inept leadership, and/ or perhaps the need to "do something" in response to an event or occurrence to which there is no obvious, effective solution. Regardless, historical practices suggest that additional changes lay ahead with regard to the organization of federal law enforcement.

Law enforcement does not occur in a vacuum and thus is subject to the effects of emergent issues, events, and sometimes political or societal whims. Such unpredictability leaves most federal agencies susceptible to organizational change. For instance, the history of the ATF has largely been shaped by societal concern for taxes, alcohol, and firearms. Accordingly, the ATF has undergone numerous reorganizations and it is suggested that additional changes are ahead. Years ago, Vizzard (1997) noted that there was a strong likelihood that the ATF would ultimately merge with another agency or would be notably reorganized. Although the ATF has not merged with another agency or been substantially reorganized, this projection remains a possibility as Representative Darrell Issa, as chairman of the House Oversight and Government Reform Committee suggested in 2011 that the ATF should be absorbed into the FBI. His suggestion was offered largely in response to the botched "Fast and Furious" operation, for which the ATF was largely criticized (Yager, 2011). Anticipated organizational reform extends beyond the ATF, as history suggests there will be some restructuring and reorganization among many federal law enforcement agencies. The creation of the U.S. Department of Homeland Security (DHS) and its organizational impact on many federal law enforcement agencies is another example.

The decentralized nature of law enforcement at all levels in the U.S., but particularly at the federal level both assists and hampers law enforcement efforts. Federal law enforcement, and law enforcement in general, have historically been decentralized in the U.S., and it is likely that they will remain that way in the years to come. Of particular note, however, is the extent to which federal law enforcement has been decentralized. The creation of the Department of Homeland Security and the general reorganization of federal law enforcement around the turn of the twenty-first century was a step toward centralization, as is the increasing creation and use of task forces that include law enforcement agencies and personnel at all levels. Nevertheless, it remains highly unlikely that the U.S. will, at any time soon, move toward a completely centralized federal law enforcement organizational approach (i.e., have one, national law enforcement agency), particularly in light of historical continuity and the specialization inherent within the charges of many federal law enforcement groups.

Entering Federal Law Enforcement

Many issues will impact the future of employment in federal law enforcement, including economic and budgetary concerns, crime and justice-based factors, technological advancements, globalism, fear of crime, politics, and many other related issues. Individuals interested in a career in federal law enforcement are strongly encouraged to consider these issues as they are expected to impact future hiring practices in federal law enforcement.

The current and anticipated roles and functions of federal law enforcement agencies dictate that high standards remain with regard to recruiting, selecting, and training personnel. Technological advancements are expected to greatly enhance these processes, which should improve the quality of individuals who enter federal law enforcement. Recruitment efforts have been, and will continue to be assisted through technological advances that enable recruiters to target larger numbers of individuals. Efforts toward better selecting employment candidates will be assisted through advanced testing and evaluation procedures that will continue to be impacted by technological developments. Evaluations that extend beyond paper and pencil tests and are practical in nature and more reflective of candidate's abilities, skills, and preparedness will continue to be used as part of the selection process of federal law enforcement agents. Training federal agents is also expected to become increasingly effective as agents undergoing initial and in-service training will be able to access more productive, convenient, and directed training resources to assist them with their preparation and deficiencies.

Tomorrow's federal agents have grown up in a society consumed with concerns for terrorism and homeland security, and are particularly dependent on — and adept at using — technology. They have been regularly exposed to the expanded responsibilities of law enforcement agencies, and are more technologically savvy than today's federal agents. The onus is on federal agencies to best understand how to use the strengths of the upcoming generation of federal law enforcement personnel in advancing the interests of federal law enforcement and criminal justice in general.

Of particular concern with regard to the future of federal law enforcement is the need for agencies to continue diversifying the ranks. Much progress has been made toward diversifying federal law enforcement agencies, and demographic projections for the U.S. suggest that continued diversification will be necessary. Historically, white males constituted the majority of federal agents. Today's federal law enforcement agents are a bit more diverse. For instance, in 1996 28.0% of federal officers with arrest and firearm authority were from a racial or ethnic minority group. That percentage increased to 34.3% by 2008. The percentage of females increased from 14.0% to 15.5% during the same time (Reaves, 2012).

Functions and Responsibilities

In light of the few major, historical transformations in law enforcement, it is anticipated that the core functions of federal agents will remain much the same. Federal agents have generally been required to investigate and respond to crime. They are ultimately responsible for ensuring that federal laws and regulations are obeyed. These functions and responsibilities will likely remain the central components of federal law enforcement agencies, however the methods by which the agents and agencies perform these functions are expected to continue evolving. Recent trends suggest that the practices and methods through which federal agents meet their responsibilities will become increasingly efficient. As evidence, compare law enforcement in the 1950s to today's law enforcement practices. Today's federal agents are much better and more efficient at what they do than they were in years past. It is anticipated that progress will continue in the field.

Criminal investigations are expected to benefit immensely from forthcoming technological advances. Extensive databases of information largely assist investigators and other personnel, as do technological advances pertaining to the analysis of evidence. Computer-generated sketches and enhanced photographic lineups will continue to progress in their effectiveness, and closed circuit monitoring should continue to enhance investigative work. With these and other advances, however, come additional concerns regarding citizen rights to privacy and freedoms, and perhaps an over-reliance on technology.

The attacks of September 11, 2001 highlighted the need for greater information and intelligence gathering and sharing among law enforcement agencies. Recent developments in law enforcement suggest that federal agencies and law enforcement groups at all levels will enhance their information and intelligence gathering and sharing practices. At the very least, technological advances will enable law enforcement to have access to more robust databases containing crime and justice-related information. Akin to the war on drugs in the U.S., the war on terrorism promises to be a long-term engagement that requires vast resources and funding.

The shift by many federal law enforcement agencies toward greater surveillance, and intelligence and information gathering was largely perpetuated by concerns for homeland security. Efforts directed toward greater surveillance are expected to become increasingly evident as concerns for homeland security persist. Such practices have generated concerns that law enforcement has or may become too invasive, and law enforcement agencies have lost sight of their primary roles.

Modern and future medical advances are expected to increasingly assist law enforcement officers with regard to stress and other health-related issues. Some federal law enforcement positions will remain stressful in nature, however it is anticipated that agents will be better prepared and more able to address the stressful nature of their work. Advancements in medicine and overall health are anticipated to help agents better address the stressful aspects of law enforcement, and agencies will likely continue to examine and address the more stressful aspects of fighting crime. Reductions in the stress levels of agents will likely stem from reductions in the contributors to stress, including depression, alcoholism, and family problems.

The use of discretion by federal agents will likely remain problematic in the future, as decision-making is sometimes controversial yet always necessary in law enforcement. The anticipated advancements with regard to identifying, selecting, and training agents will undoubtedly help in this regard, however the misuse of discretion will probably continue to generate claims of agent misbehavior, for instance in the form or racial profiling, the misuse of force, and invasion of privacy.

Better recruitment, selection, and training practices will contribute much toward reducing the amount of violence in federal law enforcement, although agents will likely remain relatively much safer than many of their law enforcement counterparts who work at the local level. Enhanced professionalism among the federal law enforcement ranks will result in agents being better able to quell situations in non-violent manners and use their judgment more wisely. Further, technological advancements such as non-lethal weaponry and computer-assisted training will continue to better protect agents from acts of violence against them, and sleeker, less restrictive body armor will continue to limit the number of agents killed on the job. Overall, it is expected that federal law enforcement will remain a generally safe field.

In light of recent trends, it appears that federal law enforcement agencies will play an increasingly significant role in confronting crime in the future. For instance, federal-level, justice-based expenditures increased from 11% of expenditures at all levels of justice in 1982 to 16% in 2007. With regard to law enforcement, federal government spending increased from 11% to 19% during the same period (Kyckelhahn, 2011). These increases are notable and suggest that federal law enforcement agencies have enhanced their efforts toward controlling crime, however, the numbers should be considered in light of the major restructuring of federal law enforcement following the 2001 terrorist attacks against the U.S.

Interagency and Intergroup Relations

Federal law enforcement agencies are expected to continuously cooperate and interact with many different groups in society. Law enforcement agencies have increasingly realized the importance of interagency and intergroup cooperation, and it is anticipated that co-operative and collaborative efforts between federal law enforcement agencies and other groups/agencies will persist. Although federal law enforcement agents will continue to interact and cooperate with many different groups in the future, relations with several groups and agencies are anticipated to notably impact the future of federal law enforcement. Those agencies include the media, young adults, racial and ethnic minorities, private security groups, and other law enforcement agencies. This is by no means a comprehensive list of groups.

Positive relations with the media are notably important for federal law enforcement agencies, and will continue to remain vital to each agency's effectiveness. Media dissemination of information has changed in recent years, and it is expected that substantial changes will continue to occur. With regard to media crime reporting practices, "the future may hold more promise for accuracy given the possibility of competing news sources and greater variety that may be available to the general public" (Jerin & Fields, 2009, p. 227). Crime news and agency actions can be shared almost instantly via internet websites, and personal phones and other mobile devices enable users to have immediate access to crime- and related-information. The importance of the media in shaping public perception of federal law enforcement is evidenced in J. Edgar Hoover's earlier efforts to ensure that the media and popular culture depicted only positive portrayals of FBI agents (Raptopoulos & Walker, 2008).

The increased competition of the media has resulted in greater accountability of federal law enforcement and the need for more formal practices regarding the dissemination of information to media outlets. It is expected that increased competition among media outlets will result in federal agencies being required to be more open with regard to their practices, for instance as investigative journalism practices become more invasive and common. Historical tensions between the media and federal law enforcement agencies have largely been attributable to the lack of understanding and respect each group has for the other's duties and responsibilities.

Federal law enforcement agents may, in the future, find that they are increasingly interacting with young adults. Juveniles are becoming increasingly adept at using high-technology, which opens up additional opportunities for crimes that didn't exist with earlier generations. File sharing and cyberbullying are among the many new types of crimes for which juveniles are well prepared and potentially motivated to commit.

Changing societal demographics will undoubtedly shape the future of federal law enforcement. The percentage and number of ethnic minority group members is increasing and expected to continue doing so. For instance, it is projected that Hispanics will constitute roughly one-quarter (24.4%) of the U.S. population by 2050 ("Hispanics in the U.S.—U.S. Census Bureau," 2010). Immigration and high birth rates are among the explanations for the increasing number of Hispanic Americans in the U.S. Continued proactive efforts to build relations with minority groups and diversify federal law enforcement will be required of tomorrow's federal law enforcement agencies. Understanding cultural practices, overcoming language barriers, and overcoming and repairing negative stereotypes of law enforcement will be even important for positive community relations in the future.

The significance of positive community relations in the future is evidenced in Lyon's (2002) suggestion that expanded powers and additional personnel are less significant in homeland security efforts than is building trust and relationships in communities most likely to support terrorism. Building positive relations in targeted areas has many positive effects, including the acquisition of information and intelligence. Building and strengthening community partnerships have recently provided many positive results for law enforcement agencies, and it is expected that agencies will continue to seek a more holistic approach to fighting crime.

The private security industry has expanded at a notable rate, and their involvement in traditional law enforcement practices is becoming increasingly visible (Nalla & Heraux, 2003; Roberson & Birzer, 2010). Historical tensions between the private security industry and public law enforcement have dissipated to some extent recently (Kresevich, 2011), as both groups continue to recognize the important roles each serves. For instance, the private industry can significantly assist law enforcement agencies with regard to technology-based crimes and general information collection and dissemination. Private security professionals serve important roles on some law enforcement-sponsored task forces.

Increased cooperation among federal law enforcement agencies, and greater interaction and collaboration with agencies at all levels of law enforcement, as well as the private security sector are likely to continue occurring. Based on recent quantitative and qualitative findings, the future of the private security industry is promising. Particularly, the private security industry has substantially grown in size and scope in recent years, and all signs suggest that the growth will continue. Currently, the number of individuals working in private security is much larger than the number of individuals working in public law enforcement, and the fiscal health of the private security industry has been consistently promising (Crank, Kadleck & Koski, 2010). It is anticipated that private security will continue to expand in the forthcoming years as public law enforcement agencies are continuously burdened with responding to traditional calls for police service, concerns for homeland security, and high-technology crimes. In light of the expansion and increasing financial well-being of the private security industry, it is expected that there will be greater interaction and cooperation between law enforcement and private police (Crank, Kadleck & Koski, 2010).

Recent efforts toward greater law enforcement cooperation with other law enforcement agencies and the general public provides evidence that many law enforcement officials recognize the need to engage others in the fight against crime. The need for greater cooperation between federal law enforcement and the private security industry is important in light of the lack of law enforcement preparedness to confront high-technology crimes and the number of private security personnel and the level of specialization maintained by many private security practitioners with regard to high-technology crime. Ultimately, private security is expected to continue assisting law enforcement in a variety of ways (Palmiotto, 2009).

Legal Aspects of Federal Law Enforcement

Recent legislative changes suggest that federal law enforcement agents will be granted additional powers to search, seize, arrest, and interrogate suspects. The USA PATRIOT Act, which was passed in response to the terrorist attacks against the U.S. in 2001, provides some evidence of the public's willingness to allow greater law enforcement intrusion into personal lives. Further evidence is found in the series of exceptions to the exclusionary rule and the relaxed restrictions on the enforcement of immigration laws.

There are two wildcards in this projection of greater law enforcement powers which could alter the likelihood of these developments occurring: (1) the occurrence of several high-profile incidents in which law enforcement overwhelmingly intrude into the personal lives of individuals, and; (2) the presence of a more civil-libertarian-minded U.S. Supreme Court bent on curbing police power. With regard to the former, enhanced legal permissiveness with regard to law enforcement is anticipated, but there may very well be a breaking point. A large-scale incident or several serious incidents in which law enforcement agents infringe on individual rights may shift public opinion regarding law enforcement powers. At this point, it is expected that law enforcement will become more restricted regarding legal procedures, primarily in efforts to quell the public's unrest.

With regard to the latter, the U.S. Supreme Court under Chief Justice Earl Warren during the 1950s and 1960s was influential in restricting law enforcement powers in several areas, although some of the impacts of the Warren Court have dissipated as new legislation has emerged. The potential for the Supreme Court to again substantially change law enforcement practices remains viable. For instance, the projection of fewer legal restrictions on law enforcement is supported by claims that the Miranda Warning is no longer needed in law enforcement as relatively few cases are dismissed due to law enforcement personnel failing to read Miranda rights to suspects in custody and subject to interrogation. It is argued that informing suspects of their rights is unnecessary and burdensome (Payne & Guastaferro, 2009). It is anticipated, however, that the increased legal freedoms expected to be bestowed upon law enforcement would be countered if the U.S. Supreme Court becomes more focused on civil liberties — a theme championed at different times by both liberal and conservative justices, but often for different reasons.

The projection that law enforcement will be granted additional rights to enforce the law is also based on consideration of the pace at which technological and other changes are occurring in society. Cybercrime in particular poses challenges for legislators who do not necessarily understand the capabilities of and complexities associated with computer technology. Nevertheless, legislators propose and vote on legislation in the area. Accordingly, they may offer and/or support broad legislation that can be interpreted in many ways, including many ways that support law enforcement efforts. The uncertainties and unpredictability associated with the nature of terrorist activities and general concern for all types of crime and injustice also result in legislators being more supportive of federal law enforcement practices.

Misconduct, Corruption, and Ethical Issues

Agent and agency misconduct is expected to persist in federal law enforcement, although perhaps not to the extent witnessed in years past. Greater accountability of law enforcement agents in the forms of citizen oversight and media practices, as well as enhanced recruitment, selection, and training practices will likely continue to reduce, to some extent, misconduct.

Among the greatest projected changes with regard to agent and agency misconduct concerns the nature of the types of misconduct committed. Particularly, it is expected that law enforcement personnel, similar to the offenders they seek to apprehend, will increasingly take advantage of technological developments. It is anticipated that a greater number of law enforcement personnel will engage in high-technology crime as they become more exposed to opportunities in this area. The increased use of high-technology within law enforcement and the enhanced focus on high-technology crimes promote agent familiarity with technology and opportunities to commit crime, and today's generation of individuals who will become tomorrow's federal agents is notably adept with regard to high-technology.

The nature of corruption and misconduct within federal law enforcement will also change, to some extent, in relation to the current and anticipated emphasis on intelligence and information gathering. Law enforcement agencies are becoming increasingly aware of the people and places they monitor and protect, which generates opportunities for the abuse of such information. The use of DNA databases, closed circuit televisions, and other methods used to collect, compile, and store personal information provide new avenues for misconduct and unethical practices. Technological advances, on the other hand, will assist with identifying problematic agency personnel. Early warning systems, which involve the use of technology to identify potentially problematic employees, provide evidence of the contributions of technology in detecting potentially problematic agents over a period of time (DeCrescenzo, 2005). Agents' personal files can be more easily compiled, stored, and analyzed through the use of automation, which enables supervisors to quickly identify problematic behavior. It is anticipated that technology-based applications will continue evolving and help reduce agent and agency corruption (Henry & Campisi, 2009).

Administration

The future of federal law enforcement with respect to administration is anticipated to generate more effective law enforcement practices. Among other factors, the increased use of high-technology will greatly assist law enforcement administrators, and enhance professionalism within the field. Further, the current grooming of leaders in academic institutions is expected to result in more effective leadership. High schools, colleges, and universities across the U.S. have recently stressed the importance of leadership skills, and many have increasingly promoted leadership qualities in their students. This investment is anticipated to pay dividends as these students eventually assume roles as law enforcement agency administrators. Of particular interest to the future of federal law enforcement administration is the potential adoption of more progressive styles of administration.

Law enforcement agencies have long been organized according the hierarchical, chain of command approach. Some scholars suggest that the time has come for the law enforcement to adopt a new organizational approach. The emphasis on community involvement and the limitations of the historical organizational approach to law enforcement suggest that agencies in the future may be more participatory in nature. It is anticipated that agents will be more instrumental in focusing the overall approach of their agencies, as supervisors increasingly realize the importance of input from individuals working directly in the field. This trend may be somewhat mitigated by the push by some organizations to return to a professional model.

Many administrative positions within federal law enforcement have been made easier and more effective through the use of automated computer systems. Hours of paperwork can now be completed with a few simple clicks of buttons. Files and other sources of information are better stored, accessed, and utilized as a result of technological advances, and it is expected that technology in this area will continue to evolve. Technology will continue to assist administrators with regard to cooperative efforts with other agencies, and it can be used to train administrators or enable them to more easily understand and perhaps emulate administrative practices in other departments or agencies.

Today's recruits and agents will become tomorrow's administrators. These individuals have been exposed to more professional law enforcement practices, and they have been subject to greater levels of accountability than their predecessors. Based on recent trends, administrators in the future will be more accountable than were administrators in the past. This projection holds promise for more ethical, effective leadership. Greater media, government, and general public oversight of law enforcement could result in administrators being more thoughtful in their actions and more open with their decision-making. Federal law enforcement agencies, and all law enforcement groups have become increasingly exposed to society in recent years, primarily through laws supporting the freedom of information, investigative journalism, and general accountability in government agencies.

The Drug War

The limitations of recent efforts to confront the drug problem in the U.S. dictate that careful thought should be devoted toward future strategies to address drugs. Some projections regarding drug use in the future suggest that additional types of drugs will become available, including "smart drugs" and synthetic hormones. These drugs are expected to be created for medicinal use but will likely make their way to illicit markets. Smart drugs will provide users the "high" associated with some traditional drugs, although they would use vitamins as opposed to many of the substances found in today's drugs. Further, it is anticipated that drugs and medicines will be designed for specific ages, genders, and ethnicities, and personalized/customized medicines will become available (Mounteney, 2004). Synthetic drugs are anticipated to continue increasing in popularity as law enforcement officials and the criminal justice system in general continue to crackdown on drugs and drug offenses, which ultimately makes it difficult to naturally produce the products found in illicit drugs.

Drugs are anticipated to provide numerous health-related benefits and challenges for law enforcement in the future. It appears very unlikely that drug enforcement efforts will cease in the short-term future, however there appears to be some movement toward legalizing or decriminalizing some drugs (e.g., marijuana). Efforts toward decriminalization or legalization may be prompted by future medical developments that reduce the harms associated with drug use, manufacturing, and distribution. For instance, in the future there may be a drug that brings about the same effects as today's illicit drugs, although it doesn't interfere much with daily life functions. The drug would not be as socially dangerous as many of today's illicit drugs, and could be legal in which case the harms associated with producing and trafficking the drug "underground" would be mitigated. In the absence of this or any related developments, it is unlikely that all drugs will become decriminalized or legalized anytime soon, which means there will continue to be a demand for illicit drugs, suppliers of the drugs, and law enforcement efforts directed toward the drug war.

Drug prevention efforts will likely improve as technological developments may assist in several ways. Historically, drug prevention education consisted of police officers and/or other officials teaching lessons in much the same manner as school teachers. Prevention practices of the future may use more advanced approaches such as body scanning to determine which individuals are at risk of addiction. Continued scientific study of human behavior and bodies may facilitate the identification of individuals susceptible to problematic drug use.

Drug use prevention actions may be provided in a more personal, simulated environment than occurs today. Preventive practices may move beyond lecturing about the harms associated with drug use to more interactive approaches in which students or subjects are presented with computer-simulated virtual realities that highlight the problems associated with drug use. Reality-based education (or placing subjects in virtual realities) is anticipated to become more of the standard in all forms of education, including drug use prevention efforts.

Technology and Criminalistics

As noted throughout much of this chapter, federal law enforcement practices are expected to become more technological in nature. Part of this development will stem from federal law enforcement agencies needing to more directly focus on high-technology crimes, and the anticipated, continued developments with regard to high-technology that will assist law enforcement. Recent law enforcement efforts have been limited by many factors, including a lack of resources, to address electronic crimes and jurisdictional issues (Burns, Whitworth, & Thompson, 2004). It may be the case that law enforcement agencies enhance their ranks with an increasingly large number of personnel devoted to high-technology crimes. Or, the need to address high-technology crimes may be designated to other groups, such as private industry or specific law enforcement agencies that are strictly devoted to high-technology crime. Regional enforcement efforts are also a possibility.

Advancements in high-technology have contributed to many different types of crime, including currency counterfeiting, as current computers, copiers, and printers enable counterfeiters to produce currency that appears legitimate. The U.S. Secret Service estimated that $40 million worth of counterfeit currency is confiscated annually in the U.S., and over 90% of counterfeiting reported in the U.S. is the result of readily available technology (Morris, Copes, & Perry-Mullis, 2009). The latter finding suggests that expensive tools and sophisticated criminal networks are no longer needed to replicate U.S. currency. An analysis of counterfeiting using data from the Secret Service in a southern jurisdiction of the U.S. suggested that counterfeiting was committed by a diverse group in terms of age, gender, race, and criminal history. Most counterfeiting cases involved multiple offenders, especially among female counterfeiters (Morris, Copes, & Perry-Mullis, 2009).

Other evidence of the increasing significance of high-technology crime is found in a recent U.S. Department of Justice report which noted that 7% of households in the U.S. (or about 8.6 million households) experienced one or more types of identity theft victimization in 2010. This finding represents an increase from the 5.5% of households that were victimized in 2005. The increase was largely attributable to the more frequent use or attempted misuse of credit card accounts (Langton, 2011).

The immediate future regarding the control of technology-based crimes appears somewhat disheartening. Recent trends and current practices offer little hope for the immediate future. Law enforcement efforts remain highly fragmented and disjointed, and no law enforcement agency seems capable or prepared to directly tackle high-technology crime. It is anticipated that high-technology crime will continue to occur largely under the radar of law enforcement officials and society in general, and will do so until the problem reaches a breaking point at which the public becomes notably frustrated. At this point, it is uncertain as to what will occur following the public's display of frustration. Federal and state law enforcement agencies are too small in size to appropriately address high-technology crime, which shifts the burden to local authorities. However, the local police are currently overburdened with many other responsibilities.

It is anticipated that one of three events will occur in response to the problems associated with high-technology crime. First, government action may result in the creation of a large federal law enforcement agency devoted to high-technology crime. There are several benefits to taking this approach, for instance as it addresses jurisdictional issues which have long challenged efforts toward addressing high-technology crimes. A second anticipated development is the regionalization and pooling of resources by various law enforcement agencies. This approach currently exists in some areas, however it may become the norm across the U.S. A final projected approach to addressing high-technology crimes in the future is for local police agencies to invest more in high-technology crimes units and provide the personnel within the units the necessary resources and training to effectively confront these types of crime.

Federal law enforcement agencies have largely been receptive to new technologies that are proposed to enhance their work, as evidenced in the greater use of high-technology by agencies throughout the U.S. The willingness of agencies to incorporate technological advancements suggests that law enforcement personnel in the future will rely more heavily on high-technology to assist them. Advancements with regard to high-technology will help law enforcement with regard to addressing crime both domestically and abroad. Internationally, "New technologies will continue to enhance the ability of states to collaboratively police the cross-border movement of cargo, information, money, and people" (Andreas & Nadelmann, 2006, p. 248). Domestically, technological advancements are expected to assist law enforcement at all levels in almost all aspects of their job. Many creative minds are currently at work seeking means by which technology can assist law enforcement, and the results of these efforts will likely be recognized in the future.

One variable difficult to account for in the continued incorporation of technology in federal law enforcement concerns the budgetary restraints often placed on government agencies. Technology comes with a price, and the most recent, up-to-date technology-based devices are generally the most costly. Budgetary concerns with regard to technology have proven problematic for many law enforcement agencies, including the U.S. Marshals, who recently faced 10% and 15% budget cuts in recent years, which hampered their efforts to update their information technology. The Marshals proposed to update outdated PCs and software, centralize the agency's email services and prisoner-tracking application, strengthen its information technology security, and consolidate data centers into a new facility shared with and operated by the Drug Enforcement Administration (Foley, 2011). Budget cuts, however, curtailed these efforts.

It is expected that continued developments in forensic science and criminalistics will also further influence federal law enforcement, and more generally the criminal justice system. The enhanced public interest in forensic science has encouraged individuals to seek careers in the area, which will contribute to more individuals studying the field. Scientific methods in crime and criminal justice have existed for some time, although forensic science has recently had an increasingly notable impact on the criminal justice system. Future developments in forensic science may include more effective and thorough forms of identifying suspects/individuals and evidence, and more advanced evidence collection practices and analyses. With regard to the latter, it is expected that more crime labs will be available and the problem of backlogged cases (e.g., Durose, 2008) will diminish.

Homeland Security and International Crime

The notable concern for homeland security in the United States following the 2001 terrorist attacks generated a host of new positions, policies, practices, and responsibilities for federal law enforcement agencies. To be sure, homeland security and international crime are distinct from one another, yet they overlap in many ways. For instance, societal and law enforcement concerns for terrorism often center around international groups, although domestic terrorist groups have been responsible for many harms in the U.S., including the Oklahoma City bombing in 1995.

The 2001 terrorist attacks notably changed the nature, scope, and organization of law enforcement at all levels, particularly at the federal level. The major restructuring and expansion of federal law enforcement, including the creation the DHS, have generated greater expectations from our federal law enforcement agencies. Terrorist threats and related concerns for homeland security have generated increased societal fear, and greater accountability of federal law enforcement. Terrorism exists in many forms, and the threat of terrorist activities remains and will continue to remain. Terrorists have been quite clever with regard to the means by which they wish to and do harm others. In response, law enforcement agencies have to remain alert to a wide array of threats and potential threats.

International crime, as it both relates and doesn't relate to terrorism, is becoming increasingly prominent in today's society. International terrorism and drug trafficking have long been international crime concerns. However other types of offenses are becoming more prevalent in society, including cybercrimes and human trafficking. Globalism has contributed to many domestic crimes being committed on an international scale (Muraskin & Roberts, 2009).

Federal law enforcement agents have the largest geographical jurisdiction among all levels of law enforcement in the U.S., thus many in society look to the federal agencies to address international crimes. Increased international commerce, communication, travel, and general interaction have resulted in greater opportunities and involvement in crimes that cross national borders. International crimes have become increasingly facilitated by technological advancements. Unfortunately, international law enforcement cooperation and interactive efforts have been limited (e.g., O'Connell, 2008). Nevertheless, it is anticipated that federal law enforcement agencies will respond and become increasingly involved in international affairs, primarily as they pertain to crime and deviance.

Immigration concerns certainly fit within the realm of homeland security and international concerns, primarily as the U.S. seeks to better control which individuals enter the country. Enhanced immigration enforcement at the U.S.-Mexico border has notably influenced federal law enforcement practices and is expected to continue doing so. Immigration arrests by federal agents increased at an annual rate of 23% between 2005 and 2009, and immigration arrests (49%) were the most common of all arrest made by federal agents in 2009, followed by drug (17%) and supervision (13%) violations. Immigration arrests constituted only 27% of all arrests in 2005 (Motivans, 2011).

The future of federal law enforcement appears promising; however the future is never certain. Unexpected events, behaviors, and general societal developments can severely alter any forecast of the future. Even so, failing to prepare for the future often leaves any agency, organization, or individual in a reactive position. Having solid strategic and contingency plans are necessary in federal law enforcement, and the most successful agencies in the future will likely be those that have been proactive as opposed to reactive.

References

Andreas, P., & Nadelmann, E. (2006). *Policing the globe.* New York: Oxford University Press.

Burns, R. G., Whitworth, K.H. & C.Y. Thompson (2004). Assessing Law Enforcement Preparedness to Address Internet Fraud. *Journal of Criminal Justice,* 32(5), pp. 477–493.

Crank, J., Kadleck, C., & Koski, C. M. (2010). The USA: The next big thing. *Police Practice and Research,* 11(5), 405–422.

DeCrescenzo, D. (2005). Early detection of the problem officer. *FBI Law Enforcement Bulletin, 74*(7), 14–17.

Durose, M. R. (2008). *Census of publicly funded forensic crime laboratories, 2005* (NCJ 222181). Washington, DC: U.S. Department of Justice, Bureau of Justice Statistics.

Foley, J. (2011). Marshals Service invests in IT, then faces cuts. *Information Week,* 9: 5.

Henry, V., & Campisi, C. V. (2009). Current and future practices and strategies for managing police corruption and integrity. In R. Muraskin & A. R. Roberts (Eds.), *Visions for Change: Crime and Justice in the Twenty-First Century* (5 ed., pp. 328–349). Upper Saddle River, NJ: Pearson Prentice Hall.

Hispanics in the U.S.—U.S. Census Bureau (2010). Accessed online December 7, 2011 at: http://www.census.gov/population/www/socdemo/hispanic/files/Internet_Hispanic_in_US_2006.pdf.

Jerin, R. A., & Fields, C. (2009). Murder and mayhem in the media: Media misrepresentation of crime and criminality. In R. Muraskin & A. R. Roberts (Eds.), *Visions for Change: Crime and Justice in the Twenty-First Century* (5th ed., pp. 217–229). Upper Saddle River, NJ: Pearson Prentice Hall.

Kresevich, M. (2011). Law enforcement and retail partnerships: Working together for common goals. *Loss Prevention,* 10 (1), 41–44, 46, 48.

Kyckelhahn, T. (2011). *Justice expenditures and employment, FY 1982–2007—statistical tables.* U.S. Department of Justice, Bureau of Justice Statistics. NCJ 236218.

Langton, L. (2011). *Identity theft reported by households, 2005–2010.* U.S. Department of Justice, Bureau of Justice Statistics. NCJ 236245.

Lyon, W. (2002). Partnerships, information, and public safety. *Policing: An International Journal of Police Strategies & Management,* 25(3): 530–543.

Mounteney, J. (2004). Nerds and narcotics: Drug use in a global future. *Drugs and Alcohol Today, 4*(4), 14–20.

Morris, R. G., Copes, H., & Perry-Mullis, K. (2009). Correlates of currency counterfeiting. *Journal of Criminal Justice,* 37, 472–477.

Motivans, M. (2011). *Federal justice statistics, 2009.* U.S. Department of Justice, Bureau of Justice Statistics, NCJ 234184.

Muraskin, R., & Roberts, A. R. (2009). The future of criminal justice: Today and tomorrow. In R. Muraskin & A. R. Roberts (Eds.), *Visions for change: Crime and Justice in the Twenty-First Century* (5th ed., pp. 1–11). Upper Saddle River, NJ: Pearson Prentice Hall.

Nalla, M. K. & Heraux, C. G. (2003). Assessing goals and functions of private police. *Journal of Criminal Justice,* 31: 237–247.

O'Connell, P. E. (2008). The chess master's game: A model for incorporating local police agencies in the fight against global terrorism. *Policing: An International Journal of Police Strategies & Management, 31*(3), 456–465.

Payne, B. K., & Guastaferro, W. P. (2009). Mind the gap: Attitudes about Miranda warnings among police chiefs and citizens. *Journal of Police and Criminal Psychology, 24*, 93–103.

Raptopoulos, K. & Walker, J. T. (2008). J. Edgar Hoover and the FBI. pp. 117–141 in J. Bumgarner (ed.), *Icons of Crime Fighting: Relentless Pursuers of Justice,* (vol. 1). Westport, CT: Greenwood.

Reaves, B. A. (2012). *Federal law enforcement officers, 2008.* U.S. Department of Justice, *Bureau of Justice Statistics.* NCJ 238250.

Roberson, C., & Birzer, M. L. (2010). *Introduction to private security: Theory meets practice.* Upper Saddle River, NJ: Pearson Prentice Hall.

Stephens, G. (2005). Policing the future: Law enforcement's new challenges. *The Futurist, March–April,* 51–57.

Vizzard, W. J. (1997). *In the cross fire: A political history of the Bureau of Alcohol, Tobacco, and Firearms.* Boulder, CO: Lynne Reinner.

Yager, J. (December 2, 2011). Rep. Issa examining ways to reorganize ATF. *The Hill.* Accessed online December 20, 2011 at: http://thehill.com/homenews/house/196865-issa-wants-to-reorganize-atf.

Index